Sleep Works

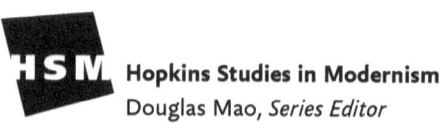

Hopkins Studies in Modernism
Douglas Mao, *Series Editor*

Sleep Works

Experiments in Science and Literature, 1899-1929

Sebastian P. Klinger

Johns Hopkins University Press
Baltimore

© 2025 Johns Hopkins University Press
All rights reserved. Published 2025
Printed in the United States of America on acid-free paper
9 8 7 6 5 4 3 2 1

Johns Hopkins University Press
2715 North Charles Street
Baltimore, Maryland 21218
www.press.jhu.edu

Library of Congress Cataloging-in-Publication Data

Names: Klinger, Sebastian P. (Sebastian Paul), 1991- author.
Title: Sleep works : experiments in science and literature, 1899-1929 / Sebastian P. Klinger.
Description: Baltimore : Johns Hopkins University Press, 2025. | Series: Hopkins studies in modernism | Includes bibliographical references and index.
Identifiers: LCCN 2024021290 (print) | LCCN 2024021291 (ebook) | ISBN 9781421450797 (hardcover ; acid-free paper) | ISBN 9781421450803 (paperback ; acid-free paper) | ISBN 9781421450810 (ebook)
Subjects: LCSH: Sleep in literature. | Literature and science—History—20th century. | LCGFT: Literary criticism.
Classification: LCC PN56.S577 K58 2025 (print) | LCC PN56.S577 (ebook) | DDC 809/.93353—dc23/eng/20240723
LC record available at https://lccn.loc.gov/2024021290
LC ebook record available at https://lccn.loc.gov/2024021291

A catalog record for this book is available from the British Library.

Special discounts are available for bulk purchases of this book. For more information, please contact Special Sales at specialsales@jh.edu.

Contents

Acknowledgments vii

Introduction. At the Borders of Consciousness 1

1. **The Science of Sleep** 16
2. **White Nights, Brown Pills** 35
3. **Dangerously Glamorous** 58
4. **Proust's Sleep Experiments** 73
5. **Undreaming Kafka** 98
6. **Rilke and Rest** 115

Conclusion 134

Notes 139
Works Cited 201
Index 237

Acknowledgments

This book was made possible by generous funding from Princeton University, the G. Wallace Ruckert Fellowship, the Donald and Mary Hyde Summer Fellowship, the Harold W. Dodds Fellowship, the Princeton Institute for Regional and International Studies, the network Literatur—Wissen—Medien at Humboldt University (Berlin), New College (University of Oxford), the Eugene A. Ludwig Fund, the Oxford Research Centre in the Humanities, and the University of Vienna.

Furthermore, I would like to thank Michael Jennings and Joseph Vogl for their ardent and unwavering support throughout the years. Mike, I am very grateful for your savvy advice, your encouragement, and your belief in me from the outset. Joseph, I am very appreciative of the countless conversations we've had about this project, for your inspiration, and for your many illuminating questions. I would also like to express my gratitude to Katja Guenther. From her, I learned how to think (more) like a historian of science, and her perspicuous comments often helped me to see things in a new light. My scholarship has also immensely benefited from discussions with many others at Princeton and elsewhere, especially Devin Fore, Tom Levin, Inka Mülder-Bach, Sally Poor, Jamie Rankin, Adam Oberlin, Johannes Wankhammer, Barbara Nagel, Brigid Doherty, Gen Creedon, Ingrid Christian, Eric Engstrom, Andreas Strasser, Ron Sadan, Diba Shokri, William Stewart, Denise Koller, Paul Babinski, Carolina Malagon, Hannah Hunter-Parker, Alexander Draxl, Ruo Jia, and, of course, Rubén Gallo. Ann Marie Rasmussen's patience and feedback have been vital to me. The members of the History of Science Program Seminar and the members of the Program in Media and Modernity commented on parts of the book, and I was struck by their generosity and insights. During regular extended stays in Berlin, the PhD-Net at Humboldt University offered a second intellectual home. Thanks go to

Anatol Heller, Klaus Wiehl, Marius Reisener, Robert Loth, and many others. I would also like to take the opportunity to thank Burkhardt Wolf and Ethel Matala de Mazza, in whose colloquia I presented parts of the book.

New College, Oxford, generously provided time for revising and expanding the manuscript in addition to sparking countless productive exchanges. At Oxford, I was extremely fortunate to have met Karen Leeder, who has inspired and supported me ever since. I am also greatly indebted to Andrew Counter and Ludmilla Jordanova for numerous discussions. Nari Shelekpayev read a decisive chapter and most kindly invited me to Yale University to test out my ideas. Charlie Louth took time away from his own work to engage my research. Carolin Duttlinger, Ben Morgan, Peter Bergamin, Andrew Marshall, Tita Chico, and Ritchie Robertson were always willing to chat. Special thanks are due to Sally Shuttleworth and Russell Foster, from whom I learned a lot about both sleep and collaboration across disciplines. Sally and Russell also worked extra hard to keep up the research network we cofounded when I moved to the University of Vienna. I am grateful to Eva Horn for her advice on the title of this book and her support of my scholarship.

I feel most fortunate to have had the opportunity to discuss this project with Douglas Mao. His perfect pitch and precision were crucial to developing and shaping the book. To the anonymous reviewers, I owe a great deal of thanks for their comments and feedback, which I found tremendously helpful. An earlier version of chapter 3 appeared in *Deutsche Vierteljahrsschrift für Literaturwissenschaft und Geistesgeschichte* 98, no. 1 (2024), 83-104. I would like to thank the anonymous reviewers of this article for their transformative suggestions. I greatly appreciate the work of Matt McAdam, Charles Dibble, Adriahna Conway, MJ Devaney, Jolanta N. Komornicka, and the team at Johns Hopkins University Press.

Many people generously provided help with archival materials. Thore Grimm opened the doors of the Schering Archive, Berlin (now part of the Bayer AG Corporate Archives) and kindly permitted the reproduction of images. Janine Reinert and her colleagues at the Bayer AG Corporate Archive, Leverkusen, unlocked a treasure trove of fascinating documents for me and facilitated my work even long after the actual visit to the archive. Gudrun Kling and Leander Diener at the Archive for Medical History, University of Zürich, were happy to discuss their rich holdings during two visits. For granting permission to reproduce material, I extend my gratitude to the Albertina Museum (Vienna), the Bayer AG Corporative Archives, the Fondation Martin Bodmer (Geneva), the Wellcome Collection (London), Carcanet Press (for

Acknowledgments

Stephen Cohn's translations of Rilke's *Sonnets to Orpheus*), North Point Press (Macmillan), Penguin Random House UK, Princeton University Press, Rowman & Littlefield Publishing Group, Vanessa Gaunt and all beneficiaries from Mark Treharne's estate, and *Deutsche Vierteljahrsschrift*. Moreover, this manuscript could not have been written without the unparalleled services provided by Princeton's Firestone Library, especially during COVID-19. Rex Hatfield procured sources for me, no matter how arcane or expensive. Christopher Skelton-Foord and Katharina Krčal also kindly added titles to their respective libraries to facilitate my research. To Daniel Tortora, special thanks are due.

Many generous, startingly intelligent friends responded to my work as it evolved. Till Greite taught me to ask questions I could not have posed without him. Elena Zanichelli can always be counted on. Talking shop with Peter Makhlouf is illuminating. And Sophie-C. Hartisch inspires me time and again.

Every day, I am overjoyed that Marie-Irène Igelmann is with me. My parents and family have constantly supported me, for which I am very grateful. My grandmother Sophie passed away while I was writing the penultimate chapter. She and my grandfather, Herbert, had been married for more than sixty years; they truly went through thick and thin together. *Liebe Großeltern, dieser Text ist für euch.*

Sleep Works

Introduction
At the Borders of Consciousness

Epicurus once quipped that "when we exist, death is not present, and that when death is present, we do not exist."[1] The same could be said of sleep. Human beings spend one-third of their lives sleeping. Yet since we cannot observe ourselves sleeping, sleep marks the boundaries of what we can subjectively experience, control, and know. When we are sleeping, we are typically not conscious. So how can we know the state in which we are immersed? What kind of activity is sleep? Is it an activity at all or is it rather a passivity? How can we describe the experience of sleep if sleep amounts to an absence of experience?

Around 1900, three groups of people began to raise such questions for the first time. Scientists and physicians ruminated on psychoanalysis and novel sleep disorders. Employees of the pharmaceutical industry, recognizing that sleep—or lack of it—could bring in big business, devoted time and effort to conquering insomnia. Literary writers such as Franz Kafka and Marcel Proust, often themselves struggling with insomnia or an addiction to sleeping pills, harnessed the creative potential of sleep states in their works of art. By looking closely at the historical entanglements and interactions of these fields, we can gain an understanding into modernist culture that the familiar study of dreams does not supply. Literature (and literary studies) offer insights into sleep that are not available in the sciences. When it comes to the terra incognita within us, experiments with writing are as powerful as electrodes.

Instead of presupposing clearly demarcated scientific and literary ways of writing about sleep, this book analyzes how these two cultures were established by their engaging with the problem of how to represent this elusive state. Today's sleep science defines its object by measuring electrical activity patterns across the brain, since even if we are slumbering, the communication among billions of neurons generates voltage changes that can be recorded from the surface of the scalp. But before scientists were able to analyze brain waves, knowledge about sleep generated problems of representation that in turn constituted the problem of understanding sleep in the first place.[2]

In early twentieth-century Europe, the challenge of how to think about sleep sparked inquiries that reached well beyond psychoanalytic interpretations of dreams. No longer regarded as the mythic sibling of death, sleep was viewed through the analytic lens of the life sciences. As a result, sleep dissolved into a vast array of disparate inquiries. It was subjected to quantitative measurement and psychological experiments and explored in connection with the subjective realms of imagination literary topoi. To make sense of the elusive phenomenon of slumber, scientists and authors experimented with the language of sleep, breaking open existing linguistic structures, epistemic genres, narratives, and conceptions. It therefore stands to reason that studying sleep in the early twentieth century requires looking at a panoply of diverging perspectives simultaneously.[3]

Sleep Works joins ranks with scholarship emphasizing that the exchange between literature and the sciences is mutual. Thus, the study can be productively read from many angles because it firmly grounds the analysis of modes of representing sleep in an exploration of cultural phenomena and the history of knowledge. Nevertheless, its major contribution is to literary studies. It shows how the medical and pharmacological production of subjectivities brought forth new ways of narrating the I—an I that is alert to ruptures of self-identity in states such as insomnia, semiconsciousness, or sleep inertia—by unpacking how creative uses of language defined sleep around 1900. Experiments with language—rather than with media technology—were essential to knowledge about sleep. In all the sleep experiments that the book explores, scientific and literary elements are inextricably entangled. Each domain functions according to its own rules and inner logic, yet scientific and literary sleep experiments connect, reference, restage, and complement each other. Their experimental designs, test situations, and technical media; their observations, interpretations, and interpretations of interpretations; their pharma-political handling of material substances and effects all depend on words. One key but forgotten mantra of modernist writers is true: poetic uses of words create our world.

Sleep without Dreams

Sleep Works is grounded in more than two decades of scholarship on the history of sleep. Sleep has become an urgent concern in the humanities and social sciences, as they critically responded to neoliberal imperatives of self-optimization and the "cultural turn."[4] In addition to Roger Ekirch's *At Day's Close* (2005) and Jonathan Crary's 24/7 (2013), my main point of reference is French anthropologist Marcel Mauss's programmatic insight that "the notion that going to bed is something natural is totally inaccurate. . . . Here are a large number of practices that are both techniques of the body and that also have profound biological echoes and effects. All this can and must be discovered."[5] Mauss diagnoses an essential technicity of human beings: human biology has become inseparable from the interplay of discourses, media technology, cultural techniques, and their social and "biological echoes and effects." These trailblazing studies by Mauss, Ekirch, and Crary inspired an ethnography of sleep, a historiography of sleep, a philosophy of sleep, and a small body of literary criticism on sleep—small because literary scholars continue to approach the phenomenon almost exclusively in terms of dreams.[6] *Sleep Works* weaves all these strands together and explores the consequences of such a blended perspective, paying special attention to the poetics of sleep.

Although dreams are an important part of sleep and are relevant to the subject of representation, the present study focuses on what Paul Valéry calls the "part of sleep not made up by dreams."[7] This focus on the part of sleep not made up by dreams is not motivated by the fact that we already have abundant scholarship on dreams; it is, rather, animated by pressing systematic, epistemic, and historical concerns that cut to the very core of the phenomenon at stake.[8] No one makes this clearer than Sigmund Freud, who excluded sleep from his study of dreams in the opening pages of *Die Traumdeutung* (1899, predated to 1900), breaking with the conventions of nineteenth-century scholarship that typically considered sleep and dreams together.[9] Freud enforced this split because he understood that sleep was notoriously elusive. As *Hysterie-Studien* (1895), the book Freud coauthored with Josef Breuer, puts it: "We cannot gain any direct insight into the deepest sleep, sleep without dreams, since the complete obliteration of consciousness in this state precludes any observation and experience."[10]

Freud realized that sleep, "the unconscious of the unconscious," posed a triple problem of experience, observation, and representation.[11] As it is impossible to give a reliable firsthand account of what the condition of being asleep feels like, sleep is only accessible through its edges, borders, transitional states, and metaphor. We simply cannot grasp the phenomenon's mysterious core without substantial mediation; all representations of sleep are inextricably shot through with fiction. This is not to suggest that the sleep sciences are hocus-pocus. It just means that their findings depend on technologies of observation, mediation, and interpretation and that literary writing provides insights precisely because it dramatizes such processes of representation.

A Drop of Grammar

The possibility of differentiating between sleep and dreams is tied to linguistic affordances in different languages. In contrast to a language such as Spanish, which uses the same term to refer to both dream and sleep ("sueño"), English, German, and French employ distinct terms to refer to these phenomena.[12] Even though this sample is small and cannot be universalized, it strongly suggests that representations of dreams and sleep do not overlap completely, however much they have in common—at stake is precisely the "différance" between dreams and sleep.[13] Let me illustrate this claim: to speak of "dreams" generally poses no problem, but even though American children might inquire "How many sleeps until Christmas?," in many languages—such as German—the noun "sleep" cannot be ordinarily used in the plural without bending grammar. Likewise, lucid dreamers can say "I am dreaming," but the statement "I am sleeping" constitutes a paradox. As Ludwig Wittgenstein might have it, sleep provides a "whole cloud of philosophy condensed into a drop of grammar."[14]

Sleep states, in other words, in no way mark the limits of representation, as some literary scholars have suggested.[15] Rather, authors who depict sleep states other than dreams often push the limits of what can be represented by devising strategies to elucidate that which eludes representation. Such depictions function in a way that recalls Michel Serres's concept of the parasite.[16] Serres originally employed this poetic term—a synonym for the French word for noise—to advance the argument that communication involves more than the act of transmitting a message from a sender to a receiver. Senders, on this account, can pass on their message only if they consider the constitutive leaks, disruptions, and interferences of the media channel.[17] For Serres, disruptions do not limit what can be said but make it possible that something may be communicated at all. Applying this idea to representations of sleep, we can say that sleep states frequently serve as a borderline case for literary representation, and how such states end up being figured sometimes sets the course for an entire aesthetics. We might say, "Tell me how you depict sleep, and I'll tell you what kind of literature you write."

The early twentieth century is not the first, let alone the only, historical moment to which this observation applies. In *Vital Strife: Sleep, Insomnia, and the Early Modern Ethics of Care* (2022), the literary scholar Benjamin Parris points out that writers such as Shakespeare, Milton, Spenser, and others pushed back against a Renaissance humanist notion of sleep as a diminution of being and attention. Grounded in a reappraisal of certain aspects of stoic philosophy, Parris's book demonstrates that these authors offer a much more nuanced understanding of sleep's vital role, one that has ethical, theological, biopolitical, and literary implications.[18] Literary innovations around sleep are thus part of a long and rich tradition whose exploration has opened up fruitful avenues of research.[19] Around 1800, for instance, somnambulism played a crucial role in intellectual discourses. The topic was simultaneously taken up in medicine, natural science, law, philosophy, literature (including drama), and opera.[20] Somnambulism enjoyed this prominence owing to the popularity of the physician Franz Anton Mesmer's theory of animal magnetism. Staging, depicting, and discussing somnambulism, however, also allowed people from various backgrounds to interrogate the notion of the autonomous subject, which was hardening during the same period. As these examples suggest, intense political, social, epistemic, and aesthetic change seems to provoke literary interest in the multifaceted phenomenon of sleep, no doubt not least because these changes impact the phenomenon of sleep itself.

Taylorized Sleep

Transformations in social conditions over the past centuries have significantly altered common sleeping patterns in North America and Europe and indeed have altered sleep itself. Both historical and scientific research of the past two decades suggest that the present order of sleep is not naturally given but results from the far-reaching social, economic, and political developments commonly described as modernization, including industrialization, urbanization, stress, accelerated rhythms of life, perpetual change, and the rise of artificial illumination.[21]

These shifts in sleep behavior took place gradually over a long period but became especially manifest in the second half of the nineteenth century and the early twentieth century. Schematically, in the mostly agrarian premodern societies, the diurnal rotation of planet Earth and seasonal shifts in exposure to sunlight functioned as the pacemakers of the biological clock (as we now say), fundamentally shaping sleep-wake patterns.[22] The premoderns appear to have evinced a polyphasic or segmented sleep rhythm, a rhythm common to most animals. The historian Roger Ekirch has demonstrated in detail (and through collaborations with scientists) that for the premoderns this polyphasic sleep consisted of a "first sleep" and a "second sleep" and a window of wakefulness in between, which could be used for various types of activities.[23] Napping during the day was also common. This model of sleep, however, was gradually dismantled during the nineteenth century. Competing explanations aim to elucidate this development, but innovations in lighting technology alone do not suffice to account for the scale of transformations, even if they might have played an important role.[24] When industrialization took hold in the West, human sleep was uncoupled from the seasons and became pegged to the technologies and temporal regimes of capitalism.[25] One of the first social groups to experience this were factory workers. They had to work long hours during the day regardless of the time of the year; they were also often required to take on additional nightshifts. The unvaryingly long hours, the fact that workers' energy was permanently spent, and an overall changed profile with respect to exposure to sunlight brought an end to segmented sleep. The workers had to sleep in a single block, as Karl Marx already pithily observed: capital "reduces wholesome sleep which restores, repairs, and refreshes vital power [Lebenskraft] to the minimum number of hours of torpor necessary for the revival [Wiederbelebung] of a completely exhausted organism."[26] Stripped from the context of its origin in the factories, this new one-block regime of anesthetic sleep was soon nonetheless propagated by nineteenth-century bourgeois moral and medical discourses as healthy, desirable, and more productive, and it began its rise to a general model for how one should sleep.[27] Implicitly, however, the monophasic model of organizing sleep not only paved the way for an ever greater reduction of time available for sleep but also for a standardization of time itself—it did away with an inherent distinction between time for work and time for rest, thus creating the foundations of today's 24/7 societies, in which one is effectively expected to be always working or consuming.[28] It is not surprising, then, that this temporal regime made life under the conditions of modernity intensely stressful and led to a proliferation of

Introduction: At the Borders of Consciousness   7

insomnia, whose scale became apparent around 1900, as chapter 2 shows.[29] Simultaneously, modernity became associated with insomnia.[30]

In this situation, contemporaries started to become aware of the historicity and cultural specificity of sleep, observing the major shifts in the order of nighttime rest and comparing them with practices in other parts of the world.[31] It was understood that, for better or worse, modern sleep had become "taylorized"—turned from a self-evident everyday phenomenon into an "epistemic thing" that could be broken down into quantifiable components, scrutinized, explained, experimentalized, and, potentially, either optimized or dismantled.[32] From all these developments, for which dreams barely mattered at all, the *conditio sine qua non* for our contemporary sleep science emerged in 1929, when the Jena psychiatrist Hans Berger (1873-1941) published an account of his invention of the electroencephalogram (EEG), a device that would profoundly alter the ontology of sleep, identifying it with a particular kind of brain waves.[33] The advent of the EEG led to the disavowal of previous modes of inquiry in sleep research and transformed sleep into a different epistemic thing, one that eventually reunited the study of sleep and dreams, which Freud had split apart.[34] For this reason, the emergence of the EEG marks the endpoint of this study.

Chronotopos

Although humans long reflected on their sleep, in early twentieth-century German- and French-speaking Europe, the multifarious transformations of sleep coalesced into such an interlocking discursive density that it is fruitful to focus again on this generally well-studied period and geographic region.[35] In this specific European locale—the Habsburg Empire, Germany, Switzerland, and France—a rich scientific exploration of sleep developed that nevertheless diverged from psychoanalysis, which contemporaneously emerged in Vienna. German- and French-speaking Europe also hosted the leading pharmaceutical firms at the time, which began manufacturing soporifics on an industrial scale. Many of these firms have headquarters on the Rhine River, from Bayer in the vicinity of Cologne to Merck in Darmstadt to Sandoz and others in the three-state triangle around Basel. It is perhaps no coincidence, then, that portrayals of sleep figure prominently in concurrent literary writing in German and French between 1899 and 1929, that is, during the historical period often labeled "modernist."

Modernism is a notoriously loaded and slippery term with its own genealogy.[36] It has meant different things to different people at different times, often serving to advance specific aesthetic agendas (such as desire to pit "high culture" against "mass culture" or a desire to oppose modernity to an ostensible postmodernity).[37] As the new modernist studies of the past two decades have demonstrated, however, modernist literature is as multidimensional as the "multiple modernities" to which it responded. Modernist literature "takes diverse forms depending on time and place, and on different agents' specific interventions, in particular sociocultural circumstances."[38] This holds true for the four central literary protagonists of this book—Proust, Schnitzler, Rilke, and Kafka, whose texts stand as distinctive yet related instantiations of modernist writing.[39] Their writing practices must, moreover, be seen within the framework of different but interconnected modernities, signaled in shorthand by the dissimilar cities that shaped them: Paris, Vienna, and Prague.[40]

Their similarities and dissimilarities notwithstanding, Proust, Schnitzler, Rilke, and Kafka share a quintessentially modern experience: they all interacted with the contemporary medical and scientific sleep dispositive—as physicians or patients, as readers of advertisement brochures of the pharmaceutical industry, as friends of sleep scientists, as insomniacs, neurasthenics, sleeping pill addicts, or proponents of natural healing. Except for Proust, who has nevertheless been read countless times through a Freudian framework, the writers were also familiar with psychoanalysis, to which they responded with characteristic ambivalence and even criticisms.[41] The sleep scenes so prevalent in the works of Proust, Schnitzler, Rilke, and Kafka cannot be accounted for through the traditional approach of the interpretations of dreams. Grounded in the knowledge and experiences of their time, these writers complicate the equation of sleep and death as well as question the modern norms of sleep, as they explore the myriad facets of states of slumbering, like dozing off, half sleep, hypnagogic experiences, sleep inertia, awakening, and sleep induced by soporifics. While authoritative studies of literary modernism(s) schematically stress that formally innovative writings of this period manifest a "tendency to center narrative in the consciousness of its characters, and to create those characters through the representation of their subjective thoughts and feelings rather than describing them objectively," few scholars have explored how this literature was often equally obsessed with moments when consciousness faded, fractured, or failed as result of tiredness, fatigue, semiconsciousness, and sleep.[42] The chapters that follow show how modernist authors—especially but not only Proust, Schnitzler, Rilke, and Kafka—systematically represent somnolent states in their works and, intermittently, even use them to organize their writings. In their own ways, all of them therefore recognized the problem of representation posed by sleep, and they pushed hard to devise strategies to take on the challenge of sleep.

Occasionally, these depictions of sleep serve to test the limits of literary representation. As James Joyce puts it memorably, "In writing of the night, I really could not . . . use words in their ordinary connections. Used that way, they do not express how things are in the night, in the different stages—conscious, then semiconscious, then unconscious."[43] For some modernist writers, ruminating on sleep states provides an avenue for probing new ways of writing, such as the interior monologue.[44]

Sleeping Subjects

The struggles with representing sleep are not unique to literary writing. A similar push for new ways of representing sleep occurred in the sciences during the early twentieth century. The protagonists of the nascent field of sleep science recognized that sleep states proved strangely resistant to conceptualization and introspection, as they evaded experimentalist approaches that had proven so powerful for the life sciences. In the words of a contemporary, "Sleep represents a bundle of somatic and psychic phenomena that one can barely unravel. Thus, causal-experimental research struggles significantly with elucidating the phenomenon of sleep."[45] Or as Ernst Trömner put it in 1912: "The scientific disciplines of experimental physiology, experimental psychology . . . , and the clinical examination of sleep disorders . . . must all come together to make the inquiry into sleep fruitful."[46]

Scientists who wanted to peep behind the veil of sleep first had to devise innovative ways to capture this elusive phenomenon, and their concepts and devices fundamentally shaped the representation of sleep. Sleep, then, complicates one of the key epistemic premises of the human sciences—as Michel Foucault would call the assembly of disciplines exploring the human subject—based on the belief that objectivity results from an abstraction of the first-person point of view.[47] The smooth epistemic shift from the first-person perspective to the third-person observer and back collapses in the case of sleep. The view of the first-person remains systematically untrustworthy. To quote Wittgenstein again, "Imagine an unconscious man (anaesthetized, say) were to say 'I am conscious'—should we say 'He ought to know'? And if someone talked in his sleep and said 'I am asleep' should we say 'He's quite right'?"[48] What can be known about sleep given the absence of conscious experience? How does one thematize one's own act of sleeping without awakening? Is the one who sleeps still me? Two things are certain: there are no easy answers to these questions, and what answers there are rattle the phantasma of an autonomous, rational, and self-identical subject.

Versions of these questions have a well-established pedigree in the history of German and French philosophy. Figures such as Denis Diderot (1713-84) and Georg Wilhelm Friedrich Hegel (1770-1831) consider the (dis-)continuity of the self during sleep and dream states. They draw not only on metaphors of somniloquy and sleepwalking, but also—in Diderot's case—on the highly performative and literary genre of the dialogue.[49] I take up Hegel's account of the sleeping self in my reading of Proust.[50] In addition to thinking about the philosophical subject, however, it is also important to embed the study of the sleeping self within broader cultures of subjectification, to use a sociological term for the making of subjects and identities in historically specific cultural milieus. I am specifically interested in how the modern rise of insomnia, the concurrent medicalization of sleep, and the proliferation of synthetic soporifics inflect discussions about the discursive formation, therapy, and optimization of sleep. What does it mean to produce subjectivities using medical and pharmaceutical means? How do synthetic soporifics change the ontology of consciousness? What side effects accompany cultures of sedation? How does one achieve "good" sleep? Through its consideration of such questions, this book approaches a cultural dispositive that could be called the sociotope of the pharma industry. Riffing on the term of the biotope, the habitat to which different species must adapt in their own ways to survive and thrive, the parlance of a sociotope of the pharma industry offers an analytic tool for describing the cultural milieu that emerges with the advent of a mass market for soporifics. *Sleep Works* thus examines not only the formation of social types related to sleep and the implications of attributing diagnostic identities (which often involve class and gender) but also the politics of their representation.

Poetics of Knowledge

Sleep Works brings methodological approaches from the joint field of literature and science to bear on the study of sleep, opening new vistas in both fields. Methodologically, it draws on the "poetics of knowledge," developed and practiced in German literary studies and connected to longstanding international concerns about a "cultural poetics of science," with which it is closely aligned.[51] Like the cultural poetics of science, the poetics of knowledge charts the irreducible yet inextricable, manifold yet unpredictable conjunctions and interdependences between literature and science, as manifested in the circulation, adaptation, and mutual exchange of forms of representations. The poetics of knowledge documents the reciprocal and symmetric impact of literature (literary, linguistic, and performative elements) on scientific practices and vice versa and is similar to models proposed by scholars such as Gillian Beer, Laura Otis, Sally Shuttleworth, Steven Meyer, Henry S. Turner, and many others.[52]

Literary writing does not provide a counterdiscourse to scientific knowledge, nor does it illustrate, dumb down, or popularize scientific knowledge. The truth is more complicated. The poetics of knowledge highlights the many forms of both literature and science, the discursive and historical specificity of their practices, and the messiness of their interrelations. Literature and science generate their respective representational practices by way of a continuous interchange with other discourses, as they assimilate, absorb, and reinforce, for example, narrative patterns, metaphorical meaning making, epistemic genres, writing scenes, media, language games, and ways of experimentation. The poetics of knowledge not only paves the way for a nuanced understanding of how literary and scientific texts operate but also challenges binary distinctions between nature and culture, soft and hard sciences, and facts and fictions in favor of a historically, theoretically, and aesthetically informed analysis of the generation, communication, and application of knowledge about sleep.

In this spirit, *Sleep Works* draws on a wealth of literary, scientific, and cultural sources. It offers interpretations of German and French literary writing, with side glances at texts in English; historic scientific documents from the disciplines of psychology, neurology, physiology, pharmacology, and medicine; and a range of materials from cultural history, from health care advice books to contemporary self-help and advertisement materials. To complement published documents, the study makes use of archives across Europe, including the archives of the pharmaceutical industry, such as the Bayer AG Corporate Archives, and archives pertaining to the history of medicine, for example, the collections housed at the Wellcome Trust in London.

Because this study considers such a broad variety of materials together, it cannot cover everything in each individual field. To make up for that, it offers a compromise: for example, it focuses on four pertinent literary authors so that it can provide in-depth analyses, but it situates those authors in a much larger field of modernist writers who come up in passing. The figures touched on incidentally include, among others, Peter Altenberg (chapter 2), Gottfried Benn (chapter 2), André Breton (chapter 5), Hermann Broch (chapter 2), Thomas Mann (chapters 4 and 5), Italo Svevo (chapter 3), Georg Trakl (chapter 4), Paul Valéry (chapters 4 and 6), Edith Wharton (chapter 3), and Virginia Woolf (chapters 4 and 6). This means that the surrealists are treated only briefly in this study, because dreams rather than sleep per se are central to their poetics.[53] Given the strong body of scholarship on feature films, only a focused discussion of medical film seemed necessary in the context of this study.[54] Likewise, specialists in the history of sleep science may argue that some figures cast in minor roles here deserve more stage time. A prominent example is the French psychologist Henri Piéron (1881-1964), who played an important role in establishing sleep science institutionally.[55] But as he conducted experiments very similar to those undertaken earlier by the Franco-Russian physiologist Marie de Manacéïne, I chose to foreground her contribution.

Chapter Outline

All in all, *Sleep Works* considers three main questions. What kind of activity is sleep? Who sleeps? How can we represent sleep? Each chapter of the book explores these puzzles through the lens of a different discourse, identifies explicit and implicit responses, and traces how their configuration reverberates and changes across fields. This entwinement of literature and science runs through the chapters of *Sleep Works* and holds the book together.

At the beginning of the twentieth century, sleep generated novel empirical inquiries that reached well beyond psychoanalytic interpretations of dreams. Sleep was no longer regarded as the mythic twin brother of death, yet it continued to prove strangely elusive to scientists. Chapter 1, "The Science of Sleep," analyzes how interdisciplinary sleep science emerged in the process of researchers' thinking through the problem of representing sleep by way of grammar. The psychologist Édouard Claparède, a former student of Freud, distinguishes sleep from related states such as fatigue, hypnosis, and coma, by drawing a distinction between "passive" and "active sleep," which he explicitly conceptualizes in linguistic terms. The neurologist Constantin von Economo built on this account after he encountered the enigmatic sleeping sickness encephalitis lethargica, which struck the world between ca. 1915 and 1927 and affected up to one million people worldwide.

Introduction: At the Borders of Consciousness   13

From his diagnostic encounter with this epidemic, Economo concludes that sleep is indeed active and must be regarded as an autonomous process of the nervous system. This insight emerged from grammatical experimentation and connected sleep to deep philosophical questions regarding agency. For example, if sleep is understood as active, does it consist of an activity of the sleeper, an activity of sleeping, or an activity during sleep? Who is doing the sleeping? As early sleep scientists raised such questions, they discovered that sleep exposed the extent to which modern subjects were confronted with the limits of their self-control, which instigated attempts to restore agency.

Chapter 2, "White Nights, Brown Pills," uncovers how pharmaceutical giants such as Bayer repurposed these fictions of agency, realizing that those experiencing "sleep anxiety" constituted an enormous market. Insomnia and other sleep disorders were difficult to cure. With the advent of synthetic sleep medication, however, an entire industry emerged that promised to do away with white nights and to repair selfhood. These drugs can thus be read as a quintessentially modern technology of the self. Drawing on corporate archives, period medical literature, self-help books, and fiction, chapter 2 backs up this idea by tracing the rise of the world's most iconic and popular soporific well into the twentieth century—Veronal, the first barbiturate. The drug achieved blockbuster status by bolstering its innovation as a pharmaceutical with a cutting-edge brand identity and by offering the product in the then-novel form of the sleeping pill, which changed how soporifics were taken. *Sleep Works* lays bare how applied science, business strategy, marketing, and advertising worked together to constitute the somnific faculties of Veronal and to fill each sleeping pill with its suggestive power.

The innovations of the pharmaceutical industry unleashed a dialectics of agency, as the invention of Veronal simultaneously implied the invention of Veronal addiction and Veronal suicides. Many of these suicides were accidental, though; the drug's dosage was based on the male body, proved highly addictive, and could be overdosed unintentionally. Women were disproportionally affected; many died. But instead of producing a critical debate about "white market drugs,"[56] the public discourse was quick to blame allegedly "hysterical" women for waves of "Veronal suicides." Chapter 3, "Dangerously Glamorous," homes in on this constellation more closely. It analyzes a paradigmatic narrative of Veronal poisoning in the work of the Austrian physician and author Arthur Schnitzler, whom Freud famously called his "doppelgänger." Based on a discovery in the corporate archives of the pharmaceutical giant Bayer—a document showing that the company took notice of (and issue with) the role of the soporific Veronal in Schnitzler's novella *Fräulein Else* (1924)—the chapter suggests that the text must be understood as a case narrative that integrates contemporary medical and pharmacological knowledge and from which a specific literary agency for Veronal can be extrapolated. Providing the first reading of *Fräulein Else* with a focus on the soporific, the chapter reveals that the novella makes a literary intervention into debates about public health and uses the drug to explore the limits and possibilities of the interior monologue.

Proust radicalizes this exploration of how to represent sleep states in literature based on contemporary knowledge. Due to his patient history as an insomniac, his addiction to soporifics, and his personal contacts with physicians and sleep researchers, he considered himself an expert on the new sciences of sleep, as well as on Veronal. Chapter 4, "Proust's Sleep Experiments," demonstrates that Proust's exposure to contemporary scientific, medical, and pharmacological discourses about sleep prompted him to undertake his own inquiries into sleep—he systematically used literary writing as an experimental instrument for investigating this state. To elucidate his findings, *Sleeps Works* interprets the key sleep scenes that structure his seven-volume *À la recherche du temps perdu* (1913-27). This provides a fresh account of the experimental methods with which the novel explores sleep states. Chapter 4 raises several questions. In what ways does the *Recherche* grapple with the seemingly impossible task of portraying sleep's profusion of absences? How does the text deal with the challenge of reporting on sleep from a first-person perspective? The answers not only provide a better understanding of Proust's literary self-experiments but also an account of somnolent subjectivity; as a sleep researcher, Proust bids farewell to the autonomous subject that has become the norm in the 24/7 society.

Whereas chapter 4 investigates perspectives on sleep in the oeuvre of an author who was intimately familiar with contemporary debates on the topic, chapter 5, "Undreaming Kafka," goes one step further and asks what the work of a writer who did not have access to such knowledge can teach us about sleep. For this reason, it turns to Kafka, a writer who adamantly refused to take soporifics such as Veronal and insisted that his rejection of sleep hygiene, as well as his insomnia, were essential to his writing. Why is Kafka's creativity so closely tied to his allegedly disordered sleeping patterns? What sort of perspectives on sleep emerge from his texts that are obsessed with various types of it? In Kafka's nocturnal workshop, sleep deprivation, hypnagogic experiences, and half-conscious states forge a writing practice that resembles both surrealist automatic writing and sleep talking. Close readings of Kafka's diaries, his fragmentary novel *Das Schloss* (1922), and his story "Der Bau" (1923-24) reveal how Kafka's fascination with the edges of sleep undermines the supposed ontological stability of wakeful existence; his texts lay bare the irreducible contingency of being and staying oneself and problematize the boundaries between waking and sleeping.

Sleep Works opens with science, but it ends with poetry. Chapter 6, "Rilke and Rest," which provides a comprehensive account of Rilke's overlooked sleep-focused poetry, does double work: it not only binds together the central argumentative strands of the book but introduces a poetics of good sleep that complements the emphasis on insomnia and creativity in the preceding chapters. Based on a corpus of more than thirty sleep-related poems that traverse Rilke's oeuvre from the middle period to his later bilingual work in German and French, the chapter analyzes Rilke's texts against the backdrop of contemporary scientific and medical debates about sleep. Close readings demonstrate that Rilke's poems intersect with these discourses on a thematic and formal level. He discovers that under the conditions of modernity, excellent sleepers are those who pay the least attention to it: cats, plants, and things, all of which he suggests we venerate as deities of sleep.[57] To descend to this divine sphere of sleep, we must traverse the realms of science, pharmacology, and literary writing.

1 The Science of Sleep

For most of human history, sleep and dreams were typically considered together. But Sigmund Freud begins his 1899 field-defining *The Interpretation of Dreams* with a sweeping move that severs the link between dreams and sleep, the latter of which he almost entirely excludes from his project:

> Until recently most writers on the subject have felt obliged to treat sleep and dreams as a single topic. . . . I have had little occasion to deal with the problem of sleep, for that is essentially a problem of physiology, even though one of the characteristics of the state of sleep must be that it brings about modifications in the conditions of functioning of the mental apparatus. The literature on the subject of sleep is accordingly disregarded in what follows.[1]

Sleep, on Freud's view, poses a problem of representation he seeks to bypass: "We cannot gain any direct insight into the deepest sleep, sleep without dreams, since the complete obliteration of consciousness in this state precludes any observation and experience."[2] If sleep comes up at all in *The Interpretation of Dreams*, it is because sleeping is a specific psychophysical state necessary to "dream work," whose mechanisms Freud seeks to elucidate in order to shed light on the functioning of the psychic apparatus in general.[3] Freud does not entirely succeed in purging *The Interpretation of Dreams* and his other texts from references to sleep, which he calls a "subject unsuitable for psychoanalysis."[4] Still, he succeeds in divorcing his study of dreams from debates about sleep as well as from late-nineteenth-century debates on hypnosis and sleeplike states that hinged on a schematic distinction between waking as an "active state of the soul" and sleep as a "passive state of the soul," where mental activity, attention, and volition cease.[5] Psychoanalysis's astute analyses of dreamlife made it increasingly implausible to maintain such dichotomic boundaries, though Freud was keen on limiting the activity of sleep to dreams proper.[6] Breaking with conventions of nineteenth-century scholarship that opposed waking and dreaming but treated sleep and dreams together, Freud began considering waking life and dreams together and juxtaposed them with the study of sleep.

While the history of dream research has by now been well studied, we know much less about the second branch, the history of sleep science, although significant scholarship—especially new books by Kenton Kroker and Hannah Ahlheim—have appeared in recent years. Even prominent practitioners of sleep science genuinely believe that this discipline came into being only after World War II and that sleep was considered an "inactive or 'idling' state" until this moment.[7] This chapter debunks such ideas and reveals that the interdisciplinary field of sleep science is not only much older but also inextricably tied to an understanding of sleep as "active." If sleep was not simply the opposite of being awake, what was going on in this state? Is sleep an activity of the sleeper, an activity of sleeping, or an activity during sleep? And how was the investigator to penetrate the veil of sleep to answer this question?

Physiologies of Fatigue

At the time when Freud tried to exclude sleep from the study of dreams, it was indeed a "problem of physiology."[8] Starting in the second half of the nineteenth century, research into sleep became the object of a highly technical niche debate within the discipline of physiology, where it served as "a viable testing ground for physiologists wanting to turn mind into body"— but to little avail.[9] It was, as one scientist put it, "the crux or the calvary of physiology."[10] The debate centered on the question of how the perceived diminishing of consciousness during sleep could be theorized in physiological terms. Although various theories had been propounded, most scientists believed that either a neural shutdown occurred during sleep or that an accumulation of chemical fatigue substances in the organism caused the onset of sleep.

Around 1900, scientists compared sleep to a combustion engine that had run out of coal. This conceit, which was ubiquitous, indicates a thermodynamically inspired understanding of the organism as a "human motor."[11] Following Anson Rabinbach's classic study, the image of the motor "fused the diverse forms of labor in nature, technology and society into a single image of mechanical work."[12] Within this framework, exhaustion featured as a key trope, pinpointing an inability to work. Preeminent figures such as Angelo

Mosso (*La fatica* [1891]) and Emil Kraepelin (*Ermüdung und Erholung* [1895]) who embraced a thermodynamic theory of labor legitimized a distinction between objective fatigue (*Ermüdung*) and subjective tiredness (*Müdigkeit*).[13] They also affirmed the idea that sleep represents a break in the function of the organism. The sleeping subject ceased all activity so that it could rebound from the repletion of its energy when awake.

From this perspective, one could regard sleep as a special case of the physiochemical notion of exhaustion that Mosso and Kraepelin proposed, although questions abounded. How much sleep was needed for optimal performance? Was all sleep equally restorative? Did variances among individuals exist? Was it possible to sleep too much or too little? A further investigation of sleep focused in particular on exhausted white-collar professionals performing intellectual labor thus promised insights that could contribute to a faster rebound after physical and mental overwork and increase productivity.[14] Mosso and Kraepelin never offered definitive answers to all these questions, but they realized that the framework of fatigue could only partially make sense of sleep.

For example, Mosso reports on this insight in his popular book *La paura* (1884), where he recounts his experiments with the consenting worker Bertino, whose skullcap had been cracked open by a falling brick. This fracture allowed Mosso "to look into the skull" (75) to record the pulsations of the sleeping brain with the help of the "graphical method"—a technical apparatus that inscribed every pulsation onto a cylinder, creating undulating curves (see fig. 1.1). Mosso "discovered, to his surprise, that even though Bertino appeared to be in deep sleep, his brain registered an immediate response to any external sound, and the excitation increased if his name was uttered, and even more so if he was spoken to severely."[15] This experiment, which tested responses to sound, evidently challenged an understanding of sleep as passive, for there were clear responses to stimuli. It was not missing instruments that prevented Mosso from articulating the consequences of this insight; it was that he had no language that allowed him to go beyond the framework of exhaustion—he announced that he was writing a work on sleep, but he never published such a book.[16]

A New Phenomenology of Sleep

The experimental psychologist Édouard Claparède (1873-1940) offered a way forward, and during the first decades of the twentieth century, virtually no one could write about sleep without taking his work into account.[17]

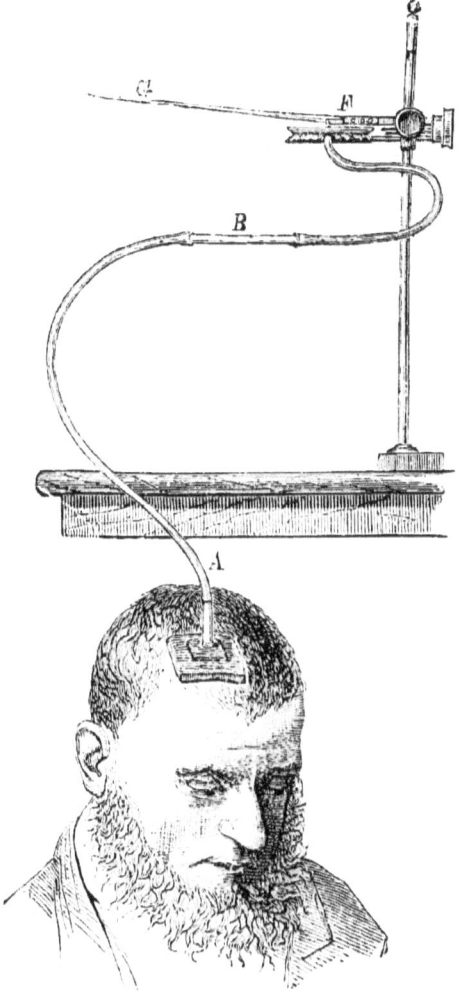

Figure 1.1. The graphical method in use on Bertino (Mosso, *La fatica*, 86).

Although the scientist had fallen under the spell of Freud, his much-cited 1905 study "Esquisse d'une théorie biologique du sommeil" (Sketch of a biological theory of sleep) established the parameters of a new discussion that liberated sleep from both psychoanalytic and physiological debates on dreams and exhaustion, even if it drew on both.[18] To reconceive the "phenomenology of sleep," as Claparède put it, he first had to popularize a new conceptual language ("La question du sommeil," 434).[19] He spearheaded what Nicolas Vaschide calls "invented concepts" ("mots inventés") of passive and active sleep, making the case that one must understand regular sleep not "as the result of some sort of fatigue" but as a genuinely "active process" ("La question du sommeil," 434).[20] To demonstrate this counterintuitive claim, Claparède critically reinterpreted the key evidence that seemed to prove the identity of sleep and exhaustion: Marie de Manacéïne's experiments with sleep deprivation, whose results were published in a journal edited by Mosso.

Manacéïne's experiments are remarkable not only because they were conducted by a female investigator but also because they sought to define sleep through sleep deprivation.[21] Still, her work has been almost forgotten today, in part because the influential and well-connected contemporary French scientist Henri Piéron repeated her experiments.[22] Both Manacéïne and Piéron examined the physiological effects of a "complete deprivation of sleep" on puppies.[23] Conceptually, these experiments aimed to strip all aspects from sleep that could not spring from the biochemical effects of fatigue, so they violently enforced a distinction between the subjective feeling of sleepiness and physical exhaustion. Barred from giving in to weariness for more than a week, the puppies in Manacéïne's experiment were finally overpowered by total physical exhaustion and sagged.[24] A quantifiable amount of fatigue substances rather than subjective impressions of sleepiness seemed to prompt sleep, the subjective impressions appearing to count for very little. In the eyes of her contemporaries, these experiments confirmed "that normal periodic sleep results, without any doubt, from exhaustion."[25]

In the "Esquisse," Claparède redescribed what the evidence of these experiments suggested. Because all puppies had died after the sleep deprivation experiment, a final opportunity to rest in its aftermath notwithstanding, Claparède argued that the experiment established no distinction at all between subjective and objective weariness.[26] What it established was a distinction between exhaustion and sleep: if "exhaustion makes us fall asleep, then we fall into a kind of sleep from which we may not wake again" ("Esquisse d'une théorie biologique du sommeil," 275). Too direct a causal relationship between exhaustion and sleep was dangerous, not normal. Thus, sleep caused by exhaustion could barely constitute regular sleep. In other words, the "passive theories" ("Esquisse d'une théorie biologique du sommeil," 313) that "perceived sleep as the result of some sort of fatigue" ("La question du sommeil," 437) made one crucial methodological error, Claparède argued: they glossed over the distinction between experiments and experience, the word for both of which in French is the same ("expérience"). Seen through the mechanical inscriptions of the laboratory, he intimated, the phenomenology of sleep disaggregated to a nonexperiential, quantitative category bereft of the qualities of the lifeworld. This yielded an impoverished concept of sleep that mistook the traces of technical inscriptions for a representation of "quotidian sleep" ("sommeil quotidien") ("La question du sommeil," 422).[27]

In contrast, Claparède describes sleep not as the result of exhaustion but as a defense against exhaustion. This argument mobilized a psychoanalytic term ("defense") but to a different end, as Freud himself noted in a letter about Claparède's "Esquisse."[28] "We do not sleep because we are intoxicated or exhausted," Claparède claims; rather "we sleep so as not to become intoxicated or exhausted."[29] In this aphoristic statement, which soon became a much-cited commonplace, Claparède employs a rhetorical chiasmus to turn the causal relationship between exhaustion and sleep upside down: the sensation of fatigue, not fatigue itself, points to a need for sleep ("besoin de sommeil") and fosters a desire to go to bed. Ignoring the sensation of sleepiness for too long, by contrast, threatens one's health, as Manacéïne's experiment illustrates vividly. Claparède's psychoanalytically inspired conception of sleep as a defense against fatigue rehabilitated the relevance of the subjective feeling of tiredness. It also brought back another figure that exhaustion theories had sought to eclipse: the acting subject.

The return of the subject in Claparède is again closely bound up with his passive and active sleep language game. If in fatigue theories one is overpowered by sleep, in Claparède's theory, the tired subject has to actively initiate sleep:

> What characterizes the "activity" of a process? . . . To be honest, it is rather difficult to define the notion of activity. . . . "Active" implies the idea of a reaction. But reaction implies in turn an activity, and then we are in a circle. Thus, let's put the term "reaction" differently—let's call it a movement elicited by a stimulus that

> enables a constitutive disposition of the organism. Then, the term "active" signifies that which implies a participation of a subject; the active process is a process to which the potentialities of the subject itself give rise, potentialities that the subject has in reserve, potentialities that are only triggered but not created by the stimulus. The more the subject participates, the more active can a process be called. ("La question du sommeil," 438-39)[30]

Although Claparède tries out several biological terms to describe this process, he remarks that the "question of terminology is only of secondary importance" ("la question de mot n'est que secondaire" ["Esquisse d'une théorie biologique du sommeil," 296]) as long as it confers "the idea of activity" ("La question du sommeil," 439). Like in the linguistic active voice, where the subject by default appears in the acting position, the subject must figure as the agent if we are to call sleep "an active process" ("La question du sommeil," 437). This idea is already implied in common French expressions such as "chercher le sommeil," which literally translates as "to seek sleep," and figures prominently in the first paragraph of Proust's *À la recherche du temps perdu*.[31] As Claparède suggests treating "language as the expression of thought," it goes without saying that he evokes this idiom himself.[32] For example, he employs it when describing the steps of the ritual that lead to falling asleep: "the search of a sleeping place, the adoption of an attitude appropriate to sleep," followed by "the action of making oneself fall asleep" ("l'action de s'endormir") ("Esquisse d'une théorie biologique du sommeil," 284).[33] The activity of the subject becomes evident in the reflexive verb "s'endormir," to put oneself to sleep. Claparède takes the reflexive structure of the verb as a cue, interpreting it as an act of unconscious detachment from the environment in favor of a return to oneself. To fall asleep thus requires taking an active disinterest in the world.

The Labor of Staying Asleep

Claparède was, of course, not the first person to describe sleep as an active disinterest in one's surroundings. Around 1900, this idea circulated in the work of Freud and the philosopher Henri Bergson, two figures with whom Claparède corresponded about sleep. But what made his idea of sleep as active disinterest different and interesting was that he pictured the detachment during sleep as extraordinarily fragile. On this view, half sleep ("sommeil partiel"; "être demi-endormi") rather than deep sleep ("Esquisse d'une théorie biologique du sommeil," 314) describes what sleep is. Again transmogrifying Freud's ideas, Claparède paints sleep as the site of an intrapsychic conflict about unplugging from the world: sleep is permanently under the threat of early awakening ("sommeil menacé"; "siège") ("Esquisse d'une théorie biologique du sommeil," 315).[34] In light of permanently inrushing sensations from both the outside world and the unconscious, it takes "constant activity" to focus one's subliminal "attention" ("Esquisse," 315) on "maintaining the sleeping state" ("La question du sommeil," 437). One technique to sustain sleep is dreaming, and here Claparède quotes Freud's idea of the dream as the "guardian of sleep (*Hüter des Schlafes*)" ("Esquisse d'une théorie biologique du sommeil," 323). In this oblique passage in *Die Traumdeutung*, Freud argues that we do not sleep in order to dream but dream so that we are able to continue sleeping. As "guardian[s] of sleep," dreams serve to protect our time of slumber against intrusions that could lead to awakening.[35] Claparède goes even further. For him, dreaming represents only one "special case of the action . . . of sleep" ("Esquisse d'une théorie biologique du sommeil," 324-25) geared toward sustaining a restorative state. Sleep literally represents a form of work—one that goes beyond Freud's dream work:

> The graphics published on the curves of sleep resemble very much the curves of work . . . , whose recording Mosso and Kraepelin have instigated. . . . It does appear that sleep, like work, must pass an onset period to reach its apogee. Here's a second parallel . . . : The sleep curves . . . show a series of oscillations . . . ; it is as if the organism, sensing that its sleep is threatened . . . , tries to reinforce the inhibitive process—just like a worker distracted by noise from the street, makes a constant effort to reinforce attention. . . . All these things happen as if the sleep centers which have been proposed to explain the maintenance of sleep are becoming increasingly exhausted so that one wakes up because one is too tired to continue sleeping. ("Esquisse d'une théorie biologique du sommeil," 315)[36]

Maintaining disinterest in the world during sleep is literally hard work. Claparède comes to this conclusion through an uncanny semblance of experimental findings: the sleep curves that various scholars collected remind him of the curves on work efficiency in Mosso's and Kraepelin's studies. One does not wake up because one's energies are restored but because one is tired of fighting off the world. From this perspective, modern sleep consists not of inner peace but of endangered rest.

Still, the concept of active sleep poses a significant problem of agency. Who sleeps during sleep? Claparède's answer: sleep centers in the brain. With his gesture toward the existence of one or many sleep regulation centers in the brain, Claparède offers a cue to what would soon feature as the central controversy in sleep science. When the strange sleeping sickness encephalitis lethargica struck wartime Europe about ten years after the publication of Claparède's "Esquisse d'une théorie biologique du sommeil," the relation of active sleep to sleep centers suddenly became the key talking point of sleep science and the discipline of neurology. To what extent was sleeping an action by the subject's brain?

Learning from Pathologies

The enigmatic sleep sickness encephalitis lethargica (EL), which came to be known as the "greatest medical mystery of the 20th century," struck the world beginning in around 1915 and wound down in around 1927 and affected up to one million people worldwide.[37] This disease received its name from the Sleeping Beauty type of slumber to which many patients succumbed; it could last for days, weeks, or months.[38] The film *Acute encephalitis lethargica*, recorded at the Institute for Medical Cinematography at the Charité Berlin in 1926 and based on a clinical case study of the book *Acute encephalitis lethargica*, offers a visual representation of the disease (see fig. 1.2).[39]

In an iconography reminiscent of Jean-Martin Charcot's medical photographs, the still shows how a doctor awakens a woman suffering from the sleeping sickness and makes her perform the finger-to-nose test.[40] Does the sick woman recognize herself? Is she able to identify her nose by pointing to it? In a long close-up shot of the woman's face, the film shows how she "goes to sleep," while performing the test, as an intertitle comment reveals.

EL "earned sleep a place in the biomedical science of the twentieth century."[41] In his history of sleep science, Kroker notes that EL attracted funding from private donors and, consequently, the attention of bacteriologists, physiologists, psychologists, and psychiatrists. Still, to grasp how the epidemic outbreak of EL advanced the concept of active sleep, we must examine the clinical, theoretical, and neuroscientific work of the Vienna-based psychiatrist and neurologist Constantin von Economo (1876–1931). Encountering patients lingering in a strange somnolence in a Viennese war hospital—just a few hundred steps away from Freud's headquarters yet seemingly in a different world—Economo concluded that a new diagnostic framework was needed to capture the mysterious nature of this clinical picture. Economo started to believe that this disease provided the master key to explaining sleep as a hardwired function of the brain. He was thus more than the first

The Science of Sleep 25

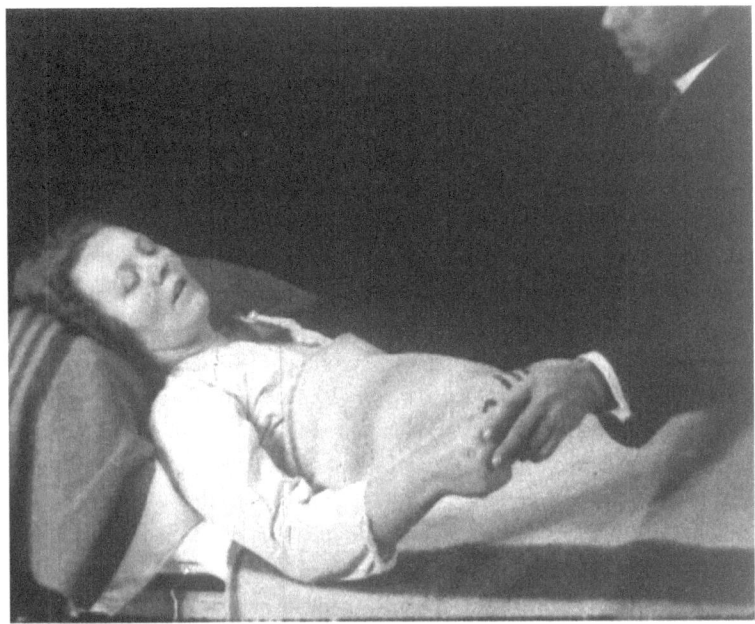

Figure 1.2. Encephalitis lethargica patient being tested for "sleep inebriation" at the Charité Berlin, film still taken from *Acute encephalitis lethargica*, directed by Friedrich Heinrich Lewy, at the University of Berlin in 1925 (Wellcome Collection, London).

clinician to diagnose EL and the foremost authority on the sleeping sickness.[42] Economo went on to make the investigation of sleep the "theme of his life."[43] Even today, Economo is credited with providing "the first evidence for an active mechanism of sleep regulation."[44] But despite this legacy, the history of how the idea of active sleep emerged from EL remains to be written, and the consequences of this conceptual shift have yet to be explored.[45]

EL was not the first sleeping sickness to provoke a reconsideration of the contested question of what sleep was and how it worked. During the late nineteenth century, the diagnosis of narcolepsy and outbreaks of African trypanosomiasis in colonial territories had led to multiple inquiries into the nature of sleep through pathologies.[46] Building on this approach, Economo framed the pathology of the sleeping sickness as a way of investigating "the ancient but still unanswered question . . . what is sleep?" ("Die Encephalitis lethargica," 25). His approaching normal sleep via an instance of nonnormal sleep situates Economo in the tradition of nineteenth-century clinical pathology, whose genealogy has been critically reconstructed by Georges Canguilhem.[47] As Canguilhem has shown, this tradition essentially aimed to reduce pathology to biology.[48] From this perspective, normal and pathological states consist in "nothing more than quantitative variations, greater or lesser according to corresponding physiological phenomena."[49] For nineteenth-century physiology, "all morbid states show us under a magnifying glass certain states that are normal—but not easily visible when normal."[50] Economo believed that the sleeping sickness had presented him with a living model of how sleep functioned.

And this model delivered results. According to Economo, EL established a definitive link between sleep and the brain, as already reflected in the name he selected: encephalitis lethargica identifies a site (encephalon, the brain), a pathological state (-itis, an affliction or inflammation), and a primary symptom (a deep lethargy).[51] Specifically, EL provided evidence that a specific inflammatory profile "in the tegmentum of the midbrain, close to the diencephalon" ("Der Schlaf als Lokalisationsproblem," 47) could produce a bouquet of sleep disorders: sleeping sickness, insomnia, and sleep inversion (reversal of periodicity), as well as a long-lasting altered reaction to sleep-inducing psychopharmaceuticals ("Schlaftheorie," 329). Based on this clinical evidentiary material, Economo concluded that the "peculiar character of the disease" ("Der Schlaf als Lokalisationsproblem," 47) is irreducibly tied to its localization. EL functions like a marker, so to speak, circumscribing the region in the brain that regulates sleep "in a primary and immediate manner" ("Der Schlaf als Lokalisationsproblem," 47). A defect in this area thus "interferes with sleep directly" ("Die Encephalitis lethargica," 1336). Economo deduced that a "sleep regulation mechanism" ("Schlafsteuerungsmechanismus im nervösen Grau" ["Der Schlaf als Lokalisationsproblem," 48]), a sleep center, must exist in the gray matter of the brain.

Every medically trained contemporary would have recognized in an instant the assertion of a "sleep regulation mechanism" as a highly controversial one, as this idea seemed to have been repudiated thoroughly in the neurological debates prior to the Great War. Indeed, the idea of a sleep center evoked the antiquated atmosphere of the nineteenth century, as in the 1880s, both clinicians and scientists began suggesting that sleep operated based on a center in the brain.[52] That this idea developed in the 1880s indicates that the hypothesis of a sleep center rose to prominence during the heyday of the paradigm of functional localization, or *Zentrenlehre*.[53] Neuropsychiatrists who embraced this theory argued that sensory and motor "centers" existed in the brain, and they set out to produce an anatomical map of the cortex that localized functions such as language organically.[54] In the second half of the nineteenth century, Carl Wernicke's research on aphasia, in particular, yielded clinical findings that seemed to undergird functional localization. In this intellectual climate, the diagnosis of previously unknown sleep disorders such as narcolepsy commonly pointed to an organic lesion. French neurologist Jean-Baptiste-Édouard Gélineau and subsequent scholars of narcolepsy, for example, argued that the clinical picture of narcolepsy resulted from a shock to the mid-brain region, which they supposed was the site of a sleep center.[55]

After 1900, however, the vogue of functional localization had temporarily come to an end.[56] Although the methodology persisted in many subfields of the neuro disciplines and even briefly flourished again in the neurosurgical clinics of World War I, the idea that functional localization was relevant to explaining sleep had been almost entirely abandoned. Francophone literature, specifically, rejected the sleep center hypothesis.[57] Ensuing studies established an international consensus that a sleep center was no more than a chimera, a finding in line with both observations on sleep-wake periods in plants and living beings born without a neocortex (anencephaly).[58] Moreover, fundamental criticism of the paradigm of localization, which had arisen from more recent theories of neuroplasticity, necessitated a different explanation of sleep. Because of these developments, support for the idea of a sleep center petered out, and new theories came to the fore that stressed sleep's periodicity and its rhythmic element, understood to be the result of human evolution.[59] Science thus returned to offering a minimal definition of sleep as a periodic phenomenon, its periodicity being what Wilhelm Wundt had once called the one and only thing that was certain about sleep.[60]

To understand how thoroughly the idea of a sleep center had been refuted after 1900, one must remember that Economo, too, was highly skeptical of the sleep center hypothesis when he first encountered EL. Although he immediately realized that the localization of the virus was "grist to the mill of this understanding of sleep" ("Neue Beiträge zur Encephalitis lethargica," 876) he insisted that "doubts" about the existence of a sleep center "remain." He thus called for rigorous experimental examination ("Die Encephalitis lethargica," 292). However, after EL had spread globally and therefore appeared to have already conducted "a cruel experiment in a laboratory of gigantic scale" ("Die Encephalitis lethargica Epidemia," 67)—as Economo paraphrases Claude Bernard's famous dictum that illnesses are natural experiments—the hypothetical existence of the sleep center received, as if it were, "the seal of clinical approval."[61] Six years after Economo's doubtful first account, he felt that the time was ripe to bring back the sleep center hypothesis and to base a sleep theory on his clinical observations. The appearance of EL therefore enabled the resurgence of a research program that had already been considered terminated. The new objective was to reexamine the central thesis of the sleep center paradigm in a way that would make it possible to account for sleep's periodicity. In this context, the concept of active sleep received new prominence.

Mechanisms of Active Sleep Regulation

Even if Economo's theoretical writings on sleep return to the question of a sleep center, he does not brush over the highly contested status of this entity. He concedes that the claim of a "so-called sleep center" appears "as an extraordinarily strange imposition at first" and even compares it to an obsolete quest "for the seat of the soul" ("Der Schlaf als Lokalisationsproblem," 38).[62] In fact, he responds to the problem of the sleep center's anachronicity with a far-reaching refurbishment of the concept. Thus, the introduction of a dichotomy between passive and active sleep serves as a key marker distinguishing Economo's new take on the sleep center from previous models: if the prewar sleep center hypothesis perceived sleep as "the passive consequence of discontinued stimuli," Economo proposes the existence of a "sleep regulation center that actively brings about sleep" ("Schlaftheorie," 322, 388). Note the subtle terminological distinction that signals this shift: the outmoded term "sleep center" ("Schlafzentrum") has given way to a "sleep regulation center" ("Schlafsteuerungszentrum"). As the verb "steuern" (to steer, to govern, to regulate) intimates, this new concept is inextricably married to the claim "that sleep constitutes an active process" (Über den Schlaf," 876).[63]

Economo's embrace of a localized, active sleep regulation center has three consequences. First of all, the sleep center becomes a complex regulating armature, or, as Economo has it, a "biological multitude" ("biologische Vielheit") ("Der Schlaf als Lokalisationsproblem," 45). To that end, he extends the notion of the center substantially and allows for a certain degree of fuzziness in terms of regional circumscription.[64] For instance, a center may well comprise a "larger area" composed out of "various parts" ("Der Schlaf als Lokalisationsproblem," 52). For Economo, then, the term "center" basically refers to clusters of gray nervous matter that are of "immediate and direct importance for the manifestation of its function" and are very selective about impulses to which they respond; in contrast to simpler centers that respond less selectively to stimulation, such distributed centers only respond to a "very specific constellation of sensations" ("Der Schlaf als Lokalisationsproblem," 39). In other words, it is the biological function of a center as such that takes center stage, displacing the idea of functions that fit into a predefined brain area, even if Economo continues to insist that functions have to be localized.

Second, Economo's localization of the sleep regulation center in the mesencephalic region of the brainstem indicates how this active regulation of sleep is supposed to function. The site situates the sleep regulation center in "direct vicinity" ("Schlaftheorie," 329) to "numerous sympathetic, parasympathetic and vegetative centers, which recent research has relocated to the adjacent bottom of the diencephalon" ("Pathologie des Schlafs," 607). The very topology of the brain therefore suggests that "the periodicity of sleep belongs to the same group of changes in the vegetative state" ("Schlaftheorie," 330). Within this framework, active sleep refers to the observation that the sleep regulation center coordinates a plethora of nocturnal processes. As a "complex biological state" ("Schlaftheorie," 314), sleep impacts the entire organism, as physiological studies on metabolic changes showed in detail. To capture this holistic effect on the organism, Economo introduces a new terminological distinction:

> In our definition, brain sleep [*Hirnschlaf*] refers exclusively to the state of the nervous and psychic functions of the brain. In contrast, the term "body sleep" ["*Körperschlaf*"] encapsulates the state of all other bodily organs during sleep, as well as changes in metabolism and the streaming of blood and lymph. With the term "body sleep" we thus capture all anatomical, chemical, and additional processes in the brain which do not find immediate expression in nervous or psychic effects. ("Pathologie des Schlafs," 593)[65]

Economo conceptually divorces the psychic and the vegetative dimension of sleep to underscore that sleep comprises more than just a diminution of mental activity, an obnubilation of consciousness, or an absence of attention. The localization of the sleep center in the mesencephalon rather than in the cortex, Economo argues, means that one must conceive of sleep as a fundamentally different state than waking, a state that results in a "qualitative transposition of a significant share of all body functions" ("Der Schlaf als Lokalisationsproblem," 45).[66] Against this backdrop, a symmetry between waking and sleeping emerges that suggests the existence of a complementary relationship between diurnal and nocturnal life: "Sleep must be seen as the complement to being awake. It is neither the opposite nor the negation of wakefulness" ("Über den Schlaf," 878). Neither being awake nor being asleep comprises a state that can be articulated in terms of the logic of the other. As a "fundamentally different" state from waking life, sleep turns into an "activity" that unfolds based on an *Eigengesetzlichkeit,* or an "autonomous logic of its own."[67]

Third, this "autonomous logic" becomes crucial to explaining the basic observation of sleep's periodicity, that is, the alternation of sleeping and waking, which had proven elusive in earlier hypotheses of a sleep center.[68] To tackle this problem, Economo divides his sleep regulation center into two discrete but interrelated parts: within the sleep center, he juxtaposes the sleep center proper with a waking center, whose "counterpoint" brings about "the alternating periodicity of sleeping and waking in concert with still other elements" ("Schlaftheorie," 313). Of course, the idea to fold two centers into one can be counted as an innovation, but the really significant new idea is the suggestion of an autonomous mechanism regulating sleep.[69] Previously, the sleep center functioned within a human-environment continuum and tied sleep to changes in the environment. This is especially apparent in Oskar Vogt's earlier model of the sleep center (1895–96): on his model, the brain passes on pertinent incoming sensations via an associate mechanism until they reach "the subcortical sleep center," whose stimulation gradually shuts down sense perception and effects sleep.[70] By contrast, Economo propagates an autonomous sleep-wake regulation system that generates endocrine rhythms. Although the periodic alteration of sleeping and waking had once been linked to the "day-night periods of our planet" and had been seen as dependent on exposure to sunlight, temperature, air pressure, radioactivity, and electricity, human evolution leads to "an easing of this dependence." That is to say, "the rhythms of the organisms adhere to their inner autonomous fluctuations ["eigenperiodischen Schwankungen"] . . . similar to high and low tide" ("Pathologie des Schlafs," 591–92). What is crucial, then, is that this endocrine sleep-wake rhythmicity not only resembles the periodicity of other vegetative functions such as body temperature but, more importantly, that it functions potentially independently from the environment. Sleep cycles become self-regulating. This was quite forward thinking; if there was jet travel at that time, the notion of circadian rhythms would have come into play as well.

Autonomous Sleep

Still, the true explosiveness of Economo's argument that sleep has its own autonomous logic only becomes evident if we relate another problem associated with EL to this claim: if sleep emerges from a self-regulating armature in the brain, who is the one who sleeps? In the most radical version of his position, Economo suggests that all sleep patterns are socially conditioned throughout ("anerzogen") ("Pathologie des Schlafs," 592) and that a fissure splits the allegedly autonomous subject.[71]

The key to understanding this argument is Economo's hint that the sleep regulation center functions analogously to reflexes in Pavlov's famous experiment. For Pavlov, reflexes are conditioned responses to stimuli (for example, the dog that begins to salivate every time a bell rings). Although Economo hedges this connection between sleep and reflexes with a provisional caveat, he underlines that it appears "very likely" that the sleep center works based on reflexes ("Pathologie des Schlafs," 607). In asserting a link between neuroanatomic localization and reflex theory to explain how the sleep center might work, Economo takes up an already-well-established idea. His idol and role model, the Viennese neuropsychiatrist Theodor Meynert (1833-92), argued that functional localization was bound up closely with reflex theory.[72] Reflex theory allows Economo to attribute to the nervous system those quasiautomatic actions that do not rise to the level of consciousness.[73] Historically, this argument was used not to explain sleep but rather psychic phenomena that volition could not account for. Some figures, such as the physiologist Sigmund Exner (1846-1926), at whose institute Economo started his academic career, even went so far as to develop a general theory of the psyche that featured the reflex as a kind of "Anti-Cogito."[74] According to Exner, "I think" or "I feel" are incorrect utterances. What is correct is "It thinks within me" or "It feels within me."[75] From this perspective, Economo's reflex-oriented sleep theory claims that it's not me who wants to sleep. Instead, one should say, "It sleeps within me." Economo explains:

> Recent insights gleaned from encephalitis have shown us that volition [*Willen*] constitutes a complex function of our being. One part of it occurs not only outside of conscious processes but also outside of the psyche in general, that is to say, it occurs not within the domain of psychology at all. This part of volition is susceptible to disruptions—interferences—that probably occur at a specific loca-

tion in the subcortex. Psychologists will have to come to terms with this. The field of psychiatry, however, gains new insights. Physiology is now able to explain functions which we once regarded as psychological processes, as processes of volition . . . and which used to prove elusive to physiology. ("Encephalitis lethargica," 1338)[76]

EL, then, opened up "physiologically and psychologically altogether unexpected insights into the mysteries of psychic mechanisms . . . , insights which will perhaps have a huge impact outside of the medical profession" ("Encephalitis lethargica," 1338).[77] What makes EL so relevant to the nonmedical world is its contribution to questions of willpower. For Economo, approaches to EL demonstrate that volition has both a psychic and a physiological dimension. Although vegetative phenomena such as sleep "are considered actions by the subject from a psychological point of view," at their inner core there sits an impersonal "it" ("Encephalitis lethargica," 1337). To use Economo's example:

> A patient who suffers, say, from Jacksonian seizures [*Jackson-Anfälle*] in one hand will explain that "it twitches in my hand" [*es zuckt in meiner Hand*]. Such a patient objectifies the movement in the hand and does not regard it as a part of themselves. An encephalitis patient who continues to flutter with one hand, however, says about it: 'I just have to move my hand like this all the time.' In other words, the encephalitis patient describes the movement as a subjective one and psychologically recognizes it as part of themselves. ("Encephalitis lethargica," 1337)[78]

Regarding sleep, too, the physiological "it" that sleeps within gets dressed up and psychologically attributed to the subject, if we follow the Viennese neurologist. In light of this finding, I suggest that the grammatical active voice is inadequate to express the full complexity of what is going on in sleep. Instead, one ought to describe sleep using the middle voice, which renders the subject neither as agent nor patient but as a combination of both. The self takes on a sort of reflexive sense: the subject acts on or for itself.

Economo's contemporary figures had already expressed ideas that ran along these lines. For example, the Austrian psychiatrist Otto Pötzl, a colleague of Economo, came up with an especially remarkable grammatical rendering. Explicitly "harkening back to the ideas and results of Economo," Pötzl realized that the invocation of a sleep regulation center profoundly challenged traditional notions of who sleeps.[79] To capture the impact of the sleep center, he presents an odd translation of a Czech expression: "'Es will sich mir schlafen.'"[80] This agrammatical and profoundly untranslatable turn of phrase radicalizes the central idea of the reflex-theoretical rendering of "It sleeps within me," from which it adapts the impersonal "it."[81] The clause combines a dummy subject (as in "it rains") with a dummy modal verb that transforms "to sleep" into a reflexive verb with a dative object. The effect is a construction in a faux middle voice: a process determines the action that is performed for the subject. Sleep becomes a matter of the reflexes of the vegetative nervous system; it also displays a massively complicated agency.

Rhythms, Curves, Lines

In the same year Plötzl theorized about the grammar of sleep, there was another decisive development: a new media technology emerged whose inventor explicitly embraced the idea that sleep is an "active achievement."[82] This new media technology was the electroencephalograph (EEG) (fig. 1.3). Developed by the Jena psychiatrist Hans Berger (1873-1941) through a circuitous process during the 1920s and first made public in 1929, the EEG refers to the graphical trace that registers incessant discharges of accumulated electrical energy of the brain in regular patterns.[83]

From the outset, Berger was interested in the "question of whether different electroencephalograms can be demonstrated during the state of wakefulness and during the state of sleep."[84] He discovered that the EEG recorded two distinct rhythms, which he called alpha rhythms and beta rhythms. He also discovered that alpha rhythms disappeared whenever his test subjects responded to stimuli, made mental efforts, or simply opened their eyes. In a relaxed state of wakefulness, with eyes closed, alpha rhythms were present. In states of sleep (including sleep on soporifics), alpha rhythms were still present, even though in attenuated form.[85] Berger correctly concluded that lower alpha rhythms continue during sleep, a finding that "corresponds with

Figure 1.3. Encephalogram of a sleeping man. The curve on top shows the alpha rhythm, the curve on the bottom is a time measure (Berger, "Über das Elektrenkephalogramm des Menschen: Dritte Mitteilung," 35).

our assumption that psycho-physical processes are by no means extinguished during sleep."[86] In the visual inscriptions of the EEG, Berger recognized active sleep—an activity complicated by the fact that making too much of a deliberate effort interfered with it.

The EEG "proved itself capable of transforming the study of sleep," as scholars of sleep research have shown in detail.[87] During the second half of the twentieth century, the EEG became the "authority to define the nature of sleep."[88] This ascent was possible because the EEG made good on the promise that an experimental, quantitative method could finally penetrate the elusive domain of sleep, which "seems to be inaccessible by way of subjective evaluation and all other objective ways of inquiry," as one scientist put it.[89] While researchers such as Claparède and Economo had stabilized the notion of active sleep as an epistemic thing, the EEG rendered this epistemic thing manifest in the form of objective, automated, and universally accepted inscriptions that visually represent (and constitute) the activity of the brain during sleep. The EEG transformed both practices of sleep researchers and the ontology of sleep itself: sleep became active sleep, but in the form of alpha rhythms that required a relaxed state to appear.

2 White Nights, Brown Pills

Sleeplessness must have existed since the beginning of history. Yet the onset of high modernity turned it into the signature of an age. In *24/7: Late Capitalism and the Ends of Sleep* (2013), Jonathan Crary has shown that the emergence of modern capitalist society and the type of subjectification to which it gives rise amounts to an assault on the material and psychological preconditions for restful sleep and regeneration.[1] A biopolitical regime that trains its subjects to be ever alert and productive provides fertile ground for the proliferation of insomnia, defined as a persistent inability to sleep despite best efforts. According to historical and sociological scholarship, the rise of insomnia has been part and parcel of modernization processes since the late nineteenth century. In the increasingly industrialized parts of Western Europe and the US, these processes included developments such as urbanization, electrification, and a reorganization of professional life. Everyday living became almost universally governed by the clock and was subjected to quantitative assessment.[2] What is more, with the rise of modern leisure culture, which placed heavy demands on the attention of individuals, the distinction between work and rest became increasingly blurred, effectively turning leisure into another taxing activity rather than a period of rest and relaxation.[3] Correspondingly, empirical studies have shown that the inability to sleep became ubiquitous starting in the 1880s; after the turn of the century, it constituted, as the physician Karl Lechner observed in the early twentieth century, "the most frequent ailment in the doctor's office."[4] This rampant proliferation of insomnia indirectly reveals the coveted status of sound sleep under the conditions of modernity. The Austrian poet Peter Altenberg pinpoints sleep's new prestige with the hyperbole characteristic of self-help literature and some of his writings: "Sacred sleep. . . . Being well rested, entirely well rested, is the only guarantee for you, o human being, that you will be able to perform your very best at work!"[5]

The relationship between the ability to sleep and work, however, goes both ways. After seeing countless patients, medical professionals and scientists understood that insomnia comes down to a paradox: an exhausted brain does not stop its cognitive activity. On the contrary, it begins to belabor the mental residues of the day with high intensity, giving rise to an overwhelming inner restlessness. Medical professionals often related this to weak nerves (neurasthenia), but they also marshaled metaphors to make sense of the experience. They portrayed insomnia as a state of "unrest, hurry, and chasing" ("Unruhe, Hasten und Jagen") "sensation hunger" ("Reizhunger"), and "associative thinking" ("Gedankenjagd"), metaphors that illustrate a psychological condition that actively drives sleep away, undercuts the insomniac's sense of control and self-efficacy, and infuses those who toss and turn in bed with a profound "anxiety."[6] Exploiting this festering anxiety as an economic resource, a gigantic market emerged that promised to do away with white nights, thereby strengthening weak nerves, bringing about inner peace and "restor[ing] selfhood."[7]

Then, as now, one could seek to cure insomnia and other sleep disorders with home remedies, self-guided relaxation therapies, sojourns at the sea or in the high mountains, and autogenic training and through medical approaches such as sleep hygiene that amount to nothing less than a reorganization of one's existence according to rational principles whose aim is to shelter one from the effects of modernity. Yet one could also fall back on chemical remedies sold over the counter in drug stores and pharmacies. In principle, this was no news—knowledge of sleep-inducing tinctures that contained extracts from the opium poppy or the mandrake dates back to antiquity, when the Greek term "pharmakon" still encapsulated three meanings: medicine, poison, and magic potion.[8]

The emergence of the modern pharmaceutical industry, however, fundamentally challenged the traditional regime of domestic remedies, sleep hygiene, and tailor-made established drugs.[9] In Germany, this industry began its rise in the late 1850s, when companies started to manufacture coal-tar dyestuffs. A few decades later, science-based firms such as Bayer (Farbfabriken vorm. Friedr. Bayer & Co.), BASF (Badische Anilin und Sodafabrik), Hoechst (Farbwerke vorm. Meister Lucius & Brüning), and others had turned into global powerhouses that had research laboratories, that collaborated with academics, and that used professional marketing. What is more, the

German pharmaceutical giants often cooperated with each other to bolster their power of innovation and worldwide dominance, and they eventually formed an enormous trust, I. G. Farben, in the mid-1920s that was then broken up by the Allies after the end of WWII.[10]

With the rise of this industry, sleep-inducing drugs, which worked reliably, became easily accessible to everyone, as they could be had for the price of a meal or less.[11] The invention of the earliest synthetic sleep medication in 1869, chloral hydrate, sparked an entire new market that promised to sell what Henri Piéron called "sleep in a bottle."[12] Portraying insomnia as a problem that could be solved through an act of consumption, the pharmaceutical industry began to market soporifics as a modern solution for a modern problem. The pharmaceutical industry therefore sold not only a chemical substance but also a promise: the promise that by taking synthetic sleep medication one could regain control over one's life and one's agency and become fully productive again.

Side Effects of Modern Life

The increased urgency of insomnia around 1900 corresponded with medical concerns about neurasthenia, a fuzzy catchall diagnosis that registered visceral responses to modernization processes such as acceleration, changes in social rhythms, urbanization, industrialization, and electrification.[13] The medical universe of neurasthenia, including the social types, narratives, and cultures the diagnosis produced in the wake of George Beard's *American Nervousness* (1881) is by now so well known that it hardly needs to be recapitulated.[14] Still, only scant attention has been paid to the fact that the prime symptom of neurasthenia was insomnia.[15] Almost all contemporary medical textbooks on nervousness highlight this when they survey the manifold manifestations of this diagnosis: "Sleep disorders are most likely never missing from cases of neurasthenia."[16] In addition to offering medical expertise, many authors attributed the rise of nervous insomnia explicitly to social causes and conditions, especially in the early interwar period: "As a result of the long war, its unfortunate ending, and the political and economic turmoil that has arisen in its wake and is still ongoing, the number of cases of nervous insomnia have increased dramatically."[17] The rise of sleeplessness in the German-speaking word was thus seen as going hand in hand with the advent of modern industrial capitalist society. According to the medical literature, insomnia was driven by disproportionate hours at work and unreasonable professional demands, and it manifested as a symptom of being overwhelmed in shift workers, stressed-out professionals, and "personalities who incorporate the social norms of modern society too zealously."[18] It also stigmatized those individuals who were deemed too sensitive to cope with packed, stressful days, whose workloads haunted them until the wee hours of the night like nightmares.[19] To make a long story short, the inability to fall or stay asleep at night was one of the prototypical side effects of modernization.

Yet despite obvious demand for a solution and a spate of new soporifics on offer, for a long time the pharmaceutical industry struggled to capitalize on the rampant sleeplessness and the anxieties that surrounded it. In part, this was because physicians believed that the problem of insomnia was part and parcel of problems of modernization more generally. Many physicians reasoned that the only effective antidote was a "return to a simpler lifestyle, to an earlier state of civilization, and an exodus from the big cities."[20] If this return to a simpler life was not possible, a smattering of self-help books offered alternatives, for example, by teaching soothing strategies through self-talk, breathing techniques, and muscle relaxation, although often in strikingly gendered ways aimed primarily at men (see fig. 2.1).[21]

The pharma industry also struggled because the use of chemical sleep medication commanded a universally bad reputation before 1900. Most German physicians relegated such use to asylum and hospital medicine, where sedatives served the purpose of putting restless patients in a chemical straitjacket.[22] As the author and physician Gottfried Benn (1886-1956) has it in a poem describing asylum patients: "One puts them to sleep. Day and night.—The new ones/are being told: here you'll regain your health by way of sleep.—Only on Sunday,/for the visits, one ensures that they are slightly more awake."[23] Even though the pharma industry sought to improve the image of its products through aggressive marketing and strove to position them as remedies to common insomnia, the use of synthetic sleep medicine was generally discouraged across the spectrum of health-care writing, be it in medical treatises, popular scientific publications, advice books, or anthologies of traditional home remedies. Their refrain was "prescriptions offer no cure" ("der Zettel heilt die Krankheit nicht").[24] These publications typically argued that soporifics were poisonous and that they medicalized sleeplessness, which could not be singled out through differential diagnosis. Most importantly, the health-care literature pointed out that pharmaceutical substances at best obliterated a "symptom" but still ignored the "causes"

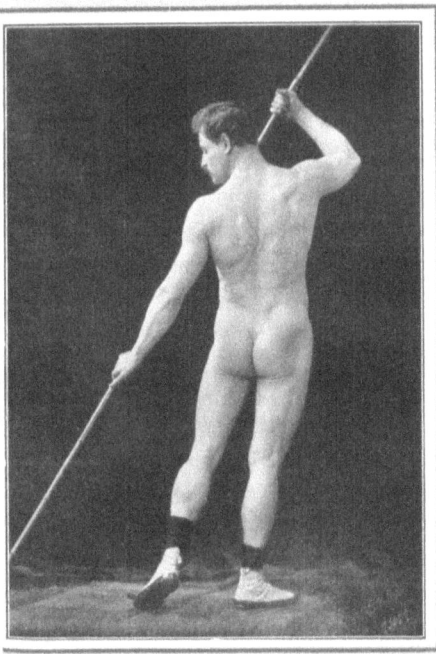

Figure 2.1. Cover page of an allegedly best-selling self-help book promising to do away with insomnia through physical exercise and breathing work. The gendered cover photo indicates that this approach is primarily geared toward men.

of sleeplessness.[25] To root out the underlying problem, physicians championed another method: sleep hygiene.

"Sleep hygiene" appears as a curious coinage, being made up of two seemingly disparate elements. Today, the word "hygiene" connotes impeccable cleanliness and aseptic rooms, but until the early twentieth century, it had a much broader meaning. It referred to a system of knowledge that described "the relationship between humans and the material conditions of their physical existence" and provided "guidelines for individuals and social institutions to regulate these conditions."[26] This notion of hygiene directly translates into a concept of sleep hygiene still in use, as an entry in 2007 sleep medicine encyclopedia indicates: "The term 'sleep hygiene' refers to habits that foster restful sleep. Several catalogues exist that spell out rules and indicate possible mistakes."[27] Such catalogues set out guidelines for

> the organization of one's day according to an adequate alternation between work, meals, and rest, the embrace of a regular order in rising and going to bed, the correct furnishing of the bedroom, the removal of all disturbing and unfamiliar sensations, overall the right and rational arrangement of one's personal life, the congruence of one's energies and one's aspirations, the mastering of one's body, the power over the directions one's thoughts are taking, the rejection of everything that is not essential.[28]

These catalogues went well beyond proposing a daily routine advantageous to the sleep-wake rhythm whose goal was to create a favorable sleep environment or devising an effective relaxation routine before bedtime. Sleep hygiene instead aimed at the rationalization of one's entire life and the production of a particular kind of subjectivity. At the core of this hygienist idea of regulating sleep by overhauling the way one lived is the belief that practices of self-care can facilitate greater agency.[29] A historic term for such practices is "dietetics."[30] One can trace hygiene and dietetics back to ancient "technologies of the self," but they gained new currency beginning in the Enlightenment, in the wake of an agenda that prized taking on responsibility for oneself.[31] For many figures in the Enlightenment era, in fact, relying on one's own understanding was inextricably linked to self-care: "People should think independently and know how to take care of their own bodies, which means that they should emancipate themselves from their guardians, be it priests or physicians."[32] The article on *hygiène* in Diderot's *Encyclopédie* (1765) espouses the Greek physician and philosopher Galen's humoral pathology, which defines light, air, nutrition, motion, metabolism, emotions, and finally sleep as *res non naturales*, all of which have a huge impact on the subject but can only be regulated in an indirect fashion, namely, by the subject implementing and maintaining a certain lifestyle or peculiar habits. That is why Galen calls them *res non naturales;* our relation to them is not determined by natural laws.[33] Good sleep is not a naturally given phenomenon but the result of a rational lifestyle choice—the choice to actively regulate and maintain social, environmental, and behavioral patterns beneficial to sleep. Hygiene thus implies indirect agency: only subjects that control themselves, the argument goes, arrive at a self-empowered subjectivity in tune with their living conditions. What therefore matters most in hygiene is self-regulation—to adopt beneficial habits, to abstain from bad ones, and to alter one's relationship to things out of one's control. On this view, an ordered life leads to ordered sleep, and regular structures plus refreshing rest leads to high productivity. And high productivity during the day, in turn, translates into good sleep during the night.

With the introduction of synthetic sleep medication toward the end of the nineteenth century, this reasoning reached a crossroads: cautions against sleep medication as dangerous and unnatural entered the corpus of hygienic literature, while the pharmaceutical industry touted sleep medication as the epitome of a new hygienic self-relation. A Bayer advertisement (fig. 2.2) shows how the company marshaled Galen and his notion of hygiene as a supporting argument for the usefulness of sleep medication. The ad assembles an idealizing bust of the physician, a quotation in ancient Greek, and a schema of a closed organic system to suggest that the advertised soporific Adalin will strengthen the self-regulation of the body. The message is clear: Galen's tried-and-true medical authority endorses the drug. The fact that this argument features in a visual advertisement rather than in a biomedical research article reveals its double objective: to link synthetic sleep aids with the authority of hygiene and to bring about a new type of consumer who would be willing to take sleep medication. The pharmaceutical companies repackaged their products in such a way to suggest that they fulfilled the demands of hygienic self-care. Their ads implied that one could now solve insomnia through an act of consumption, an act that did not demand a rejection of modernity. In purchasing synthetic sleep medication one was not only buying sleep that "worked" but also buying into the idea that through consumption one could reclaim agency and even selfhood threatened by modernity.

Figure 2.2. Galen in an advertisement for Bayer's soporific Adalin, ca. 1909 (BAL, 166/8, Adalin).

Veronal Sleep

A stylized tree diagram (fig. 2.3), dated to 1927 in the upper right corner, illustrates how the pharmaceutical giant Bayer (part of I. G. Farben at that point) imagined its range of soporifics on offer in the interwar period: as natural products with deep roots in modern industry and as a flourishing business. Most likely designed as an advertisement aimed at physicians, the tree diagram comprises eight sleep-inducing drugs whose chemical composition varied and that had different purposes: Adamon, Voluntal, Luminal, Phanodorm, Adalin, and its successor Abasin, as well as Veronal and its successor Paranoval.

The diagram can be understood in several ways. It can be seen as emphasizing that the nature of these substances was such that switching up the pharmaceutical regime regularly was advised to keep the drugs effective and safe. It can also be seen as foregrounding the composition of different types of pharmaceuticals and their individual profiles. Adamon, for example, was directed at patients who would be well served with the herb valerian but asked for (or were prescribed) a drug with the appearance of a stronger soporific.[34] Clearly, the air of a potent drug was part of the intended effect. Luminal, by contrast was a very powerful soporific and antiepileptic (indeed, these properties were exploited systematically by the national socialists to kill patients with psychiatric disorders and disabilities, who accepted the pharmaceutical because they believed it was *only* a soporific).[35] Having a broad range of soporifics on offer could thus provide benefits in reaching different audiences. The diagram can also be understood as advertising material. It assembles not only different types of soporifics in simultaneous use but also different generations of them, ranging from the seasoned Voluntal to the more current developments placed at the center. Yet another way of reading the diagram is that it testifies above all to the success of what has been called the "most important class of soporifics in the first half of the twentieth century," barbiturates. Four of the eight drugs featured in the diagram are barbituric.[36] Their success is inextricably tied to the first barbiturate in use as a sedative and soporific, Veronal, which Bayer and Merck introduced in 1903 and took off the market in the mid-1950s.

Veronal marked the starting point for the large-scale clinical application of barbiturates, a chemical class of which "more than 2500 different agents were synthesized" and that gave rise to "profound changes in the pharmacological approach to the . . . disorders of the time."[37] According to historians

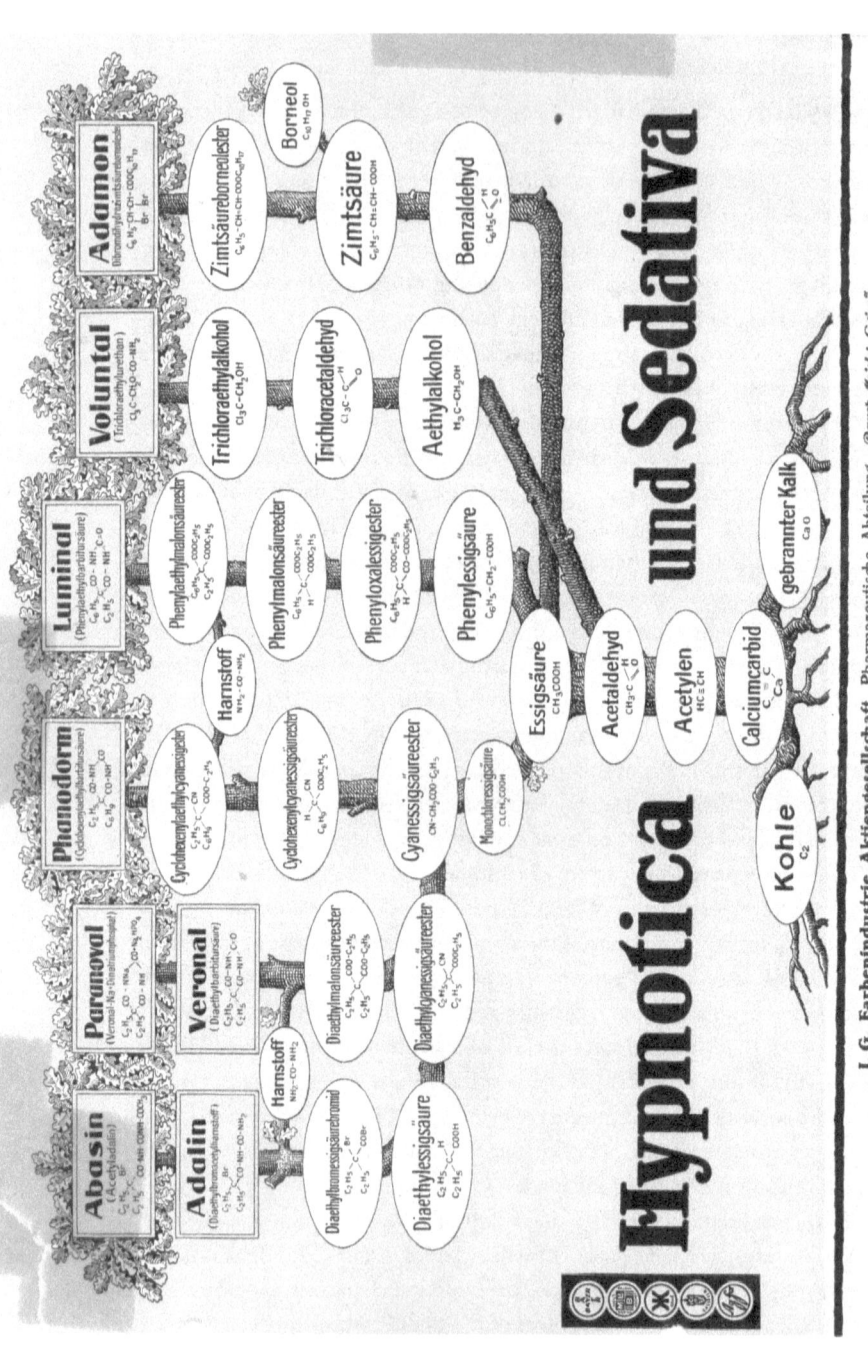

Figure 2-3. Tree diagram, "Hypnotics and Soporifics," 1927 (BAL, 166/10, Pharma, Pharmazie Allgemein, 1906–64).

of pharmacology, barbiturates commanded "substantial advantages" in comparison with earlier existing sleep medication (such as Adamon, Voluntal, Adalin, and Abasin), including greater potency, duration of action, and a wider therapeutic range.[38] To use the words of Edward Shorter, Veronal "transformed" the drug scene.[39]

Drawing on archival documents, advertisements, medical literature, and newspaper clippings, the next section explores why Veronal, as an authoritative history of pharmacology puts it, "quickly eclipsed previously used sleep medications" and succeeded in becoming a "household brand."[40] Chemistry is only one part of this story. Veronal could not have become an "expression of everyday culture"[41] without a specific historic constellation; it was the first soporific that combined an influential chemical innovation with orchestrated efforts to establish a brand name and with a distinctive new mode of consumption. This assemblage of innovations in pharmacy, marketing, and product design made it possible to position the drug as the driving force of a grand narrative of scientific progress in which Veronal featured as the "ideal soporific."[42] Moreover, Bayer positioned the new soporific as an antidote to living with the challenges of modernity more generally. What Veronal addressed was both insomnia and the quotidian effect of modern times. This shift from medicine to "lifestyle agent" crystallized in a novel material object: the sleeping pill proper. With the unprecedented commercial success of Veronal, modern Western society entered into a large-scale experiment in how to use sensitive new technologies of the self.

Veronal's rise to blockbuster status would have been impossible without clinical demand for stronger, safer, and more reliable soporifics. According to historians of pharmacology, the barbiturate Veronal offered just that.[43] Veronal also promised to do away with the experiential difference between "natural" sleep and "artificial" sleep.[44] According to advertising materials, Veronal induced an "almost natural need for sleep" and a "most tranquil slumber of several hours, without dreams, and without any differences from physiological sleep."[45] Better yet, whoever took the drug would awake "fresh and without a dazed feeling."[46] The pharmaceutical industry captured this promise with a paradoxical slogan: they called the experience "natural sleep on Veronal" ("natürlicher Veronalschlaf").[47] Most importantly, the scientific credibility of Veronal was immediately established. The discovery of the soporific qualities of barbiturates and their subsequent proliferation emerged from a cooperation between two renowned scientists: the clinician Josef Freiherr von Mering, a "pioneer in the work on diabetes," and the chemist Emil Fischer, who had just been awarded the inaugural Nobel Prize in his field (1902).[48] To commercialize their find, Fischer used his close personal ties to the pharmaceutical industry, and both Merck and Bayer were licensed to produce and sell the new drug, which was introduced in 1903. The commercialization of Veronal became a success story because the pharmaceutical industry succeeded in situating the drug as a scientific solution to the practical problems faced by clinicians.

To create a nexus between pharmaceutical innovation and clinical application was a challenge for a simple reason: even if the idea of such a nexus appealed to common sense in an age that believed in scientific progress, the nexus itself did not exist and had to be constructed rhetorically. At the outset of their introductory article on Veronal, Mering, and Fischer explicitly reference this problem, noting that while it is evident that soporifics work, so far no one has been able to make sense of why and how: "Almost as obscure as the essence of natural sleep is the link between chemical constitution and pharmacological effect, despite the existence of a significant number of synthetic soporifics."[49] In plain language, the question is why chemical soporifics have a "soporific effect" ("schlaferregende[] Wirkung").[50]

Around 1900, there were few inroads into this problem in pharmacology. The industry used around "two dozen different substances to fabricate sleep medication," substances that ran the gamut of chemical classes.[51] This suggested that many individual substances could induce sleep, even though these substances did not share a common property nor did they adhere to a common theoretical principle that accounted for their effectiveness. Nevertheless, some scientists had already advanced hypotheses regarding the chemical design of an "ideal sleep-inducing drug."[52] Using state-of-the-art chemical reasoning, Mering and Fischer began to methodically test variations of these designs and ended up with a "big new class of sedatives"—barbiturates with a carbon atom and several ethyl groups.[53] The configuration of these barbiturates showed, they discovered, "a few surprising relations between chemical constitution and somnific effect."[54] Once again, Mering and Fischer began to test these substances systematically, first using dogs and later patients in asylums.[55] Finally, the scientists decided on one substance— "Diaethylmalonylharnstoff" (100)—that they deemed to be perfectly balanced: it was stronger than any existing sleep medication but supposedly still did not cause hangovers or have side effects.[56] What Mering and Fischer claimed, in other words, was that they found the fabled "ideal soporific," whose chemical composition scientists had discussed for a long time.[57] Such an ideal soporific, physiologists and pharmacologists fathomed, would exactly reproduce the fatigue substances that the body supposedly generated during states of exhaustion.[58]

However, like the theory of the sleep center, fatigue substances constituted a scientific theory that was, paradoxically, already outdated when it started to manifest in actual material objects. Claparède published his influential problematization of fatigue substances in "Esquisse d'une théorie biologique du sommeil" (1904-5) at almost the same time that Mering and Fischer published their treatise. Nevertheless, even if the theory of fatigue substances had lost its intellectual luster, many scholars continued to take the existence of fatigue substances as gospel, especially in physiology. Two strands of inquiry held on to a modified version of fatigue substances. The first of these was the experimental modification of Claparède's theory in Piéron's *Le problème physiologique du sommeil* (1913), which contemporaries regarded as one "of the best books ever written on the subject of sleep" and that is still held in high esteem as "one of the twentieth century's most influential scientific studies of sleep."[59] Repeating Marie de Manacéïne's experiment (that Claparède had debunked as unsound) by way of an extraordinarily cruel method of strangulating dogs, Piéron managed to isolate an alleged fatigue substance—a chemical structure he called "hypnotoxin."[60] The second line of inquiry that sought to actualize the idea of fatigue substances without sacrificing Claparède's insights was tied to an uptick in interest in potential sleep hormones.[61] For instance, Economo returned repeatedly to the question of whether hormones regulated the armatures of the circadian rhythm, though it was several more decades before such substances entered into the proceedings of sleep research.[62] As a result of these developments, the metaphor of the fatigue substance was "resuscitate[d]" ("reviv[ait]").[63] In light of the scientific buzz about endocrine sleep-inducing substances—regardless of whether they consisted of outdated fatigue substances, "hypnotoxins," or sleep hormones—it becomes evident how the pharmaceutical industry could continue to capitalize on the narrative of an "ideal soporific" that was supposedly out there but had yet to be discovered.[64]

The parlance of a "soporific . . . that could be called ideal" ("das Ideal eines Hypnotikums") worked like a hinge to connect sleep science, the pharmaceutical industry, clinical application, and marketing.[65] If the vagueness of the nature of endocrine sleep-inducing substances such as hormones posed a problem to scientific discourse, for the pharmaceutical industry it unlocked an opportunity:

> According to our current knowledge, sleep is caused by specific metabolic products, so-called fatigue substances: the most ideal soporific [*das idealste Schlafmittel*] would thus be a synthetically produced chemical substance whose constitution fully matches the constitution of these fatigue substances. But because we know exactly nothing about the composition of the latter, we must fall back to different substances. . . . Among the best of those is Veronal, which was synthesized and added to therapy by Emil Fischer and J. v. Mering in 1903.[66]

This tidbit of popular science, drafted in Bayer's scientific-pharmaceutical department under the aegis of the trained chemist Dr. Ernst Lomnitz, must be regarded as a textbook example of effective scientific communication.[67] Written for an advertising brochure, it harnesses physiological discourses about fatigue substances to stage an answer to the question of how soporifics work pharmaceutically. This answer serves, first and foremost, as an argument to buy Veronal, which resembled, as Lomnitz's rhetorical prestidigitation suggests, endocrine fatigue substances: even if Veronal does not offer the "most ideal soporific," it still provides an "ideal soporific." It is thus a matter of consequence that Bayer stages the pharmaceutical mechanism of the soporific in its advertising materials. As in the famous American TV commercial for the antidepressant Zoloft, which centers on an animation of selective serotonin reuptake at a synapse, an ad prospectus for Veronal showcases the advanced nature of the drug by way of its ornamental formula (fig. 2.4).

The narrative of the ideal sleep medication constitutes the core of Veronal as a brand. It is already encapsulated in the trade name.[68] Kitchen-sink etymology traces the signifier "Veronal" back to the Latin term "verus," meaning "true," and so the name implies that the substance provided the only true sleep medication.[69] Various rumors also circulated as to the origin of the name, all of which highlighted the qualities of the substance as a soporific. For instance, it was fabled that the inventors had tested the substance during train travel to Switzerland and only woke up when they arrived at Verona, which then gave its name to the drug. Other accounts interpret the name of the soporific as a reference to the sleep potion of the lovers of Verona—*Romeo and Juliet*—as this drug puts Juliet in a very deep sleep.[70] These well-crafted stories are as important as the chemistry itself.

Veronal.

Diaethylmalonylharnstoff.

Es dürfte unter den neueren Heilmitteln wohl kaum ein zweites Präparat zu finden sein, das in gleicher Weise das Interesse der Aerzte sich zu erobern gewusst hätte wie das Veronal. Unter günstigen Auspizien, als das Ergebnis der planvollen Zusammenarbeit eines hervorragenden Chemikers und eines Klinikers von Ruf in die Therapie eingeführt, zählt das neue Schlafmittel heute nach zwei Jahren zu den beliebtesten und am meisten gebrauchten Medikamenten. Mehr als 130 fast durchweg günstige Publikationen über Veronal legen Zeugnis davon ab, dass wir zur Zeit kein anderes Hypnoticum besitzen, das so viel Vorzüge und so wenig Nachteile aufweist, wie dieses Präparat. Freilich darf man von einem Hypnoticum, welches in die Zirkulationsverhältnisse im Zentralnervensystem so gewichtig eingreift, dass zuverlässig Schlaf eintritt, auch nicht absolute Harmlosigkeit erwarten; „ein wirksames Hypnoticum, das gefahrlos ist und in Drogerieen in beliebiger Menge von Jedermann gekauft werden kann wird von der Wissenschaft niemals erfunden werden." *(Stein).*

Figure 2.4. Bayer's prospectus for Veronal, ca. 1905 (BAL, 166/8, Veronal).

As Walter Benjamin puts it, "Today, brand names contain the phantasies that were once associated with the treasuries of a 'poetic' vocabulary."[71] A magical aura surrounded the talismanic phrase "Veronal," an aura that evoked the narrative of the ideal sleep medication and attached it to the soporific, so that it not only had a chemical but also a suggestive effect.[72]

This aggressive branding of Veronal was a product of modernity and would not have been possible just a few years earlier. Its prerequisite was the Federal Law for the Protection of Commodity Brands (*Reichsgesetz zum Schutze der Warenbezeichnungen*), which came into being in 1894 and established the legal foundations for modern practices of branding in Germany. The introduction of a central trademark list (*Warenzeichenrolle*) allowed companies to prevent competitors from using both name brands (*Wortmarken*) and brand icons (*Bildmarken*).[73] The pharmaceutical industry, however, used these new options to "make up specific trademarks" for their products and to establish brand-name drug identities. Branded medication allowed customers to distinguish among potentially similar products by way of aspects such as name, design, and manufacturer.[74] The advantages of selling branded medications were obvious: they simplified and accelerated communication about products, and they were easier to remember. Veronal, for example, became so deeply engrained in the cultural memory that the name of the drug became a synonym for sleep-inducing drugs per se, in texts ranging from serialized novels to entertainment journals to Dadaist works, for example, *En avant dada* by the trained physician and artist Richard Huelsenbeck (1892–1974) that famously proclaimed that culture resembled "Veronal for the consciousness."[75]

New Pills, New Consumers

Bayer and Merck tied the influential chemical innovation and the orchestrated efforts to establish Veronal as a brand name for sleep medication to the introduction of a novel material object. Soporifics had traditionally been administered as powders, pastilles, drops, tisanes, tinctures, or theriacs, but Veronal launched the career of the sleeping pill.[76] The distribution of soporifics as pills led to three major developments: First of all, an aesthetics of consumption took hold in a domain that was previously structured primarily by a medical economy. Second, sleeping pills became designed objects. Finally, the pill made soporifics a staple of the family medicine chest and was specifically targeted at a previously disregarded group of potential customers: women. In other words, the sleeping pill turned soporifics into a "lifestyle agent."[77] Not unlike contemporary drugs such as Viagra, sleeping pills no longer served primarily as remedies for a specific medical symptom but rather as devices to shape one's own life.

The introduction of the sleeping pill in Germany would have been impossible without historical changes that transformed the country's healthcare system into a mass market. In the nineteenth century, a general shift had taken place whereby pharmaceuticals were no longer made by artisans in an apothecary shop but became proprietary medicinal products supplied by pharmaceutical wholesalers that used industrial production methods.[78] In Germany, the introduction of the social insurance system under Chancellor Otto von Bismarck (1883) boosted the sales volume of proprietary medicinal products. But to work smoothly, a mass market for pharmaceuticals required commodities that were easy to mass produce, store, distribute, administer, and invoice—it basically called for the invention of the pill. Coincidence or not, only one year after the introduction of the German social insurance system in 1883, the British company Burroughs, Wellcome & Co took out a patent for a "tablet" or "tabloid." These neologisms designated medicinal substances with a round, biconcave surface that contained a concentrated pharmaceutical agent.[79] Refunctioning industrial technology originally designed to fill cartridges with ammunition, the mass-produced tablet quickly replaced more traditional modes of administering pharmaceuticals.[80]

Despite the general popularity of pills, a considerable amount of time passed before the preproduced tablets managed to take hold in sensitive and potentially dangerous domains such as sleep medicine. In Germany, a distribution monopoly for potent substances (*Apothekenpflicht*) had been in existence since the mid-nineteenth century, and the powerful apothecary lobby was up in arms over the demotion of the pharmacy to a mere point-of-sale kiosk of drugs, a shift that implied the deskilling of a profession that had previously provided individuals with tailor-made medicinal products, since now everyone could sell premade pills.[81] Acknowledging the resistance from pharmacists, Bayer continued to deliver newly introduced soporifics as powders to the pharmacies. For instance, both the soporific Sulfonal, introduced in 1888, and the soporific Hedonal, which was first offered ten years later in 1898, were only available as powders contained in "glasses or cardboard boxes, or in bags made from parchment."[82] When Veronal came out in 1903, the introduction of sleep-inducing medication as pills was thus a long-overdue innovation. To put it differently, the sleeping pill introduced a novelty whose features were not actually new to anyone, as patients had

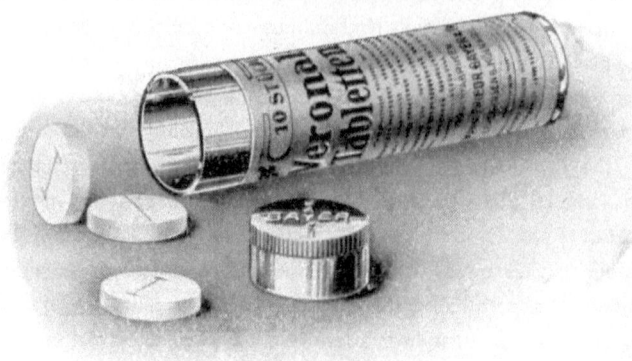

Figure 2.5. Veronal tablets in an advertisement catalogue, mid-1920s (BAL, 465).

been trained in how to take tablets for more than a decade. The polemics of the apothecary lobby against industrially produced sleeping pills testify to how quickly they had transformed the market for soporifics. In 1908, the daily *Berliner Tageblatt* published an article entitled "Die Tablettenseuche" (The pill plague) lamenting that the patients of "all social classes" had "recently" started to consume "sleep-inducing pharmaceuticals almost exclusively as pills."[83]

With the distribution of sleeping pills, an aesthetics of consumption started to take hold that would have been impossible just a few years earlier. On the one hand, the tablet made it possible to link drugs like Veronal to a specific graphical representation—to give it "thingness," as it were—and to shift advertising strategies from dense, text-heavy explanations to more visually enticing images (see fig. 2.5).[84] On the other hand, critiques (such as the article on the pill plague) register with seismographic precision how the success of the sleeping pill changed the everyday practices associated with the use of soporifics as a cultural technique at large. Here and elsewhere, the boilerplate charge against distributing soporifics in tablet form culminated in the claim that the shift from powder to pills obfuscated the medical purpose of these drugs. Pulverized soporifics, critics argued, were not subject to nonmedicinal consumption because they were rather cumbersome to use. Moreover, they came with an abominable flavor that chemists described as bitter and soapy; patients had difficulty rendering the taste into words but were sure that they strongly disliked it.[85]

In stark contrast to this unpleasant procedure of taking an unpleasant substance, sleeping pills in tablet form seemed to suggest that one could simply consume them "as easily as a bonbon."[86] As a matter of fact, the pharma industry owned the bonbon. It started to foreground the pleasures of consumption and introduced "Veronal pills with cacao," tablets in which the bitter pill received a sugarcoating in the most literal sense.[87] Even if medical professionals were concerned about sugarcoating as a practice, this move opened new markets, targeting customer groups with different tastes and diversified sources of health-care advice. The health and well-being pages of the woman's magazine *Blatt der Hausfrau* (Journal of the housewife), for instance, lost no time recommending the "Veronal chocolate pills" to women.[88]

Long before the Rolling Stones would be able to write songs about tranquilizers like valium, there was already Veronal if "Mother needs something . . . to calm her down," a little pill even "though she's not really ill."[89] The introduction of the sleeping pill turned this type of drug from a product that was medically administered into a "lifestyle agent."[90] These drugs "promise[d] a power to reshape life pharmaceutically that extends way beyond what we previously understood as illness."[91] In fact, sleep-inducing drugs began to serve as a means of enhancing "our capacities to adjust and readjust our somatic existence according to the exigencies of the life to which we aspire."[92] In an advertising brochure aimed at physicians, Bayer makes a very similar argument:

> Today, in this restless hurrying time, with its increased strain on all intellectual and somatic faculties, a physician will often face the necessity of prescribing his patients—regardless of their social standing—a sedative or soporific. There may be multifarious causes for the condition, from simple insomnia and restlessness to states of profound excitation. Therapy must be as individualized as the causes.[93]

The copy in the brochure suggests that life under the conditions of modernity deregulates a traditional economy of rest and excitement and that physicians must attend to the resulting psychophysical tensions with a genuinely modern technology of the self: pharmaceutical antidotes that restore harmony. Furthermore, Bayer suggests that these remedies could enter into the physician-patient relationship as tools of individualization. Specific assemblages of drugs and doses supply the patients, "regardless of their social standing," with a sense of incommensurable somatic uniqueness; they also integrate the symptoms into the patients' subjecthood. Finally, sedatives and soporifics serve to restore social functionality. In stark contrast to the regimes of hygiene and dietetics that demanded the complete reorganization of one's life to make the symptoms disappear, these drugs reorganized the symptoms according to one's aspirations. Veronal, then, tapped into new modes of consumption at the intersection of health and lifestyle.

Clashing Narratives

The combination of a significant chemical innovation, aggressive marketing, and the modes of consumption the sleeping pill afforded turned Veronal into an immediate commercial success story. One year after the drug became available in 1903, the pharmaceutical industry announced with a triumphal tone that "if one has ever been able to say a new medicinal drug has taken the world by storm, this most certainly holds true for Veronal."[94] This commercial success extended to Veronal's scientific reputation. Around 1900, a pharmaceutical novelty got three reviews in medical journals on average.[95] Yet Veronal received more than 20 in the first months; two years after it appeared, more than "130 unequivocally positive publications" existed on the drug; and a 1909 "bibliography on Veronal," which Bayer circulated to physicians for PR purposes, listed more than 200 entries.[96]

The story of the ideal soporific fit seamlessly into a nineteenth-century positivist narrative of unbound scientific progress, and it helped to position the pharmaceutical industry as the agent of this progress. The great market success of Veronal, however, also exposed the inherent risks of marketing a substance using such a narrative. The dissemination of this allegedly ideal soporific that had no side effects—whose discovery even dailies covered as a newsworthy triumph of scientific reason and that drugstores initially sold over the counter—quickly started to produce media events that went against the grain of the carefully curated grand narrative of the pharmaceutical industry.[97] If the industry narrative dominated scientific and professional communication, a different take on this story began to form in the back pages of local German newspapers. Here, scattered news about suicides, accidents, and abuse started to crop up, *faits divers* that were only linked by a single feature: Veronal.

Hermann Broch's novel *Die Schlafwandler* (1930) is one of many contemporary novels that testify to this experience. When an outed gay figure commits suicide in the novel, the mere mention of Veronal suffices to convey what has happened: "This noon . . . and now we have found him . . . Veronal."[98] To be sure, the ubiquity of Veronal suicides and accidents certainly demonstrated that the substance had not been adequately tested or regulated. Around 1900, Germany did not interfere with the offering of new drugs, and a consensus existed among legislators that "new drugs could . . . basically be put to the test in the medical offices of general practitioners."[99] Moreover, it took German legislators more than five years to remove Veronal from the category of over-the-counter drugs, putting it on a blacklist that included extrapotent drugs such as cocaine. Even when it finally got designated as a "poison," this classification only meant that one technically required a prescription to buy it.[100] But countless court cases whose records survive in Bayer's archives demonstrate that it was still common among pharmacists to sell Veronal over the counter, to issue pills on forged prescriptions, or to allow a single prescription to be used ad infinitum in multiple pharmacies.[101] The company archives also document that this happened not just in the case of Veronal but also comparable products sold by their competitors, such as Medinal (based on a derivative of Veronal and licensed to the Schering company of Berlin), although these products never gained the notoriety of the original.[102]

The case of Veronal thus paradigmatically shows that new substances and technologies always unleash profound effects that no one anticipates. These unforeseen effects render distinctions visible that had previously been of little conceptual importance. With Veronal, this becomes clear in the case of female bodies that required a different dosage from the one suggested on the package, which was calculated with male bodies in mind. Later, Veronal came with additional instructions on how to dose the drug for female bodies (the suggested dose was up to four times lower). Still, the break lines prescored in the pills, which were geared toward male bodies, made it difficult for women to take only the suggested dose. Their physical makeup also made them respond differently to accumulated residues of the soporific in the body, a problem that was further acerbated in cases of Veronal addiction or simply drug use on successive days, because the long half life of the drug could increase the effective dose massively. It thus hardly comes as a surprise that fatal accidents with soporifics—as Weber has noted in his history of psychopharmacology—occurred all too frequently with women.[103]

Nevertheless, this did not lead to a public debate but resulted in Veronal

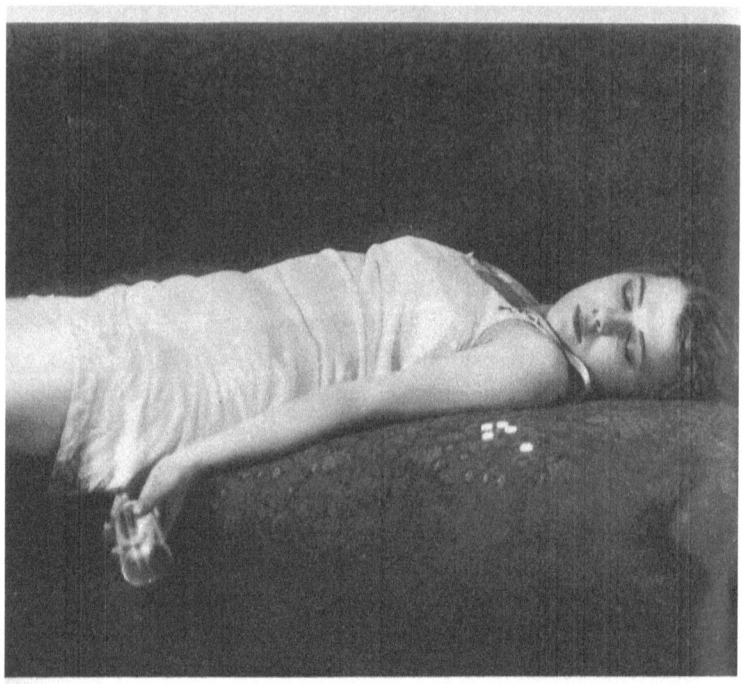

Figure 2.6. Eduard Birlo's glossy photograph "Veronal," printed in *Das Kriminal-Magazin* 3, vol. 25 (1931): 1288.

accidents being coded as a problem of female irresponsibility, lack of self-control, and suicidality. In public discourse, figurations of women dying by suicide with Veronal almost entirely eclipsed a more nuanced debate about the substance. A high-gloss image by the little-known Berlin-based photographer Eduard Birlo illustrates the case in point (see fig. 2.6).[104] Printed as a full-page contribution to the popular illustrated journal *Das Kriminal-Magazin*, the photo with the title "Veronal" explicitly links the sleeping pill to gendered problems of agency. In a profile shot, the black-and-white photograph shows a young woman lying on a bed or chaise lounge or sofa; her negligée has pushed up and reveals the edges of her thighs; her head rests on the bolster, facing the viewer with closed eyes; she seems to be on the brink of losing consciousness, as her left hand still holds onto a glass, which will fall to the ground when her muscles relax. The trigger for her state is evident enough—a handful of white pills of Veronal next to her shoulder. But what has happened? One could read the ambiguity of Birlo's photo as a dramatization of the question of causality. Was it an accident? Suicide? Date rape? Or murder? Regardless, the polyvalent image replaces a debate about the substance with a debate about the behavior of the woman.

Based on these developments, discourses, and figurations, one could tell Veronal's story as a scandal deeply interwoven with gender norms. One might also recall the dialectics of the Enlightenment, in which the success of reason unhinges all boundaries and ultimately turns into its opposite. One could also add another twist to this story about Veronal, one that transgresses the common lines of interpretation and that specifically applies to life under conditions of modernity: with the wide distribution of Veronal, modern societies embarked on an open-ended self-experiment, as it were, conducted on a large scale by and on unintentional participants. This Veronal culture turned into a hotbed of stories and media events that competed and clashed with the official narrative of the "ideal soporific."[105] Veronal not only offered a new substance and new modes of interacting with psychoactive drugs but provided new storylines that were deeply intertwined with the question of what it meant to live in modern times.

3 Dangerously Glamorous

In 1924, the notoriety of Veronal reached a new peak. At the same time that the pharmaceutical industry was launching a successor product for the soporific whose recognizability had become bad for business, the Austrian author and physician Arthur Schnitzler published his novella *Fräulein Else*.[1] The novella quickly attracted scrutiny from the pharmaceutical industry. As a memo discovered in the corporate archives of the pharmaceutical giant Bayer reveals, the research officers at the company sensed that this literary text written by a practicing doctor had implications for their core business of innovating and selling drugs.[2] *Fräulein Else* mobilizes Veronal to put the novella's protagonist into a somnolent state at the edges of consciousness, thus connecting pharmaceutical and literary experiments. The chapter at hand demonstrates that the drug is central to grasping the novella's formal work—contemporary gender politics—and that it critically intervenes in corporate discursive strategies.

In literary history, *Fräulein Else* features as a modernist classic for two reasons: for its dialogue with Sigmund Freud, who famously called Schnitzler his "doppelgänger," and for "perfecting" the interior monologue, a narrative technique that relates thoughts, feelings, and sense perceptions of characters without marked auctorial mediation.[3] This technique creates the impression that the reader is able to witness all mental events in Else's consciousness, including her experience of the Veronal poisoning at the end of the novella. Sweeping studies have examined *Fräulein Else*'s narrational strategies, gender and sexuality in it, and its historical contexts, but scholars have never attempted to read the novella with a focus on Veronal.[4] In what ways does Schnitzler—a physician with the reputation of writing literary case studies that were "'correct' from a clinical point of view"—integrate the medical and pharmacological knowledge of his time?[5] How does Schnitzler's use of Veronal inflect female agency in the text? To what extent does *Fräulein Else* present an intervention into public health debates?

Schnitzler's *Fräulein Else* presents a critical rewriting of contemporary discussions about Veronal: the text negotiates a public health crisis caused by a "white market drug," a market that supplied medically and legally approved substances that assumed agency.[6] Agency is here understood in terms of Thomas de Quincey's definition given in his quintessential drug narrative: "Not the opium-eater, but the opium is the true hero of the tale; and the legitimate centre on which the interest revolves. The object was to display the marvellous agency of opium."[7] *Mutatis mutandis*, this chapter centers on Veronal and seeks to shed light on its cultural, medical, and literary agency in Schnitzler's work.

Scholars have long been aware that the literary and medical writings of the author-physician are inextricably intertwined, but they have paid too little attention to the role of medicinal drugs in his oeuvre, although they feature frequently in his writings.[8] Veronal in *Fräulein Else*, for example, has been mainly considered a suicide prop; in particular, it has elicited speculation as to whether the ingested dose of Veronal suffices to kill the protagonist.[9] But if one approaches *Fräulein Else* with a main focus on the medicinal drug, it becomes evident that Veronal plays a foundational role for the text (and the culture from which it emerged) and that Schnitzler's engagement with issues of public health was by no means limited to questions of sexual and social hygiene but also reaches into the social scaling of pharmacology.[10]

Read alongside Schnitzler's medical writings, *Fräulein Else* reveals that he considers medicinal substances to be an attempt to provide a "techno-fix" that, on a societal level, cannot address the deeper social issues that have given rise to many diseases in the first place; instead of providing a cure, drugs generate new problems such as addiction or accidents. The large-scale distribution of pharmacological substances effectively covers up symptoms, causes, and social side effects by effectively turning them into manifestations of individual suffering. To unmask these systematic shrouding mechanisms, Schnitzler turns not to psychoanalysis but to literature. *Fräulein Else* serves to render visible the problems associated with Veronal in their social situatedness; the novella reads like a case study that stages these problems within the framework of a dramatic conflict, one that emphasizes that the creation of Veronal entails the Veronal accident.

Newspaper Report, Novella, Case Study

In accordance with the drug culture of the early twentieth century, when the consumption of soporifics such as Veronal registered as a normal "expression of popular culture and the social climate,"[11] the drug is evoked almost from the outset of the novella, which is set in fin-de-siècle Austria. It makes its first appearance during the nervous wait for the announced letter from Else's mother that sets the plot into motion (*FE*, 14; *E*, 196). Veronal serves as a quotidian complement to Else's desire to try "hashish" (*FE*, 14; *E*, 196), which connects the text to contemporary drug narratives such as Walter Benjamin's hashish protocols.[12] In addition, Else relies on Veronal to counter the onset of her menstrual pain *(FE*, 14).[13] She also uses the drug as a tranquilizer (*FE*, 35; *E*, 207) and a soporific (*FE*, 96-97; *E*, 235).

The soporific thus holds the dramatic structure of the plot together as the novella systematically builds up to a lethal overdose of the drug. Else, the nineteen-year-old daughter of a debt-ridden Jewish lawyer from Vienna's upper-class circles, is tasked by her mother with fending off the imminent collapse of her family's social and economic capital while she sojourns in the Dolomites. Else is hoping to secure a significant loan from her wealthy acquaintance, Dorsday. The aging beau is willing to supply it, but at a price. In exchange for the loan, he solicits a strip show. Feeling betrayed and trafficked by her family, Else decides to cause a scene: she disrobes in public, falls into a trance, and commits suicide with an overdose of Veronal.

Despite this spectacular plot, *Fräulein Else* is neither the only nor the first modernist text to feature a Veronal suicide. To name just one canonical and one popular example, Italo Svevo's novel *La coscienza di Zeno* (1923), set, like Schnitzler's novella, in the Italian part of the Habsburg Empire and published slightly earlier than *Fräulein Else*, connects the death of the businessman Guido to a miscalculated dosage of Veronal.[14] Veronal suicides also came up regularly in serial novels, such as Ludwig Wolff's *Die Kwannon von Okadera* (1920).[15] Nevertheless, when one of Bayer's internal press informants broke the news that the "prominent author and Viennese physician Dr. Arthur Schnitzler" had published a story that culminates in a "'Veronal poisoning,'" the company responded with horror. Alarmed that a wide circulation of Schnitzler's *Fräulein Else* could undermine the "trust" in their product and shift the narrative, Bayer decided to try to persuade the author that it would be better to refrain from this negative publicity for our drug in the future and to choose a different manner of death for his heroes and heroines, whom he wants to kill off for whatever reason, and to eliminate the reference to Veronal by all means if a reprinting becomes necessary.[16]

We do not know whether an emissary from Bayer ever knocked on Schnitzler's door. To be sure, the author's subsequent *Traumnovelle* (1925-26), which also includes a poisoning, drops any references to specific brands.[17] Nevertheless, Veronal continues to feature in all further reprints of *Fräulein Else* and even showed up in a close-up shot when it was turned into a silent film a few years later.[18] Veronal's significance in the novella is further highlighted by the fact that its appearance constitutes an anachronism; in 1896, when *Fräulein Else* supposedly takes place, the drug was not yet available.[19] Given that Schnitzler knew his medical history and deliberately set his novella *Sterben* (1894) at a moment before a particular therapy was invented that would have impacted the plot, the importance of this anachronism cannot be overstated. The text deliberately blends the interwar period with the prewar Habsburg Empire through its depiction of Else as consuming a drug that was not available at the time (and consuming it, moreover, as a powder).[20] The brand name Veronal is indispensable to the novella both because it links it with newspaper reports about Veronal suicides and because it updates the theory of public health crises developed in Schnitzler's earlier medical writings, which is based on morphine. Without Veronal, the text's ending would look very different.

Paradoxically, the nexus between Schnitzler's novella and contemporary newspaper reports on cases of people who used the drug to kill themselves becomes most evident in the documents in Bayer's corporate archives. Here, the note on the publication of *Fräulein Else* sits among clippings of Veronal poisonings that had appeared in the press.

This conjuncture was not an accident. Schnitzler regularly mined the press to find new subjects on which he could write; over the years, he amassed a rich archive of newspaper clippings.[21] *Fräulein Else* was the product of his rewriting of a news report. Schnitzler's diaries show that he took note of several cases of Veronal poisoning; he especially noticed a Viennese case whose text he excerpted from the *Neue Freie Presse*: "5/17 (Holiday.) Note in N. Fr. Pr.: 'The thirty-year-old unmarried Stephanie Bachrach took ... etc. Morphine and Veronal ... died. ... The cause of her suicide is unknown.'"[22] This sparse note made a deep impression on Schnitzler because he knew this woman well: she was the girlfriend of a close friend, and they had been moving in the same circles for years; Bachrach had even provided the model for a character in his novel *Der Weg ins Freie* (1908).[23] Despite his private grief, Schnitzler—an author who specialized in covering social hot-button issues—was, however, ultimately less interested in documenting this specific case than in converting it into a "case study" of a Veronal suicide that could circulate more widely and raise societal awareness.[24]

As a seasoned writer of popular books and plays, Schnitzler immediately understood how to get a gripping story out of a reticent press report that resembled an uncounted number of other notes on Veronal suicides, and he rewrote it using the interior monologue. Instead of presenting a narrative *on* Else, the text foregrounds her point of view.[25] The use of the interior monologue thus seeks to make good on the promise that fiction can render transparent the inmost motives of a person, revealing the web of delicately interwoven impulses, affects, and social dynamics at play.

Fräulein Else does not just use the newspaper report as catalyst. Through Else's incessantly describing her own motives and actions as if print media were going to report on them, we see the way a human subject can be mediatized. In her imagination, she stages fictional versions of her suicide that seem to come straight out of an operetta, a cheap novella, or a gossip magazine, genres that she herself evokes to describe her self-fashioning (*FE*, 29, 34, 67; *E*, 203, 206, 225), slipping into the diction of the yellow press when she ponders her suicide options:[26]

> I'll drink the Veronal. Just a little swallow, then I'll be able to sleep well . . . But I could also go outside to the front of the hotel . . . and then flit farther, farther over the meadow, into the woods, climbing, higher and higher, all the way to the top of the Cimone, lie down, fall asleep, freeze to death. *Mysterious Suicide of a Young Lady of Viennese Society. Dressed only in a black evening coat, the beautiful girl was found dead in an inaccessible location behind the Cimone della Pala.* (*FE*, 109-10; *E*, 246-47, emphasis in Margret Schaefer's translation)[27]

In this novella set less than two hundred kilometers from Verona, Else tries to slip into a different role than that of the bartered bride.[28] She always wanted to go "on stage" (*FE*, 29; *E*, 204), and she draws on a familiar repertoire of melodramatic role models that speak to her. Else thus turns into the "author" of her own death, not unlike Emma Bovary in Gustave Flaubert's *Madame Bovary*.[29]

Else's desire for glamour is not only evident in her fantasies of sunbathing on an imagined future property on the Riviera (*FE*, 8, 78; *E*, 193).³⁰ It is also apparent in her bedtime reading: Guy de Maupassant's novel *Notre Cœur* (1895). This book explicitly associates the glamorous persona of the socialite Michèle de Burne with the use of narcotics such as chloroform and morphine.³¹

Veronal has a highly ambiguous part to play within these fatal self-experiments of becoming glamorous—the soporific comes with the reputation of being the suicide aid of the stars. In the year in which the novella appeared, for instance, a suicide attempt by the "famous film actor Max Linder" made big headlines in 1924.³² Even years later, Veronal's image of being dangerously glamorous persisted—for example, in the 1932 film *Grand Hotel*, the Academy Award-winning film version of Vicki Baum's novel *Menschen im Hotel* (1929) and an early Hollywood movie with an all-star cast. Here, Greta Garbo shines in the role of an aging actress who tries to take her life with Veronal but is rescued by a gentle diamond thief. Else grapples with the power and sway of such prefabricated cultural scripts. They lure her by implying that she could leave behind her difficult social position as a "young lady from a good family" (*FE*, 32; *E*, 206) and assume the dazzling role of the diva. In other words, readers notice what Schnitzler calls Else's "Mittelbewusstsein"—a preconsciousness of the extent to which the privileged young white woman is the product of the conditions under which she lives.³³ Else perceives the world through the internalized norms, scripts, and codes of a society that actively works against her flourishing, even though it has simultaneously inculcated her with a "cruel optimism" about attaining happiness in the future.³⁴ Veronal embodies this double bind.

Schnitzler's Theory of Public Health Crises

All this leads to the heart of Schnitzler's thoughts about pharmaceutical drugs from a public health perspective. The trained physician immediately understood that Veronal presented more than a problem of irresponsible use by individual patients, as the pharmaceutical industry framed the issue. For example, Bayer's case officers argued that references to Veronal ought to be purged form *Fräulein Else* because such references allegedly encouraged "feeble characters" to undertake similar "suicide attempts with Veronal."³⁵ The company therefore not only mobilized theories of mimetic imitation— "example and imitation," as Ferdinand Flury has it in his statistics regarding death by poison.³⁶ The company feared a "Werther effect," a wavelike causal relationship between a suicide as a model and subsequent suicides as imitations, as was allegedly instigated by Goethe's *Die Leiden des jungen Werthers* (1774).[37] However, for physicians like Schnitzler who opposed pharmacological "techno-fixes," irresponsible individual users were not the problem; rather it was the effects of the social scaling of legally and medically approved drugs and the close connection of the medical to the industrial apparatus in particular that was to blame.

Although Schnitzler does not explicitly comment on the scaling of Veronal prescriptions, his earlier medical reviews strongly suggest an implicit public health theory based on his argument about morphine.[38] One key aspect of these reviews is that they strive to ground the practice of medicine in a deeper social awareness, to further "not only the medical knowledge of the physicians but also their societal understanding."[39] In particular, Schnitzler's reviews of pharmacological works (including his review of a book by the coinventor of Veronal, Josef von Mering) reveal a stark ambivalence about a medical profession that put treatments with drugs front and center: "We have more drugs than in the past, but we fail to achieve an equally great proportion of cures."[40] In contrast to physicians like the preanalytical Freud, who proposed curing morphine addiction through the prescription of additional drugs such as cocaine, Schnitzler contends that drug treatments cover up symptoms instead of effectively addressing the root problems.[41] He generally believes that it does more harm than good to prescribe drugs without first considering a patient-specific holistic approach. In a review of a medical book on morphine addiction for the medical journal *Internationale klinische Rundschau*, he observes that morphine

> is still highly regarded, and yet it must be considered the best example of our inadequacy. Morphine, this souverain reliever of pain, is all too often a false friend of those who suffer; it demands too high a price for its favors, and over time, it costs one's freedom, sometimes even one's life. . . . Still, there can be no doubt that we must expect to learn about similar cases soon. After enormous intellectual efforts, we have wrested healing powers from poisonous substances. In some of these drugs, their original spirit will take over again, and they will reveal themselves to a fooled humankind, showing us what they really are: poisons.[42]

Schnitzler describes a dangerous dynamic inherent in the use of morphine. The drug pretends to be a healing force, yet it develops an agency of its own and tends to drag its users into dependency and even death. In making this argument, Schnitzler recovers the original ambivalence of the Greek term "pharmakon," which can refer both to a poison and medicinal substance.⁴³ In ancient thought, the fine-tuning of the dose governs the relationship between the poisonous and the healing aspects of the *pharmakon*; for Schnitzler, it seems evident that an addictive substance will, in the long run, develop its own agency and transform any potential remedy into a poison. If a drug is to continue exerting an effect on a body used to it, the dose must necessarily be steadily increased, until it eventually becomes poisonous. One is reminded of Paul Virilio's insight that the invention of the car implies the car crash, the invention of the train implies the train wreck, and—to spell out the analogy—that the invention of morphine implies morphine addiction and morphine death.⁴⁴ By the same token, Schnitzler predicts that Veronal will necessarily produce Veronal poisonings and Veronal suicides.

Fräulein Else is not the first literary text in which Schnitzler stages fatal drug incidents arising from an alleged misfunctioning of the medical system, aided and abetted by physicians and pharmacists. The drama *Der Ruf des Lebens* (1906) and the novella *Der Mörder* (1911) are two other examples. In the drama, the physician Dr. Schindler persuades the young Marie Moser to administer morphine to her terminally ill father so that she can go out for a night on the town without having to worry about him. After Marie inadvertently injects too much morphine and kills her father, she insists that this accident was inevitable given the pharmacological agency of the drug.⁴⁵ Schnitzler's drama frames the death as both the result of medical malpractice and of having too much confidence in pharmaceutical treatments. *Der Mörder* (1911) elaborates further on this point by extending the responsibility from physicians to pharmacists. In the story, Alfred, a jurist, goes the rounds "from one physician to the next, and from one pharmacist to next" in order to procure enough morphine to get rid of his mistress Elisa, who has become a nuisance to him. Alfred soon gets hold of the required dose by playing the medical system:

> He ... subsequently went to three physicians. At all three, he presented himself as a man tormented by unbearable pain who has been used to depending on morphine for many years, but now had run out of supplies. He received the requested prescriptions, filed them in several pharmacies, and was ... in possession of a dose which he deemed more than sufficient for his purposes.⁴⁶

Schnitzler, of course, is neither the first nor the only modernist who pens scenes like this. For instance, Edith Wharton's novel *The House of Mirth* (1905) offers a detailed account of how a young woman surreptitiously obtains soporifics on a borrowed prescription, which proves fatal when she overdoses on the "queer-acting drug" chloralhydrate despite a warning from the pharmacist.[47] In this regard, Veronal was no different from chloralhydrate and morphine. Many people who "had no suicidal intentions were comforted by the possession of fatal quantities of barbiturates; they felt empowered at times of emotional disablement."[48] This raises the question of whether Else takes her life with Veronal or whether Veronal take Else's life. Schnitzler's text dramatizes a dialectics of agency in which the same drug that seems to empower Else in a psychologically challenging situation entangles her in a dynamic that ultimately leads to a fatal chain of contingent events.

Does Else Wake Up Again?

Raising the question of whether Else takes her life with Veronal or whether Veronal take Else's life assumes that Else does not recover from the amount of Veronal she ingests toward the end of the novella. But some scholars argue that a suicide would require a higher dose of the soporific than Else has at her disposal and that she will wake up again when the interior monologue of the novella breaks off.[49] Schnitzler's novella briefly alludes to the typically "lethal dose" of ten grams of Veronal, as established by medical and juridical cases (see *FE*, 88; *E*, 235).[50] Other contemporary medical case reports, however, document much lower lethal doses—as low as 4.5 and 5 grams—which is less than what Else most likely ingests.[51] Ultimately, the text remains ambiguous about Else's specific dose.[52] Given the contextual framing that grounds the novella in newspaper reports about Veronal suicides, Schnitzler's implicit theory that positions pharmaceuticals as a public health issue, and the author's repeated narratives about fatal morphine abuse, it is possible that Schnitzler seeks to showcase that even a relatively mild overdose might turn out deadly. To what extent does the novella's depiction of Else's liminal state of consciousness correspond to the symptomatology of fatal poisonings in contemporary medical literature?

To answer this question, a close reading of its dénouement is necessary, which begins when Else is back in her hotel room, where she has been carried after her public disrobing and subsequent blackout in the music room. She hovers in a strange twilight state and is being attended to by the physician Paul and his lover Cissy, who comment on every change in her condition. When Dorsday, the wealthy man who solicited the strip show from her, appears in the doorway, Paul and Cissy briefly leave their watch to talk to him. Unobserved, Else immediately gulps down the prepared glass of Veronal.[53] Schnitzler himself insisted that Else consumes the soporific only in this very last scene.[54] He was adamant about the sequence, because it generates a contrast between the representation of consciousness in the final scene and two earlier moments of clouded consciousness—Else's daydream on a park bench and the odd twilight state she falls into after her disrobement in the music room. In the final scene the change in Else's condition is tied to her consumption of a pharmacological substance.

Many scholars have offered interpretations of the last scene of *Fräulein Else*, yet even the most persuasive readings have overlooked the fact that Schnitzler systematically integrates the clinical symptomatology of Veronal poisoning.[55] To ensure that these symptoms are noticed and correctly named, he positions the physician Paul at Else's bedside. This approach via medical symptomology is particularly significant because it distinguishes Schnitzler's novella from other representations of suicides with soporifics, such as Wharton's *The House of Mirth*. To depict the fatal overdose of Lily Bart, its protagonist, Wharton makes intense use of narrative modes and the temporal progression of the text. She also exploits the difference between what Lily knows and what the narrator knows to depict Lily's progressive loss of consciousness.[56] Wharton, then, displays little interest in integrating the clinical signs of a poisoning with Lily's drug of choice, chloralhydrate; other figures infer the cause of death from a found bottle of the drug.[57] By contrast, the clinical picture of Veronal poisoning provides the essential backbone of the last scene of Schnitzler's *Fräulein Else*.

The passage divides into four sections of varying length that capture the gradual onset of Veronal's effects. A slight variation of the phrase "I drank the Veronal" (*FE*, 131, 131, 132, 132; *E*, 261, 261, 262, 263) marks the beginning of each of these four sections: latency, first effects, full effects, and the threshold of death. During the period of latency, the impact of the soporific is barely perceptible, as Else herself remarks, "I drank the Veronal. I'll die! But everything is just the same as it was before. Maybe it wasn't enough . . ." (*FE*, 131; *E*, 261).[58] She first registers the effects of Veronal when she begins to get tired ("müde") (*FE*, 131); at the same time, Paul comments on Else's pulse, which is "steady" (*FE*, 131; *E*, 261) and "almost regular" (*FE*, 131; *E*, 262).[59] In the next section, the effect of the soporific has become so strong that Paul cannot wake Else up, even though he makes no fewer than nine attempts. She enters a state described as dreamlike (*FE*, 133; *E*, 262). In the last section, Else starts to shiver (*zittern*) (*FE*, 135), before she succumbs to a loss of consciousness that causes the interior monologue to break off; in the first printing, Schnitzler additionally marked this moment with the paratext "the end" (*Ende*) (*FE*, 136) so that the text grinds to a halt in three steps: Else loses consciousness, the interior monologue breaks off, and the paratext ends the narrative.[60]

It is clear that Schnitzler integrated what the medical literature and reassuring leaflets from the pharmaceutical industry call the "characteristic clinical picture" of Veronal poisoning: it consists of "a profound loss of consciousness despite relatively strong breathing," accompanied by physiological processes such as shivering ("Zittern"); interventions such as "calling" ("Anrufen") can no longer arouse the patient.[61] If one believes the testimony of the pharmaceutical industry, this specific clinical presentation is uncommon. In their words, Veronal poisonings are "rather rare" and result from "enormous dosages which have been ingested due to either an unfortunate accident or (more often) with the intention of committing suicide."[62] In light of the novella's integration of the symptomology of poisoning, there can be little doubt that the novella does not end well for Else.

The Body of Language

The textual nature of Else's body raises another question. How do the effects of the soporific impact the formal presentation of the scene? Linguistic changes in the interior monologue become especially apparent when Veronal comes into its full effects, acting forcefully on Else's consciousness. At the outset, this intensifies structures of displacement and condensation and gives rise to an even more prominent, associative logic through which images are linked, recalling the dream scene earlier in the novella where Else is under the impression that she has poisoned herself with hashish (*FE*, 72; *E*, 228). Furthermore, fragments of phrases used earlier in the novella flare up in Else's consciousness, such as "filou," "Fiala," "convict[]," "Matador" (*FE*, 133; *E*, 262). This generates a kind of temporal regression, which calls up half-coherent quotes and voices from ever more distant moments in Else's adolescence and childhood (*FE*, 134; *E*, 262). This culminates in her memories of lullabies (*FE*, 136; *E*, 263-64).[63] When the events take their course, the sixfold repetition of the verb "to run" (*FE*, 134-35; *E*, 263) unmistakably evokes the German idiom "das Geschehen nimmt seinen Lauf" (meaning "to run its course"). As she succumbs to Veronal, her language seems to warp, as, for example, in the case of Veronal turning into "Veronalica" (*FE*, 134), a phrase that recalls the female name Veronica and assigns Else the role of the *vera icon* of the soporific.[64]

In the final sequence of the novella, the impact of Veronal on the body of the text intensifies. Up to this point, the text has only alluded to changes in Else's perception—for example, that the voices at her bedside have registered as mere noise or "buzz" (*FE*, 142; *E*, 261). But now, *Fräulein Else* incorporates this voiding of semantic meaning at the level of form, foregrounding the possibilities and limitations of the interior monologue. This literary technique can create the impression of consciousness in the present moment, but it struggles with the representation of temporal lapses and is only able to show moments in which the mind appears blank or empty by drawing on typographical devices such as punctuation marks, hyphens, or special characters, and syntactical ellipses. This interplay between the *Sprachkörper* (body of the text) and the *Schriftkörper* (textual body) stands out in the last paragraph of the novella (*FE*, 136; *E*, 263-64):

> Else! Else!
> They're calling from so far away. What do you want from me? Don't wake me up. I'm sleeping so well. Tomorrow morning. I'm dreaming and flying. I'm flying . . . flying . . . flying . . . sleeping and dreaming . . . and flying . . . don't wake me . . . tomorrow morning . . .
> El . . .
> I'm flying . . . I'm dreaming . . . I'm sleeping . . . I'm drea . . . drea—I'm flying . . .
> (*FE*, 136; *E*, 263-64)[65]

In this passage, the attempts to wake Else fail. The insistent calls demonstrate how the young woman succumbs to the soporific effect of Veronal, and her sleep deepens to a point where her interior monologue finally breaks off. The text is shot through with explicit typographic signs that serve to highlight the fact that black print on white paper constitutes Else's voice. Her language crystallizes into signs that act as placeholders for other signs that cannot be uttered; the marked visuality of the ellipses exposes the artificiality of the perspective; a void appears within the interior monologue. If Else's consciousness is captured in the *Sprachkörper*, Veronal seems to control the *Schriftkörper*, and the passage shows precisely how typography takes precedence.

Consequently, the syntagmatic structures of the text come apart. The sentence construction becomes elliptical and fragmented, and what remains loses meaning. Statements such as "I'm sleeping" pinpoint a psychophysical state that troubles language; these enunciations also evoke paradoxical phrases from Else's earlier dream, such as "I'm wearing black mourning clothes because I'm dead" (*FE*, 73; *E*, 228). Her language loses the capacity to produce meaning and only retains a gestural quality, before it peters out in empty repetitions, dots, and dashes.

Finally, the metaphors of physical, mental, and somatic activity that accompany Else's ingestion of Veronal drive the prose forward but gradually flatten into self-referential cues to intertextual references. The assorted verbs "to fly," "to dream" and "to sleep" clearly stem from a line in a lullaby by the romantic writer Clemens Brentano (1778-1842) that reads "Sleep, dream, fly, I will wake/you soon and be overjoyed."[66] Sleeping, dreaming, and flying evoke a strongly aestheticized way of dying, one that is still heavily colored by with romantic ideas of death. Such ideas pervade the genres with which Else's imagination has proven to be intimately familiar: operettas and cheap novellas (*FE*, 29, 34, 67). Yet one could also read "flying" as a reference to the physiological dream theory of the English psychologist Havelock Ellis, whom Schnitzler had read. Ellis contends that dreams involving flying indicate "trouble with breathing and the heart or an anesthesia of skin sensations during sleep."[67] This somatic interpretation suggests reading the metaphors of movement and especially the experience of flying as an effect of Veronal poisoning. Still, why does Schnitzler quote a romantic lullaby to indicate Else's death? The quotation reminds the reader that Else must be understood as a body made from text. As a displaced soothing mechanism that seems to arise from a flashback of childhood memories, the lullaby also reinforces the cruel optimism of the protagonist who is unaware that she will not wake up the next morning. Most importantly, however, the lullaby with its stress on monotonous repetition empties out meaning; what remains is the breakdown of form that foregrounds the typographic system. All in all, Else's Veronal sleep dismantles the apparatuses of language and reveals the technical underbelly of representation implicit in the interior monologue: hermeneutic reading, literary form, grammatical conventions, and the materiality of signs.

Ending and the Interior Monologue

Finally, it is necessary to discuss how the portrayal of the Veronal suicide in *Fräulein Else* makes use of the potential of the interior monologue. The "range of possibilities" and "limitations" characteristic of this form have already been systematically explored in Dorrit Cohn's classic study *Transparent Minds*, but revisiting her book in the context of this study complicates at least one common assumption about the interior monologue.[68] According to Cohn's authoritative account, interior monologues can come close to simulating a psychic transparency of the main figure, but to be successful, this mode of presentation must operate within a tight spectrum of restraining parameters—a conventional narrator cannot be deployed, the text must adhere to a strict dramatic unity of time, self-address must be legitimized, and nonmediated statements have to be minimized.[69] Although this account of the interior monologue has become canonical, it overstates the necessity of an exact simultaneity of experience and enunciation, which means that on its account those moments in Schnitzler's interior monologues when narrated time outpaces the time of narration stand as undesirable "irregularities."[70] Rather than see such moments as evidence that allegedly flawed interior monologues are necessarily haunted by conventional narrators, I suggest that these "irregularities" point to an inherent potential of the interior monologue to speed up or slow down time, which comes to the fore in moments of diminished consciousness.

This is apparent in the dénouement of *Fräulein Else*. The protagonist's attempt to kill herself with Veronal reinforces the challenge of how to depict the loss of consciousness, a challenge the novella has hinted at twice already: first, during Else's dream on the park bench, which becomes fully legible as a dream only after her awakening; and second, during her blackout in the music room, characterized, on the one hand, by the insertion of a musical score that subsequently falls silent, and, on the other hand, by Else's insistence on her sense of ongoing wakefulness.[71] In all three cases, it is evident that the interior monologue cannot step away from its focalization on the experience of the protagonist. For this reason, Veronal is an ingenious device: it allows the text to evoke and delay the imminent loss of consciousness, dramatizing the emerging interval. The staggering of different phases is the key to this logic of deferral, in which the suspension of consciousness is itself suspended time and again. Comparable to death scenes in the opera dragging on and on, Veronal prolongs the threshold state between consciousness and unconsciousness in ways that the interior monologue has not yet explored.

At the same time, losing consciousness doubtlessly provides an elegant ending for an interior monologue.[72] It also poses the question of whether the text must necessarily end, since the rich textual corpus of interior monologues offers many examples in which figures lose their consciousness but awaken again. The protagonists in Vsevolod Garshin's 1877 *Four Days* (Четыре дня), Édouard Dujardin's 1887 *Les lauriers sont coupés*, and Schnitzler's *Leutnant Gustl* of 1900 provide case in points. Still, *Fräulein Else* differs from these examples, because the loss of consciousness happens at the end of the novella. What is more, Schnitzler explicitly places the paratext "end" ("Ende," *FE*, 136) right after this final scene. This is not to say that "end" is unambiguous; it could signify the formal end of the quoted monologue just as well as Else's demise. Consequently, phrases such as "——He slept" ("——Er schlief") with which Schnitzler's friend Richard Beer-Hoffmann represents and authorizes the onset of sleep in the third-person narrative *Der Tod Georgs* (1900), are off the table in the interior monologue; no monologue novella can depict an unequivocal death of the protagonist, because that would require a final intervention by a narrator, which interior monologues, by definition, do not have.[73] From a formal perspective, then, the ending of the interior monologue in *Fräulein Else* remains ambiguous, despite the paratext. The impression that Else could wake up again therefore appears as an inadvertent artifact of the text's way of closure, another side effect, as it were, of portraying Veronal in the interior monologue spun out of control.

Understood as a text with a literary and a public-facing function, Schnitzler's novella therefore exposes an important aspect of Veronal: the immense commercial and cultural success of the drug was not only tied to an effective combination of chemistry, business strategy, and marketing but also hinged on the public buying into the narrative of the pharmaceutical industry, which postulated that Veronal was the scientifically proven "ideal soporific," without significant side effects or risks.[74] To legitimate this narrative, the pharmaceutical industry relied, above all, on medical authority. But as a prominent writing physician, Schnitzler challenged this framing. His novella *Fräulein Else* instead magnified a more complicated competing narrative that increasingly came to the fore in both medical journals and the press. It revealed that Veronal's success went hand in hand with countless Veronal accidents and that women had to bear the brunt of the drug's safety failures. In drawing attention to this counternarrative through advanced literary techniques, Schnitzler demonstrates that literature can offer a meaningful intervention into debates about public health.

4 Proust's Sleep Experiments

For more than a century, readers have been puzzled by immense amount of attention Marcel Proust's autofictional novel À la recherche du temps perdu (In Search of Lost Time) dedicates to the elusive "world of sleep" (RTP 3:629; ISOLT 5:108).[1] No other book in the history of European literature "reserves so much space for a sleeping hero;" no other book relates "with equal skill the infinite gradations that make up sleep"—a state whose richness the interpretation of dreams cannot capture.[2] From the somnolent overture onward, the Recherche obsessively charts sleep states ranging from insomnia to leaden sleep, from sleep inertia to reveries, from semiawakening to sleep talking, from hypnagogic trance at the threshold of losing consciousness to what it feels like to take sleep-inducing drugs. In what ways does the Recherche grapple with the seemingly impossible task of portraying sleep's profusion of absences? How does the text deal with the challenge of reporting on sleep from a first-person perspective? This chapter demonstrates that Proust's engagement with sleep medicine and period sleep science shapes the Recherche, buttresses the representational strategies of the text, and complicates our understanding of sleep. The novel reveals that infinite facets of consciousness extend from somnolence to wakefulness and blur the boundaries between inside and outside, mind and body, subject and nonsubject, raising the question of whether the self that sleeps is still the same person.

While a few scholars have addressed Proust's "inquiries into the depths of sleep" from literary, philosophical, psychoanalytical, and biographical perspectives, the literature has yet to connect the poetic practices of the Recherche to the nascent empirical sleep sciences of his time and to the cultural milieu of the pharma industry.[3] It is all the more urgent to address this gap because a growing amount of evidence suggests that Proust was acutely aware of these developments by way of his own patient history as an insomniac and a sleeping pill addict, as well as through his encounters, readings, and exchanges.[4] Nevertheless, if the present chapter analyzes how the sleep sciences feed into the play of signs in Proust's novel, it also highlights the abyss of representation that sleep's elusiveness opens up. How does one thematize one's own act of sleeping without awakening?

Whenever Proust portrays sleep, he interrogates the nexus of sleep's elusiveness and its representation. Philological work on the manuscripts of the *Recherche* reveals that the author pored over the sleep passages of the novel until the "very last weeks of his existence"; his final publications, two preprints from *La prisonnière*, again explicitly engage in the depiction of sleep.[5] The novel thus opens and ends with sleep.

Between these framing scenes, each of the seven volumes contains at least one elaborate bedroom scene that serves as a springboard for narrative, theoretical, and metapoetic discourse about sleep. The existence of these scenes and the textual infrastructure they create have been first commented on more than two decades ago, but they have never been used as a systematic matrix with which to approach the *Recherche*.[6] This chapter unlocks their potential to illuminate the structural function of sleep within the novel. It supplements the discussion with readings of other scenes across the text and draft versions of the *Recherche*, such as the narrative essay *Contre Sainte-Beuve* (1895-1900), as well as Proust's essays and correspondences.

In depicting sleep in the age of soporifics and sleep science, Proust's writing does not just dramatize the possibilities, modalities, and boundaries of literary representation of slumbering consciousness. Sleep is the primary structuring element of the *Recherche* and is also at the center of a new poetics that breaks with reading for the plot, with privileging content over form, and with substituting recovered memory for the ruminating interior monologue during half sleep. This means that in writing about sleep, Proust always writes about writing.

"I'm falling asleep"

Before the electroencephalograph (EEG) allowed scientists to register, read, and analyze brain waves, it was evident that knowledge about sleep was tied to questions of representation.[7] As Georges Canguilhem puts it, if the "essence of sleep . . . is to let life go without calling it into account," its "norms are recognized as such only when they are broken."[8] Ruptures to regular sleep, such as insomnia or sleep inertia during awakening, can render visible the otherwise hidden conditions, principles, and implications of sleep. Early on, the *Recherche* stages the recurring "theatre and drama of my bedtime" (*RTP* 1:44; *ISOLT* 1:47), a performance in which the speaker struggles to fall asleep. Later, the novel explicitly reflects on its portrayals of insomnia as inroads into exploring the elusiveness of sleep:

> Well, Monsieur, the fact is that this malady alone causes us to take notice of and to learn, and enables us to analyze, the mechanisms of which we would otherwise be ignorant. A man who drops into his bed each evening like a dead weight and lives again only at the moment of coming awake and getting up, will that man ever dream *of* making, if not great discoveries, then at least some minor observations, concerning sleep? He hardly knows whether he sleeps. A spot of insomnia is not without its uses for appreciating sleep, for projecting a certain light into that darkness. (*RTP* 3:51-52; *ISOLT* 4:57)[9]

This passage echoes period scientific theories maintaining that "pathologia illustrat physiologiam" ("pathologies elucidate physiological processes"). Propagated by prominent scientific experimenters like the physiologist Claude Bernard (1813-78) and the psychologist Théodule Armand Ribot (1839-1916), two authors whom Proust had read, this adage suggested that disorders can shed light on seemingly normal everyday phenomena. The pathological makes norms visible by straying from them, but this deviance only counts as a difference in grade, not as a difference in kind. Like period science, Proust's novel turns to alleged sleep disorders to penetrate sleep's opacity.

From this perspective, the overture of the *Recherche* appears in a new light; the text opens with the depiction of an extraordinary, ambiguous state on the fringes of consciousness. The exact nature of this state remains shrouded in darkness; some scholars speak of insomnia and others of a state of semiawakening, while still others have related it to a medical diagnosis such as "neurasthenic half sleep."[10] As detailed in the accounts of contemporary physicians—and especially in the hygienic textbook written by Proust's father—neurasthenic half sleep refers to "fall[ing] asleep soon after going to bed" but then "quickly awaken[ing]" again: "This process—soon falling asleep, soon waking up—may, under certain conditions, repeat itself countless times within the course of a single night."[11] The protagonist of the overture indeed dozes off quickly (*RTP* 1:3), awakens (*RTP* 1:3), falls back asleep (*RTP* 1:4), awakens for the blink of an eye (*RTP* 1:4), falls back asleep (*RTP*

1:4), and awakens again. He struggles to determine where, when, and even who he is (*RTP* 1:5), before being carried away by the "long reveries" of the multithousand-page novel (*RTP* 1:7; *ISOLT* 1:11).

As the gateway into the fictive world, the allusive overture of Proust's *Recherche* determines the further course of the novel and showcases its logic of narration. Turning what could be a reductive medical case history into a literary narrative, the novel discovers that this peculiar state prompts the interior monologue, sets memory into motion, and launches the text with a gesture of reaching back into the past, which makes what follows appear as if it were "a subjective fragment, a flash from the stream of consciousness."[12] Proust thus nests his novel in the twilight zone between falling asleep and fully waking up. This twilight zone is close to revery, but it cannot be fully captured through revery, as it leads to a foregrounding of psychology rather than form.[13]

Many novels begin with scenes of waking up but rarely with depictions of falling asleep. Even the strongest readings of the dialectic of sleeping and awakening in the overture—those by Annelies Schulte Nordholt and Hans Blumenberg—still oversimplify the threshold of sleep and, by extension, the opening of the *Recherche*.[14] Rendered in the iterative tense of the *imparfait*, the overture describes much more than a single night—it depicts a scene that repeats itself over and over. This repetition is not limited to the threshold of the text: Proust staggers "nights of insomnia" (*RTP* 1:376; *ISOLT* 1:387) throughout the novel in a way that matches the "multiplication of beginnings" that Gérard Genette has shown to pervade Proust's text.[15] These sleepless nights evoke, reprise, and continue the beginning, giving rise to a process of writing and rewriting that cannot reach closure.

The *Recherche* perpetually points back to the sleep scene of the overture, with at least one bedroom passage in each of the seven volumes reiterating the beginning of the text—in scenes set in Combray in *Du côté de chez Swann*, in Balbec in *À l'ombre des jeunes filles en fleurs*, in Doncières in *Le côté de Guermantes*, in Balbec again in *Sodome et Gomorrhe*, in Paris in *La prisonnière*, in Venice in *Albertine disparue*, and finally in Tansonville in *Le temps retrouvé*.[16] These scenes have been described as "digressions" and may appear as mere signposts for key moments in the narrative (such as the saint's day of the protagonist, the first encounter with Albertine, and the acknowledgment that his grandmother has died).[17] Still, the bedroom passages matter because they form a quasiautonomous and interconnected text within the text, an armature of self-reflection, a constant reminder of the narrative situation of the novel. Like parentheses, the bedroom passages disrupt, delay, and amend the linear progression of the text; they interpolate a metapoetic commentary and serve as a substitute for the initial night scene: "It is not possible to describe human life without bathing it in the sleep into which it plunges and which, night after night, encircles it like the sea around a promontory" (*RTP* 3:384; *ISOLT* 3:82). For this reason, it is problematic to assume that the *Recherche* moves from unconsciousness to consciousness, from oblivion to the epiphany of the Madeleine, from nonmemory to recovered memory, and from nonwriting to writing.[18] Instead, the text perpetually circles back to the elusive twilight of the bedroom, reentering the in-between of falling asleep and awakening over and over again.[19] Proust situates his novel on the verge of consciousness, treating his text as if it consisted of a series of hypnagogic images flickering and vanishing as he moves in and out of sleep.

Proust's novel inscribes this gliding threshold into the very fabric of its opening. Scholars have proposed that the overture occurs during the narrator's second stay at a sanatorium and have identified this stay with Proust's own stay at Paul Sollier's clinic in 1906, where he underwent a six-week isolation treatment with the goal of curing him of his own neurasthenic half sleep and his addiction to soporifics after the death of his mother.[20] Yet the "first temporal section of the *Recherche*," as Genette has pointed out, "evokes a moment that is impossible to date with precision."[21] The overture is thus set in no specific place and time at all.

The extraterritoriality and extratemporality of the overture coincides with uncertainty about the identity of the speaker who uses the first-person singular while he drifts in and out of sleep—it is a person at a stage of life that neither corresponds to the protagonist of the novel (a boy who strives to become an artist during the course of the book) nor to the narrator (the artist who writes the story of how he became the artist who writes the story of becoming an artist). In first-person narrative, narrating I and narrated I typically coalesce in one and the same person, but the narrator of the overture instead exhibits precisely the discrepancy between these two poles, thereby demonstrating an internal void or mismatch between them—the impossibility of transforming a narrative voice into an anthropomorphic homodiegetic narrator.[22]

To bridge the unbridgeable gap between protagonist and narrator in the overture, Marcel Muller came up with the idea of what he calls "intermediary subject." Muller defines this hypothetical figure as an I that "constitutes an indispensable hinge for the narrator who remembers the protagonist."[23]

The intermediary subject serves a clearly demarcated function: it creates a round subject with memories the text can recuperate after the famous Madeleine episode, identifying the I who will narrate the I in order to narrate the I. But what if this identity could never be established? What if the disjunction of I and me, of narrator and narratee, of subject of enunciation and enunciation of the subject, which the first sentence of the book inaugurates—"Longtemps, je me suis couché de bonne heure" (*RTP* 1:3)— persists across the text? Let us reread the opening paragraph of the *Recherche* to get a better understanding of the full scope of the problem:

> For a long time, I went to bed early. Sometimes, my candle scarcely out, my eyes would close so quickly that I did not have time to say to myself, "I'm falling asleep." And, half an hour later, the thought that it was time to try to sleep would wake me; I wanted to put down the book I thought I still had in my hands and blow out my light; I had not ceased while sleeping to form reflections on what I had just read, but these reflections had taken a rather peculiar turn; it seemed to me that I myself was what the book was talking about: a church, a quartet, the rivalry between François I and Charles V. This belief lived on for a few seconds after my waking; it did not shock my reason but lay heavy like scales on my eyes and kept them from realizing that the candlestick was no longer lit. Then it began to grow unintelligible to me, as after metempsychosis do the thoughts of an earlier existence; the subject of the book detached itself from me; I was free to apply myself to it or not; immediately I recovered my sight, and I was amazed to find a darkness around me soft and restful for my eyes, but perhaps even more so for my mind, to which it appeared a thing without cause, incomprehensible, a thing truly dark. (*RTP* 1:3; *ISOLT* 1:7)

This opening portrays a recurring event; after the first sentence, the tense immediately shifts to the iterative *imparfait*, which describes actions that have repeated themselves. Although the *imparfait* could also be interpreted as providing background information or as an indication of indefinite time, what is central here is the shift of emphasis from narrated time to time of narration. This becomes most evident in the iterative temporality of the *imparfait*. On this reading, the pan from the *passé composé* to the *imparfait* splits the narrated time from its chronological organization. For an analysis at this level, we need the French original:

> Longtemps, je me suis couché de bonne heure. Parfois, à peine ma bougie éteinte, mes yeux se fermaient si vite que je n'avais pas le temps de me dire: 'Je m'endors.'

> Et, une demi-heure après, la pensée qu'il était temps de chercher le sommeil m'éveillait; je voulais poser le volume que je croyais avoir encore dans les mains et souffler ma lumière; je n'avais pas cessé en dormant de faire des réflexions sur ce que je venais de lire, mais ces réflexions avaient pris un tour un peu particulier; il me semblait que j'étais moi-même ce dont parlait l'ouvrage: une église, un quatuor, la rivalité de François Ier et de Charles Quint. Cette croyance survivait pendant quelques secondes à mon réveil; elle ne choquait pas ma raison mais pesait comme des écailles sur mes yeux et les empêchait de se rendre compte que le bougeoir n'était plus allumé. Puis elle commençait à me devenir inintelligible, comme après la métempsycose les pensées d'une existence antérieure; le sujet du livre se détachait de moi, j'étais libre de m'y appliquer ou non; aussitôt je recouvrais la vue et j'étais bien étonné de trouver autour de moi une obscurité, douce et reposante pour mes yeux, mais peut-être plus encore pour mon esprit, à qui elle apparaissait comme une chose sans cause, incompréhensible, comme une chose vraiment obscure. (*RTP* 1:3)

What is happening here? A narratorial voice states that an I went to bed early for a long time. This going to bed early sometimes led to a peculiar event: after dozing off quickly, the I was awakened again but still hovered in a state of half sleep or half awakening, that was accompanied by confusion as to who, when, and where the I was. At the center of the passage sits a temporal ellipsis. In the very first sentence, the phrase "Je m'endors"—"I'm falling asleep"—pinpoints a moment that sits on the verge of what can be experienced consciously. The text highlights the paradoxical nature of this event. It is rendered in direct speech (although this speech act was never uttered), in present tense (although it has been skipped and does not catch up with the speed of the passing moment), and in the first person (as if falling asleep would not radically sever the experiencing I from the narrating I, for it is impossible to be falling asleep and to relate it simultaneously). The first lines of the text, therefore, split the first person in two, in "je" and "me"— "je me suis couché," "je n'avais pas le temps de me dire," "je m'endors"— breaking apart the subject and cleaving asunder the syntax of its reflexive agency, as sleep paradoxically turns into the actant: "Le sommeil m'éveillait" ("sleep would wake me"). A moment later, the I will fall back asleep. In crossing the thresholds of sleep, the passage unmoors the agency of the self.

An awareness of mediating instances frames the entire passage; verbs mark fluctuating beginnings and endings of events. Nothing is fixed. As if in slow motion, intervals become increasingly precise, as they pass from an extended period to a set of repetitions, to a half hour, and to the span of a few seconds. No anthropomorphic narrative perspective glues these intervals together. But who or what articulates the strange utterance "Je m'endors"? How could anyone be almost asleep and at the same time articulate this condition so eloquently? Roland Barthes dedicated an entire article to this problem, continuing a debate with Jacques Derrida and Genette about the question of what constitutes a literary statement: "To say 'I am asleep' is indeed, literally, just as impossible as to say 'I am dead'; writing is precisely that activity which tampers with language—the impossibilities of language—to the advantage of discourse."[24] Even though Barthes exacerbates the problem at hand when he equates Proust's "Je m'endors" ("I am falling asleep") with the paradoxical "Je dors" ("I am asleep"), his point is still well taken: to write literature means to create utterances that often make little to no sense in everyday discourse but are possible in writing: literary writing showcases language being pushed to the limits.

Barthes only addresses certain aspects of the strangeness of "Je m'endors," however. We can go further and claim that this enunciation empties out what it enunciates. In her definitive study *The Logic of Literature* (1968), Käte Hamburger argues that a phenomenon such as the epic preterit (the fictive past tense in which literary works are conventionally written) does not refer to a past tense at all but reads as the present. Proust himself advanced a similar argument in his essay *À propos du "style" de Flaubert* (1920), which bears directly on the *Recherche*, amounting, as Renate Schlesinger points out, to a "revelation of the principles of construction" of his novel.[25] Commenting on Flaubert's use of grammar, Proust's essay argues that the author of *Madame Bovary* and *L'éducation sentimentale* furnishes his readers with a new vision of the world by spearheading "an entirely new and personalized way" to use the French tense system.[26] What matters most to Flaubert is the "rhythmic value" ("valeur rythmique") of the tenses—and for this reason, he often blurs the distinction between the *imparfait* and *present* tense.[27] Venturing beyond orthodox interpretations of the essay, I propose that this blurring of tenses, which Proust describes as a "grammatical beauty" ("beauté grammaticale"), is similar to the quasipresent tense that is no present tense of Hamburger's epic preterit.[28] The puzzling use of the *passé composé* in the very first sentence of the *Recherche*—"Longtemps, je me suis couché de bonne heure" (*RTP* 1:3)—illustrates the case in point.

From this perspective, the present tense of "Je m'endors" captures more than a present tense—even more than an iterative present tense. It pinpoints a "now" of narrated time that never occurs "now"; when the sentence is read, however, it will always have happened to the me in this instant. In the same vein, the I does not refer to me; this instant does not mean this instant; in the moment of falling asleep, the I is awake. Proust therefore quipped that literature speaks a "foreign language," deriving its particular characteristics from liminal statements such as "Je m'endors" (*RTP* 1:3).[29] The portrayal of sleep in the overture of the novel, then, introduces the reader to the lands of literature, lands in which language does things it cannot do in everyday speech. The *Recherche* dwells in the twilight of fiction.

Sound Sleep

The *Recherche* displays an almost capricious awareness of the connection between sleep and writing that manifests especially in states that are "intermediate between waking and sleep" (*RTP* 3:375; ISOLT 4:381). When a journalist asked Proust to comment on the state of literature, he gave an elaborate response pointing to sleep as a metapoetic trope for writing. In the first part of his answer, he stresses literature's potential to unearth and make visible the natural laws of fragile, unconscious states such as sleep, without destroying them. In the second part, he introduces self-observation of one's sleep while sleeping as the core figure through which this can be captured:

> It's a matter of wresting from the unconscious to bring it [the truth/*une réalité*] within the domain of the intelligence, while trying not to mutilate it but to keep it alive by preserving it as far as possible from degradation, a truth [*une réalité*] which, seemingly, the pure light of intelligence would be enough to destroy. To succeed in this task of salvage takes nothing less than all the forces of the mind, even of the body. It's not unlike the . . . effort incumbent on a sleeping man who wishes to make a conscious study of his sleep without waking himself up in the process.[30]

Proust does not have dreams in mind here—in his response to the journalist, he, in fact, effaces the reference to dreams explicitly, even if scholars have yet to take note of this: his final sentence overwrites an almost identical statement by Henri Bergson in the essay *The Dream* (first published in 1901), an overwriting that works like a palimpsest.[31] The final sentence thus demands a different reading: repurposing a term coined by the sociologist Niklas Luhmann in a different context, one might speak of a "reentry"[32] to describe the effort incumbent on a sleeping man who wishes to make a con-

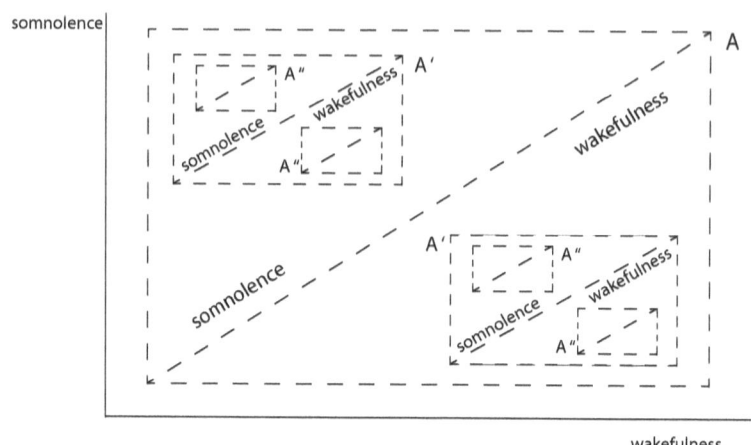

Figure 4.1. Reentries of somnolence and wakefulness (my diagram).

scious study of his sleep without waking himself up in the process." In the context of this passage, I use the term "reentry" to point out how the distinction between waking and sleeping creates a distinction between two states of consciousness. The distinction gets then reiterated within sleep— it again introduces the distinction between somnolence and wakefulness within the state of sleep. Deep sleep thus now figures as the sleep within sleep, while the prelude to awakening represents wakefulness within sleep, but these two states are nested within a smaller box, as it were, and both remain on the sleep side of the initial distinction between sleep and waking. In this sense, the reentry resembles the nesting of layers in the figure of the mise-en-abyme, which places a copy of itself within itself, with the possibility of an infinite regress: A, A', A'', and so on (see fig. 4.1).

The *Recherche* returns to the recursive, mise-en-abyme-like structure of reentry to depict sleep time and again. Proust's novel even uses the image of reentry: "I entered sleep, which is like a second apartment that we have and into which . . . we go in order to sleep" (*RTP* 3:370; *ISOLT* 4:376). A paraphrase highlights reentry: "Going to sleep is like entering a place where we go sleep, which is like entering a place where we go to sleep."[33] He also uses this device to describe falling asleep as a reentry of reflection on the sleeping side of the distinction between waking and sleeping, thus introducing an "intelligence" into sleep that does not cause an awakening:[34]

[In the afternoon,] my parents would tell me to go to bed for a while and try to get some sleep. It takes no great thought to know how to go to sleep, but habit is very useful, and even the absence of thought. But during these afternoons, I lacked both. Before going to sleep, I spent so much time thinking that I should be unable to do so that even after I had gone to sleep, a little of my thought remained. It was no more than a glimmer in almost total darkness, but it was enough to cast its reflection into my sleep, first the idea that I could not sleep, then, as a reflection of this reflection, that it was in my sleep that I sensed I was not asleep, then, by a further refraction, my awakening . . . to a new state of drowsiness in which I was trying to tell some friends who had entered the room that, a moment ago, when I was asleep, I had thought I was awake. (*RTP* 2:443-44; *ISOLT* 3:142)[35]

Here the speaker reflects on the idea of "searching" for and "finding" sleep, problematizing the extent to which falling asleep can be accomplished intentionally. The border between waking and sleeping disintegrates; it becomes fluid and uncertain. How can one notice during sleep that waking thoughts linger? Does one cross the border to sleep at one moment or, somehow, over the course of a certain timeframe? Proust's text tackles such questions by way of syntax, that is, by constructing sentences in such a way that they pass the border of sleep without ever really passing it. The passage presents sleep as a house of mirrors, as a labyrinth of reflecting surfaces that repeat, displace, and distort one's own subject position. When the protagonist is convinced that he will be unable to fall asleep, he dozes off; when he realizes that he is no longer awake, he wakes up; and when he thinks that he is awake, he has entered a more profound slumber. What could be a waking up to clarity of consciousness could just as well turn out to be a plunge into a deeper layer of sleep.

This aspect of Proust's work recalls and complicates contemporary experiments by sleep scientists who strove to determine arousal thresholds—the point where the distraction from the outside world is intrusive enough to awaken the sleeper. Proust knew about such experiments by way of the scientist Nicolas Vaschide, who presents a succinct account in his 1911 monograph *Le sommeil et les rêves*: "A method has been proposed . . . to determine the depth of sleep" that "consists in producing noises of different intensity" with the goal of ascertaining "the minimal intensity necessary to wake up the test subject."[36] The experimenter gradually increases the volume of a sound until it is loud enough to disrupt even the firmest sleep of the test subject. The recorded series of arousal thresholds could be compiled into a single curve showing how profoundly the sleeper had slumbered at any given point in the night.[37] Arousal threshold experiments revealed that liminal consciousness was a zone composed of many verges rather than a simple, immobile boundary between wakefulness and sleep. Set against this backdrop, it becomes clear how Proust's novel traces the borders of sleep with sound events. For example, the novel introduces a scenario that closely resembles the setup for an arousal threshold experiment during the protagonist's sojourn in the garrison town of Doncières. Around the same time every morning, a military band passes by with fifes and drums. While the noise is usually loud enough to wake up the protagonist, sometimes it is not. Proust explores what happens on those days when the protagonist seems to sleep through the martial music:

> Once or twice . . . the intervening barrier of sleep was resistant enough to withstand the impact of the blare and I heard nothing. On other mornings its resistance relaxed for a moment; but my consciousness, still smoothed over by sleep—like those organs which, after a preliminary anaesthetic, react to a cauterization first as something unfelt then, at the very end, as something like a faint smarting—was touched only gently by the shrillest notes of the fifes, which caressed it distantly with a cool early-morning warble; and after this minimal intrusion in which the silence had turned to music, it joined my sleep again even before the dragoons had gone by [*avant même que les dragons eussent fini de passer*], depriving me of the last blossoming sprays of the bouquet of surging sound. And the zone of my consciousness that had been brushed by its springing stems was so narrow, so hemmed in by sleep, that later on, when Saint-Loup asked me if I had heard the band, I was not certain that the sound of the brass had not been as imaginary as that which I heard during the day rising up, after the slightest noise, above the paved streets of the town. Perhaps I had heard it only in a dream, out of fear of being awakened, or else of not being awakened and so not seeing the dragoons [*le défilé*] march past. For often, when I remained asleep at the very moment when I had supposed that the noise would have awakened me, for the next hour I would imagine I was awake, while in fact I was still dozing, and I played out to myself in frail shadows on the screen of my sleeping consciousness the various scenes of which it deprived me but which I had the illusion of witnessing. (*RTP* 2: 384-85; *ISOLT* 3:82)[38]

Here the individual features of singular events in a series are used to foreground what is typical about them. What is more, the French original marshals iterative narration to describe incidents that may not have occurred. The protagonist may have slept right through them, but it's also possible that the events described unfold in an anesthetized, if not cauterized, semiconscious state in which distinctions between real and unreal have become fluid. In such a state, one cannot even distinguish whether dragoons or dragons are passing by—the French word "dragons" (*RTP* 2:384) refers to both soldiers and mythical creatures. One of Proust's earliest advocates and translators—Walter Benjamin—remarks that "the contrary opposition of sleep and waking has no validity for the empirical forms of human consciousness."[39] He instead points to an "infinite variety of concrete states of consciousness, which are conditioned by all possible centers, through all conceivable degrees of being awake."[40] In other words, acoustic events create the distinction between outside and inside in the first place, as they mark the fluctuating edges of sleep, translucent and dim zones at the interstices of sleep and wakefulness, with margins that resemble reversible figures. The borders of sleep are thus coconstitutive with ambiguous sensual events. In the *Recherche,* then, sleep and waking overlap, blur, and change into each other as they coagulate in "an intermediary zone almost beyond definition."[41]

Psychonautics

We have seen that Proust's writing does away with any clear-cut differentiation between the world of sleep and the waking world. The role of soporifics in the *Recherche* further complicates the dissolution of seemingly clear boundaries. To be sure, the appearance of drugs in modernist texts often goes hand in hand with a perforation of the allegedly fixed contours of the self, as, for instance, in Walter Benjamin's hashish protocols, the opium diaries of Proust's friend Jean Cocteau (1889-1963), Gottfried Benn's (1886-1956) invocations of cocaine, Antonin Artaud's (1896-1948) obsession with laudanum, and the drug experiments of the poet and trained pharmacist Georg Trakl (1887-1914), who took Veronal regularly.[42] To grasp the full significance of soporifics for Proust's texts, then, we need to consider their function in what could be called the author's "scene of writing."[43] Without an obligation to report for a job, the wealthy Proust was not in sync with the conventional rhythm of work and rest and withdrew into his womb-like bedroom at the Boulevard Haussmann, with its sealed shutters and cork-insulated walls, slumbering during the day and writing in a semirecumbent position in bed during the night.[44] A self-professed "man accustomed to depend on sleeping drugs" (*RTP* 3:631; *ISOLT* 5:110), Proust regulated his daily wake-sleep rhythm with the help of copious amounts of "sinister caffeine" ("funeste caféine") and a variety of additional uppers, whose effects he then offset through a "pact with impious Trional" ("pacte avec l'impie Trional") and other, even more powerful downers such as opium and Veronal.[45] Barthes suggests that in Proust's simultaneous use of stimulants and soporifics, inspiration has given way to regulating energetic inputs and outputs; in writing, "the body feels simultaneously and contradictorily sleepy, opaque, 'out of it,' sluggish, lazy, uninventive—it has to be roused, stimulated, and yet at the same time the stimulation has to be controlled, for it has the tendency to go on interminably: insomnia."[46] Proust's use of soporifics and his ability to write are closely related. More importantly, they are central both to the experiments with the subject position and to the poetic procedures of the *Recherche*.

Soporifics allow Proust's novel to experiment with depictions of otherwise inaccessible states of consciousness. On the one hand, soporifics give rise to experiences beyond the control of the subject. On the other hand, soporifics open an avenue for the exploration of mechanisms of the mind that are ever present in the background but rarely in focus. Cocktails of sleep-inducing drugs thus serve a psychonautical purpose, if we understand psychonautics as subjective explorations of the functioning of the mind by means of state-altering substances.[47] At the same time, psychonautics point to a constitutive split of the subject: in embarking on experiments with one's own consciousness, a movement of distancing, detachment, and doubling takes hold, destabilizing the first-person perspective. What is more, psychonautics transforms self-relations into object relations, so that one experiments with oneself as with a thing in a seemingly "objective" fashion. The pharmacological self-experiments in Proust's novel therefore question the subject position and suggest the extent to which experimentation can do away with subjectivity.[48]

The sleep scenes of the *Recherche* touch on such problems everywhere, but their exploration of the self culminates in the portrayal of the insomniac writer Bergotte, who explores altered states of consciousness and novel facets of himself by experimenting with different dosages of soporifics.[49] This scene is informed by Proust's own self-experiments with soporifics. His housekeeper and secretary, Céleste Albaret, reports that the author once swallowed a precisely calculated, nonlethal overdose of Veronal to find out what a similar experience would feel like for one of his characters: "Yes, I'm convinced that he wanted to experience death and that he wanted to experiment with the greatest possible loss of consciousness. Still, knowing him as well as I have known him, I'm convinced that he had meticulously calculated the dosage of the drug—most likely Veronal—so that he could rest assured his analysis remained wholly lucid."[50] From Albaret's report, we can assume that Proust's novel uses soporifics to discover the extent to which the subject could be dismantled, which state the "greatest possible loss of consciousness" would yield. Now consider the Bergotte scene:

> Bergotte . . . tried, with success but to excess, various sleeping draughts [*différents narcotiques*], confidently reading the leaflet which accompanied each one. . . . Bergotte tried them all. Some are of a different family from the ones we are used to, being derived, for example, from amyl and ethyl. One swallows the new product, with its different chemical composition, in delicious anticipation of the unknown. Where will the newcomer take us, towards what unknown kinds of sleep, of dreams? Now it is inside us, controlling the direction of our thoughts. How shall we fall asleep? And once we are asleep, down what strange paths, to what peaks or unexplored abysses will the all-powerful master lead us? (*RTP* 3:691; *ISOLT* 5:168)[51]

Guided by the package inserts whose heady prose the fictional writer takes in with utmost attention, Bergotte undertakes self-experiments to track how different products change his inner experiences. The effects of these soporifics often did not match the descriptions in the advertisement material; to find out, one had to try the drugs, as one period physician remarked.[52] For Bergotte, testing out novel psychoactive substances such as barbiturates is as vitalizing as going on a first date. The unique thrill of taking unfamiliar medications comes from the novelty of these encounters; it arises from deviating both from habitually used pharmaceuticals and from testing the accuracy of the account of the drug offered in the accompanying leaflet. Although these psychonautical adventures are very risky and will eventually kill Bergotte, they create inroads to previously unexplored modes of existence and ways of being.

What distinguishes the epistemology of such self-experiments from regular experiments is not only their risk but also the fact that they cannot bypass the subjectivity of the experimenter. As the *Recherche* puts it, the seeker "is also the obscure country where it [the seeker's mind] must seek and where all its baggage will be nothing to it. Seek? Not only that: create. It is face to face with something that does not yet exist and that only it can accomplish, then bring into its light" (*RTP* 1:45; *ISOLT* 1:48). Deeply personal, self-experiments promise knowledge that is only to be had firsthand, and literary writing serves as a method for investigating a notoriously elusive domain.

Like an "experimental psychologist," Proust teases out the connection between the conditions under whose influence a person has fallen asleep and the properties of the resulting slumber.[53] The *Recherche* brims with suggestive descriptions of "various forms of sleep" (*RTP* 3:631; *ISOLT* 5:110) brought about by certain soporifics. In an exemplary passage, the narrator walks the reader through "the private garden in which various kinds of sleep, so different from each other, grow like unknown flowers: sleep induced by datura, by Indian hemp, by the multiple extracts of ether, the sleep of belladonna, of opium, of valerian" (*RTP* 2:383; *ISOLT* 3:83). This flower imagery is often used in contemporary medical writing to describe altered states of the mind.[54] Although the passage foregrounds metaphors of highly individual experiences, the substances serve to pinpoint typologies, taxonomies, and topologies of sleep states: "Only through the repetition of diverse circumstances can one find out their basic elements. This variation of circumstances . . . allows a writer to discern the permanent properties by means of a kind of experimental setup."[55] This strategy could serve to erase the particularities of the experiencer; it corresponds to a rhetoric that foregrounds general classes of experience rather than individual encounters. For this reason, impersonal pronominal forms such as "on" intersperse the account in the first-person description of sleep states; the text also reorients the presentation of events from a chronological order to iterative repetition in the *imparfait*, so that the portrayal of a singular experience already implies its further iteration.[56] Proust's goal is to discover "general laws" ("lois générales") that will uncover the existence of classes of possible sleep states and the conditions of their appearance.[57] At the same time, there remains little doubt that these typologies are ultimately subjective—they are different for everybody and change with every new discovery. Distinctions between different sleep states thus multiply ad infinitum. The *Recherche* certainly refines its own classifications further and further through ever-new experiments:

> Varying the time and place where one goes to sleep, inducing sleep by artificial means, or, on the other hand, returning to natural sleep—the strangest of all for

those accustomed to rely on sleeping draughts—will produce varieties of sleep a thousand times more numerous than any gardener's varieties of roses or carnations. (*RTP* 3:631; *ISOLT* 5:110)[58]

The most mundane sleep is perceived as the most marvelous. This approach means that the *Recherche* turns the relationship between natural and artificial sleep on its head: it is not natural sleep that sheds light on artificial sleep but the other way around. Proust explicitly defines "natural sleep" (*RTP* 3:631; *ISOLT* 5:110) in relation to his experiments with soporifics: "I have always said—and proved by experiments [*expérimenté*]—that sleep is the most potent of hypnotics. Having slept deeply for two hours . . . , it is far more difficult to come awake than after taking several grams of veronal" (*RTP* 3:373; *ISOLT* 4:379, trans. corr.). According to Proust's narrator, natural sleep provides an even stronger soporific than pharmaceuticals, but natural sleep and artificial sleep are distinguished from each other by the side effects they each produce (*RTP* 3:374; *ISOLT* 4:380). The differing experience of artificial and natural sleep, then, shapes one's perception of alertness and somnolence so that one starts to recognize what had remained invisible earlier:

> I was still enjoying the last remains of sleep [*débris du sommeil*], that is to say, the only originality, the only novelty which exists in the telling of stories, since all waking narratives, even those embellished by literature, lack the mysterious incongruities which are the true source of beauty. It is easy to speak of the beauty created by opium. But for a man accustomed to depend on sleeping drugs, one unexpected hour of natural sleep will uncover the morning immensity of a landscape just as mysterious and far fresher. (*RTP* 3:630-31; *ISOLT* 5:110)[59]

The habitual use of soporifics gives rise to experiences with "natural sleep" whose nuances would not register otherwise. These alterations are of utmost poetic interest to the *Recherche*—the experimental setup of the novel generates differences through repetition. Proust's text discovers variances by restaging a phenomenon. The quoted passage recapitulates this experimental procedure in Proust's novel in a nutshell. His writing begins by repeating something known, but then a contingent event shifts the results, creates differences, and sparks more writing. From this perspective, the "only innovation, the only regeneration which exists in the mode of narration" reads quite literally as the repetition of earlier scenes, as it is only this repetition that then produces difference and continues the novel. Proust knew that one must regularly swap soporifics to maintain their effectiveness, minimize their dosage, and control their addictive potential. He varies his text just like his drugs: the *Recherche* moves from the establishment of habituation to disruption, to variation, to new habituation, to new disruption, and so on. For example, the novel first narrates the interruptions of insomnia; then it maps out the kinds of sleep afforded by different soporifics, only to delve again into the semisomnolent states created by turning away from soporifics. Proust's novel shows that even the most quotidian phenomena, such as sleep—"after so many centuries, we still do not know very much about it" (*RTP* 4:295; *ISOLT* 6:23)—are not well understood at all. Yet they can become better so with the help of literature.

The Angel of Certitude

In Proust's novel, soporifics give rise to experiments with ways of falling asleep and explorations of various kinds of sleep states. Yet sleep on soporifics is also tied to reflections on awakening, which the text in turn links to questions of memory. Since the *Recherche* often presents sleep as a temporary interruption and suspension of the self, awakening resembles its recollection. Yet this return of the self to itself in awakening is no straightforward process, because "on sleep's chariot, we descend into depths where the memory can no longer keep pace with it and where the mind stops short and is forced to turn back" (*RTP* 3:370; *ISOLT* 4:376). Proust expounds: "From these deep sleeps we then awake in a dawn, not knowing who we are, being nobody, quite new, prepared for anything, our brain finding itself emptied of the past that had hitherto been our life" (*RTP* 3:371; *ISOLT* 4:377). Or, to quote another striking formulation: "Waking is barely experienced, without consciousness, as a pipe might experience the turning off of a tap" (*RTP* 3:630; *ISOLT* 5:109). Proust asks, "What hammer-blow has this person or thing that is here received that it should be aware of nothing, be stupefied, up until such time as the memory comes hurrying back, and restores its consciousness or personality?" (*RTP* 3:371; *ISOLT* 4:377) It is evident that these remarks encapsulate a philosophical problem. Who or what is absent during sleep and returns thereafter? How are we to understand this alleged absence of the self? Is it an absence or rather a transformation? What are we to make of awakening as a restoration of personhood, couched in the vocabulary of memory?

Proust was fully aware of the philosophical problem he was laying out. He knew that he was not the first or only author to explore analogies of awakening and remembering and to connect them to inquiries into subjecthood. Arthur Schopenhauer's *Die Welt als Wille und Vorstellung,* a book Proust devoured in translation, explicitly presents awakening as a scene of remembrance:[60]

> Every morning, upon awakening, the mind is a *tabula rasa,* even though it fills up quickly again. First, the now-reappearing surroundings of the previous evening make us recall [*welche uns erinnert*] what we have been thinking in these surroundings: through association, links to the events of the previous days are established, and thus one thought swiftly leads to another, until everything which mattered to us yesterday is there again. . . . We can only tell from individual glitches [*einzelnen Unvollkommenheiten*] of this operation that sleep interrupts the thread of memory [*Faden der Erinnerung*] completely, with the result that it must be reattached each morning; for example, a melody of which we couldn't rid ourselves in the evening can no longer be recalled in the morning.[61]

Schopenhauer portrays the recollection of the subject after awakening as a mostly nonproblematic process, even though he hints both at the profoundness of the interruption and potential glitches that shed light on the very act at stake. Proust complicates this description further. A scene in *Sodome et Gomorrhe* recounts a conversation, supposedly relayed through word of mouth, between Henri Bergson and a "Norwegian philosopher" (*RTP* 3:373; *ISOLT* 4:379) that centers on the effects of sleeping pills on memory. It riffs on a few philosophical ideas by Bergson, such as metempsychosis and the distinction between memories stored in time and memories retained in the brain, in order to establish that sleeping pills often leave behind a dazed feeling after awakening, making it difficult "to seize hold of some memory of our everyday life" (*RTP* 3:374; *ISOLT* 4:380).[62] On such days, some parts of us just never seem to wake up, still in the hold of soporifics.

For an analytical vocabulary that reveals the complexity of the problem of awakening as recollection, however, it is instructive to complement Proust's own take with recent continental philosophy, such as the philosophy of Jean-Luc Nancy, that typically draws on Hegel's *Enzyklopädie der philosophischen Wissenschaften im Grundrisse* to distinguish between the sleeping subject and the soul.[63] The distinction serves to pinpoint the entity that is sleeping but is no longer identical with the waking self. In this understanding, the notion of the soul carries no religious meaning but refers to the "individual identity that has not acquired or conquered or produced its identity—and that will nevertheless endure throughout the whole process of the subject."[64]

In other words, Hegel postulates an underlying state of somnolent dedifferentiation. In this state, the distinctions between the self and the other, between the self and itself, and between the self and its gender assigned during waking life are dissolved, even though the sleeper has not become a different person to the outside observer. For Hegel, awakening, then, restores several distinctions that falling asleep has undone: between sleeping and waking, between soul and subject, between genders, and between the various senses and the categories of perception.[65] As Peter Schwenger observes, this means that awakening amounts to nothing less than a "quotidian reenactment of what, according to Hegel, is involved in the primal process of becoming a self-conscious subject."[66]

Still, in Schopenhauer, Hegel, Bergson, and Nancy, this process of awakening as a recollection of subject formation is ultimately never fully fleshed out. Literary writers, by contrast, often pay meticulous attention to the minutiae of this process.[67] To be sure, Proust is not the first author to offer an insightful account of awakening. For instance, Fyodor Dostoyevsky's 1846 novel *The Double* (Двойник) depicts a "man who is not yet quite sure whether he is awake or still asleep" before the gradual process of awakening recomposes the familiar environment of Dostoyevsky's protagonist from impressions of colors and objects.[68] Nevertheless, no other text matches the *Recherche* in the extraordinary depth and detail with which it analyzes the intricate transition from being asleep to being awake and the composition of the subject in its course. Take this passage:

> The great modification brought about by awakening is not so much our entry into the clear life of consciousness as the loss of all memory of the slightly more subdued light in which our mind had been resting, as in the opaline depths of the sea. The half-veiled thoughts on which we were still drifting a moment ago involved us in quite enough motion for us to refer to them as wakefulness. But then our awakenings themselves involve an interruption of memory. A short time later, we describe what preceded them as sleep because we no longer remember it. And when the bright star, which, at the moment of wakening, lights up behind the sleeper the whole expanse of his sleep, begins to shine, it creates the momentary illusion that he was not sleeping but awake; a shooting star in reality, which dispels along with its fading light . . . the illusory existence . . . and enables the waking man to say: "I've been asleep." (*RTP* 2:631; *ISOLT* 3:334)[69]

The awakening of the subject is less a transition to consciousness than a forgetting of the state that preceded it. Awakening forms an event that always incurs a delay: one must be wide awake to declare oneself awoken and to distinguish one's condition from sleep. The statement "I was asleep," then, paradoxically, amounts to a self-reflection of being awake, as it actually means 'I am awake,' rather than 'I was asleep,' because sleepers cannot gauge their condition properly: "'I wasn't asleep,' I answered as I awoke" (*RTP* 2:631; *ISOLT* 3:333). In other words, I have slept, thus I must be awake.

In the *Cahiers*, Paul Valéry succinctly outlines this problem of awakening: "One should not say *I wake*, but—*There is waking*—for the *I* is the result, the end, the ultimate QED. of the congruence-superimposition of what one finds on what one must have been expecting to find."[70] According to Valéry, one should replace the statement "I awake" with an impersonal form, on the lines of how French speakers say "il pleut" and English speakers say "it rains."[71] As it awakens, the I emerges from the depth of the third person; it is a scene of becoming oneself. But why do I awaken as myself and not as someone else? What happens in waking up? How does sleep end? Proust's novel explicitly raises such questions:

> We call that a leaden sleep, and it seems as if, during the few minutes after such a sleep has ended, we have ourselves turned into mere figures of lead. Identity has vanished. So how then, searching for our thoughts, our identities as we search for lost objects, do we eventually recover our own self rather than any other? Why, when we regain consciousness, is it not an identity other than the one we had previously that is embodied in us? It is not clear what dictates the choice nor why, among the millions of human beings we might be, it is the being we were the day before that we unerringly grasp. What is it that guides us when there has been a genuine interruption (whether it be that we have been totally taken over by sleep or that our dreams have been utterly different from ourselves)? What has happened really is a death, as when the heart has ceased to beat and a rhythmical traction of the tongue revives us. . . . No doubt the room, even if we have seen it only once before, awakens memories to which older memories cling; or possibly some of them lay dormant inside us and we now become conscious of them. The resurrection that takes place when we wake up—after that beneficent attack of mental derangement we call sleep—must in the end be similar to what happens when we recall a name, a line of poetry, or a refrain we had forgotten. (*RTP* 2:387; *ISOLT* 3: 84-85)[72]

Proust approaches sleep as an intermittence of the self. Here and elsewhere, the novel depicts sleep as a domain dismantling one's personal identity, disbanding one's gender in favor of an allegedly primordial "androgynous" state (*RTP* 3:370; *ISOLT* 4:376). (No wonder that Virginia Woolf was devouring the *Recherche* while she was drafting her novel *Orlando: A Biography* (1928)—here the eponymous protagonist undergoes several changes of gender during episodes of extended sleep.)[73] Because sleep also appears as a descent into the underworld for Proust, even as death (*RTP* 2:387; *ISOLT* 3:85), awakening turns into a full-fledged metaphysical incident—a "miracle" (*RTP* 3:630)—associated with allegorical figures such as the "good angel of certainty" (*RTP* 1:8; *ISOLT* 1:12) and the "goddess Mnemotechnia" (*RTP* 3:631; *ISOLT* 5:109). One cannot take the success of awakening for granted; "the half-awakened sleeper" must put in "the same effort as someone who jumps from a moving train and runs along the track beside it . . . to keep his balance" (*RTP* 3:629; *ISOLT* 5:108). Thus, an intermedial zone emerges at the fringes of sleep in which "the half-awakened sleeper" has entered a waking state but is still governed by the physics of sleep.

Sleep that continues into awakening—reflecting the sleeper's "ignorance of the waking moment" (*RTP* 1:8; *ISOLT* 5:12)—only yields to the intervention of memory. In the analysis of awakening in the *Cahiers*, Valéry highlights such an alliance between memory and awakening and connects it to a specific verbal structure: "The capital fact of memory consists in recovering oneself in waking, recovering one's own body and oneself."[74] Valéry's attention to the grammatical aspects of the ends of sleep sheds light on two important aspects of the *Recherche*. Valéry stresses that awakening is triggered by verbs with a reduplicative prefix: "What is awakening? It is re-covering. This RE [is the] essential notation."[75] Still, Proust's novel rarely employs "retrouver" ("to recover") or "se retrouver" ("to recover oneself") in descriptions of awakening. The text instead portrays the bared, blocked, and delayed awakening as an awakening from which the reduplicative prefix has been purged, as in, for example, "Quand je m'éveillais au milieu de la nuit, comme j'ignorais où je me trouvais, je ne savais même pas au premier instant qui j'étais" (*RTP* 1:5). Proust employs the verb "se trouver" ("to find oneself") to mark a condition of awakening that is characterized by radical uncertainty, giving rise to an irreducible ambivalence hovering between objective discovery and subjective perception that recalls Kafka's *Die Verwandlung* (1915), in which Gregor Samsa finds "himself changed in his bed into a monstrous vermin."[76] It also evokes a scene in Thomas Mann's *Der Zauberberg* (1924) in which the protagonist, Hans Castorp, loses his way during a blizzard and succumbs to an "impersonal desire to lie down and sleep" after he downs a beer, with the effect that he drifts off in the cold.[77] To describe

Hans Castorp's *Schlaftrunkenheit* (sleep inertia; literally, "sleep inebriation") after his fortunate awakening a few minutes later, Mann likewise turns to the phrase "to find oneself": Hans Castrop "found himself [*fand er sich*] lying in the snow," even though this "was not a genuine awakening; he simply lay there blinking . . . and he went on dreaming, as it were—no longer in visions, but in thoughts hardly less perilous and tangled."[78] In all these cases, the phrase "to find oneself" marks an awakening that remains incomplete and is thus distinguished from awakening understood as a straightforward "recovering" of the self.

Proust's *Recherche* complicates the process of awakening even further by associating "se trouver" not only with a confusion of identity, time, and location but also with a shift from the first to the third person:

> A sleeping man holds in a circle around him the sequence of the hours, the order of the years and worlds. He consults them instinctively as he wakes and reads in them in a second the point on the earth he occupies, the time that has elapsed up to his waking; but their ranks can be mixed up and broken. . . . [When] I woke thus, my mind restlessly attempting, without success, to discover where I was, everything revolved around me in the darkness, things, countries, years. My body, too benumbed to move, would try to locate, according to the form of its fatigue, the position of its limbs in order to deduce from this the direction of the wall, the location of the furniture, in order to reconstruct and name the dwelling in which it found itself. Its memory, the memory of its ribs, its knees, its shoulders, offered in succession several of the rooms where it had slept, while around it in the invisible walls, changing place according to the shape of the imagined room, spun through the shadows." (*RTP* 1:6; *ISOLT* 1:9-10)[79]

At the end of sleep, the need for orientation in space and time sparks a search movement by mind and body, depicted in slow motion. Proust portrays the struggle of finding oneself as an experience of being placed on "the revolving disc of awakening" (*RTP* 2: 386; *ISOLT* 3:84), which manifests in metaphors of uncertain perception such as swiveling, turning, and gyrating. They reveal the world of waking to be a series of "revolving, confused evocations" unfolding like the flickering images of an early cinematic projector (*RTP* 1:7; *ISOLT* 1:11). Awakening thus appears as a detective novel of the unreal, which sorts out discombobulated possibilities and misleading clues: "One often has at hand, in those first minutes when one is letting oneself slip towards awakening, a range of different realities from which one thinks one can choose, like taking a card from a pack" (*RTP* 3:630; *ISOLT* 5:109).

Leading from the possible worlds of the dream to the world of possibilities in waking, awakening frames a strange scene of recognition. Here, the "corps conscient" ("consciousness of the body") reenters the "corps matériel" ("material body") (*RTP* 2:27). Orientation, consciousness, and a sense of self emerge from an organic memory; they arise from unconscious reminiscences of past dwellings that are called up: "No doubt the room, even if we have seen it only once before, awakens memories to which other, older memories cling; or possibly some of them lay dormant inside us and we now have become conscious of them" (*RTP* 2:387; *ISOLT* 3:85). The consciousness of awakening is thus tied to specific places; it reconciles potential and actual sites. Moreover, it recomposes consciousness through assembling the parts of the body into a whole, a whole that then becomes a synonym of the I:

> And even before my mind, which hesitated on the thresholds of times and shapes, had identified the house by reassembling the circumstances, it—my body—would recall the kind of bed in each one, the location of the doors, the angle at which the light came in through the windows, the existence of a hallway, along with the thought I had had as I fell asleep and that I had recovered upon waking. (*RTP* 1:6; *ISOLT* 1:10)[80]

In a compressed form, Proust dramatizes a twofold event. While the process of awakening aligns the end of sleep with a specific locale, the I receives a body, a body that is simultaneously related to the first and to the third person, both "my body" ("mon corps") and it ("lui"). An extensive support structure of subjectivity comes to the fore that makes it possible for awakening to reassemble "my self's original features" (*RTP* 1:6; *ISOLT* 1:9). This entanglement of mind and body undoes Cartesian dichotomies of *res extensa* and *res cogitans*, as it shows an I that emerges from nonthinking and nonidentity; the first person does not cause awakening but is, on the contrary, a consequence of having been awoken. Like Valéry, Proust reassigns the phrase "Je m'éveille" a different meaning: he shows that "to awake" ultimately carries a hint of the middle voice, the grammatical mode in which the subject acts on itself and is being acted on—not "I awake" but rather "I find myself awoken."

This reading of the *Recherche* in the context of contemporary sleep science, medicine, and pharmaceuticals, then, highlights the specific labor of Proust's literary language, its sleep work: one cannot peep into the state of slumber without reflecting on the fictions involved in this endeavor. While the *Recherche* flaunts an almost lascivious awareness of its artistic devices, this awareness ultimately serves to examine sleep as a "metamorphosis" of the self (*RTP* 2:383; *ISOLT* 3:85).[81] When entering the "unconsciousness of sleep" (*RTP* 2:385; *ISOLT* 3:83), forces take hold that spellbind the sleeper and dissolve any perceived coherence of the self. This means that Proust's embodied subject exemplifies the exact opposite of a common understanding of the self—with sleep, the subject can no longer be seen as master in its own house and cannot be reduced to any substrate; its individuality only comes into view through processes of decomposing and recomposing its supposed identity, such as falling asleep and awakening.

5 Undreaming Kafka

Like Proust's *À la recherche du temps perdu*, Kafka's literature inhabits the night. Between 1910 and 1924, fourteen years that span almost his entire career as a writer, nighttime provided him with his most productive hours, and his embrace of nighttime writing was reinforced by a fantasy of "writing the entire night without restraints" and "sleeping the entire day without restraints."[1] Kafka never succeeded in inverting the conventional social rhythm, but nocturnal writing determined his everyday schedule as a regulative idea; he systematically organized his entire life around it. Early in the morning, he got up to toil in his bread-and-butter job as an insurance lawyer. Around 2 P.M., he left the office for good to have lunch and to "make it possible to continue the literary work until very late at night by getting much sleep in the afternoon."[2] Around 7:30 P.M., he got up again and began to shake the tiredness out of his body; his exercise regime consisted of "10 minutes gymnastics, naked at the open window," and an hour-long walk. After a late dinner with his parents, in whose apartment he lived, Kafka finally sat down at his writing desk, sealed his ears with plugs made of cotton and wax, and embarked on his poetic projects that occupied him "until 1 A.M., 2 A.M. or 3 A.M." and sometimes until "6 A.M." (*Briefe, 1900-1912*, 203-4).[3] Why did Kafka believe that insomnia was paramount for his literature? How does the literary "night work" (*Briefe, 1900-1912*, 258) shape the poetics and narratives of Kafka's literature? What do Kafka and his texts teach us about sleep?

The century-old tradition which deciphers Kafka's texts as expressions of a "dream logic" cannot help us answer these questions.[4] In that tradition, the author's works appear as landscapes of the unconscious that subvert expectations of objectivity, causality, and verisimilitude by way of strategies similar to those Freud outlines in *The Interpretation of Dreams*—association, displacement, deferral, distortion, metalepsis, and interpretative openness.[5]

Even if the dream hypothesis has generated many important insights and close readings, Kafka—a self-professed foe of psychoanalysis—explicitly rejected this approach: "It was no dream" ("Es war kein Traum"), *The Metamorphosis* states prominently.[6] What is more, the dream hypothesis cannot do justice to the gamut of different sleep states that Kafka weaves throughout his texts. While even a generous count yields "only three literary dreams"[7] in Kafka's oeuvre, his texts constantly grapple with work-related sleep issues. Time and again we encounter characters who still work in their beds; some suffer from chronic sleep disorders that have become part of their everyday lives after extended periods of overwork; others try foregoing rest altogether to get more done.[8] Kafka charts the gradations of restless, semiconscious sleep. His texts are obsessed with the edges of sleep, with half sleep, slumbering, dozing, reveries, twilight states, and situations of being half awake, falling asleep, and waking up. This obsession asks us to consider of why he thematizes sleep and awakening over and over, how he portrays such intangible states, and what his writing reveals about sleep.

Kafka was fully aware that the elusiveness of these sleep states often required elaborate ways of representation. But because he simultaneously sought to purge overt metapoetic reflection from his writing, Kafka frequently removed theoretically charged passages on sleep from his work (which the back matter of critical editions recover).[9] This chapter joins ranks with recent scholarship that does not regard Kafka's texts as autonomous units but rather as works in progress, as bundles of fragments that do not necessarily coalesce into a whole.[10] We therefore need to look more closely at creative processes and the messiness of the manuscripts, which shed new light on Kafka's literary techniques and thus on the presentation of sleep. The present chapter considers an assortment of Kafka's texts, including novels, stories, notebooks, and letters, paying special attention to canceled passages. Its close readings focus on the fragmentary novel *Das Schloss* (1922) and the late fragmentary story "Der Bau" (1923–24). This attunement to the specific procedures of Kafka's writings is necessary to elucidate his poetics of sleep.

In the Nighttime Workshop

As Roland Barthes points out in *The Preparation of the Novel*, Kafka's literary "night work" conjures up "mythical images" of a productive imagination, indeed, "the whole mythical space of Wanting-to-Write."[11] The question of how one organizes writing cuts to its very core. Nevertheless, few authors deliberately scheduled writing for the night. Some even advised explicitly against it. When journalists invited Thomas Mann to comment on the question "Does one need sleep and cigarettes for writing?," he referred readers to an earlier essay of his, which gives an unequivocal answer: "The greatest writer is most certainly the one who is loyal to the night and keeps longing for the night but accomplishes the most enormous deeds during daytime."[12] According to Mann, then, the artist must resist the urge to write during nocturnal hours in order to get things done during the daytime.[13] For Kafka, however, writing proper had to take place at night. Thus, his nighttime workshop can neither be described as a makeshift arrangement nor as a bureaucratization of creativity, that is, simply working after hours.[14] Kafka adopted the writing schedule he did because he was not interested in completing another day of work measurable in word counts and revisions but in an exceptional literature that could emerge only during the nocturnal hours: "Again realized that any text is of inferior quality if it is produced in a fragmented fashion and not mainly written in the course of a single night (or even written entirely in the course of this night)" (December 8, 1914, Kafka, *Tagebücher*, 706). The emergence during an exceptional night characterizes almost all of Kafka's major literary achievements, for example, his famous story "Das Urteil," written in 1912 and published in 1913 (September 23, 1912, *Tagebücher*, 460-61). Kafka even believed that only the "burning electric light, the silent house, the darkness outside, the last waking moments" gave him "the right to write" (December 25, 1910, *Tagebücher*, 139; *Diaries*, 45). Paradoxically, the fantasy of writing in one nighttime sitting had the opposite effect from what Kafka intended, forcing him to build larger narratives from quasiepisodic, self-sustained pieces. Instead of producing completion, the nocturnal writing scene saturates Kafka's texts with gaps, voids, and cul-de-sacs, trapping his literature in an irreducible fragmentariness and a state of becoming that can never reach closure.

Kafka's embrace of nocturnal writing left him with a glut of sleep disorders—above all, insomnia. Scribbling under the electric light, which, like Kafka himself, burned on and on, the author traded both his nighttime rest and his health for the sake of writing—as some sleep scientists note, Kafka systemically cultivated sleep deprivation as a creative technique.[15] He was fully aware that he maintained an "inadequate sleep hygiene" which suffused his daytime with a leaden tiredness and engendered an unending struggle with falling and staying asleep at night: "I believe my insomnia is a side effect of my writing" (October 2, 1911, *Tagebücher*, 51).[16] Still, as he wrote to

Grete Bloch, he refused to give up his "quite erroneous way of life" to go to bed "early and at regular hours" and equally rejected options to normalize his sleep disorders with the aid of pharmaceutical sleep aids such as Veronal, in accordance with the doctrine of natural healing to which he subscribed (*Briefe, April 1914-1917*, 71).[17] Kafka understood that sleep deprivation seriously affected his body, but he was willing to carry on because he saw it as sparking his creativity: "Perhaps a different way of writing exists, but I know only this one. In the night, when anxiety does not let me sleep, I know only this one. And I am fully aware of its infernal nature"[18] (see fig 5.1). As he allegedly noted in a personal conversation, "If it were not for these horrible sleepless nights, I would never write at all."[19] For Kafka, writing, not pills, is the way to deal with anxieties that drive sleep away.

During his insomniac nights, Kafka learned that sleep was more than just a blackout, which can be briefly haunted by evanescent images. At least since his early self-portrait as a somnambulist, Kafka devoted considerable thought to the subject of sleep—and the question of who is active during sleep: "The kind of sleep I have is . . . rather more wakeful and exhausting than being awake. There are moments in the office—talking or dictating—in which I sleep more deeply than during sleep" (*Briefe, 1913-März 1914*, 330).[20] He also once quipped that his insomniac nights consisted of two parts—"a waking part and a sleepless part" (*Briefe, 1913-März 1914*, 204). The diary spells out what he meant, recording a condition in which hallucinatory images "radiate into the state of wakefulness" before one falls asleep (October 2-3, 1911, *Tagebücher*, 49-53). The visual metaphor calls up the jittering mirages that sometimes emerge at the thresholds of sleep. They reference sensual experiences the period psychologist Alfred Maury classified as "hypnagogic images," dreamlike states that are no dreams.[21] Scholarship on hypnagogic experiences pervades the psychological literature of the nineteenth and early twentieth centuries. From there, the discussion spilled over into texts by many philosophical writers that informed Kafka's life and thought, including Arthur Schopenhauer, Friedrich Nietzsche, Ernst Mach, and his close friends Max Brod and Felix Weltsch.[22] André Breton also explores hypnagogic hallucinations, crediting experiences at the edges of sleep with inspiring the artistic practices of surrealism.[23] For all of these figures, hypnagogic images foreground an encounter with endogenic phantasmagorias, which foreshadow the moment of finally dozing off—the Greek term "hypnagogia" literally denotes an experience that hands the self over to sleep. In Kafka's personal case, the situation of being handed over to sleep is perpetual

Figure 5.1. Franz Kafka, *Self-Portrait as a Somnambulist*, pencil drawing, ca. 1905-1907, 11.2 x 6.6 cm (Albertina, Vienna, item 31339r).

and never-ending: "Basically, I stay all night in the same frame of mind, in which a healthy person remains just for a little while before falling asleep" (October 2, 1911, *Tagebücher*, 50). Something remains awake in him and struggles against sleep, something that is, paradoxically, only instigated by the onset of sleep. In Kafka's wakeful nights of insomnia, "certain powers which, at a depth inaccessible under normal conditions, shape themselves into literature...." (*Briefe, 1913-März 1914*, 209).[24] In these nights, the voice of literature awakens.

Kafka's diary insightfully theorizes this connection between writing and sleeping: "[Gestern] im Bett hat mir der Brief im Kopf gekocht" ("Yesterday in bed, the letter was simmering in my mind") (October 15, 1913, *Tagebücher*, 583).[25] The entry conceives of the processes in bed as an inroad to textual production. In coupling the "letter" with the verb "kochen" (literally "to cook"), Kafka employs an ergative-like construction—in which a direct object in a transitive construction becomes the subject in an intransitive or passive construction—in this case "The letter simmered" as opposed to "I cooked the letter." If Kafka writes, "im Bett hat mir der Brief im Kopf gekocht," who cooks the letter? Does the letter cook itself? Does the letter get cooked in the bed? Does the mind cook the letter? The result is a diffusion of agency, blurring traditional concepts of activity and passivity. This fissure transforms sleep into a metaphor for writing:

> What I need for my writing is detachment [*Abgeschiedenheit*], not "like a hermit," that would not be enough, but like the dead. Writing, in this sense, is a sleep greater than death, and just as one would not and could not tear the dead from their graves, so I must not and cannot be torn from my desk at night. (*Briefe, 1913-März 1914*, 221)[26]

For Kafka, writing resembles a "sleep greater than death." To define writing as sleep cuts all ties to a "poetics of dream" that foregrounds an increase in imagination. The image of a deathlike sleep for an experience of writing harkens back to medieval mysticism. Most importantly, it takes center stage in Kafka's choice to introduce the term "Abgeschiedenheit" as the essential denominator of his writing. The apposition "not like a hermit" leaves no doubt that for him, "Abgeschiedenheit" means "detachment" and not "seclusion." This distinction goes back to Meister Eckhart, a medieval mystic whom Kafka had read.[27] Kafka's appropriation of mystical detachment as a way to think through his poetics raises important questions. Which dimensions of consciousness, reason, and affective life are being put to sleep in writing that amounts to a "sleep deeper than death"? Which parts of the self must be sedated to write? How does this sedation work? What is at stake in a detached mode of writing? In his diary, Kafka gives an open answer to these questions:

> I have never understood how it is possible for almost everyone who writes to objectify his sufferings in the very midst of undergoing them; thus I, for example, in the midst of my unhappiness, in all likelihood with my head still smarting from unhappiness, sit down and write to someone: I am unhappy. . . . And it is not a lie, and it does not still my pain; it is simply a merciful surplus of strength at a moment when suffering has raked me to the bottom of my being and plainly exhausted all my strength. But then what kind of surplus is it? (September 19, 1917, *Tagebücher*, 834; *Diaries*, 578-79, trans. corr.)[28]

The idea of writing as a surplus that emerges while in a state of anguish and sedation raises the question of writing's preconditions more generally, and Kafka meditates on what it means to write in this paradoxical state and on what this paradoxical state means for writing. Kafka's contemplation reveals, most importantly, that a peculiar self-reflexive faculty sits at the heart of literature: if one experiences anguish during times of unhappiness, it is possible to distract oneself from it by writing about it, by making it into the object of literature. To thematize one's anguish in writing does not diminish the affliction, but it nonetheless comes with a neutralizing power that puts oneself at a distance from one's own experience; it turns "my anguish" into anguish that is correctly attributed to me but is not mine anymore, giving rise to a paradoxical literature in which an exploration of one's inmost experience provides a distraction from it, in which effects of "self-anesthesia," as Kafka once described it, are created by one's writing about anguish.[29] It is a literature that is both all about oneself and not about oneself at all, rendering it fictional. As Kafka puts it himself: "It is night and no one will hold against me whatever I could say now because it might be uttered in a state of sleep."[30] In his nocturnal workshop, sleep deprivation, hypnagogic experiences and trance give rise a writing practice that transgresses the control of the subject. Kafka suggests nothing less than understanding his literature as a sort of sleep talking.

Kafka's literary night work, then, has three direct implications for his literature. One, it privileges fragmentary writing, in which completable, coherent, and linear narratives give way to an infinite repetition and revision of a beginning. Two, Kafka systematically taps into insomnia as a creative technique. He is willing to suffer from a spate of different parasomnias to have new hypnagogic experiences that are crucial to his writing because they deprive the self of control. During sleepless nights, a literary voice awakens in him. Finally, Kafka captures the force of that which awakens in him with a poetics of quasi-somniloquy. Therefore, while one part of him struggles with shutting down the overflow of language, another part becomes ever more awake; while one part seeks solace and peace, another part defies rest; while one part wrestles with detaching itself from the world, another part becomes ever more closely enmeshed in its retreat. How does this nighttime writing shape Kafka's texts? And which perspectives on sleep do these texts in turn open up?

Awakenings without Awaking

Scenes of awakening play a key role in Kafka's literature. Kafka's stories often emerge from a twilight zone at the edges of sleep or lead back into it, imbuing his texts with irreducible contingency. If there are different ways waking up can go wrong, we find them assembled in his oeuvre. Time and again, Kafka's texts start with a scene of awakening that goes amiss; the end of sleep catapults the protagonists straight into days resembling nightmares. In *The Metamorphosis*, Gregor Samsa sleeps over the ringing of the clock. When he emerges from "unsettling dreams," he finds "himself changed in his bed into a monstrous vermin."[31] In *The Trial*, Josef K. opens his eyes on his thirtieth birthday. Still snug in the softness of the pillow, his world comes apart; he gets arrested in bed, "without having done anything wrong."[32] In *The Castle*, the protagonist arrives at an inn late at night. Having just dozed off, he is treated to a rude awakening; an official gives him a new identity— he is proclaimed land surveyor, or, worse, the messiah.[33] Overnight, a single difference has taken hold, a single parameter has shifted, and yet everything is off. Awakening thus features as a "fissure or rupture that divides time and perspectives, giving birth to both a fictional world and a story with one and the same narrative act."[34] When Kafka's texts open with an opening of the eyes, they repeat and restage a beginning that has always already begun, a beginning whose latent and unrealized possibilities the story is about to unfold. In *The Trial*, the protagonist says as much in a passage Kafka later eliminated as part of his effort to expunge metapoetic reflection from his stories.[35] The literary and philosophical contingencies associated with waking up in Kafka's writings turn this moment into the "riskiest moment in the day":

> Someone . . . said to me that it is strange that when we wake up in the morning, generally everything is still in the same place as the night before. It seems that while sleeping and dreaming, one has been in a state that is fundamentally different from waking life, and it takes . . . a boundless presence of mind or, better, quick-wittedness [*Schlagfertigkeit*] to grasp with the opening of the eyes [*mit dem Augenöffnen*] everything in the same place, as it were, where one had relinquished it [*losgelassen*] the previous night. Thus, the moment of awakening is the riskiest moment in the day [*der riskanteste Augenblick im Tag*]; once one has come through without having been dragged away from one's place, one must not be afraid for the rest of the day.[36]

What makes awakening so risky is the looming danger of that one might miss the right moment to wake up. Kafka treats waking up as a figure of the middle: in the temporal order of the narrative, something precedes it and something follows it.[37] Whatever begins with the figure of awakening has started long before it. It happens "too late" or "too early" or it happens too slow or too fast to capture the beginning of the beginning, which, in turn, necessitates another beginning that imitates the beginning.[38] Kafka shares this fixation on reiterative beginnings with other modernist writers such as Gertrude Stein.[39] Yet in Kafka's work, the figuration of the beginning as a repetition of a prior beginning throws the protagonists off balance; it initiates an event time that does not make any progress but that rather continuously lags or gets ahead of itself. To put it differently, the story of Gregor Samsa always remains the story of his metamorphosis; the story of Josef K. never gets past his arrest, and the land surveyor is always "just" arriving in the village.[40] Kafka's characters are never able to come to full wakeful consciousness—they find themselves in a process of awakening they must undergo again and again. Awakenings in Kafka are therefore never in sync with clock time; they undercut and disperse the momentous presence of the now, as Peter-André Alt remarks: "Time signals a disrupted order which can be grasped no longer[;] . . . it signals the construction of a temporality of perpetual beginning which can never come to an end, because it does not move forward."[41] Whenever Kafka's characters try to enter the narrative while they are asleep, they get stuck in a metaleptic awakening process and turn into Sisyphuses of sleep doomed to struggle forever.

Because Kafka treats awakening as a figure of the middle, he sometimes uncouples it from the portentous beginning so characteristic of his work. But even in these instances—as in the novel *Der Verschollene* (1911-14), in the story "Blumfeld, ein älterer Junggeselle" (1915), and in the story "Der Bau" (1923-24)—waking up still features as the "riskiest moment." In "Der Bau," for example, awakening dissolves the temporal logic of the text. The fragmentary story is told from the first-person perspective of an indeterminable animal with mole-like features. It inhabits a labyrinthine underground burrow of its own labor that protects it from enemies and allows it to live an almost autarkic life until a piping or hissing sound appears that triggers all its latent anxieties.[42] The story conforms to the iterative mode until the first manifestation of the sound in the middle of the text that coincides with a scene of awakening:

> But now I am overcome by a certain sluggishness, and I curl up in a loose ball in one of my favourite clearings; I haven't inspected everything, not by a long way, but I do want to continue my inspection to the end; I don't want to go to sleep here, only I yield to the temptation of settling myself down as if I did; I want to see whether that will still succeed as well as it used to. It does, but I don't succeed in rousing myself: I stay here deep asleep. I have probably been sleeping for a very long time. I am woken out of the last traces of sleep only as they begin to fade; it must have been a very light sleep, for a scarcely audible piping rouses me. (*Nachgelassene Schriften und Fragmente II*, 1:605-6; "The Burrow," 168)[43]

The awakening breaks open the defensive works of the story, inserts a caesura into its labyrinthine texture, and fissures the "now" character of the narrative. Once again, it ties in with missing the right moment—in awakening, the "quick-wittedness" is absent, although the burrow animal would have required its help when returning to consciousness.[44] The animal is unable to hold things in place, and the peacefulness of the burrow goes amiss overnight. The barely audible hissing sound creeps into the inmost sleep of the animal.[45] Cutting through several layers of sleep, it points to a consequential event within deep sleep whose specifics are never revealed.

Three aspects of this observation deserve further scrutiny. First, the gradual passages of sleep in the story—from sleep-like dozing to deep sleep to retreating sleep—call into question to what extent the animal awakens. Instead of transitioning into clear-eyed consciousness, it lingers in a trancelike state and never leaves behind its sleep inertia. Long after the scene of awakening, the animal is still "on the brink of sleep" ("Halbschlaf" [*Nachgelassene Schriften und Fragmente II*, 1:614; "The Burrow," 173]) which overshadows the actions of the animal. It does not stop here, either. Repeated moments of falling asleep and waking up again are woven through the text, occurring, as the story puts it, "frequently" ("öfter" [*Nachgelassene Schriften und Fragmente II*, 1:614; "The Burrow," 173]). For the same reason, the metaphors used to describe the animal's perception of the burrow continue to draw on the semantic field of awakening and rising, for example, when the passageways' "stillness is aroused" at the arrival of the animal ("deren Stille aufwacht bei meinem Kommen" [*Nachgelassene Schriften und Fragmente II*, 1:621; "The Burrow," 176]). It is therefore no exaggeration to say that the animal never wakes up from a state of half sleep that makes it dawdle in the borderlands of sleep. The delayed and incomplete awakening points to a profound confusion of where sleep begins and where it ends.

Second, the appearance of the hissing sound "between dozing and unconscious sleep" ("zwischen Hindämmern und bewußtlosem Schlaf" [*Nachgelassene Schriften und Fragmente II*, 1:580; "The Burrow," 155]) dissolves principles of causality and decouples cause from effect. In a world of effects without causes and of causes without effects, anything may "flip into its opposite" at any time.[46] The impact on the agency of the animal is profound; the transition from deep sleep to semiwakefulness wavers between passive and active, between the animal's being roused without an agent and its getting roused by a potential hallucination. This rift becomes even starker when the animal later notes, "I feel . . . as if I were looking . . . at myself as I sleep, and as if I had the good fortune to be both deep asleep and at the same time able to observe myself keenly" (*Nachgelassene Schriften und Fragmente II*, 1:591; "The Burrow," 160; trans. corr.).[47] Here a first-person speaker describes a subjective experience as if it were a detached object.[48] And yet the narrator clearly stages this linguistic transgression between inner and outer experience. To put it differently, one cannot distinguish between figurative speech and the event proper; figurative speech is the event. At the edges of sleep, it is impossible to distinguish who says "I."

Third, the awakening is couched in a paradoxical temporality. The first and second invocation of the "now" both invoke a present moment in the present tense. In draft versions of "Der Bau," this does not register, because the verb between these instances also takes on the present tense: "I probably sleep . . . for a long time" ("ich s[ch]lafe . . . wohl sehr lange").[49] But then Kafka substitutes the perfect tense for the grammatically tenuous verbal form, a decision that ruptures the continuum of the present, suspending the identity of the speaker, the burrow, and the tense. A fizzling space of contingency opens in the conjugation of "to sleep," a dramatization of contingency in its most literal inflection (the Latin "contingere" means to tie together two elements without necessity). The story brims with these strange temporal fissures, as J. M. Coetzee has shown in his essay "Time, Tense and Aspect in Kafka's 'The Burrow'" (1981). He argues that the focalized "now" in the story does not move parallel to a linear timeline. This is because the (often iterative) verbal constructions in the text suggest competing timelines, over and over, giving rise to a temporal structure composed of contingent instances: "There is one moment and then there is another moment; between them is simply a break."[50] Coetzee makes this point again even more explicitly: "Between then and now is always a break."[51] In awakening, a latent discontinuity of time becomes manifest. Coetzee remarks that throughout the story, the "empathic use of deictics like now, this, here" homes in on these fissures, constructing what he calls the "stance in a present moment" or an idiosyncratic "event time."[52]

The moment of awakening thus busts open the ground zero of spatiotemporal orientation in the world, whose central and all-determining horizon is the experience that I am here, right now. The literary theorist Käte Hamburger has called this the "origin of the now-here-I-system" ("Origo des Jetzt-Hier-Ich-Systems").[53] In awakening, the subject does not hold its world together; it does either not yet hold it together or it no longer holds it together. To put it differently, "Der Bau" dramatizes the dissolution of the now-here-I system. When the animal returns from the outside, it dozes off in any one of the more than "fifty" clearings (*Nachgelassene Schriften und Fragmente II*, 1:580; "The Burrow," 155). It could be virtually anywhere in the burrow, even though the animal uses deictic markers such as "now" and "here" obsessively (*Nachgelassene Schriften und Fragmente II*, 1:605-6; "The Burrow," 168). In Kafka's work, the indeterminacy of half sleep sucks up certainties; it unmoors the beginning and gives rise to a strange event time, whose paradoxical agency undercuts the autonomy of the subject.

On the Verge of Sleep

Since awakening typically catches Kafka's figures off guard, undermines temporal coherence, and leads into a diegesis replete with uncertain causal relations, it should come as no surprise that his figures do not tend to fall asleep blissfully. Often, a sense of doom besets Kafka's texts when going to sleep comes into purview. These moments render evident what Baudelaire means by saying that "humans fall asleep every night with an audacity that is only intelligible because we know that it results from an ignorance of the danger."[54] When Kafka's figures doze off, they often do so in bizarre positions—on a heap of clothes, on a straw mattress in a taproom, in a tent camp in a desolate area, in a makeshift night quarters on the floor of a primary school on the edge of a bed, but not in the bed itself.[55] These physical positions already indicate that something is off. In "In der Strafkolonie" (1914), for example, a soldier dozes off while on guard—as a punishment, he is tortured to death while being strapped to what is called the "Bed" (*Bett*).[56] In the early fragmentary novel *Der Verschollene* (1911-14), Karl Roßmann feels that he must ward off sleep for several nights to protect a suitcase, his only possession.[57] Other figures, too, struggle with letting go and only dare entering half sleep states that are shot through with latent wakefulness.[58] This copresence of sleep and nonsleep generates narratives imbued with a pervasive drowsiness. According to Carolin Duttlinger, Kafka's attention to such somnolent states affects the "style, mode and structure of his narratives" and undercuts "fixed boundaries, identities and categories."[59] Instead of creating fictional worlds, Kafka's narratives decompose their condition of possibility, implementing a "progressive de-creation" that results in opaque storyworlds brimming with trancelike states, mirages, and liminal scenes and that raises the question of what kind of threshold sleep constitutes.[60]

The fragmentary novel *The Castle* (1922)—apparently conceived in the aftermath of a three-week-long spell of insomnia—grapples with this question from the get-go.[61] The novel's protagonist, K., arrives at an inn during a winter night. Having been allowed to "sleep on a straw mattress" (*S*, 7; *C*, 5) on the floor of the taproom, K. dozes off but gets awakened almost immediately; he goes back to sleep, only to be aroused again.[62] This pattern continues with some interruptions until the morning (*S*, 13; *C*, 8). When K. finally leaves the inn to walk over to the castle, he is still "very tired" (*S*, 20; *C*, 13) and has to retreat into the "twilight" (*S*, 20; *C*, 13) of a farmhouse, where he falls asleep and wakes up one more time. As this pattern highlights, the world of *The Castle* emerges from intervals between being awake and being asleep, intervals that do not correspond to the logic of the dream.[63] They rather serve to introduce the novel's idiosyncratic logic of the "as . . . if" (*S*, 8). When a castle deputy rouses K. for the very first time, K. encounters one instance of this "as if" in the guise of legal fiction: "This village belongs to the castle, so anyone who stays or spends the night here is, so to speak, staying or spending the night at the castle" (*S*, 8; *C*, 5). Did someone who sleeps over in the village already enter the castle, even if one needs a permission from the castle to do so, a permission K. does not have but would have required to do what he did? What sort of metaleptic limbo is being produced here, in the process of falling asleep and awakening? What does it mean to find one's way into this textual world while falling asleep? One thing is certain: the protagonist of *The Castle* never escapes the borderlands of sleep. K.'s identity incessantly points back to the initial loops of falling asleep, waking up, and falling asleep again. Kafka therefore situates his text within sleep's indeterminate zone—the series of immersions into and reappearing from slumber couches the novel in an etui of derealization.

At the climax of the novel, K. again encounters the castle's bureaucracy on the threshold of sleep. This liminal setting is further reinforced by the troubled textual status of the scene. For example, Brod excluded it in his first edition of the novel on the grounds that Kafka had lost control over the plot.[64] Yet it is the only moment in the novel when the land surveyor comes close to establishing contact with the castle. But a recognition of his status does not happen, as the land surveyor is intermittently awake, asleep, and hovering in between instead of making use of the opportunity. (In this sense, the episode resembles the "Snow" chapter in Mann's *Der Zauberberg*, in which the protagonist Hans Castorp falls asleep during a blizzard and experiences an existential illumination during a dream that vanishes from his mind and that he does not act on.)[65] These puzzles have generated many insightful scholarly readings, but even the strongest interpretations cannot make sufficient sense of K.'s sleep states.[66] Does the land surveyor get closest to the castle while he is asleep? The answer to this question is no, since the Bürgel episode reiterates the opening scene of the novel—it serves to undermine the possibilities to which it seems to have given rise. The sleep states of the passage mark the ultimate dissolution of distinctions.

K.'s encounter with Bürgel results from an unlikely chain of contingent events. Nevertheless, the stark correspondences with the opening of the novel overdetermine the entire episode. The land surveyor receives a request for a so-called nocturnal hearing (*Nachtverhör*) at the castle inn, but the interrogation does not take place as scheduled because the designated official is found to be asleep at the time of the hearing.[67] When K. returns later in the same night, he misses the right door and stumbles into a room almost entirely made up by a bed, rousing a different official, Bürgel. Instead of dismissing the land surveyor, Bürgel insists that K. keep him company, allegedly to improve his chances of going back to sleep. The ensuing conversation inverts this proposition: it is not the official who is put to sleep but the land surveyor (S, 406; C, 226).

The Bürgel episode thus repeats the beginning of the novel: K. looks for a place to sleep and finds one, even if he does not get a room for himself (S, 7-8, 403; C, 5, 224-25). In each case, he enjoys a "nightcap" ("Schlaftrunk") (S, 13, 403; C, 8, 224). Even the representative of the castle here corresponds: Bürgel is most likely a deputy of the same official who has appointed K. as land surveyor in the opening scene.[68] Most importantly, however, K.'s slumber follows the same pattern: as soon as he falls "half asleep," his slumbers are "disturbed again" (S, 413; C, 230), he falls asleep again (S, 415; C, 231), he is roused once more (S, 416; C, 231-32), he balances on the threshold between being half asleep and half awake, he dozes off again, "this time without any dream or other disturbance" (S, 419; C, 233), he enters into a yet deeper sleep (S, 424; C, 236), and then he awakes again, dazed "from being woken suddenly" and "still in dire need of more sleep" (S, 426; C, 237). Instead of bringing K. closer to the castle, the Bürgel episode rather returns him to the indeterminate in-between that characterizes the beginning: the land surveyor is trapped in a liminal sphere where there is no "difference between ordinary time and time spent working" (S, 411; C, 228); his position at the edge of the bed does not qualify as an official work place (*Amtsplatz*) (S, 406; C, 226) but is also not a place suitable for sleep, and he deals with an official who proclaims to "have in fact stopped being an official" (S, 422; C, 235) but still acts as one because he needs to engage in official communication in order to drift off into slumber (S, 407; C, 226-27). Everything hovers in between.

The defining poetic principle of the episode, then, consists in the elimination of distinctions. To be sure, a refined legal scholasticism characterizes Bürgel's discourse, but the flow of the text leaves no doubt that it primarily matters as a sort of ambient noise, as an interference that becomes part of K.'s sleep: "K. was asleep. It was not real sleep; he could hear what Bürgel was saying perhaps better than during his early period of wakeful exhaustion; word after word came to his ear, but his troublesome consciousness was gone; . . . he was not yet deeply immersed in slumber, but he had taken the plunge" (S, 415; C, 231).[69] Here and elsewhere, Kafka's use of free indirect discourse leads to confusion among voices and perspectives with the effect that they cancel each other out; the uncertainty of the "perhaps" (S, 415; C, 231) abounds at the verges of sleep; meaning evaporates, becoming meaningless: K. "knew so little, he didn't even make out whether Bürgel was asking the question seriously or only rhetorically" (S, 411; C, 229, trans. corr.). The sleep states of the land surveyor bring about a "fall of distinctions" if we apply this felicitous turn of phrase by Jean-Luc Nancy to *The Castle*:[70]

> K. nodded with a smile. He thought he understood all about it, not because it troubled him but because he was now convinced that he would fall properly asleep in the next few minutes, and this time without any dream or other disturbance; between the secretaries responsible on the one side and those not responsible on the other, and in view of the whole crowd of fully occupied members of the public, he would fall into a deep sleep and thus escape it all. By now, he was so used to Bürgel's quiet, self-satisfied voice, as he obviously endeavored in vain to fall asleep himself, that it was more likely to send him to sleep than disturb his slumbers. Clatter, mill-wheel, clatter, he thought, clatter on for me. (S, 419; C, 233)[71]

Falling asleep downgrades Bürgel's voice to noise in the background, making it so unimportant that it does not even have to be integrated into a dream anymore. The faculty of comprehension happily turns blank. For K., this lullaby to hermeneutics recalls an aphorism by the hygienist Christoph Wilhelm Hufeland, which explains how noises, counterintuitive as it may seem, can be helpful sleep aids: "The miller wakes from his sleep when his mill suddenly stops."[72] Bürgel's voice, in other words, opens a void: things turn into their opposites and then dissolve.

The narrative pattern at play in this passage is by no means limited to K.'s experience. It dominates the entire episode, recurring in almost every single motific strand. It suffices to highlight this operative principle using only the most obvious example: the text embarks with the proposition that the conversation with the land surveyor would put Bürgel to sleep. But then Bürgel puts K. to sleep. Then K.'s sleep turns out to be "not real sleep" (S, 415; C, 231). Then K.'s pseudosleep turns out to be sleep (S, 424; C, 236). Then, the land surveyor is called off "in dire need of more sleep," and Bürgel is confident enough to doze off now (S, 426; C, 237). And so on. This series renders the underlying mechanism evident: the initial proposition to be explored is withdrawn at the end. Indeed, not only is the proposition withdrawn but the passage also falls back to before its starting point, the conditions of possibility required to make the start in the first place being erased. One of Kafka's images illustrates this succinctly: the land surveyor gulps down a "nightcap" (*S*, 403; *C*, 224) with the paradoxical effect that he feels at first more energetic but ultimately ends up entirely depleted. The threshold of sleep traps Kafka's figures in situations exceeding their control and notions of causality, situations in which everything seems possible until it is not.

All in all, the sleep scenes that pervade Kafka's texts—states of insomnia, half sleep, twilight sleep, parasomnias, and restless sleep, as well as liminal situations such as awakening and falling asleep—rarely prompt the reader to reflect on a supposed resemblance of Kafka's writings and dreams. In these scenes, we rather recognize fragments of today's 24/7 society, a society whose elimination of boundaries between working and resting hours leads to a proliferation of sleep issues that undercut any notion of an autonomous subject. Kafka's literary nightwork provides an attempt to work through the anxieties generated by such a social order. These elusive realities that can be rendered invisible through adaptive therapies and pills become visible in Kafka's "sleep works," even though we could also call them "nonsleep works."

6 Rilke and Rest

Baladine Klossowska's 1922 *Rilke on His Sofa in Muzot* (see fig. 6.1), a watercolor in earthy and reddish hues, depicts Rainer Maria Rilke in a pose that diverges from the iconic images of the poet with their air of intense concentration and their focus on acts of looking.[1] Klossowska instead captures Rilke in an intimate moment with his eyes closed, nestled on a red sofa, asleep. In a letter from that time, Rilke describes such a scene as divine worship: "That great god: Sleep; I sacrifice to him without any time avarice—what does time matter to *him*!—ten hours, eleven, even twelve, if he wants to accept them in his lofty, mildly-silent way!"[2] The watercolor thus depicts Rilke's sleep as a zone of contact between a human and a transcendent world that gives rise to creativity and inspiration. At the top of the page, Rilke has jotted down a poem, making it seem as if it emerges from the borders of sleep, as it were.[3] Like the sign the surrealist Saint-Pol-Roux is said to have placed on his bedroom door that read "Le poète travaille" ("The poet is at work"), the painting connects Rilke's sleep to his writing.[4] In other words, the watercolor of the dozing Rilke hints at a poetics of sleep that differs from the practices of Proust and Kafka, two authors whom Rilke read and venerated early on. How do sleep states play out in Rilke's poetry?

Scholarship on Rilke has never raised this question systematically, even though his poetry is well equipped to provide eloquent answers.[5] From his early writings and *Neue Gedichte* to his late and last work, Rilke's poetry in German and French frequently features sleep scenes.[6] Here, Rilke grapples with many of the same questions as contemporary scientists, but he does so in ways that cannot be understood without a close consideration of his engagement with the work of Paul Valéry and the forms employed in Rilke's poetry.

Figure 6.1. Baladine Klossowska, *Rilke on His Sofa in Muzot*, 1922, aquarelle and pencil, with the poem "Der Gram ist schweres Erdreich" added in Rilke's hand, 20.8 x 28 cm (Fondation Martin Bodmer, Geneva).

Tossing and Turning

Like many of his contemporaries, Rilke first discovers the urgency of portraying sleep by way of encounters with insomnia and the medical apparatuses built around it. In his letters, the poet recalls an episode from his adolescence, in which "excruciating sleeplessness" led to him being sent "as 'highly nervous' to Salzburg for a salt cure," an event that made him an oversensitive neurasthenic and established sleep as a recurring problem in his life and work.[7] The topic remains latent in most of his juvenilia and early texts, but sleep and insomnia proliferate in his writings after he moved from the countryside to Paris. His novel set in the metropolis, *Die Aufzeichnungen des Malte Laurids Brigge* (1910), for example, represents urban life under the conditions of modernity as an attack on sleep. The text's opening scene depicts the soundscape of an almost sleepless night in the city, whose incessant tramway traffic and other noises register as visceral experiences and leave the protagonist, who "can't give up sleeping" with his "window open," tossing and turning in bed:

> Electric trams hurtle through my room with their bells ringing. Automobiles drive over me. A door slams shut. Somewhere a pane of window glass shatters and falls, I can hear its large shards laughing, the smaller splinters giggling. . . . Towards morning there is even a cock crowing, and that feels good, immeasurably good. Then I suddenly fall asleep. (*KA*, 3:455–56; *Notebooks*, 87)[8]

While in this scene, sleep difficulties are directly linked to a clash of rural and urban modes of life, sleep disturbances recur throughout the novel, often in close connection to states of nervousness. The text evokes, for example, anxious awakenings from sleeplike states, states in which distinctions between waking and sleeping blur (*KA*, 3:477; *Notebooks*, 115).[9] It also depicts medical scenes of diagnosis in which physicians interpret and evaluate the protagonist's trouble with sleep (*KA*, 3:494; *Notebooks*, 137).[10] Rilke's text solves the problem of sleep disturbances in its own way: as in Proust's and Kafka's work, the first-person narrator starts writing at night (*KA*, 3:611; *Notebooks*, 291).[11] In light of this fictional writing scene, the novel emerges from insomnia in a literal sense; the text works through the anxieties that keep its protagonist up at night.

Considering the thrust of *Die Aufzeichnungen*, it comes as no surprise that insomnia and its antidote, the (synthetic) production of rest, are the aspects of sleep that dominate several poems in Rilke's middle period. For example, Rilke's volume *Der Neuen Gedichte anderer Teil* (1908) clusters several poems around this theme. They range from a scene of trauma-haunted tossing and turning ("The Bed," *KA*, 1:572; *New Poems*, 335) to a dramatization of the repetitive sleep-inducing sound structures of a lullaby ("Lullaby," *KA*, 1:576; *New Poems*, 349) to evocations of the somnific properties of medicinal plants cultivated in the remote corners of botanical gardens ("Opium-Poppy," *KA*, 1:574; *New Poems*, 343) to "Lady before the Mirror" (*KA*, 1:570; *New Poems*, 331), a sonnet featuring causal and gendered use of soporifics.[12] In this sense, Rilke's texts are both autonomous and products of their time; as works of art, they capture and reflect social reality on the level of aesthetic form.

"All things must be written departing from sleep"

A few years later, however, Rilke's poetics of sleep underwent a significant shift. This change coincided with the transitional phase from his late to his last work, after he moved to the Swiss countryside, completed the *Duino Elegies* and the *Sonnets to Orpheus* during two weeks of manic nighttime writing in January 1922, and discovered the work of Paul Valéry. This encounter was "the most important event in the late years of his existence as an artist."[13] To Rilke, Valéry stood out as a poet and literary theorist because he paid so much attention to thinking through sleep.

Sleep states intrigued Valéry because they provided an inroad to studying the ontology of consciousness through moments of its interruption, receding, and recomposition, as we have already seen: "I find nothing more striking than the essential property of the human system ["système de l'homme"] to unmake and dissolve itself during sleep and to reconstitute itself upon awakening—after an intermission."[14] As Nobutaka Miura and others have observed, the French theorist was fascinated by the fact that humans are as much defined by experiencing what it means to be conscious as they are by being able to let go of consciousness temporarily. Throughout his life, Valéry puzzled over these experiences testifying to an intense connection of mind and body: "The phenomenon of falling asleep and that of awakening have been occupying me for a long time. . . . What marvel is this ability of not being, a property of this which is."[15] To be sure, although Valéry referred to sleep as miraculous and considered it the epitome of an absent presence, there was nothing metaphysical about his interest. He rejected psychoanalytic approaches to dreams and once described himself as "the least Freudian of all" ("le moins freudien des hommes").[16] He instead preferred what he considered a scientific approach to making sense of sleep—for him, the *via regia* to the unconscious was a precise language that could capture the elusiveness of the phenomenon at stake. To this end, his writing systematically draws on metaphors lifted from mathematics, physics, and chemistry, as Miura has pointed out, employing, for example, the physicochemical term of "phase" to differentiate between solid, liquid, and stable states during sleep.[17] Likewise, Valéry draws up mathematical formulas to track these transitions and interprets them in the language of thermodynamics.[18]

Even though Valéry never compiled a systematic account of sleep, an antipsychological theory of unconscious states emerges from his sprawling web of bold ideas, examples, cases, and formulas, suggesting that we regard sleep as the dynamic baseline of the self. Valéry developed this reading of sleep in his posthumously published intellectual diaries, the *Cahiers*—some of them are devoted entirely to related issues, for instance, the so-called *Somnia* notebook (1911). What is more, Valéry's literary writings are almost as intensely theoretically imbued as his intellectual diaries. Few other writers of the modernist period—or of any period—have centered their literature in a similarly unabashed fashion on the work of the intellect as Valéry: his texts are all about poetics.[19] In literary writings such as the narrative essay *La soirée avec Monsieur Teste* (1895), the prose fragment "Agathe" (1898), and the long poem *La jeune parque* (1917), Valéry employs sleep as a device to explore the boundaries of representation, the properties of narrative voice, and the constitution of the speaking subject: "Upon awakening, one doesn't know where one is, who one is, being just there—; one is a plurality of questions."[20] Or as Valéry puts it elsewhere: "All things must be written departing from sleep—the origin and point zero."[21]

Forms of Sleep

We can only speculate how familiar Rilke was with these thoughts and texts, although he spared no effort to get his hands on "those of Valéry's writings which were difficult to obtain."[22] He corresponded with the French writer and met Valéry repeatedly in person, occasions during which the two men might have discussed questions of sleep. Moreover, "Valéry's poems, prose pieces, and dialogues impacted his work more strongly than anything else," and at times, Rilke even "preferred translating them to furthering his own literary production."[23] Instead of tracing potential or assumed influences based on conjectures, however, let us look at Rilke's translation of Valéry's sonnet "La dormeuse," as a consideration of its immanent poetics brings to light how Rilke parses Valéry's approach to sleep.

Rilke encountered "La dormeuse" in Valéry's collection *Charmes*, whose sixteen lyrical texts he translated between March 1921 and February 1923.[24] With characteristic attention to form, Valéry arranged the collection in such a way that long poems are interspersed with clusters of short ones; moreover, all employ different metrical structures. The internal coherence of the volume, then, is created by an artfully organized impression of disorganization. Valéry even explicitly regrouped the poems to stress their autonomy within the larger structure and to maximize the potential of readers' being enchanted by the individual texts in *Charmes*.[25] For this reason, "La dormeuse" can be read on its own:

Quels secrets dans son cœur brûle ma jeune amie,
Âme par le doux masque aspirant une fleur?
De quels vains aliments sa naïve chaleur
Fait ce rayonnement d'une femme endormie?

> Souffle, songes, silence, invincible accalmie,
> Tu triomphes, ô paix plus puissante qu'un pleur,
> Quand de ce plein sommeil l'onde grave et l'ampleur
> Conspirent sur le sein d'une telle ennemie.
>
> Dormeuse, amas doré d'ombres et d'abandons,
> Ton repos redoutable est chargé de tels dons,
> Ô biche avec langueur longue auprès d'une grappe,
>
> Que malgré l'âme absente, occupée aux enfers,
> Ta forme au ventre pur qu'un bras fluide drape,
> Veille; ta forme veille, et mes yeux sont ouverts. (*Œuvres*, 3:110)

Rilke's German translation is titled "Die Schläferin":

> Welches Geheimnis da in der jungen Freundin glüht vor sich hin,—
> Seele, die einer Blume Duft durch die sanfteste Maske genießt?
> Aus was für nichtiger Nahrung erschließt
> ihre arglose Wärme das Schimmern der Schläferin?
>
> Atem, Traum, Schweigen—, unbezwingliche Stille, drin
> Du den Sieg hast, Friede, der stärker als Weinen fließt,
> wenn der volle Schlaf, der sich ernsthaft und breit ergießt,—
> einer solchen Feindin bewältigt den Eigensinn.
>
> Schläferin: Hingabe, Schatten und Goldes ein Hauf,
> aber dein furchtbares Ruhn tut so große Begabungen auf,
> langhin, o Hindin, bei einer Traube gestreckte,
>
> daß, wird die Seele, dir fern, auch im Hades betroffen,
> doch deine lautere Form, die ein Arm wie Fließen verdeckte,
> wacht; sie wacht deine Form, und meine Augen sind offen. (*Übertragungen*, 349–51)

David Paul's English translation is titled "Sleeping Woman":

> What secrets in her heart is my young friend burning,
> Soul through the tender mask inhaling a flower?
> From what vain aliments does her naive warmth
> Create this radiance of a sleeping woman?
>
> Breath, dreams, silence, lull invincible,
> You triumph, oh tranquility keener than a tear,

> When the solemn wave, the breadth of that full slumber
> Conspire on the breast of such an enemy.
>
> Sleeper, golden mass of shadows and surrenders,
> Your formidable quiet is loaded with such powers
> —Oh fawn languid with length alongside a vine-cluster—
>
> That though the soul is absent, absorbed in the underworld,
> Your form with the pure belly draped by a fluid arm
> Is awake: it watches, and my eyes are open. (*Poems*, 139, trans. corr.)

Valéry's poem pairs a male gaze and a sleeping woman without critically reflecting on the gender norms and iconographic traditions that this setup reiterates. Still, the poem offers a philosophical reading of the scene it stages: the poem successively moves from images to sounds to semiosis to form. In the first stanza, the speaker watches a sleeping woman and mediates on her secrets. In contrast to the narrator in Proust's *Recherche* who jealously speculates about the sleeping Albertine's infidelities in a comparable scene, the speaker of this sonnet appears more concerned with the physiological secrets of sleep.[26] The poem highlights metabolic processes depicted in thermodynamic metaphors and the rhythm of respiration—one hears the regularity of the breath in the first four lines. In the second stanza, the sound pattering becomes even more striking, given the prominent use of somnolent alliterations and assonances (s-s-s-s-s-, t-t-t, p-p-p-p-p). In this stanza, the speaker directly addresses the woman's sleep. He associates it with a state of peace and rhythmically organized, repetitive phenomena such as breathing. In other words, the sonnet links sleep with actions that typically happen automatically and without conscious control. In the third stanza, the poem shifts its attention from sleep as a state to the female sleeper to the processes of signification that make up her sleep, playing almost systematically on C. S. Pierce's distinction between iconic, indexical, and symbolic semiosis— icons being signs that claim to represent the depicted object (e.g., pictograms), indices being signs that point to a phenomenon (no smoke without fire), and symbols being signs with a conventionalized (but not necessarily transparent) meaning. The third stanza of Valéry's poem begins with staging a movement of decomposition that turns the woman from the object of love (given that one can hear "amas doré" equally as "âme adorée") into an aggregate ("amas") of absences.[27] Like an icon, the woman is represented by the aggregate of absences. Next, however, nouns such as "ombres" ("shadows") point toward another element whose absence they make legible as an absence—"shadows" are the prototypical indexical signs that require, both causally and locally, a body in close vicinity. When Valéry addresses the sleeping woman as a deer, he adds yet another type of signification: symbolic images. The fact that it remains unclear what the deer with the cluster of vines symbolizes emphasizes the tenuousness of symbolic semiosis. The concluding terzet draws all these aspects together and reformulates them as a question about form, the poem's key concept, which is mentioned twice. To prepare for the thematization of this concept, the poem evokes a plethora of distinctions typically unsettled by the idea of form, such as that between inside and outside and body and soul before it explicitly states that the form has been concealed by the draped arm. In the final movement of the poem, then, the form becomes manifest and opens the speaker's (and the reader's) eyes not only to the presence of the male gaze but also to the fact that the form is wide awake, even if the woman is still sleeping.

Rilke's translation takes some liberties, but the most striking deviation from the original (apart from its omitting Valéry's dedication to French novelist Lucien Fabre) illustrates how carefully Rilke has worked out the turning point implied in Valéry's French poem, the point when the poem shifts to reflecting on form. To stress this turning point, Rilke inserts an "aber" ("but") and a "doch" ("yet") in his translation of the poem, conjunctions that do not appear in Valéry's text.[28] These conjunctions are, however, characteristic of Rilke's own poetics: his sonnets in *Neue Gedichte* are frequently constructed around turning points marked with them, as Judith Ryan has demonstrated in a classic study.[29] In other words, it is precisely this turning point Rilke finds interesting about Valéry's poem and his approach to sleep. With regard to sleep, this therefore suggests that transitions from one state to another—from being awake to falling asleep, from sleeping to awakening—are relevant to Rilke's poetry. He is specifically interested in them as phenomena through which form can be perceived.

Thresholds of Perception

The turning point is the most important formal feature in several of Rilke's poems dedicated to cat sleep. In fact, this structure is so central that Rilke would abandon even promising drafts of poems if he found he could not deliver the pivot. In the fragmentary poem "Divinité du sommeil des chats," for example, which plays with the idea of creating a sanctuary for a "deity of cat sleep" in language, Rilke predicates its pivotal moment on a risky substitution of French tenses (simple past for present subjective) that does not work.[30] He scrapped the fragment after only five lines and made a fresh start in German. Thus, the resulting poem, "Idol," counts among Rilke's so-called double versions, or double poems, which exist both in a German and French version and interpret the same theme within the possibilities of another language.[31] In "Idol," the turning point is the imperative instruction not to read the poem as a lullaby:

> Gott oder Göttin des Katzenschlafs,
> kostende Gottheit, die in dem dunklen
> Mund reife Augen-Beeren zerdrückt,
> süßgewordnen Schauns Traubensaft,
> ewiges Licht in der Krypta des Gaumens.
> Schlaf-Lied nicht, — Gong! Gong!
> Was die anderen Götter beschwört,
> entläßt diesen verlisteten Gott
> an seine einwärts fallende Macht. (KA, 2:395)

> (God or goddess of cat sleep,
> savoring idol who squeezes
> ripe eye-berries in the dark mouth,
> grape juice of now-sweetened glances,
> eternal light in the crypt of the gums.
> No sleep-song, — Gong! Gong!
> What evokes the other gods,
> releases this cunning god
> to its inward falling power.)

According to prominent scholars, the poem adapts Valéry's poetics from *Charmes* but develops its own mode of poetic incantation.[32] Ulrich Fülleborn calls this mode of incantation the "evocative" to characterize a fictional grammatical case that hovers "somewhere at the interstices between the vocative and nominative case" and calls forth the evoked object by way of poetic address, not unlike a magical spell.[33] Here, however, the evocation is immediately complicated by the fact that the addressee, the eponymous idol, is pulled back into sleep.

From the outset, then, the poem (which consists of a single stanza with nine tetrameters, divided into three sentences of unequal length) subverts the common understanding of sleep. This version of sleep presented here is shot through with synesthesia. "Idol" systematically takes stock of various descriptors of sense organs, including taste ("kosten," "reif," "Traubensaft"), touch ("zerdrücken"), smell ("süßgeworden"), sight ("Schaun"), and sound (the silence of the crypt). From the appositions of the opening line onward, these senses blend into each other, most strikingly in the agglomeration of contradicting nouns. The poem eventuates in a stark sound event, which is both doubled ("Gong! Gong!") and overdetermined. The gong—on which Rilke elaborated in another double poem—could be read as an onomatopoetic sound and as a German or a French word.[34] But even if the gong is parsed as a reference to a percussion instrument originating in the Far East, "Idol" encapsulates pure sound: the gong's metal discs produce hums that hover between music and auditive event. In fact, the gongs reverberate, producing vibrations that the poem seems to capture or even anticipate when it initially presents several *g-* and *go-*sounds which are followed by *n-*sounds and then again by *go-*sounds. Sleep in "Idol" features an explosion of sense perceptions, but they remain strikingly overdetermined.

The very appearance of the gong in "Idol" is overdetermined, as this instrument has a special place in the history of the sleep sciences that chapters 1 and 4 touch on, namely, that since the nineteenth century, gongs and gong-like instruments had been used to determine the so-called threshold of awakening (*Weckschwelle*). The researcher gradually produced louder and louder sounds until the drumbeat was noisy enough to awaken the sleeping test subject. Rilke likely knew about this research through the works of the philosopher and experimental psychologist Gustav Fechner (1801–87), whose work was popular in the poet's social circles.[35] Fechner studied the interdependence of mind and body and investigated the relationship between quantifiable external sensations and subjective experience. For instance, he postulated that external sensations (such as the brightness of a light bulb) would turn from unconscious to conscious perceptions if they surpassed a quantifiable threshold of intensity. In *Elemente der Psychophysik* (1860), Fechner explicitly extends this approach to the study of sleep, referencing the nascent dissertation research by his student Ernst Kohlschütter.[36] This work made a seminal contribution to the scientific study of sleep, in asking how loud the sound of a "Schallpendel" (sound pendulum, a gong-like instrument) had to become to wake up a sleeping person.[37] Kohlschütter's experiments revealed that this threshold changes during a given night, according to what sleep phase—although this terminology did not exist—the subject was in and showed that the deeper the sleep, the louder the sound needs to be. Until the sleeper awakens, however, the sounds make noise but are not heard. As Rilke puts it, "Sound, no longer measurable/with the sense of hearing."[38] The poem confronts the reader with the thresholds of perception.

The second line in "Idol" renders this apparent in showcasing a distinctly intensified use of punctuation. It brings into play a host of punctuation marks whose notation is visible but not necessarily audible, such as the hyphen that binds together the composite "Schlaf-Lied" ("lullaby"), the comma that adds a caesura between the first and the second half of the sentence, the dash prolonging the caesura, and the two exclamation marks which follow the evocation of the gong. This emphasis points to a simultaneous marking and unmarking of distinctions—the poem posits and then denies the existence of a difference between lullabies and gongs, sounds and noise, signs and signification, foreground and background. In doing so, Rilke refers to but turns inside out the genre of the lullaby, which is driven by regular and predictable sound structures and a stable addressee who might or might not doze off during the poem.

A structural feature of "Idol" is that it dramatizes such a transformation of the redrawing of distinctions over and over. The gendering of the deity of cat sleep provides the most striking example: at first, the poem does not specify whether the god is male or female and explicitly presents both options to the reader. In a second step, it turns the deity into a fully androgynous god.[39] Here and elsewhere, a strong connection between sleep and an undoing of gender is implied. As we have seen, this idea appears in texts by Hegel, Proust, and Virginia Woolf, whose novel *Orlando: A Biography* (1928) situates the transformations of the protagonist's gender in sleep states. Like Woolf, Rilke associates sleep with a state of potentiality. Rilke's poems hold on to this potentiality as long as possible, as expressed in the line "let me be undetermined" ("laissez-moi diffus") in the poem "Le dormeur" (*KA Supp.*, 176). The poem "Idol," however, finally replaces the neutral "deity" of cat sleep with the masculine "god" ("diesen verlisteten Gott"). It seems that, in German, the god must be male when sleep has not yet taken over. Still, it is not clear whether we should parse the neologism "verlistet" as meaning "cunning," "outsmarted," or "according to the listed rules of grammar," three diverging options that result in a blurring of boundaries even during sleep's onset.

Rilke's poem "Idol" attributes a unique agency to sleep in its last sentence that pinpoints a principle of causation governed by contradistinction: the same event that evokes "the other gods" hands the deity of cat sleep over to "its inward falling power." Here, sleep appears as an inherent force that brings about an implosion, an implosion that literally affects the architectural metaphors of the vault evoked in both "Idol" and its "Divinité du sommeil des chats." If one reads this implosion as a collapse onto itself, then it reveals a peculiar meaning of the relinquishing ("entlassen") that can be seen as characterizing both the crashing down of an architectural structure and the act of going to sleep. The dissolution of agency brings forth an instance of lightness, an alleviation that frees itself from a weight.

Therefore, when "Idol" insists on sleep as an overlooked realm of intense sensual activity, when it hints at religious imagery, when it erases firm boundaries between the inside and outside of slumber, when it dramatizes gender transformations, and when it suggests that sleep amounts to an overpowering of the agency of the subject, making it implode like an overburdened vault, it inextricably ties our understanding of sleep to movements and distinctions of language.

Bending Grammar

It is not surprising, then, that sleep states are depicted several times in Rilke's *Sonette an Orpheus* (written in 1922), poems that are—if we follow Christoph König—imbued with Valéry's French throughout.[40] But even on more conventional readings, these poems continue the "orphic explanation of the Earth," as the symbolist Stéphane Mallarmé, an important mentor of Valéry, has called the exegesis of the world by means of poetic language.[41] Rilke situates himself vis-à-vis this French tradition that is highly conscious of linguistic constructions but simultaneously pushes the symbolist strategies of writing to their very edge, as the sleep scenes highlight.[42] The most significant evocation of sleep in the *Sonette* occurs right at the outset, in the second poem, which, together with the first poem, constitutes what has been called the double frame of the collection. What kind of sleep does this poem depict, and how does it do it? Let's read the poem.

> Und fast ein Mädchen wars und ging hervor
> aus diesem einigen Glück von Sang und Leier
> und glänzte klar durch ihre Frühlingsschleier
> und machte sich ein Bett in meinem Ohr.
>
> Und schlief in mir. Und alles war ihr Schlaf.
> Die Bäume, die ich je bewundert, diese

fühlbare Ferne, die gefühlte Wiese
und jedes Staunen, das mich selbst betraf.

Sie schlief die Welt. Singender Gott, wie hast
du sie vollendet, daß sie nicht begehrte,
erst wach zu sein? Sieh, sie erstand und schlief.

Wo ist ihr Tod? O, wirst du dies Motiv
erfinden noch, eh sich dein Lied verzehrte?—
Wo sinkt sie hin aus mir? . . . Ein Mädchen fast . . . (KA, 2:245)

(And almost a girl it was and came forth
from this glad unity of song and lyre
and shone brightly through her springtime veils
and made herself a bed within my ear.

And slept in me. And all things were her sleep.
The trees I forever marvel at, these
palpable distances, the deep-felt meadows,
and an entire life's astonishment.

She slept the world. Singing god, how did you
so perfect her that she never once
had need to be awake? Look, she arose and slept.

Where is her death? Ah, will you introduce
that theme before your song expires?—
I can feel her drifting off . . . to where? . . . A girl almost . . . [Sonnets to
   Orpheus, 9])

Due to the difficulty of the sonnet, it seems helpful to begin with a paraphrase. The first stanza has a maiden figure emerge from orphic music and embed herself in the ear of the speaker, as if she were an earworm, a catchy tune. (This idea links in with the first poem of the *Sonnets*, where orphic song creates "temples in the ear" for beasts.) The second stanza dwells on the observation that the maiden figure slept in the speaker, which means that she accompanied and coexperienced the speaker's impressions, feelings, and actions. The third stanza asks what kind of existence can consist only in sleep. In the fourth stanza, the speaker asks Orpheus when (if at all) this sleep will turn into death, but instead of answering this question, the finale of the poem stages the intermittent vanishing of the maiden figure from the cycle, before she is remembered toward the end of the first part (in sonnet I.25) and returns and dances in the second part of the collection (in sonnets II.18 and II.28).[43]

Scholars have long noted the prominence of sleep in the poem.[44] Hermeneutic accounts interpret the poem's presentation of sleep as a general alternative to an instrumentalizing worldview, championing passivity.[45] More recent scholarship, however, has pointed to the idiosyncratic transitive use of the verb "to sleep" in third stanza: "She slept the world" ("Sie schlief die Welt"). The phrase is puzzling. German does not allow one to sleep *something*; at best, German and English allow such phrases such as "to sleep a long sleep."[46] One of Rilke's cherished authors, François-René de Chateaubriand (1768-1848), uses the French intransitive verb "dormir" in a similar way: "I've slept life [*j'ai dormi la vie*] in the bosom of my mother."[47] In both Rilke and Chateaubriand, instances of sleep reshuffle the valency of verbal constructions, resulting not only in the bending of grammatical rules, but also in a foreground of the "active nature of this sleeping."[48]

Indeed, the third stanza of the poem features two processes with different actors coalescing in sleep: the singing god is creating a girl who enters the ear to sleep there. In this context, the imperative "look" takes on a deictic function and emphasizes the connection between entering the ear and sleeping there while also stressing that the conjunction "then" is not used in a consecutive sense but as "and." The speaker stresses that the girl "arose and slept" simultaneously. This may sound puzzling, but it is an idea that often recurs in Rilke, for example, in the lines "Since the marvelous days of creation/the God has been sleeping: we are his sleep,/accepted, dully endured by him/under stars which he transcended" in the poem "[Seit den wunderbaren Schöpfungstagen]" (*KA*, 2:93).[49] The almost girl exemplifies autonomous creation; in putting herself to sleep in the ear, her sleep turns into the poem. One could thus conclude that Rilke—in a very different framework and with different consequences—arrives at a finding that parallels the key discovery of the contemporary sciences: that sleep was not, as had previously been suggested, an absence or a stand-in for death.

Because Rilke's sonnet I.2 serves as a point of access for the maiden figure, it does not treat sleep as death, despite the prominence of the ancient idea of sleep as a sibling of death. The finale of the poem says as much, as the shift from the third to the fourth stanza is accompanied by a change from the preterit to the present tense and from an account of sleep to a thematization of the act of speaking. Indeed, the poem omits the motif of death in an overly explicit manner. Even if the *Sonette an Orpheus* were conceived as a "tomb for Wera Ouckama Knoop" (*KA*, 2:237), Rilke suppresses the temptation to conceal death in aesthetically pleasing images, as Gotthold Ephraim Lessing famously refers to the practices of portraying death as sleep and of describing sleep as death.[50] Instead, sleep in Rilke's sonnet calls up figures of withdrawal: "I can feel her drifting off . . ."[51] It remains unsaid whereto the girl drifts off; the "song" slows down when the *o*-assonances associated with death (*Tod*) come into play; the dash and the ellipses interrupt the poem, which retreats to the beginning, continuing sleep, as it inverts the figure of the almost girl—"A girl almost"—and restarts the poem anew with intense repetitions of "and": "And almost a girl it was." If death marks an artificial arrest of the ever-changing play of forms in the *Sonette an Orpheus*, sleep is a state without such a moment of arrest, amounting instead to "an immersion in constant cyclical changes."[52] The difference between beginning and end in sonnet I.2 is replaced with a loop: the girl appears as a figure who over and over emerges and sleeps, sleeps and emerges anew. In other words, in Rilke's writings, sleep does not simply appear as a motif, theme, or poetic figure. His texts also associate sleep with a specific textual order generated by somnific states.

Sleep without Sleepers

In other poems, too, Rilke tests out to what extent he can override conventional notions of sleep. In sonnet II.XIV, for example, he not only associates plants and sleep but also seeks to use this association to pry open the "interpreted world" ("gedeutete[] Welt"; see *KA*, 2:201). With a riff on the German verb "bedeuten" ("to assign meaning"), one could call this recourse to sleep "entdeuten" ("to unravel meaning"):

Siehe die Blumen, diese dem Irdischen treuen,
denen wir Schicksal vom Rande des Schicksals leihn, -
aber wer weiß es! Wenn sie ihr Welken bereuen,
ist es an uns, ihre Reue zu sein.

Alles will schweben. Da gehen wir umher wie Beschwerer,
legen auf alles uns selbst, vom Gewichte entzückt;
o was sind wir den Dingen für zehrende Lehrer,
weil ihnen ewige Kindheit glückt.

Nähme sie einer ins innige Schlafen und schliefe
tief mit den Dingen -: o wie käme er leicht,
anders zum anderen Tag, aus der gemeinsamen Tiefe.

Oder er bliebe vielleicht; und sie blühten und priesen
ihn, den Bekehrten, der nun den Ihrigen gleicht,
allen den stillen Geschwistern im Winde der Wiesen. (*KA*, 2:264)

(Look at the flowers, keeping good faith with the world,
to whom we at destiny's margins presume to lend destiny.
Who can be sure they do not regret how they fade?—
for to be their regret is perhaps our own duty.

Things that are pining to float we burden with ballast,
adding ourselves to their load and exulting in weight:
to the things of our world. O we are envious tutors
for they happily dwell in a childhood that lasts.

Imagine one who brought things into the innermost heart
of his sleep: from the depth he had shared in the night
would he not differently wake to a different day?

But if he stayed, as he might, flowers would blossom and praise
him, the converted, now become one of their kind,
silent as one of their siblings blown by the meadow wind. [*Sonnets to Orpheus with Letters to a Young Poet*, 95, trans. corr.])

The scholarly consensus holds that this ornate poem advocates for resistance against anthropomorphic interpretations of nature. For a nuanced understanding of this resistance in the context of sleep, however, we must examine the performative reversal at the core of the poem more closely than previous scholarship. In the first stanza, the lyrical subjects ("we") attribute human destiny to flowers; in the fourth stanza, the poem, in turn, attributes the destiny of flowers to the lyrical subjects and thus inverts subject-object relations. This hypothetical becoming thing-like is of a piece with an alleviation and letting go of gravitas: the poem rhymes authoritative interpretation in the form of tutors ("Lehrer") with ballast and complainers ("Beschwerer").[53] On a formal and thematic level, sleep is then important to the poem because it marks its central turning point: the right kind of sleep seems able to turn heavy-handed exegesis of existence into an alleged lightness of being. Consequently, the "determinate indeterminacy" of the sonnet allows us to read the pronominal structures in the third stanza in various ways.[54] Does the poem encourage the first-person plural speaker to take childhood into the "innermost heart/of his sleep" ("innige Schlafen und schliefe")? Does it propose that "we" take the "things" into the "innige Schlafen"? What is "innige[s] Schlafen," anyway, and does it imply a successful transformation of the "he" imagined in the poem?[55] There can be no definite answer to these questions, because the poem evokes them to dramatize a deanchoring of sense and to eschew definite interpretations. The poem says as much: "Everything is pining to float" ("Alles will schweben"). In the same way in which determinate meanings dissolve and fade away when one drifts off, the onset of sleep clouds the referential clarity of the poem. The cloud is Rilke's metaphor. He uses it in another poem to replace the notion that we "fall asleep"—an idea which Rilke explicitly rejects in his novel—with a different image, the image of sleep as a hovering state: "But from the sleeping one [*dem Schlafenden*]/like from a cloud standing still/rains an abundance of heaviness" (*KA*, 2:383).[56] The floating sleep state, then, means not only taking the world and its meanings lightly but also becoming light oneself.

There are, however, still boundaries to the erasure of distinction. The French prose poem *Cimetière,* for example, unfolds as a series of open questions that say as much: "How can you not be *our* flowers? Does the rose use all its petals to fly away from us? Does it want to be only a rose, nothing but rose? No one's sleep under so many eyelids? [*Sommeil de personne sous tant de paupières?*]" (*KA Supp.*, 290).[57] These lines testify to an overarching programmatic attempt to step away from encasing the world in a web of anthropocentric ideas. Is there a way that the roses could not be ours, not be seen from a human perspective? The last question establishes a parallel between anthropomorphism and the problem of sleep: "No one's sleep under so many eyelids?" The question suggests the sleep of the roses can perhaps not be captured in anthropocentric terms at all. Do roses sleep, and are they the agents of their sleep? Period scientists certainly took such questions very seriously, building on scholarship about "plant sleep" (Carl Linnaeus) that reached back well into the eighteenth century.[58] As early as the 1720s, naturalists realized that the flower *Mimosa pudica* folds up its leaves when night comes but opens them again in the morning. Intrigued, Jean-Jacques d'Ortous de Mairan (1678-1771) put the flower to a test and observed that it continues to display these "rhythmic folding and unfolding leaf movements for several days in complete darkness," laying the foundations for the development of a field known today as the study of circadian rhythms.[59] For more than 250 years, researchers puzzled over the question of what elicited these regular opening and closing rhythms that always seemed to last about a day. Was it light, temperature, moisture, gravity, genetics, another external factor such as electricity, or a combination of them? Were these rhythms related to other physiological factors with their own rhythms? Or could one regard them somehow as an expression of the "personality" of the *Mimosa pudica*, which is named for its perceived sensitivity and bashfulness (its leaves close and sag when they are being touched)? At the time when Rilke was writing, scientists did not have good answers to these questions. As the leading contemporary scholar of plant sleep, Rose Stoppel (1874–1970)—whose work was so brilliant that it eventually garnered her the first female professorship in botany in Germany—remarks in the conclusion of a handbook entry, "As we have seen, our knowledge of circadian phenomena in plants is still very incomplete. We can only make guesses about their causes at the moment. . . . Indeed, we have presently not advanced much beyond what Zinn understood in the year 1759."[60] While Rilke's "sommeil de personne" literally means the "sleep of nobody," it's possible Rilke had "sleep of a nonperson," that is, a *Mimosa pudica* or a rose, in mind.

From this perspective, "sommeil de personne" radicalizes the earlier attempt to withdraw human characteristics in sleep and thereby dissolve gender in "Idol." and brings to the fore the question of whether there can be sleep without a sleeper. Rilke addresses this question in one of his most famous poems, which he selected as his epitaph in his will. Situated at the crossroads of languages (the poem's first word could be either German or French),[61] Rilke's short poem (*KA*, 2:394) revisits the paradox of the "sommeil de personne."

> Rose, oh reiner Widerspruch, Lust,
> Niemandes Schlaf zu sein unter soviel
> Lidern.
>
> (Rose, oh pure contradiction, pleasure
> of being Nobody's sleep under so many
> eyelids.[62])

Rilke explicitly highlighted the phrase "Niemandes Schlaf" by capitalizing the initial letter in the manuscript, which he otherwise does not do after a line break.[63] Sleep sits at the center of this hermetic poem, which condenses many of Rilke's key concerns but thwarts any definite readings.[64] The poem consists of three lines without a finite verb. It orbits around an artfully incomplete syntax made up of nouns and appositions, making it impossible to know how to weigh the words. Scholars have thus often attempted to approach the poem in terms of its generic form: as a puzzle, as an epitaph, as an intermedial emblem that can only be understood in concert with the gravestone that also bears a crest and Rilke's name, and as a haiku after the French symbolist tradition.[65] Due to the context and the roses as closed eyelids, it seems obvious that "Niemandes Schlaf" must be parsed as a metaphor for death, but the poem complicates such an interpretation in making manifold competing readings possible. For instance, if the rose as a nonperson is sleeping and experiencing this sleep as pleasure, it suggests a state of the in-between, a sort of sleep that does not correspond well to anthropomorphic ideas and therefore stands at the threshold of human consciousness. If sleep already presents an elusive state, the impenetrability of the poem magnifies it, as the depicted sleep is nobody's, the sleep of a nonconscious entity.

We may conclude that Rilke's thinking is in line with that the sleep sciences of his time, especially with respect to ideas regarding wake-sleep thresholds, the active nature of sleep, and plant sleep. In attending more closely to his encounter with Valéry and to the formal and linguistic strategies of his poems, however, we have seen that very few of the sleep states Rilke's poetry discusses can be mapped directly onto our everyday understanding of these states. In his lyrical texts, for example, sleep appears much less deathlike than death appears sleeplike, creating an elusive and ambiguous state of the in-between and raising hermeneutic questions as to how knowledge about sleep and its sleepers is possible.

Conclusion

This study has brought together three ways of thinking about sleep: a scientific way, a pharmaceutical way, and a literary way. Rather than being mutually exclusive, literary and scientific ways of knowledge are closely entwined: wrestling with the question of how to represent an elusive phenomenon such as sleep, the protagonists of this book—scientists, physicians, employees of the pharmaceutical industry, and literary writers—not only drew on sleep experiments conducted in different fields but also established their own mode of reasoning in permanent integration of and differentiation from these experiments. Each chapter of *Sleep Works* documents, unpacks, and refines the link between aesthetic and scientific modes of representing sleep from a different perspective. Literary and scientific writings on sleep draw on each other more often than one might have expected.

What emerges is a comprehensive account of how sleep can be understood. In other words, *Sleep Works* demonstrates how sleep is simultaneously coproduced by several interlocking representational systems (texts, images, films, sound-producing media apparatuses, the semiotic "différance" of languages), epistemic modes of inquiry (experiments, psychonautical self-experiments, insomnia, medical case studies), body politics (the shaping of biorhythms through urban modernity, medical and pharmaceutical authorities, advertisements), technologies of the self (drug regimes, sleep hygiene, home remedies) and the devices spearheaded in literary writing (interior monologue, automatic writing).[1] All these aspects contribute—according to their own inner logic—to constructing sleep as a scientific, aesthetic, philosophical, and political object, an object with a trove of concomitant implications for understanding what it means to be a self.

This analysis of the cultural production of sleep is rooted in the history of science: at the core of *Sleep Works* sits a thoroughgoing exploration of the

Conclusion

scientific, medical, and pharmaceutical history of sleep around 1900. I show how a sleep science that distinguished sleep from related states such as fatigue, hypnosis, coma, narcosis, and dreams emerged from a heterogenous group of disciplines in the early twentieth century. Instead of focusing on "dream work," as psychoanalysis did in the wake of Freud, the sleep scientists focused on what could be called "sleep work." They challenged the conception that sleep was essentially a passive state—an inert backdrop for restoration and dreaming—and furnished it with its own vital power and agency, one that called into question whether the subject was sleeping or being slept. The discursive independence from dreams and the autonomy that sleep gained as a result is most obvious in the contemporaneous sleep business of the pharmaceutical industry—one manufacturer of soporifics literally received the moniker "slumber factory with a stock market listing" ("Schlummerfabrik auf Aktien").[2] The highly lucrative sleep industry successfully positioned sleep-inducing drugs as desirable solutions to the pressures of and anxieties provoked by urban modernity, which symptomatically coalesced in a proliferation of insomnia and threats to the agency of stressed-out and overworked modern subjects. By way of a seamless collaboration of pharmaceutical research, business strategy, and marketing, the pharmaceutical industry forged a narrative that presented soporifics as an easy way to fight insomnia and restore both labor power and full subjecthood. *Sleep Works* traces this development via the interdiscursive career of Veronal, arguably the most famous sleeping pill of the early twentieth century, from hygienic and medical writings into the laboratories of the pharmaceutical industry and from there in the broader public discourse and into literature.

The book then turns to literary "sleep works," offering fresh perspectives on some of the most canonical modernist writers and their strategies for writing sleep. The author and physician Arthur Schnitzler intervened in the public health debates about the soporific Veronal with his novella *Fräulein Else* (1924). Simultaneously, he tested out how to represent Veronal sleep and other somnolent states with the interior monologue. Marcel Proust's literary sleep experiments, too, were aided and abated both by his knowledge of sleep science and by his self-experiments with sleep-inducing drugs. Like his pharmaceutical regime, the experimental setup of the *Recherche* generates ever-new sensations by reiterating familiar situations and introducing variety, which results in the discovery of new facets of what used to be a familiar experience. If Proust employs scenes of awaking to think through how a subject is constituted, the poetry of Rainer Maria Rilke poses the question of whether there can be sleep without a sleeper. He arrives—like Hegel, Proust, and Virginia Woolf—at the conclusion that sleep makes and unmakes personhood but that one's soul endures during sleep. Franz Kafka, for one, conceived his important works in nighttime writing sessions like Proust, but—unlike the great French writer—categorically refused to regulate his insomnia with soporifics. Kafka's texts thus brim with depictions of restless slumbering, dozing, reveries, twilight states and situations in which characters are half awake, falling asleep, and waking up, while basic narrative structures are undone: coherent temporality dissolves, the point of view goes blind, and a split severs the enunciation of the subject from the subject of enunciation.

These and other modernist writers (discussed in passing throughout the book) question the modern norms of sleep as well as the familiar equation of sleep and death. According to classic scholarly accounts, sleep and death used to be regarded as part of "a series of discrete states on the same spectrum which potentially seem to merge into each other: drunkenness, sleep, unconsciousness, asphyxia, and actual death."[3] *Sleep Works* explores in detail how scientists and writers reconceptualized this notion between 1899 and 1929 when they started describing sleep as an activity rather than as a passive state. As a result, sleep appeared no longer as a homogenous element in a "vertical" series of states characterized by diminished consciousness, making it possible to scrutinize the heterogeneity of sleep's "horizontal" multiplicity in much greater detail. States which were phenomenologically known but notoriously difficult to investigate with scientific experimental methods, such as twilight states, being half conscious, slumbering, hypnagogic states, and insomnia, now started to promise inroads into the elusive nature of sleep as well as into well-known dream hermeneutics. We have seen how much literary writing has to offer for such an approach and how closely it is tied to being alert to the texts' fictionality.

Nevertheless, *Sleep Works* also reveals areas in which the close connection between images of sleep and death persisted: in the discourse of the early twentieth century, sleep induced by soporifics still betrayed a metaphorical (and sometimes literal) proximity to death. Proust, for instance, experimented with the amount of Veronal he could ingest before being unable to regain consciousness; his Bergotte, as well as Schnitzler's Else, Svevo's Guido, and many other figures, pass this threshold when they overdose on Veronal or another drug (such as chloralhydrate in the case of Wharton's

The House of Mirth). It therefore seems that in the early twentieth century, sleep on soporifics was still generally regarded as "deathlike sleep," as Hugo von Hofmannsthal (1874-1929) puts it when, in one of his plays, a physician offers advice on the administration of sleep-inducing drugs.[4] For some writers, this raised the philosophical question as to what extent the sleeping self remains itself. Proust, for example, worked through this issue in ways recalling the thought of Hegel, Schopenhauer, and Bergson but used his writing to offer a far more nuanced literary account of how awakening reconstitutes subjecthood.

Against this backdrop, we may lastly ask whether the changed relationship between sleep and death affected not only the understanding of sleep but also the metaphorology of death. Even though the corpus I explore in *Sleep Works* does, of course, not offer a conclusive answer to this question (which pertains more to the history of death than the history of sleep), some texts suggest that from the early twentieth century onward, death, too, could no longer always figure as sleep in a straightforward sense.[5] Thomas Mann's *Der Zauberberg*, for example, insinuates that this notion no longer has credibility and has become merely a rhetorical means of consolidation, a euphemism:

> Hans Castorp made a personal inspection of the deceased. . . . The eyes were closed unnaturally tight—pressed closed, Hans Castorp could not help thinking, not just closed. They called that the last token of love, although it was done more for the sake of the survivors than of the dead man. And it had to be done very soon, because once too much myosin had formed in the muscles, it was no longer possible, and then he would lie there staring—and that was the end of the sedate notion of "slumber."
>
> A skilled expert at all this, in his element in more than one sense, Hans Castorp stood piously beside the bed. "He looks as if he's sleeping," he said to be kind, although the considerable differences were obvious.[6]

In a nutshell, this passage provides an allegory for a historical moment in which sleep and death are no longer being represented together, a development that inadvertently testifies to new understandings of sleep. And in pointing to the agency of myosin, Castorp also suggests that literary and scientific discourses often coconstitute their subjects, as *Sleep Works* demonstrates over and over for sleep.

Notes

Introduction: At the Borders of Consciousness

1. Epicurus, "Letter to Menacceus," 29.
2. For a summary of the long-standing debates on representation, see Rheinberger, "Representation in Scientific Practice."
3. In other words, thinking about sleep requires engaging with a body of knowledge that "weder in den Wissenschaften und Disziplinen aufgehoben ist noch bloß lebensweltlichen Charakter besitzt, das vielleicht vorbegrifflich, aber nicht vordiskursiv ist, das verstreut und zusammenhängend zugleich erscheint. Dieses Wissen ist weder Wissenschaft noch Erkenntnis; es verlangt vielmehr eine Suche nach operativen Faktoren und Themen, die auf verschiedenen Territorien wiederkehren, jeweils eine konstitutive Position darin besetzen und doch keine Synthese und keine Einheit des Gegenstandes unterstellen" (Vogl, "Für eine Poetologie des Wissens," 118).
4. The felicitous phrase "cultural turn" refers to the reorientation in literary studies inspired by various once-new approaches to the study of culture (e.g., anthropology, gender studies, and indeed cultural studies). For a full account of the term, see Bachmann-Medick, *Cultural Turns*. Bachmann-Medick does not, however, address sleep.
5. Mauss, "Techniques of the Body," 467-68. "La notion que le coucher est quelque chose de naturel est complètement inexacte. . . . Voilà une grande quantité de pratiques qui sont à la fois des techniques du corps et qui sont profondes en retentissements et effets biologiques. Tout ceci peut et doit être observé sur le terrain, des centaines de ces choses sont encore à connaître" ("Techniques du corps," 285).
6. On the ethnography of sleep, see Wolf-Meyer, *The Slumbering Masses*, "What's So Natural about Sleep?," "Natural Hegemonies," "Where Have All Our Naps Gone?," and "Biomedicine." Other important contributions are Williams, *Sleep and Society*, Steger, *Inemuri*, and Reiss, *Wild Nights*. On the historiography

of sleep, see Ekirch, *At Day's Close*, Handley, *Sleep in Early Modern England*, Kroker, *The Sleep of Others*, Kinzler, *Das Joch des Schlafs*, Ahlheim, *Kontrollgewinn—Kontrollverlus*, Ahlheim, *Der Traum vom Schlaf im 20. Jahrhundert*, and Garnier, *L'oubli des peines*. On the philosophy of sleep, see Schwenger, *At the Borders of Sleep*, vii–xi, Seitter, *Geschichte der Nacht*, 163, Nancy, *The Fall of Sleep*, de Warren, "The Inner Night," Penzin, *Rex Exsomnis*, Wortham, *The Poetics of Sleep*, and Fuller, *How to Sleep*. Exceptions to the tendency of literary scholarship to approach sleep almost exclusively in terms of dreams are Kocziszky, *Der Schlaf in Kunst und Literatur*, Greaney, *Sleep and the Novel*, Montiglio, *The Spell of Hypnos*, Cohn, *Still Life*, Wallace, *Scanning the Hypnoglyph*, Uhlig, *Traum und Poiesis*, Scrivner, *Becoming Insomniac*, Schwenger, *At the Borders of Sleep*, Scrivner, "That Sweet Secession," Dufoe, "Bram Stoker's Sleep Work," Paulin and Pfotenhauer, "Einleitung," Schwenger, "Writing Hypnagogia," Pfotenhauer and Schneider, *Nicht völlig Wachen und nicht ganz ein Traum*, Pergnier, *Le sommeil et les signes*, Déchanet-Platz, *L'écrivain*, Wöhrle, *Hypnos*, Mavromatis, *Hypnagogia*, Duttlinger, "Schlaflosigkeit," Pusse, "'Unter schläfernden Lidern,'" Parris, *Vital Strife*, Parris, "Seizures of Sleep in Early Modern Literature," Parris, "'The Body Is with the King,'" Schmidt-Hannisa, "Halbschlafbilder," and Schmidt-Hannisa, "Das eiserne Szepter des Schlafes."

7. "la partie non-rêve du Sommeil" (*Cahiers*, 2:32). In another passage of the *Cahiers*, Valéry is even more explicit: "Ceux qui spéculent du rêve oublient de régler d'abord l'affaire du sommeil" (2:189).

8. A selection of instructive studies on dreams includes Krovoza and Walde, *Traum und Schlaf*, Peter-André Alt, *Der Schlaf der Vernunft*, Dieterle and Engel, *Historizing the Dream*, Neumann, "Träume als Abfederungsritual der Kultur," Blanchot, "Dreaming, Writing," Beradt, *Third Reich of Dreams*, and Chan, *Edge of Knowing*.

9. Maury, *Le sommeil et les rêves*. Here I concur with Freud researchers: "Die *Traumdeutung* knüpft direkt an die Traumforschung des 19. Jahrhunderts an, die in der Regel auch den Schlaf als physiologisches Problem mitbehandelt und daher ebenfalls meist im Titel führt" (Mayer, *Freud zur Einführung*, 49).

10. "Vom tiefsten, traumlosen Schlafe können wir directe nichts aussagen, weil eben durch den Zustand völliger Bewusstlosigkeit jede Beobachtung und Erfahrung ausgeschlossen ist" (Breuer and Freud, *Studien über Hysterie*, 168). Breuer is the author of this statement, even though Freud most likely approved it. It is also included in Freud, *Nachtragsband*, 251.

11. Fuller, *How to Sleep*, 32.

12. The distinction between sleep and dream is replicated in the metaphorical realm, where it is even more stark: in everyday language, a dreamer is characterized as insufficiently connected to reality and as falling behind in performative activity. Sleepers, by contrast, are thematized in vocabulary drawn from intelligence agencies as latent figures that may be suddenly activated to carry out pernicious actions.

13. See Derrida, *L'écriture et la différence*. Of course, Derrida does not talk about dreams and sleep.

14. Wittgenstein, *Philosophical Investigations*, 222.

15. "By the same token, sleep and other states of suspended consciousness also offer the most natural boundaries for autonomous monologues. Several texts do in fact begin as their speakers awaken, or close as they drift off into sleep" (Cohn, *Transparent Minds*, 241). More recently, Cohn indirectly gives more nuance to her earlier position in discussing the complex narratological strategies that come with the depiction of sleep states ("'I Doze and Wake,'" 96-108). Current scholarship in English studies, however, sidesteps the problem when it demonstrates that in the Victorian Bildungsroman, moments of reverie, trance, and dreams lead to incursions of lyricism that halt narrative progression. See Cohn, *Still Life*.

16. See Serres, *The Parasite*.

17. Such leaks could be the background noise that overlays the coffeehouse conversation, the unstable internet connection that attributes frazzled statements to frozen faces, wiretapping by agencies, or slow wittedness.

18. See Parris, *Vital Strife*.

19. For scholarship in this area, see note 6.

20. Relevant figures include, among others, Franz Mesmer, Heinrich von Kleist, G. W. F. Hegel, Honoré de Balzac, and Vincenzo Bellini. Many scholarly works have explored instances of somnambulism around 1800, but there is still space for a synthetic study that integrates the various strands, especially from a broad comparative perspective. For individual studies, see, for example, James, *Dream, Creativity, and Madness*, 13-66, Wortham, *The Poetics of Sleep*, 31-38, Schmidt-Hannisa, "Das eiserne Szepter des Schlafes," Barkhoff, *Magnetische Fiktionen*, 239-68, Uhlig, *Traum und Poiesis*, 129-61, Osten, "Über Wachen und Schlafen," and Osten, *Das Tor zur Seele*.

21. Scholars who have investigated the impact of modernization on sleep include, among others, Ahlheim, *Der Traum vom Schlaf im 20. Jahrhundert*, Ekirch, "Modernization of Western Sleep," Scrivner, *Becoming Insomniac*, and Kroker, *The Sleep of Others*.

22. The claim that sleep patterns in early modern Europe were bi- and polyphasic associated with Ekirch's research remains controversial, but it finds significant support in today's sleep science: "Biphasic sleep (sleeping during two periods interrupted by wake) or polyphasic sleep (multiple sleep/wake episodes) is the normal situation for most animals, and may have been for humans before the Industrial Revolution. Although there is no universal agreement, the original concept that the natural state of human sleep is polyphasic was partly developed based upon human historical research, and therefore provides a good example of how historical studies can inform contemporary science" (Foster, "Sleep, Circadian Rhythms and Health," 13). For arguments about preindustrial sleep (that push

against the idea of a "natural" state of sleep free from social moldings of rhythms), see Ekirch, *At Day's Close*, and Handley, *Sleep in Early Modern England*.

23. See Ekirch, *At Day's Close*. For a nuanced account of early modern sleep, see also Handley, *Sleep in Early Modern England*.

24. On these developments, and artificial illumination in particular, see Ludtke, "Sleep, Disruption and the 'Nightmare of Total Illumination,'" Leahy, *Literary Illumination*, Otter, *The Victorian Eye*, Sharpe, *New York Nocturne*, and Schivelbusch, *Lichtblicke*.

25. On the creation of social sleep rhythms, see Crary, 24/7, 8-18, and Wolf-Meyer, "What's So Natural about Sleep?"

26. "Den gesunden Schlaf zur Sammlung, Erneuerung und Erfrischung der Lebenskraft reduziert es [das Kapital] auf so viel Stunden Erstarrung, als die Wiederbelebung eines absolut erschöpften Organismus unentbehrlich macht. Statt daß die normale Erhaltung der Arbeitskraft hier die Schranke des Arbeitstags, bestimmt umgekehrt die größte täglich mögliche Verausgabung der Arbeitskraft, wie krankhaft gewaltsam und peinlich auch immer, die Schranke für die Rastzeit des Arbeiters" (Marx and Engels, *Werke*, 23:280). The English translation in the body of the text is mine. To be sure, there was resistance to this new organization of time from the outset. For example, Jacques Rancière explores in *Proletarian Nights* how workers in the 1830s and 1840s diverted hours earmarked for sleep to educate themselves.

27. See Ekirch, "Modernization of Western Sleep," 159-81. For Ekirch, modes of production play only a limited role in comparison to social movements and, above all, technologies of illumination. Compelling arguments against techno-determinist arguments focused exclusively on technologies of illumination have also been presented by Ludtke, "Sleep, Disruption and the 'Nightmare of Total Illumination,'" 1-8.

28. See Crary, 24/7, 8-18.

29. See Shuttleworth and Foster, "Sleep and Stress."

30. See Scrivner, *Becoming Insomniac*. Because English draws a distinction between "sleeplessness" and "insomnia," it has been possible to track the rise of the medical term "insomnia": By "the 1890s, the term was far more common in medical titles than 'sleeplessness' and 'wakefulness' combined" (Kroker, *The Sleep of Others*, 78).

31. Marcel Mauss's comments deserve particular attention in this respect. For similar remarks about the cultural construction of sleep, see, for instance, Schenk, *Versuch einer psychologischen Theorie des Schlafes*: "Der Ablauf der Wach-Schlaf-periodizität . . . ist bestimmt durch die Struktur kultureller Gemeinschaft" (98).

32. Named for the American engineer Frederick W. Taylor, Taylorism is a self-description of modernity with origins in a factory management system introduced

toward the end of the nineteenth century. In Taylorism, production processes are analytically broken down into their smallest parts. The goal is to make these parts mechanically repeatable (imagine an assembly belt) and thus more efficient. On these developments in general, see Rabinbach, *The Human Motor*. For a more detailed account of the "epistemic thing," see Rheinberger, *Toward a History of Epistemic Things*.

33. On the invention of the EEG and its impact on sleep research, see Borck, *Brainwaves*, Kroker, *The Sleep of Others*, 255-324, and Ahlheim, *Der Traum vom Schlaf im 20. Jahrhundert*, 209-26.

34. See Kroker, *The Sleep of Others*, 256.

35. For studies of non-Western sleep, see, for example, Ma, *At the Edges of Sleep*, Steger and Brunt, *Night-Time and Sleep*, Dibie, *Ethnologie de la chambre à coucher*, and Mauss, "Techniques of the Body," 467-68.

36. For a history of the understanding of modernism in the Anglophone world, see Latham and Rogers, *Modernism*, Brooker et al., *Oxford Handbook of Modernisms*, and Friedman, "Definitional Excursions." In recent Anglophone literary criticism, "modernism" has assumed a broader meaning than in German and French scholarship. Modernism in anglophone writing now extends beyond the period between circa 1890 and 1945, it encompasses writers from regions beyond North America and certain parts of Europe; it also covers more than so-called high culture. For an introduction to new modernist studies, see Mao, *The New Modernist Studies*, and Mao and Walkowitz, "The New Modernist Studies." In referring to Proust, Kafka, Schnitzler, and Rilke as modernists, I am not challenging this more expansive definition of modernism.

37. Various handbooks and companions provide an overview of the scholarly landscape; their number testifies to the fact that modernist studies is a heterogenous enterprise with many centers and peripheries. See, for example, Lewis, *Cambridge Introduction to Modernism*, Lewis, *Cambridge Companion to European Modernism*, Sherry, *Cambridge History of Modernism*, Rabaté, *Handbook of Modernism Studies*, Brooker et al., *Oxford Handbook of Modernisms*, and Wollaeger and Eatough, *Oxford Handbook of Global Modernisms*. My focus on Anglophone companions and handbooks owes to the fact that the term "modernism" is not as prominent in German and French scholarship, which tends to focus on more localized accounts of smaller movements (naturalism, symbolism, expressionism, etc.), even though the term "klassische Moderne" is sometimes used in scholarship in German.

38. Brooker et al., "Introduction," 4.

39. For exemplary discussions of the respective "modernism" of these four authors, see Compagnon, *Proust between Two Centuries*, Ryan, *Rilke, Modernism and Poetic Tradition*, Jürgensen, Lukas, and Scheffel, *Schnitzler-Handbuch*, esp. 291-346, and Engel, "Kafka und die moderne Welt."

40. For a more comprehensive portrait of the modernisms afforded by these very different cities, see, for instance, Harvey, *Paris*, Schorske, *Fin-de-Siècle Vienna*, and Spector, *Prague Territories*.

41. For more detailed and nuanced accounts, see Surprenant, "Freud and Psychoanalysis," Le Rider, "Tiefenpsychologie und Psychiatrie," Duttlinger, "Psychology and Psychoanalysis," and Fiedler, "Psychoanalyse." Note that these accounts typically play up the importance of psychoanalysis for these writers.

42. Lodge, *Consciousness and the Novel*, 57. Similar statements from important studies are easy to produce. Lodge himself refers to Erich Auerbach. To be sure, I am not claiming that there is no scholarship on these states; my point is that they have yet to be adequately thought through with regard to their formal ways of representation. This is especially apparent in studies that discuss such states, for example, Schwenger, *At the Borders of Sleep*, Wallace, *Scanning the Hypnoglyph*, and Greaney, *Sleep and the Novel*. In "Terribly Strange Beds," Greaney comes close to articulating a similar insight but does not follow up on it (see especially page 5).

43. Quoted in Lane, "Falling Asleep in the Wake," 163.

44. "Many of the formal innovations and psychological discoveries of Modernist literature—stream-of-consciousness narrative, interior monologue, the absent-minded trance of involuntary memory—can be read as dispatches from the hinterlands of sleep, the effusions of a hyperactive mind in a substantially deactivated body" (Greaney, "Terribly Strange Beds," 5). See also Niehaus, *"Ich, die Literatur, ich spreche . . . ,"* 138, 150. For additional striking examples, see Cohn, "'I Doze and Wake.'"

45. "Da der Schlaf einen kaum entwirrbaren Komplex somatischer und psychischer Erscheinungen darstellt, ist er der kausal-experimentellen Forschung äußerst schwer zugänglich" (Renner, *Schlafmittel-Therapie*, 2).

46. "[Die] experimentelle Physiologie, experimentelle Psychologie, die Entdeckung der hypnotischen Phänomene, die klinische Beobachtung von Schlafstörungen an Nervösen und Geisteskranken, alle diese Wissenschaftszweige müssen zusammengefasst werden, wenn eine Untersuchung über den Schlaf fruchten soll." (Trömner, *Das Problem des Schlafes*, 3).

47. For an elaboration of this argument, see Daston and Galison, *Objectivity*, and Daston and Galison, "The Image of Objectivity." Foucault addresses the same problem in *The Order of Things*. For a helpful commentary, see Reckwitz, *Subjekt*.

48. Wittgenstein, *Zettel*, 396.

49. Denis Diderot's dialogue *Le rêve de d'Alembert* was authored in 1769 but appeared in print only in 1830. The word "dream" in the title has numerous meanings, but one of them is "somniloquy." Intricately structured, the philosophical dialogue is divided into three interwoven parts that require a reading sensitive to style and composition. In the middle section, d'Alembert has had enough of the philosophical discussions that make up the first part and retreats to bed. He is

sleeping behind a screen and is sleep talking. Mademoiselle de l'Espinasse records his words and then calls for Bordeu, the doctor, to help her make sense of the notes she has produced. Readers immediately recognize that they show a connection between d'Alembert's earlier philosophical discussion and a figure called Diderot, thus establishing continuity between d'Alembert's sleeping and waking selves, even though he assumes a different position in each state. In fact, the conversation quickly turns to the argument that the self is composed of exchangeable smaller units, assigning a key role to memory for maintaining the perceived unity of the self. While Bordeu and Mademoiselle de l'Espinasse are chatting, d'Alembert is intermittently sleeping and waking. Occasionally, he offers an interjection. Eventually, he gets up and demands to know what the doctor thinks about sleep. The doctor replies that sleep is a special mode of the functioning of the mind, one in which internal instead of external stimuli are being processed, and he specifically refers to nocturnal emissions and dreams. Since *Le rêve de d'Alembert* also refers to sleep talking as dreaming, Diderot is clearly using this passage to clarify the title and the poetic conceit of the text. The doctor's emphasis on the epistemology of dream states also indicates that Diderot's concerns are different from mine. For the text, see Diderot, *Entretien entre D'Alembert et Diderot*, 285–371. For a comprehensive philosophical commentary, see Duflo, *Diderot philosophe*, 189–270, and Anderson, *Diderot's Dream*. For a reading with a focus on sleep talking, see Hansen, *Somniloquies*, 41–86.

50. Sleepwalking for Hegel does not illuminate the normal state of mental processes during sleep but constitutes a pathology, which contrasts with Diderot's view of somniloquy. Hegel argues that sleeping and walking must alternate regularly; thus, sleepwalking is a failure to wake up at the appropriate interval. On this question, see Wortham, *The Poetics of Sleep*, 31–38. For a general exposition of the sleeping subject in Hegel, see Schwenger, *At the Borders of Sleep*, vii–xii. I discuss Hegel's argument in more detail in the Proust chapter.

51. For an overview of the field and literature and science, see Turner, "Lessons from Literature for the Historian of Science (and Vice Versa)," and Biagioli, "Post-disciplinary Liaisons." Several handbooks, companions, and encyclopedias map the field—for example, Borgards et al., *Literatur und Wissen*, Clarke and Rossini, *The Routledge Companion to Literature and Science*, Meyer, *The Cambridge Companion to Literature and Science*, and The Triangle Collective, *The Palgrave Handbook of Twentieth and Twenty-First Century Literature and Science*. German and Anglophone approaches to literature and science have so far not been theorized together, although they are evidently aligned. For an overview of the approaches in the Anglophone world and its history, see Bono, "Making Knowledge," and Bono, "Science Studies as Cultural Studies." For an overview of the specifically German approach, see Vogl, "Für eine Poetologie des Wissens," Schäfer, "Poetologie des Wissens," and Brandt, "Kulturwissenschaften und Wissenschaftsgeschichte", 97–100.

52. Important scholarly works that expound on this claim include Beer, *Darwin's Plots*, Biagioli, *Galileo's Instruments of Credit*, Griffiths, *Age of Analogy*, Shuttleworth, *The Mind of the Child*, and Otis, *Membranes*.

53. Robert Desnos might represent one exception, although his staged sleep talking is couched in the terminology of somnambulism and dreaming by his fellow surrealists. On Desnos, see Conley, *Robert Desnos*, 15-23.

54. For scholarship on silent feature films such as *Das Cabinet des Dr. Caligari* (dir. Robert Wiene, Germany, 1920), *Nosferatu* (dir. F.W. Murnau, Germany, 1922), and *Paris qui dort* (dir. René Clair, France, 1924), see Kaes, *Shell Shock Cinema*, Andriopoulos, *Possessed*, and Saint-Amour, "Stillness and Altitude."

55. Kroker, *The Sleep of Others*, 155-77; Gottesmann, *Henri Piéron and Nathaniel Kleitman*.

56. For the term, see Herzberg, *White Market Drugs*. Herzog discusses Veronal in the US, focusing on a later period than this book.

57. As Greaney notes, "the very best sleepers—babies and young children—are those who know or think least about it" ("'Observed, Measured, Contained,'" 64).

Chapter 1. The Science of Sleep

1. Freud, *The Interpretation of Dreams*, 40. For the original, see Freud, *Die Traumdeutung*, 2:33: "Bis vor kurzem haben die meisten Autoren sich veranlaßt gesehen, Schlaf und Traum in dem nämlichen Zusammenhang abzuhandeln. . . . Ich hatte wenig Anlaß, mich mit dem Problem des Schlafes zu befassen, denn dies ist ein wesentlich physiologisches Problem, wenngleich in der Charakteristik des Schlafzustands die Veränderung der Funktionsbedingungen für den seelischen Apparat mit enthalten sein muß. Es bleibt also auch die Literatur des Schlafs hier außer Betracht."

2. Breuer and Freud, *Studien über Hysterie*, 168. For the German and a comment on the passage, see note 10 in the introduction.

3. In *The Vocabulary of Psychoanalysis,* Pontalis and Laplanche explain that according to Freud, "two separate functions may be distinguished in mental activity during the construction of a dream," first, "the production of the dream-thoughts" and second, "their transformation into the [manifest] content of the dream" and that "it is this second operation, constituting the dream-work proper, whose four mechanisms Freud analysed: *Verdichtung* (condensation), *Verschiebung* (displacement), *Rücksicht auf Darstellbarkeit* (considerations of representability) and *sekundäre Bearbeitung* (secondary revision)" (125).

4. See Freud, *Vorlesungen zur Einführung in die Psychoanalyse*, 11:85. The most significant exception to Freud's general intellectual eschewal of sleep can be found in a passage in *The Interpretation of Dreams* where he seems to turn the relationship between sleep and dreams on its head when he defines dreams as the "guardian of

sleep" (253-54). Other texts in which sleep plays a role are *On Narcissism* (1914), the *Metapsychological Supplement to a Theory of Dreams* (1916), and the *Introductory Lectures on Psycho-Analysis* (1916-17). For an integrative overview of Freud's theory of sleep, see Solms, "Sleep," and Wortham, *The Poetics of Sleep, 39-56*.

5. See, for example, Liébeault, "Das Wachen." Many studies have explored contemporary debates regarding hypnosis and their consequences. See especially Mayer, *Sites of the Unconscious*, and Andriopoulos, *Possessed*.

6. Freud, *Vorlesungen zur Einführung in die Psychoanalyse*, 11:85. On the idea of dreamless sleep as the best sleep, see Ahlheim, *Der Traum vom Schlaf im 20. Jahrhundert*, 40-46. Ahlheim situates this idea within the historic context of late nineteenth-century theories of sleep as interruptions in mental life.

7. Dement, "The Study of Human Sleep," 2. In the meantime, some sleep scientists have begun to collaborate with humanists and social scientists, an exchange that has been proving fruitful for both sides. See, for example, a special issue of *Interface Focus*, the journal of the Royal Society, coedited by Sally Shuttleworth and Russell G. Foster titled "Sleep and Stress."

8. Freud, *The Interpretation of Dreams*, 40.

9. Kroker, *The Sleep of Others*, 81. He refers to Daston, "British Responses to Psycho-Physiology."

10. Lhermitte, *Le sommeil*, 204. Trömner, *Das Problem des Schlafes*, 3-4, makes similar claims.

11. See Rabinbach, *The Human Motor*, and Sarasin, *Reizbare Maschinen*. Rabinbach and Sarasin do not discuss sleep explicitly.

12. Rabinbach, *The Human Motor*, 38.

13. See Rabinbach, *The Human Motor*, 43-44. See also Rabinbach, "Ermüdung, Energie und der menschliche Motor."

14. Several scholars have pointed out that this project is mainly geared toward white-collar professionals and less toward blue-collar workers. See Shuttleworth, "Fagged Out," 1-4, and Ahlheim, *Der Traum vom Schlaf im 20. Jahrhundert*, 84-103.

15. Shuttleworth, "Fagged Out," 3. On the graphical method, see Borck, "Writing Brains."

16. See Mosso, *Die Ermüdung*, 202.

17. For a contemporary assessment, see Lhermitte, *Le sommeil*, 64. For a first scholarly take on Claparède, see Kroker, *The Sleep of Others*, 148-61, and Claparède, "Édouard Claparède."

18. Claparède edited the first French-language review of *The Interpretation of Dreams* and translated some of Freud's psychoanalytic writings for a Francophone audience. To do so, he initiated a dialogue with Freud, both via correspondence and in person. Freud, in turn, was happy to have Claparède among his followers. See Freud to Claparède, May 24, 1908, Sigmund Freud Papers, General Correspondence, mss39990, box 20, Library of Congress, https://www.loc.gov/item

/mss3999000507. On Freud's early reception in the Francophonie, see Scheidhauer, *Freud et ses visiteurs*.

19. The possibility of a "phenomenology of sleep" has been contested by Nancy, *The Fall of Sleep*. For phenomenological considerations on sleep, with extensive commentary on Husserl's thoughts on the subject, see de Warren, "The Inner Night," and König, "Erwachen."

20. Vaschide, *Le sommeil et les rêves*, 137. In referring to invented concepts, Vaschide intends to point out that Claparède's theory of active sleep does in fact rely on words, not on positivist facts, noting that in "La question du sommeil," Claparède himself asks, "Où sont les faits?" (143). To be sure, Claparède is not the first to speak of sleep as active, but he is commonly credited for this reconceptualization. For an earlier usage in the context of hypnotism, see Oskar Vogt, "Zur Kenntniss [sic]," 318: "Alle diese Erscheinungen weisen darauf hin, auch in dem Schlaf einen activen Vorgang zu sehen, auch ihn auf eine neurodynamische Erscheinung zurückzuführen." It is possible that Claparède was aware of Vogt's work.

21. Manacéïne, a Russian-born physiologist who published mostly in French and German, was among the first cohort of women that received a European university education in medicine and, subsequently, the sciences; she also counts among the first generation of researchers who practiced sleep science. For more details and a bibliography, see Kovalzon, "Some Notes on the Biography of Maria Manasseina," 312-19.

22. On Piéron's experiments and his subsequent disagreement with Claparède, see Kroker, *The Sleep of Others*, 161-78. For Piéron's position in the historiography of sleep science, see Gottesmann, *Henri Piéron and Nathaniel Kleitman*.

23. Manacéïne, "Quelques observations expérimentales." On this experiment, see also Bentivoglio and Grassi-Zucconi, "The Pioneering Experimental Studies on Sleep Deprivation."

24. Manacéïne, "Quelques observations expérimentales," 323.

25. See, for example, Pawlow, "Innere Hemmung," 46.

26. When Henri Piéron repeated Manacéïne's experiment, he solved this problem by cruelty: the act of finally being overpowered by sleep would strangulate the dogs (which were equipped with a gallows noose). See Piéron, *Le problème physiologique du sommeil*.

27. In one instructive polemic passage, Claparède argues that laboratory life invariably constructs its research objects through theoretical, methodological, and experimental practices, bearing out Bachelard's suggestion that "phenomena emerge that bear the stamp of theory throughout" (*The New Scientific Spirit*, 13).

28. Freud himself suggests that we must read Claparède's notion of defense psychoanalytically. After having "studied" the "Esquisse" "diligently" in its year of publication, Freud dispatched a congratulatory note on April 1, 1905, stating his

approval of Claparède's repurposing of "the idea of a psychic 'defense,'" which, he points out, he himself had "highlighted with regards to neurosis" for a new "'theory of sleep'" (Library of Congress, Sigmund Freud Papers, General Correspondence, mss39990, box 20, https://www.loc.gov/item/mss3999000507).

29. "Ce n'est pas parce que nous sommes intoxiqués, ou épuisés, que nous dormons, mais nous dormons pour ne pas l'être" ("Esquisse d'une théorie biologique du sommeil," 347).

30. "Qu'est-ce qui caractérise l'"activité' d'un processus? . . . A vrai dire, le concept d'activité est assez difficile à définir . . . . 'Actif' implique l'idée d'une réaction. Mais réaction implique à son tour activité, et nous tournons dans un cercle. Disons donc, au lieu de réaction: mouvement déclanché par un stimulus en vertu d'une disposition constitutionnelle de l'organisme. Actif signifie donc: qui implique une participation du sujet; le processus actif est celui qui se déroule grâce aux potentialités du sujet, que le sujet possède en réserve, potentialités qui sont seulement déclanchées, et non créées par le stimulus. Plus cette participation du sujet est large, plus le processus sera dit actif" ("La question du sommeil," 438-39).

31. "Longtemps, je me suis couché de bonne heure. . . . Et, une demi-heure après, la pensée qu'il était temps de *chercher le sommeil* m'éveillait" (Proust, *À la recherche du temps perdu*, 1:3, emphasis mine). I analyze this sentence at length in chapter 4.

32. Schneuwly, "La psychologie appliquée à l'enseignement du français," 146.

33. Claparède transposes the entire process into the grammatical active. He also bases his ideas on multilingual comparison and even coins neologisms that require the French original to make sense:

> The term "endormissement" [a nominalization of "s'endormir," "the making oneself fall asleep"] . . . would be preferable in comparison with "assoupissement" [a nominalization of "s'assoupir," "the dozing off"] as the latter has the passive meaning of "light sleep" and not that of an "action to make oneself fall asleep" (the term "Einschlafen" in German). —The neologism "endormie" would be . . . better still, as it is constructed by analogy to the verb "sortir," which indicates an action.

> (Le mot *endormissement* . . . serait préférable à *assoupissement*, qui a le sens passif de "sommeil léger" et non celui de "action de s'endormir" [das Einschlafen des Allemands]. —Le néologisme *endormie* vaudrait . . . mieux encore, étant construit de façon analogue à *sortir*, qui indique une action. ["Esquisse d'une théorie biologique du sommeil," 284]).

34. The metaphor of the siege comes up several times ("Esquisse d'une théorie biologique du sommeil," 311, 315, 321).

35. Freud, *The Interpretation of Dreams*, 253-54: "All dreams are in a sense

dreams of convenience: they serve the purpose of prolonging sleep instead of waking up. *Dreams are the guardians of sleep and not its disturbers. . . . Thus the wish to sleep . . . must in every case be reckoned as one of the motives for the formation of dreams, and every successful dream is a fulfilment of that wish*" (emphasis in the original).

36. "Les graphiques publiés de courbes de sommeil ressemblent beaucoup aux courbes de travail . . . , édifiées à l'instigation de Mosso et de Krœpelin. . . . Il semble que, pour arriver à son apogée, le ` sommeil, comme le travail, doive passer par une phase de mise en train. Voici encore une autre analogie qui ressort de l'examen de ces courbes : Les courbes de sommeil, notamment celles publiées par Michelson, par de Sanctis et Neyroz, présentent une série *d'oscillations* . . . ; c'est comme si l'organisme, sentant son sommeil menacé . . . , faisait un effort pour renforcer le processus inhibitif, — comme le travailleur dérangé par le vacarme de la rue, fait de constants efforts pour renforcer son attention au fur et à mesure qu'il la sent se relâcher. Dans de nombreuses courbes on constate aussi, vers la fin de la nuit . . . une brusque augmentation de la profondeur du sommeil, qui fait songer au *coup de collier* (Schlussantrieb) des courbes de travail. . . . Le coup de collier est une réaction contre la fatigue. . . . Les choses se passent tout à fait comme si les centres préposés au maintien du sommeil se fatiguaient peu à peu et que l'on se réveillât parce que l'on est fatigué de dormir" ("Esquisse d'une théorie biologique du sommeil," 315).

37. Vilensky, *Encephalitis Lethargica*, 7. For a discussion of potential causes, including the influenza pandemic of 1918, see Vilensky, *Encephalitis Lethargica*, and Foley, *Encephalitis Lethargica*. They report that one scholar counted approximately nine thousand publications dedicated to the sleeping sickness during the interwar period. For a near-complete reconstruction of the interwar discourses on encephalitis lethargica, see Foley, *Encephalitis Lethargica*. Credible estimates of the number of people affected range from around fifty thousand to one million, based on the assumption that most cases have not been officially reported. On the credible estimates, see Vilensky, *Encephalitis Lethargica*, 40. Despite its reach, the "two ultimate goals" of encephalitis lethargica research were "unfortunately never attained: identification of the pathogen, and the development of effective therapies" (Foley, *Encephalitis Lethargica*, 12). Kenton Kroker argues that encephalitis lethargica allowed health authorities to construct the concept of an epidemic ("Configuring Epidemic Encephalitis"; "The First Modern Plague").

38. For all the prominence of extended sleep, encephalitis lethargica named a protean and polymorphic condition. It could also trigger protracted insomnia, petrification, seizures, and even a range of altogether different symptoms. Worse still, survivors of the sleeping sickness often developed a malicious sequel— postencephalitic parkinsonism, the condition of being locked in a catatonic state described in Oliver Sacks's *Awakenings* (1973) and portrayed in the Hollywood film

Awakenings: Based on a True Story. For a clinical description, see Vilensky, *Encephalitis Lethargica*, and Foley, *Encephalitis Lethargica*. For contemporary clinical accounts, see esp. Economo, *Die Encephalitis lethargica*, and Stern, *Die epidemische Encephalitis*.

39. The film is available online; see Friedrich Heinrich Lewy, *Acute encephalitis lethargica* (Wellcome Collection, https://wellcomecollection.org/works/dcpe3h6a). Lewy wrote an accompanying article on the film titled "Akute Encephalitis lethargica." The film was part of a larger project to record medical case histories at the Charité Berlin. See Degner, "Das medizinisch-kinematographische Universitäts-Institut," and Degner, "Medizinische Kinematographie." The journal can be accessed in the archive of the Deutsche Kinemathek, Berlin. For biographical background on F. H. Lewy, see Rodriges e Silva, "Das Leben von Prof. Dr. Fritz Jakob Heinrich Lewy (1885–1950)."

40. On Charcot's medical photographs and his theatrical medicine, see Didi-Huberman, *Invention of Hysteria*, and Marshall, "Dynamic Medicine and Theatrical Form." For Charcot's own encounters with sleeping patients see his *Leçons du mardi à la Salpêtrière*, 63–71.

41. Kroker, *The Sleep of Others*, 191.

42. In the 1920s, there had been a controversy about the primacy of diagnosis (the so-called *Prioritätenstreit*). In any case, the ICD-10 still registers the sleeping sickness as encephalitis lethargica, Von Economo-Cruchet disease. It also notes that it has been called "Economo's disease." See ICD-10, A85.8, https://www.icd10data.com/ICD10CM/Codes/A00-B99/A80-A89/A85-/A85.8, accessed January 11, 2024. In the ICD-11, however, it is only registered among "viral encephalitis not elsewhere classified" (http://id.who.int/icd/entity/956664712, accessed November 28, 2023). See also Berger and Vilensky, "Encephalitis Lethargica."

43. Economo, "Professor Emil Redlich (†)," 327. For Economo's work on sleep, see especially "Encephalitis Lethargica," "Über den Schlaf," "Pathologie des Schlafs," "Schlaftheorie," and "Der Schlaf als Lokalisationsproblem."

44. Drucker-Colín and Merchant-Nancy, "Evolution of Concepts of Mechanisms of Sleep," 3. See also contemporary textbooks in biology, for example, Pinel, *Biopsychology*, 400. Sleep researchers have paid homage to Economo's work. See Triarhou, "The Signaling Contributions of Constantin von Economo," Triarhou, "The Percipient Observations of Constantin von Economo," and Lavie, "The Sleep Theory of Constantin von Economo."

45. For an overview of the historic debates about passive and active sleep, see Lhermitte, *Le sommeil*. The role of encephalitis lethargica in deciding this controversy has occasionally been acknowledged in relation to active sleep; see, for instance, Borbély, *Das Geheimnis des Schlafes*.

46. On the history of narcolepsy, see Dement, "The History of Narcolepsy and Other Sleep Disorders." On the history of African trypanosomiasis, see Gradmann, "Africa as a Laboratory," Bloom, "Diagnosing Invisible Agents," and Lyons, *The*

Colonial Disease. Both diseases are evoked in the description of encephalitis lethargica, most importantly in Economo, *Die Encephalitis lethargica*.

47. Canguilhem, *On the Normal and the Pathological*.

48. Canguilhem, by contrast, insists that differences in quantity are differences in kind. For him, the discourse on the pathological serves less to render "biological ideals" visible than to introduce practices of normalization that institutionalize what counts as "biologically normal" in the first place (*On the Normal and the Pathological*, 123, 118). On biological reductionism in the nineteenth century, see Keating and Cambrosio, "Does Biomedicine Entail the Successful Reduction of Pathology to Biology?"

49. Canguilhem, *On the Normal and the Pathological*, 13.

50. Nietzsche, *Nachgelassene Fragmente, 1887-1889*, 13:42. Nietzsche paraphrases Claude Bernard.

51. Kroker, "Configuring Epidemic Encephalitis," 77.

52. See, for example, Gélineau, "De la narcolepsie," Mauthner, "Zur Pathologie und Physiologie des Schlafes," Dubois, "Le centre du sommeil," Claparède, "Esquisse d'une théorie biologique du sommeil," 317, and Trömner, *Das Problem des Schlafes*.

53. On functional localization, see Hagner, "Lokalisationstheorien," and Hagner, *Der Geist bei der Arbeit*, 170-79. On the importance of Vienna as a center of the localization paradigm, see Lesky, *Die Wiener medizinische Schule*.

54. Guenther, *Localization and Its Discontents*, 13. She refers to Uttal, *The New Phrenology*, 147, 103.

55. See Gélineau, "De la narcolepsie." On Gélineau, see Kroker, *The Sleep of Others*, 87. For other connections between narcolepsy and functional localization, see Redlich, "Zur Narkolepsiefrage," and Redlich, "Über Narkolepsie." Redlich counts among Economo's colleagues and mentors.

56. See Hagner, "Lokalisationstheorien," 862.

57. Vaschide, for example, remarks that "je regrette que M. Claparède se laisse influencer par la manie des neurologistes de chercher des centres à tout propos, et désire trouver un centre du sommeil" (*Le sommeil et les rêves*, 20).

58. See the studies on anencephaly by Karplus and Kreidl quoted in Economo, "Über den Schlaf," 875. Regarding studies disputing the idea of a sleep center, Economo refers to studies by Lhermitte, Dejerine, Veronese, and others ("Der Schlaf als Lokalisationsproblem," 45-46).

59. The most important study from this camp is Piéron, *Le problème physiologique du sommeil*.

60. See Wundt, *Grundzüge der physiologischen Psychologie*, 623. For contemporary work on organic and evolutionary rhythms, see also Piéron, *Le problème physiologique du sommeil*, 3.

61. Trömner, "Schlaf und Encephalitis," 787. Economo argues in a similar manner; see "Pathologie des Schlafs," 607. The idea of encephalitis lethargica as a

natural experiment on a large scale is a common one; W. R. Hess, for example, justifies it by suggesting that "die Natur selbst hat solche Experimente gemacht" ("Der Schlaf," 133). Many of Economo's contemporaries took a different approach to the disease. The German neurologist Felix Stern focused on helping patients with therapeutic remedies, the French psychiatrist Jean René Cruchet tried to limit the geographical spread of the disease, and Raymond Pearl at Johns Hopkins and Josephine Neal at Columbia considered its epidemiology, Pearl by conducting statistical analysis and Neal through an investigation into viruses. For an overview of their work, see Foley, *Encephalitis Lethargica*, and Vilensky, *Encephalitis Lethargica*.

62. On the search for the site of the soul, see Vidal, *The Sciences of the Soul*.

63. In fact, when Economo first introduces the term, he adds twofold emphasis in calling it "truly a sleep regulation center" ("ein wirkliches Schlafsteuerungszentrum" ["Pathologie des Schlafs," 592, 607]).

64. This position matches Economo's general neuroanatomic commitments that led him to engage in a protracted *Gelehrtenstreit*, or scholarly dispute, with the German neuroscientists at the Kaiser Wilhelm Institute at Berlin-Buch (especially with Cécile Vogt-Mugnier, Oskar Vogt, and Marthe Vogt), in which he argued that brain areas could have fuzzy boundaries. See Economo, "Nochmals zur Frage der arealen Grenzen in der Hirnrinde," 313–14. Unlike for Economo, there is a substantial body of research on the Vogts. See Hagner, "Gehirnführung."

65. "Unter Hirnschlaf im engeren Sinne wollen wir also jetzt bloß den Zustand der spezifisch nervösen und psychischen Funktionen des Gehirns im Schlafe verstehen, während wir demgegenüber unter der Bezeichnung Körperschlaf nicht nur den Zustand aller übrigen Körperorgane im Schlafe subsummieren, sondern auch jene Änderungen im Stoffwechsel, in der Blut- und Lymphströmung also alle diejenigen anatomischen, chemischen und weiteren Vorgänge des Gehirns selbst dazurechnen, welche nicht unmittelbar als nervöse oder psychische Effekte zum Ausdruck kommen" ("Pathologie des Schlafs," 593).

66. A few pages later, he extends this argument qualitatively and quantitatively; sleep is now described as encompassing vegetative, animalic, and psychic alterations—for example, the possibility of dream states ("Der Schlaf als Lokalisationsproblem," 49).

67. Sarason, "Zur Einführung," 6. Sarason summarizes Economo's work.

68. Sarason, "Zur Einführung," 6.

69. Still, the assumption of a waking center instead of a sleep center was not unheard of. In fact, Economo is aware of Karl Friedrich Burdach, who suggested a similar theory in the early nineteenth century.

70. Vogt, "Zur Kenntniss [sic],"323.

71. See also Economo, "Schlaftheorie," 323.

72. Guenther, *Localization and Its Discontents*, 13–38; Hagner, "Lokalisationstheorien." Guenther gives a concise definition of "reflex": "A reflex is made up of the

nervous connections between sense organs and muscles, which pass through the central nervous system (the spinal cord or the brain). Over the course of the nineteenth century, this sensory-motor system became the dominant principle for explaining nervous function" (4).

73. See Canguilhem, "Le concept de réflexe au XIXe siècle," 295.

74. Canguilhem, *La formation du concept de réflexe*, 153. On Economo's relationship with Exner, see Economo and Wagner-Jauregg, *Baron Constantin von Economo*, 8, 44. Under the tutelage of Exner, Economo conducted research that looked into reflex function. See Economo, "Die centralen Bahnen des Kau- und Schluckactes," 629-43. On Exner, see Coen, *Vienna in the Age of Uncertainty*, 91-116.

75. Canguilhem, *La formation du concept de réflexe* 153, fn. 5: "Exner, célèbre physiologiste autrichien, a construit lui aussi une explication générale de toutes les fonctions psychiques à partir du réflexe, poussant la logique jusqu'à faire du réflexe ce que nous appellerons un Contre-Cogito; on ne devrait plus dire, selon Exner: Je pense, Je sens, mais: Il pense en moi, Il sent en moi."

76. "Erkenntnisse der letzten Zeit bei Enzephalitis haben uns gezeigt, daß es sich beim Willen um eine komplexe Funktion unseres Wesens handelt, deren eine Teil nicht nur außerhalb unserer Bewußtseinsvorgänge, sondern außerhalb unserer Seelenvorgänge überhaupt, das heißt extrapsychisch verläuft und daß dieser Teil Störungen, also Beeinflussungen zugänglich ist, die an einer lokalisierten Stelle subkortikal gesetzt werden. Die Psychologen werden sich damit irgendwie abfinden müssen. Die Psychiatrie erwirbt jedoch damit eine neue Erkenntnis; Funktionen, die wir früher als rein psychisch bedingte Vorgänge, als Willensvorgänge . . . bezeichneten und die physiologisch nicht erklärbar waren, werden nun physiologisch erklärbar" ("Encephalitis lethargica," 1338).

77. "Physiologisch und psychologisch ganz unerwartete Einblicke in die Geheimnisse der seelischen Mechanismen. . . , Erkenntnisse, die vielleicht auch außerhalb der ärztlichen Welt von großer Wirkung sein werden."

78. "Während ein Patient, der zum Beispiel an Jackson-Anfällen in einer Hand leidet, darüber sagt, 'es zuckt in meiner Hand,' also die Bewegung der Hand objektiviert und als fremd empfindet, sagt der Enzephalitiskranke, der mit der Hand fortwährend herumwischt, 'ich muß halt die Hand fortwährend so bewegen,' das heißt er subjektiviert die Bewegung, er anerkennt sie psychisch als persönlich" ("Encephalitis lethargica," 1337).

79. Plötzl, "Zur Physiologie des Schlafes," 54.

80. Plötzl, "Der Schlaf als psychisches Problem," 26. The phrase appears less odd, however, when it is embedded in local usage. A contemporary study on language contact between Czech and German in the Habsburg Empire remarks à propos of loan translations that "um die Lust oder Unlust an etwas zu bezeichnen, bedient man sich oft der Redensart: 'Es will sich mir' mit folgendem Infinitiv nach

Analogie des Slavischen: Es will sich mir nicht essen, trinken, schlafen (nechce se mi jísti, píti, spáti . . .)" (Tomanek, "Ueber den Einfluss des Čechischen," 34).

81. An approximation in English would be "It wants (or is trying) to sleep me."

82. Berger, "Über das Elektrenkephalogramm [sic] des Menschen: Neunte Mitteilung," 548. Berger attributes this insight to W. R. Hess (1881-73), the Swiss physiologist and Nobel Prize-winner of 1949. Berger also read and quoted Economo ("Über das Elektrenkephalogramm des Menschen: Achte Mitteilung," 459-60, 466), but he does not name him here. On Hess, see Diener, "Krieg und Frieden im vegetativen Nervensystem," 111-15, Christian W. Hess, "Walter R. Hess (17.3.1881-12.8.1973)," Akert, "Walter Rudolf Hess (1881-1973)," Jung, "W. R. Hess und das Ordnungsprinzip in der Physiologie," and Borbély, *Das Geheimnis des Schlafes*, 74-76. Hess's papers have been preserved at the Hess Collection, Archive for the History of Medicine, University of Zürich. See also Hess, *Biological Order and Brain Organization* and "Über die Wechselbeziehungen zwischen psychischen und vegetativen Funktionen."

83. For a cultural history of the invention of the EEG, see Borck, *Hirnströme*, and Borck, "Writing Brains." Borck's monograph is now also available in English. See Borck, *Brainwaves*.

84. Berger, "Über das Elektrenkephalogramm des Menschen," 569.

85. On Berger's calibration of the EEG with stimulants (such as cocaine) and soporifics (such as Scopolamin, Avertin, Pernocton, Evipan, and Luminal), see especially Berger, "Über das Elektrenkephalogramm des Menschen: Dritte Mitteilung," 33-36, and Berger, "Über das Elektrenkephalogramm des Menschen: Achte Mitteilung," 454-59.

86. Berger, "Über das Elektrenkephalogramm des Menschen: Vierte Mitteilung," 21.

87. Kroker, *The Sleep of Others*, 256. For Kroker, the history of active sleep begins *with* the EEG, but as this chapter suggests, this is not the case. On the invention of the EEG and its impact on sleep research, see also Ahlheim, *Der Traum vom Schlaf im 20. Jahrhundert*, 209-26.

88. Kroker, *The Sleep of Others*, 257.

89. "Weder der subjectiven Schätzung noch auch sonst irgend einer andersartigen objectiven Betrachtungsweise zugänglich erscheint" (Michelson, *Untersuchungen über die Tiefe des Schlafes*, 54). Michelson was a student of Emil Kraepelin.

Chapter 2. White Nights, Brown Pills

1. See Crary, 24/7.

2. In scholarship, sociological explanations dominate the discussion of how to make sense of this historic change. These approaches center on five elements: industrialization and the onerousness of professional life, urbanization, electrifica-

tion, acceleration, and medicalization. See Ekirch, "Modernization of Western Sleep," Ahlheim, *Der Traum vom Schlaf im 20. Jahrhundert*, Scrivner, "That Sweet Secession," 280, Scrivner, *Becoming Insomniac*, Aebischer and Rieder, "Awaking Insomnia," and Summers-Bremner, *Insomnia*.

3. See Crary, *Suspensions of Perception*, and Duttlinger, *Attention and Distraction*.

4. Schulz and Salzarulo, "The Evolution of Sleep Medicine," 79; Lechner, *Die klinischen Formen der Schlaflosigkeit*, 1. All translations into English from sources in languages other than English are mine, unless credited otherwise.

5. "Der heilige Schlaf. . . . Ausgeschlafen sein, restlos, garantiert Dir, o Mensch, Deine Dir überhaupt mögliche höchste Arbeits-Leistung!" (Altenberg, *Mein Lebensabend*, 222).

6. Flatau, "Ueber die nervöse Schlaflosigkeit," 4; Siemerling, *Schlaf und Schlaflosigkeit*, 22; Renner, *Schlafmittel-Therapie*, 18. Carl Seyfarth argues that "as insomnia is most certainly in many cases only the consequence of psychic agitation, especially the appearance of anxiety, the suggestive effect of all conceivable prescriptions is, of course, most important" (*Strümpell-Seyfarth Lehrbuch*, 2:890).

7. Siemerling, *Schlaf und Schlaflosigkeit*, 7, 22, 25. Similar arguments have been advanced by Metzl, *Prozac on the Couch*, and Herzberg, *Happy Pills*. Both address American postwar culture. "Few Americans at the turn of the twenty-first century would have been surprised by this ad or its claim. The notion that pills could restore selfhood had become commonplace, pervading popular as well as medical culture" (Herzberg, *Happy Pills*, 1).

8. See Herlinghaus, "Towards a Cultural Pharmacology," 2.

9. For an overview of early synthetic sleep medication beginning with Chloralhydrat, see Müller-Jahncke, Friedrich, and Meyer, *Arzneimittelgeschichte*, 141-47, and Andretta-Purtschert, *Zur Entwicklungsgeschichte der Hypnotika und Sedativa*.

10. On these developments, see Lesch, *German Chemical Industry*, Homburg, Travis, and Schröter, *Chemical Industry in Europe*, Travis, *Determinants*, Wimmer, *"Wir haben fast immer was Neues,"* Plumpe, *Die I.G. Farbenindustrie AG*, and Beer, *German Dye Industry*.

11. The prices for soporifics are parsed in Weber, *Die Entwicklung der Psychopharmakologie*, 95.

12. Piéron, *Le problème physiologique du sommeil*, 396.

13. See Jacobsohn, *Klinik der Nervenkrankheiten*, 379.

14. For an overview of this medical universe, see Rabinbach, *The Human Motor*, 146-78, Böhme, "Das Gefühl der Schwere," Radkau, "Die wilhelminische Ära," Radkau, *Das Zeitalter der Nervosität*, Pross, Müller-Wille, and Bergengruen, *Neurasthenie*, and Gijswijt-Hofstra and Porter, *Cultures of Neurasthenia*.

15. For an analysis of insomnia and neurasthenia in nineteenth-century French medical literature, see Aebischer and Rieder, "Awaking Insomnia," and Aebischer,

"De la veille à l'insomnie." See also Beaumont, "Insomnia and the Late Nineteenth-Century Insomniac."

16. Hauptmann, "Neurasthenische und hysterische Äußerungen und Konstitutionen," 641.

17. Auerbach, *Die Behandlung der nervösen Schlaflosigkeit*, 3.

18. Auerbach, *Die Behandlung der nervösen Schlaflosigkeit*, 13; Flatau, "Ueber die nervöse Schlaflosigkeit," 6. Some physicians argued that insomnia only was worthy medical attention if it interfered with work. See also Lechner, *Die klinischen Formen der Schlaflosigkeit*, 41.

19. Richard Traugott claims that the sleep disorders of these people spring from "productive[] geistige[] . . . Arbeit," which they continue "in den Schlaf hinein" (*Die nervöse Schlaflosigkeit und ihre Behandlung*, 30).

20. Oppenheim, "Die Neurasthenie oder Nervenschwäche," 1136.

21. For a selection of contemporary self-help books on insomnia, see Kruse, *Das Büchlein zum guten Schlaf*, Sommer, *Kraft durch Ruhe*, and Starck, *Die Kunst gut zu schlafen und früh aufzustehen*. Kruse has recently been discussed in the context of early attempts of self-optimization. See Steinfeld, *Ich will, ich kann*.

22. Gaupp, "Über Wesen und Behandlung der Schlaflosigkeit," 40-42.

23. Benn, "Mann und Frau gehn durch die Krebsbaracke," 16. The original reads: "Man läßt sie schlafen. Tag und Nacht. —Den Neuen/sagt man: Hier schläft man sich gesund. —Nur Sonntags/für den Besuch läßt man sie etwas wacher." Note that my translation contains a strong interpretation of the verb "lassen."

24. Gaupp, "Über Wesen und Behandlung der Schlaflosigkeit," 43.

25. Starck, *Die Kunst gut zu schlafen und früh aufzustehen*, 20.

26. Sarasin, *Reizbare Maschinen*, 17.

27. Peter, "Schlafhygiene," 1090.

28. Gaupp, "Über Wesen und Behandlung der Schlaflosigkeit," 44: "die zweckmäßige Tageseinteilung mit dem Wechsel zwischen Arbeit, Nahrungsaufnahme und Ruhe, die Gewöhnung an Ordnung und Regelmäßigkeit im Aufstehen und Zubettgehen, die richtige Gestaltung des Schlafraumes, die Abhaltung aller störenden und ungewohnten Sinnesreize, überhaupt eben die richtige und vernunftgemäße Einrichtung des persönlichen Lebens, die Übereinstimmung unserer Kräfte mit unserem Wollen, die Beherrschung des eigenen Körpers, die Macht über die Richtung der Gedanken, die Ablehnung alles Unwesentlichen."

29. Sarasin, *Reizbare Maschinen*, 19.

30. According to Philipp Sarasin, both terms can be used as umbrella terms for the other. In general, the term "hygiene" connotes practices of preserving health (*hygieia*), while the term "dietetics" (*díatia*) refers to the regulation of one's nutrition according to individual conditions and needs, as well as to questions of conduct conducive to one's well-being.

31. The notion of the technology of the self plays a key role in the late

Foucault. On his account, ancient dietetics refer to an ensemble of prophylactic measures implemented to avoid diseases, but they ultimately encapsulate an entire art of how to live and to constitute oneself as a subject through "technologies of the self." The technique of how to live according to one's own body is meant to foster individualized ethics. On this topic, see especially Hesse, "'Ästhetik der Existenz.'" Other scholars have demonstrated that Foucault's take on ancient dietetics builds on a discursive framework determined by nineteenth-century hygienists; thus, his notion of the *souci de soi* would have been impossible without it. See Sarasin, *Reizbare Maschinen*, 452-66.

32. Sarasin, *Reizbare Maschinen*, 73. See also Kinzler, *Das Joch des Schlafs*, 224-25.

33. Sarasin, *Reizbare Maschinen*; Kinzler, *Das Joch des Schlafs*, 35.

34. See BAL, 166/8, Pharma, Produkte A-Z, Adamon, brochure entitled "Adamon (Dibromidhydrozimmtsäureborneolester) [sic]," 1.

35. See Ahlheim, *Der Traum vom Schlaf im 20. Jahrhundert*, 254.

36. Andretta-Purtschert, *Zur Entwicklungsgeschichte der Hypnotika und Sedativa*, 118.

37. López-Muñoz, Ucha-Udabe, and Alamo, "History of Barbiturates," 322, 329.

38. López-Muñoz, Ucha-Udabe, and Alamo, "History of Barbiturates," 333.

39. Shorter, *Before Prozac*, 19.

40. Müller-Jahncke, Friedrich, and Meyer, *Arzneimittelgeschichte*, 145; Shorter, *Before Prozac*, 306; Kinzler, *Das Joch des Schlafs*, 197; Ahlheim, *Der Traum vom Schlaf im 20. Jahrhundert*, 243. See also Schmitz, *Geschichte der Pharmazie*, 482.

41. Weber, *Die Entwicklung der Psychopharmakologie*, 101.

42. Anders, "Veronal."

43. López-Muñoz, Ucha-Udabe, and Alamo, "History of Barbiturates," 333.

44. "Das Mittel erzeugt ein fast natürliches Schlafbedürfnis" and is "Grundbedingung zur Erzeugung eines natürlichen Veronalschlafes" but "das Zittern während des Schlafes muss als künstlicher Schüttelfrost aufgefasst werden" (BAL, 166/8, Pharma, Produkte A-Z, Veronal, 1903-8, brochure "I," 6).

45. "vollkommen ruhigen, traumlosen, dem physiologischen Schlaf gleichenden, mehrstündigen Schlaf" (BAL, 166/8, Pharma, Produkte A-Z, Veronal, 1903-8, "neues Hypoticum").

46. "frisch und ohne das Gefühl einer Benommenheit erwachen" (BAL, 166/8, Pharma, Produkte A-Z, Veronal, 1903-8, brochure "I," 6).

47. BAL, 166/8, Pharma, Produkte A-Z, Veronal, 1903-8, brochure "I," 6.

48. "Joseph von Mering (1849-1908)," *Nature* 164, no. 4182 (1949): 1076. Mering's first name is spelled with both "ph" and "f" in the sources. I follow his choice to use "f."

49. Fischer and Mering, "Ueber eine neue Klasse von Schlafmitteln," 97.

50. Fischer and Mering, 97: "schlaferregende[] Wirkung."

51. Anders, "Veronal."

52. According to Ruth Anders, "der physiologische Chemiker Sigmund Fränkel verglich ihre Strukturen, suchte nach 'hypnophoren' Gemeinsamkeiten, war bemüht, 'toxiophore' Strukturelemente zu eliminieren und skizzierte schließlich einen hypothetischen Bauplan für ein 'ideales Schlafmittel': ein an einem Kohlenstoffatom mit zwei Etylgruppen beladener, ansonsten physiologisch völlig indifferenter Kern" ("Veronal," n.p.). While Fränkel did not consider the core, Mering proposed to use urea, which did not come with a physiological effect and had been barely researched until this moment.

53. Fischer and Mering, "Ueber eine neue Klasse von Schlafmitteln," 97.

54. Fischer and Mering, "Ueber eine neue Klasse von Schlafmitteln," 97.

55. Fischer and Mering's article mentions "testing on humans" ("Prüfung am Menschen") (100). Albrecht Renner explains that such testing was carried out in asylums by default, as its residents provided a constituency that was not typically able to opt out, especially as psychiatrists were keen on having restful patients. See Renner, *Schlafmittel-Therapie*, 22.

56. Fischer and Mering, "Ueber eine neue Klasse von Schlafmitteln," 100-101.

57. Anders, "Veronal."

58. According to Abel Bouchard, "Le corps fabrique une substance qui accumulée produirait le sommeil" (qtd. in Piéron, *Le problème physiologique du sommeil*, 397). On fatigue substances, see the extensive discussion in the Claparède section of chapter 1.

59. Kleitman, review of Piéron's *Le problème physiologique du sommeil*, qtd. in Kroker, *The Sleep of Others*, 162; Kroker, *The Sleep of Others*, 162. For a hagiographic account, see Gottesmann, *Henri Piéron and Nathaniel Kleitman*.

60. See Piéron, *Le problème physiologique du sommeil*. Piéron extracted this chemical structure from a dog's brain after the test animal had fallen prey to fatal exhaustion. He induced this state of exhaustion by way of a prolonged period of "enforced wakefulness." Then, he injected the chemical structure extracted from the dead dog (Piéron called it "hypnotoxins") into another dog. This other dog would then also die. Even though this experiment seemed to underwrite the existence of fatigue substances, Piéron tied it to a modification of Claparède's theory. On the intellectual exchange (and fraught friendship) of Piéron and Claparède, see Kroker, *The Sleep of Others*, 165.

61. See, for example, Mingazzini, "Klinischer und anatomisch-pathologischer Beitrag," 228.

62. Economo could not have used the concept a biological clock proper, even if he relied on ideas that came close, because this concept only originated much later. On biological clocks in sleep research, see Webb, "Sleep as a Biological Rhythm." For an overview of the history of melatonin in the context of research into the pineal gland from the 1950s to the 1990s, see Turek, "Melatonin."

63. Bouchard qtd. in Piéron, *Le problème physiologique du sommeil*, 397.

64. Anders, "Veronal."

65. The author here, one Dr. Sachse, is referring to Paranoval, the successor of Veronal (BAL, 166/8, Pharma, Produkte A–Z, Veronal, 1909-29, "Das neue Schlafmittel 'Paranoval': Aus dem Sanatorium Ulbrichshöhe [Chefarzt: San.-Rat. Dr. Woelm]," 1).

66. "Nach unseren heutigen Anschauungen wird der Schlaf durch gewisse Stoffwechselprodukte, die sog. Ermüdungsstoffe, hervorgerufen: das idealste Schlafmittel wäre daher jedenfalls ein synthetisch hergestellter chemischer Körper, dessen Constitution genau mit derjenigen dieser Ermüdungsstoffe übereinstimmte. Da uns aber die Zusammensetzung des letzteren noch absolut unbekannt ist, so sind wir auf andere Körper angewiesen. . . . Unter diesen steht mit an erster Stelle das im Jahre 1903 von Emil Fischer und J.v. Mering hergestellte und in die Therapie eingeführte Veronal" (BAL, 166/8, Pharma, Produkte A–Z, Veronal, 1903-1908, document 2696: draft for a brochure on Veronal and Veronal-Natrium, typescript with edits and comments in pencil, ink, and red color, ca. 1908).

67. See BAL, 271/2.1, Dr. Ernst Lomnitz personal file, object 89.

68. The name also made it possible to distinguish Veronal easily from a plethora of existing soporifics. These drugs, most of which had been launched prior to the existence of a trademark registry, still sported chemical names such as "Paraldehyd" or clumsy abbreviations of their chemical names such as "Sulfonal," which clearly betrayed its origin in diethylsulfondimethylmethan. The company had already tested this marketing strategy with the previously developed soporific Hedonal. The name Hedonal (1898) implies that patients would take the drug with joy, as most physicians would have guessed in an instant, given their predominantly humanistic education with countless hours of instruction in both Latin and Greek.

69. See López-Muñoz, Ucha-Udabe, and Alamo, "History of Barbiturates," 332.

70. See Hoffert, "Warum 'Veronal'?," 144-45.

71. Benjamin, "Das Passagen-Werk," 235: "Heute nisten in den Firmennamen die Phantasien, welche man ehemals im Sprachschatz der 'poetischen' Vokabeln sich thesauriert dachte."

72. See Wegmann, *Dichtung und Warenzeichen*, 61-62: "Im projektiven Akt der Markenbildung werden Dinge mit Eigenschaften ausgestattet, über die sie per se nicht verfügen, um so die Bindung des Subjekts an [die] Waren zu ermöglichen."

73. See Hellmann, *Fetische des Konsums*, 11, and Weyand, *Poetik der Marke*, 9.

74. Weber, *Die Entwicklung der Psychopharmakologie*, 96.

75. Huelsenbeck, *En avant Dada*, 33-34: "Kultur kann man feierlich als den Form gewordenen Geist eines Volkes . . . , aber auch als Kompensationserscheinung, als Verbeugung vor einem unsichtbaren Richterstuhl, als Veronal für das Gewissen bezeichnen."

76. On modes of administration, see Müller-Jahncke, Friedrich, and Meyer, *Arzneimittelgeschichte*, 22-34. See also Jorek, *Das Pulver als Arzneiform*.

77. Healy, *Creation of Psychopharmacology*, 377. Viagra is Healy's example.

78. See Weber, *Die Entwicklung der Psychopharmakologie*, 86.

79. See Müller-Jahncke, Friedrich, and Meyer, *Arzneimittelgeschichte*, 32. The term finally designated "Komprimate mit hochwirksamen Arzneistoffen in konzentrierter Form" (32).

80. See Weber, *Die Entwicklung der Psychopharmakologie*, 93. For example, the Erlangen-based entrepreneur Isidor Rosenthal ventured into this new segment of the market. After the end of the Franco-Prussian War, he transferred his method for the industrial filling of cartridges with ammunition to medicinal products, a strategy that was internationally successful, as Weber remarks: "Der Durchbruch der Tablette als Nachfolger der herkömmlichen Tropfen, Pulver, Decote oder Arzneiweine erfolgte aber erst 1884 nach der Patentierung der 'tabloids' des englischen Herstellers Sir Henry Solomon Wellcome . . . auf der technologischen Basis einer 1873 von Remington entwickelten Preßmaschine" (93).

81. See Kinzler, *Das Joch des Schlafs*, 196.

82. BAL, 166/8, Pharma, Produkte A-Z, Sulfonal: Bayer, Riedel, Schering und Hofmann & Schoeten communiqué (1888).

83. "Unter der sehr bezeichnenden Überschrift 'Die Tablettenseuche,'" 389. This article quotes a Dr. Zehden in *Berliner Tageblatte*, who writes that the "schlafbringenden Mittel . . . neuerdings fast ausschließlich in Tablettenform genommen werden. Sie werden von allen Schichten der Bevölkerung nicht nur gegen die durch das Großstadtleben geschädigten und angestrengten Nerven angewendet, sondern gegen alle möglichen Schmerzen und fieberhaften Erkrankungen, bei den sie häufig direkt Schaden anwenden." Clippings and notes commenting on the ensuing debate are preserved in BAL, 166/8, Pharma, Produkte A-Z, Veronal, 1909-29.

84. Detail in an advertisement brochure for a broad range of soporifics and sedatives, ca. late 1920s (BAL, 195 D: Sedativa und Soporifica). Note that by this historical moment, the tablet form had become the standard method of distribution and depiction of soporifics in general. In fact, these images were already being replaced by increasingly evocative images that could do without the materiality of the product altogether. For contextual imagery, see Ulrich, *"Wirkungen, die an Wunder grenzen."*

85. "Der laugige Geschmack wird von den meisten Patienten als süßlich charakterisiert: es resultiert ein unangenehmer, bittersüßlicher Geschmack" (Winternitz, *"Über Veronalnatrium"*, 2.) A private print of this article is preserved in BAL, 166/8, Pharma, Produkte A-Z, Veronal, 1903-8.

86. "leicht wie Bonbons gegessen warden" ("Im 'Bulletin de la Société Royale de Pharmacie de Bruxelles'"). An annotated clipping is preserved in BAL, 166/8, Pharma, Produkte A-Z, Veronal, 1903-8. See also "Unter der sehr bezeichnenden

Überschrift 'Die Tablettenseuche,'" 388: "Daß Kinder durch sie [the pills] zum Naschen verleitet warden."

87. "Veronaltabletten mit Kakao" ("Im 'Bulletin de la Société Royale de Pharmacie de Bruxelles'").

88. "Gesundheitsrat."

89. The Rolling Stones, "Mother's Little Helper," track 1, *Aftermath* (UK version), 1966, 0:17-0:26. Also quoted in Moser, *Psychotropen*, 11.

90. Healy, *Creation of Psychopharmacology*, 377.

91. Rose, "Neurochemical Selves," 58. Rose discusses antidepressants (selective serotonin reuptake inhibitors—SSRIs—such as Xanax, Prozac, and Zoloft).

92. Rose, "Neurochemical Selves," 58.

93. BAL, 195 D: Sedativa und Soporifica: "In der heutigen, unruhig hastenden Zeit, bei der erhöhten Inanspruchnahme aller geistigen und körperlichen Fähigkeiten tritt an den Arzt häufiger die Notwendigkeit heran, seinen Patienten, gleich welcher sozialen Stellung, ein Beruhigungs- oder Schlafmittel zu verordnen. So vielseitig auch die Ursachen dafür sein mögen, von der einfachen Agrypnie und Unruhe bis zu den schwersten Erregungszuständen, so vielgestaltig, so individualisierend muß auch die Behandlung sein."

94. Merck Inc. communication qtd. by Weber, *Die Entwicklung der Psychopharmakologie*, 108.

95. Wimmer, *"Wir haben fast immer was Neues,"* 331.

96. On the number of reviews, see Weber, *Die Entwicklung der Psychopharmakologie*, 108. He refers to sources in the Merck Corporate Archive. On the positive reviews, see BAL, 166/8, Pharma, Produkte A-Z, Veronal, 1903-8, brochure "II." For the 1909 bibliography, see "Verzeichnis der Veronal-Literatur: Zusammengestellt im Mai 1909" (BAL, 166/8, Pharma, Produkte A-Z, Veronal, 1909-29).

97. "Ein ideales Schlafmittel."

98. "Mit Ihren Reden haben Sie ihn damals ganz irrsinnig gemacht . . . er hat ihn zu sehr geliebt . . . wie er es in der Zeitung gelesen hat, hat er sich eingeschlossen . . . heute mittags . . . und jetzt haben wir ihn gefunden . . . Veronal" (*Die Schlafwandler*, 363). The scene occurs in the second of the three novels forming the *Schlafwandler* trilogy, first published as *Die Schlafwandler: Esch oder die Anarchie 1903* (1931). Two things are significant here: first, the suicide occurs in the same year in which Veronal was introduced. Second, the suicide of Harry Köhler does not result from an accidental overdose. Rather, it is directly related to the denunciation of Harry's past same-sex relationship with a wealthy and glamorous businessman, which has been reported in a newspaper. I do not discuss Broch's intriguing book in more detail, since he draws on a different conceptual framework from one the authors I focus on use. For a recent study in English, see Herold, "Paradox of Time."

99. Wimmer, *Wir haben fast immer was Neues*, 328.

100. "Erscheint es infolge der früheren bedingten allgemeinen Freiverkäuflich-

keit und der späteren freien Verkäuflichkeit des Veronals im Handverkauf der Apotheken wohl verständlich, dass auch jetzt noch von Seiten der Ärzte hin & wieder die Verordnung in Form eines Rezeptes nicht für erforderlich erachtet wird . . . , so kann es gegenwärtig keinem Zweifel unterliegen, dass Veronal und alle stark wirkenden Arzneimittel . . . nur auf jedesmalig für die einzelne Abgabe erneutes Rezept verabfolgt werden dürfen" (BAL, 166/8, Pharma, Produkte A-Z, Veronal, 1903-08, document: Sächsisches Ministerium des Innern, "Behandlung von Veronal-Rezepten," July 19, 1905).

101. See documents in BAL, 166/8, Pharma, Produkte A-Z, Veronal, 1909-29.

102. See documents in BAL, 166/8, Pharma, Produkte A-Z, Medinal. A 1918 newspaper clipping from the *Apotheker-Zeitung* (archive number BA1b) addresses this matter directly. The paper first quotes a statement by the police and then offers a comment that points out a gap in the law: "Es ist festgestellt worden, daß in hiesigen Apotheken mehrfach Medinal (Veronal-Natrium . . .) ohne Vorlage einer ärztlichen Verordnung abgegeben und von den Empfängern wiederholt zu Selbstmordversuchen verwendet worden ist. Die Apothekenvorstände werden daran erinnert, daß Medinal wie Veronal erstmalig nur auf ärztliche Verordnung abgegeben werden darf." Then the paper comments: "Eine gesetzliche Verpflichtung, die Abgabe von Medinal von der Vorlegung einer ärztlichen Anweisung abhängig zu machen, besteht jedoch nicht, auch kann eine Bestrafung wegen freihändiger Abgabe von Medinal nach dem Wortlaut des Ministerial-Erlasses vom 22. Juni 1896 . . . nicht erfolgen. Durch Ministerial-Erlaß vom 29. Februar 1908 wurde in das Verzeichnis der dem Handverkaufe entzogenen Arzneimittel Veronalum . . . eingefügt, nicht aber das Natriumsalz, das Medinal."

103. Weber, *Die Entwicklung der Psychopharmakologie*, 103. Moreover, this risk was exacerbated because women preferred soporifics as a suicide method, a preference only otherwise demonstrated by male physicians and pharmacists. See Flury, "Statistik der Vergiftungen," 56.

104. Eduard Birlo (1884-1943) has left few traces in the history of photography and cannot be regarded as a household name. The information we have suggest he was active in Berlin from the 1910s to the 1940s. He frequently contributed to illustrated magazines (especially artistic nudes, photos of "problematic" women like alcoholics, and staged crime scenes). In his day-to-day business, Birlo seems to have courted the upper classes, for example, by advertising his services as a portrait photographer in *Deutsches Adelsblatt* (see, e.g., *Deutsches Adelsblatt* 51 [1933], n.p.).

105. Anders, "Veronal."

Chapter 3. Dangerously Glamorous

1. *FE* refers to the 1925 German edition of Schnitzler's novella, while *E* refers to the 2003 English translation. Other translations are my own, unless noted otherwise.

2. BAL, 166/8, Pharma, Produkte A-Z, Veronal, 1924-26, doc. 5224, November 22, 1924. The document is signed by Dr. Lomnitz and Dr. Peiser. I would like to very much thank the archivists at Bayer in Leverkusen. Without their extraordinary openness and support, this chapter could not have been written.

3. Freud to Schnitzler, May 14, 1922, in Freud, "Briefe an Arthur Schnitzler," 96-97; Pottbeckers, "Hatte Leutnant Gustl Hunger?," 85; Cohn, *Transparent Minds*; Schmid, *Elemente der Narratologie*; Niehaus, "Zur Vorgeschichte des 'inneren Monologs.'" Freud's theories of hysteria have been discussed with regard to *Fräulein Else*, for example, in Bronfen, "1924, October." For a general overview of the relations between Freud and Schnitzler (and their works), see Worbs, *Nervenkunst*, Perlmann, *Der Traum in der literarischen Moderne*, 32-62, Thomé, *Autonomes Ich und "Inneres Ausland*," and Thomé, "Die Beobachtbarkeit des Psychischen."

4. Lukas and von Keitz, "'Stimme' und 'Partitur'"; Gess, "Intermedialität Reconsidered"; Gomes, *Gedankenlesemaschinen*; Morris, "Der vollständige innere Monolog"; Cohn, *Transparent Minds*, 232-46; Bronfen, "Weibliches Sterben an der Kultur"; Matthias, "Arthur Schnitzler's *Fräulein Else*"; Brandstetter, "Ökonomie und Vergeudung"; Caspari, "Durchkreuzungen des zeitgenössischen Hysterie-Diskurses"; Neymeyr, "*Fräulein Else*"; Lukas, *Das Selbst und das Fremde*; Thomé, "Die Beobachtbarkeit des Psychischen"; Aurnhammer, *Arthur Schnitzlers intertextuelles Erzählen*; Schößler, "Börse und Begehren"; Tacke, *Schnitzlers "Fräulein Else."* Klinger, "Veronal Sleep," a version of this chapter published in 2024, does not take up comparisons or a theoretical consideration of the interior monologue. The chapter contains the definitive version of my thinking about the subject. I would like to thank the anonymous reviewers of the article for their transformative feedback.

5. Fliedl, *Arthur Schnitzler*, 105.

6. Herzberg, *White Market Drugs*.

7. De Quincey, *Confessions of an English Opium-Eater and Other Writings*, 77. De Quincey's understanding of agency differs slightly from the currently prevailing notions of it propagated especially by the work of Bruno Latour.

8. For Schnitzler's medical writings, see his *Medizinische Schriften*. For scholarship on Schnitzler's medical writing, see Gross-Elixmann, *Poetologie und Epistemologie*, Herzog, "'Medizin ist eine Weltanschauung,'" Otis, *Membranes*, 119-47, Thomé, *Autonomes Ich und "Inneres Ausland*," 598-722, and Worbs, *Nervenkunst*. This scholarship reconstructs Schnitzler's medical training and his ongoing practice, unpacks his relationship to contemporary psychiatry and psychoanalysis, tracks his literary transformations of clinical accounts (for example, hysteria, tuberculosis, paranoia, and syphilis), uncovers the cross-fertilization among practices such as hypnosis, and illuminates the function of "epistemic genres" such as the medical review and the case history. See Pomata, "The Medical Case Narrative," and Pethes and Richter, *Medizinische Schreibweisen*.

Pharmacological and medicinal substances appear in frequently in Schnitzler,

Medizinische Schriften, such as the review of Unverricht's *Über moderne Fieberbehandlung* (1887), the review of Erlenmeyer's *Die Morphiumsucht und ihre Behandlung* (1888), the editorial "Silvesterbetrachungen" (1889), the review of Semmola's *Vorlesungen über experimentelle Pharmakologie* (1890) and in literary works such as the drama *Der Ruf des Lebens* (1906) and the novellas *Der Mörder* (1911), *Traumnovelle* (1926), and *Fräulein Else*. The only scholar who has considered this topic so far identifies only three reviews that thematize pharmacological questions, but these themes are much more rampant in Schnitzler's work. See Gross-Elixmann, *Poetologie und Epistemologie*, 73.

9. The chapter reevaluates this discussion in the sections titled "Does Else Wake Up Again?" and "Ending and the Interior Monologue." For the controversy in scholarship, see Scheible, "Arthur Schnitzler," 28–29, Tebben, "Selbstmörderinnen in der deutschen Literatur," and Aurnhammer, *Arthur Schnitzlers intertextuelles Erzählen*, 167.

10. On sexual hygiene in *Der Reigen*, see Otis, *Membranes*, 119–47. Eugenics and euthanasia are related topics that come up briefly in texts such as *Der Weg ins Freie* (1908) and *Professor Bernhardi* (1912).

11. See Weber, *Die Entwicklung der Psychopharmakologie*, 101.

12. On Benjamin's experiments with hashish, see Benjamin, "Hashish in Marseilles," and Benjamin, "Main Features of My Second Impression of Hashish," "Surrealism," 216, and "Hashish, Beginning of March, 1930."

13. "I slept so badly last night. Of course it's because it's almost that time of the month. That's also why I have cramps in my legs. Today's the third of September. So probably on the sixth. I'll take some Veronal tonight. Oh, I won't become addicted to it" (*FE*, 14; *E*, 196). The link between Veronal and menstrual pain has been noted by Rabelhofer, *Symptom, Sexualität, Trauma*, 202.

14. See Svevo, *Edizione critica delle opere di Italo Svevo*, 3:368–69, 393.

15. As in Schnitzler's case, Bayer took issue with the novel *Die Kwannon von Okadera* by Ludwig Wolff, first published in installments in the *Berliner Illustrirte Zeitung* [sic]. Here, a "glass tube with ten pills of Veronal" ["Glasröhre mit zehn Veronal-Tabletten"] serves, in the words of Bayer's case officers Dr. Krüger and Dr. Lomnitz, as "an ideal tool for suicides" ["als ideales Mittel für Selbstmörder"]. Bayer's employees further state that they "would love to go without this involuntary advertising, in the interest of Veronal." They also suggest: "Perhaps one of your men might seize on the opportunity to call on the publishing house Ullstein or the editor in charge, Kurt Korff—Charlottenburg, in order to remind him that such an appraisal of a medicinal product for illegal purposes goes too far." [Dr. Krüger and Dr. Lomnitz "möchten im Interesse von Veronal liebend gern auf diese unfreiwillige Reklame verzichten. Vielleicht nimmt einer Ihrer Herren Gelegenheit, einmal beim Verlag Ullstein vorzusprechen oder bei dem verantwortlichen Redakteur Kurt Korff—Charlottenburg, um ihn darauf aufmerksam zu machen, dass derartige Anpreisung

eines Medikaments zu ungesetzlichen Zwecken doch etwas weit geht"] (BAL, 166/8, Pharma, Produkte A-Z, Veronal, 1909-1929, doc. 477, September 16, 1920).

16. "von dieser Anti-Propaganda für unser Präparat doch in Zukunft lieber abzusehen und sich für seine Helden oder Heldinnen, die er aus diesem oder jenem Grunde in ein besseres Jenseits befördern will, eine andere Todesart auszusuchen und den Hinweis auf Veronal in einer vielleicht nötig werdenden zweiten Auflage unbedingt zu streichen" (BAL, 166/8, Pharma, Produkte A-Z, Veronal, 1924-26, doc. 5224, November 22, 1924).

17. *Traumnovelle* reports three such incidents, all of which are relayed by press reports: a poisoning with mercury (452), a first anonymous poison (467), and a second anonymous poison: "Fridolin . . . picked up an evening paper and read a few lines here and there, just like he had in another coffeehouse the night before: . . . Today a lady poisoned herself in an upscale hotel in the inner city. The remarkably beautiful lady had arrived there a few days ago and registered as Baroness D" (494). The novella then refers to this event as "morphine poisoning" (498), even though it reflects on the fact that the hero Fridolin is making up at least parts of his statement.

18. See Paul Czinner, dir., *Fräulein Else*, silent film, 90 min. (Berlin: Poetic Film Co., 1929). The film used to be available on YouTube but was removed in 2022. On the film version of the novella, see Tacke, *Schnitzlers "Fräulein Else" und die Nackte Wahrheit*.

19. The described events take place on September 3, 1896. See Bronfen, "1924, October," 738.

20. This observation builds on and complicates studies that have discussed anachronisms in *Fräulein Else* with special attention to gender roles. See Steinlechner, "*Fräulein Else*."

21. Schnitzler's archive of newspaper clippings mostly deals with the critical reception of his work, while he commonly jots down notes on his readings of the press in his diaries. On his practices, see Bellettini, "Das 'Handbuch des perfekten Rezensenten.'" For a general account of the newspaper clipping as a material object, see Heesen, *Der Zeitungsausschnitt*.

22. "17/5 (Feiertag.) Notiz in der N. Fr. Pr.: 'Die dreißigjährige Private Stephanie Bachrach nahm . . . etc. Morphin und Veronal . . . gestorben. . . . Die Ursache der That ist unbekannt.'" (Schnitzler, *Tagebuch*, May 17, 1917, https://schnitzler-tagebuch.acdh.oeaw.ac.at/entry__1917-05-17.html). The importance of this diary entry for *Fräulein Else* has been documented in scholarship, although Veronal plays no role in these studies. See especially Karsten, "Ein Urbild '*Fräulein Elses*'?"

23. For details of Schnitzler's friendship with Stephanie Bachrach, see Karsten, "Ein Urbild '*Fräulein Elses*'?"

24. Case studies have received significant scholarly attention in recent years. See, for example, Forrester, *Thinking in Cases*, Pethes and Düwell, *Fall—Fallgeschichte—*

Fallstudie, Class, "Medical Case Histories as Genre," Pomata, "The Medical Case Narrative," Pethes, "Telling Cases," and Mülder-Bach and Ott, *Was Der Fall Ist*. Notorious examples of Schnitzler's attention to controversial topics include the novella *Leutnant Gustl* (1900), which sparked an outcry in the military, and the play *Professor Bernhardi* (1912), which explores Austrian antisemitism and was banned until the collapse of the Habsburg empire.

25. To strengthen this aspect, Schnitzler explicitly transposed *Fräulein Else* from third-person free indirect speech to first-person interior monologue when he was moving from the plotting to the writing stage. The August 12, 1921, draft (ELS_S^{T}2) contains no references to Veronal and is narrated in the third person; the 1922 draft (ELS_H1), begun on December 14, 1922, contains Veronal and is narrated in the first person. For the chronology of the drafts, see https://www.schnitzler-edition.net/chronologie/9257#. See also Aurnhammer, *Arthur Schnitzlers intertextuelles Erzählen*, 176.

26. For a more complete account of these intertextual patterns, see Aurnhammer, *Arthur Schnitzlers intertextuelles Erzählen*, 166–213.

27. "Ich werde Veronal trinken. Nur einen kleinen Schluck, dann werde ich gut schlafen. . . . Aber ich könnte auch vors Hotel gehen [. . .] und dann weiter, weiterflattern über die Wiese, in den Wald, hinaufsteigen, immer höher, bis auf den Cimone hinauf, mich hinlegen, einschlafen, erfrieren. Geheimnisvoller Selbstmord einer jungen Dame der Wiener Gesellschaft. Nur mit einem schwarzen Abendmantel bekleidet, wurde das schöne Mädchen an einer unzugänglichen Stelle des Cimone della Pala tot aufgefunden . . . " (*FE*, 109-10). Several other passages could also have been selected to support this argument, e.g., "Wie uns aus San Martino gemeldet wird, hat sich dort im Hotel Fratazza ein beklagenswerter Unfall ereignet. Fräulein Else T., ein neunzehnjähriges bildschönes Mädchen, Tochter des bekannten Advokaten . . . Natürlich würde es heißen, ich hätte mich umgebracht aus unglücklicher Liebe oder weil ich in der Hoffnung war. Unglückliche Liebe, ah nein." ["According to sources from San Martino today, a lamentable accident occurred today at the Hotel Fratazza: Fräulein Else T., a beautiful nineteen-year-old girl, the daughter of a well-known attorney. . . . Of course they'll say I killed myself over an unhappy love affair or because I was pregnant. Unhappy love affair! Unfortunately not"] (*FE*, 17; *E*, 198).

28. "Die edle Tochter verkauft sich für den geliebten Vater und hat am End' noch ein Vergnügen davon. . . . Wenn ich einmal heirate, werde ich es wahrscheinlich billiger tun. Ist es denn gar so schlimm? Die Fanny hat sich am Ende auch verkauft. Sie hat mir selber gesagt, daß sie sich vor ihrem Manne graust. Nun, wie wär's, Papa, wenn ich mich heute Abend versteigerte? Um dich vor dem Zuchthaus zu retten. Sensation —!" ["The noble daughter sells herself for her beloved father, and in the end really enjoys it. . . . If I marry some day, I'll probably do it for less. Is that really so bad? Fanny as much as told herself in the end. She told me herself

that her husband makes her shudder. Well, how about it, Papa? What if I just auctioned myself off this evening? To save you from prison? What a sensation!"] (*FE*, 29–30; *E*, 204).

29. Bronfen, "Weibliches Sterben an der Kultur," 468. Schnitzler was quite familiar with Flaubert and even rewrote the plot of *Madame Bovary* in the story *Die Toten schweigen* (1897). See Aurnhammer, *Arthur Schnitzlers intertextuelles Erzählen*, 25–52.

30. For a theory of glamour, see Thrift, "The Material Practices of Glamour."

31. "Après les rêveuses passionnées et romanesques de la Restauration, étaient venues les joyeuses de l'époque impériale, convaincues de la réalité du plaisir; puis voilà qu'apparaissait une transformation nouvelle de cet éternel féminin, un être raffiné, de sensibilité indécise, d'âme inquiète, agitée, irrésolue, qui semblait avoir passé déjà par tous les narcotiques dont on apaise et dont on affole les nerfs, par le chloroforme qui assome, par l'éther et par la morphine qui fouaillent le rêve, éteignent les sens et endorment les émotions" (Maupassant, *Notre Cœur*, 56).

32. See "Selbstmordversuch oder Unfall des Filmschauspielers Max Linder," *Neue Freie Presse*, February 23, 1924. See the clipping in BAL, 166/8, Pharma, Produkte A-Z, Veronal, 1909–29. The clipping in Bayer's corporate archive notes "Neue Freie Presse, Wien," with Wien (Vienna) being underlined in red.

33. Similarly, the interior monologue *in Leutnant Gustl* has been read as an expression of the collective *Mittelbewusstsein* (best translated as subconsciousness or preconsciousness) in fin-de-siècle Vienna. The term "Mittelbewusstsein" is found in Schnitzler's posthumously published writings, where he critiques psychoanalysis and seeks to offer corrections to what he perceives as shortcomings in Freud's approach. "*Mittelbewusstsein*" is Schnitzler's attempt to assign greater value to semiconscious states that have the potential to become conscious at any moment, an idea he prefers to Freud's notion of the inaccessible unconscious. "*Mittelbewusstsein*" differs from the individual nature of the unconscious because it highlights collective patterns of thought and behavior; it pinpoints the "social history of semiconscious thought," as Walter Müller-Seidel (*Arztbilder im Wandel*, 40) puts it. Horst Thomé stresses the ethical dimension of Schnitzler's preference for *Mittelbewusstsein*, explaining that Schnitzler regards grappling with elusive dimensions of the self via introspection as a quasi-heroic act of overcoming affective resistances to facing the truth. This is closely related to the task of literature, which Schnitzler views as an instrument able to confront "the recipient with the ethical appeal to make conscious what one is actually doing and thinking" ("Die Beobachtbarkeit des Psychischen," 61, 62).

34. Here I concur with Elisabeth Bronfen, who states that Else "is in complicity with the very cultural forces that weaken and injure her" ("1924, October," 740). The term "cruel optimism" alludes to Berlant, *Cruel Optimism*. Berlant argues that

"a relation of cruel optimism exists when something you desire is actually an obstacle to your flourishing" (1).

35. BAL, 166/8, Pharma, Produkte A–Z, Veronal, 1924–26, doc. 5224, November 22, 1924; Reents, "Suicidal Tendencies in Modern German Literature."

36. Flury, "Statistik der Vergiftungen," 56.

37. Reents, "Suicidal Tendencies in Modern German Literature."

38. Schnitzler penned these texts in the 1890s, when he served as the book review editor of the medical journals published under the aegis of his father, an acclaimed and ambitious laryngologist. In writing his reviews for practicing physicians, Schnitzler read and assessed what was new in the medical field, formulating for the first time many ideas to which he would return over and over during his career as a writer. See Herzog, "'Medizin ist eine Weltanschauung,'" 232. Herzog draws on hypnosis to discuss the notion of the individual vis-à-vis role-playing.

39. Schnitzler, "Rezension zu Erlenmeyer," 143.

40. "[Es] gibt mehr Heilmittel als früher, aber nicht im gleichen Maße mehr Heilungen" (Schnitzler, "Rezension zu Erlenmeyer," 142).

41. Between 1884 and 1887, Freud published five papers on cocaine. Notably, one of them was funded by the pharmaceutical giant Merck and one by the American pharmaceutical company Parke, Davis & Co. These papers are available in Freud, *Schriften über Kokain*.

42. "Das Morphium! Noch immer steht es weit oben an, und doch darf es zugleich als bestes Beispiel unserer Unzulänglichkeit gelten. Das Morphium, dieser souveräne Schmerzenstiller, ist allzu oft nur ein falscher Freund der Leidenden; es läßt sich seine Gefälligkeiten allzu teuer bezahlen, es fordert mit der Zeit die Freiheit, zuweilen auch das Leben. . . . Es steht aber kaum zu zweifeln, daß uns in der nächsten Zeit noch ähnliche Erkenntnisse werden beschieden sein. In manchen Giften, denen man nach unsäglichen Gedankenmühen ihre versteckte Heilkraft abzuringen verstand, wird der ursprüngliche Genius neu erwachen, und sie werden sich in ihrer wahren Gestalt der betrogenen Menschheit zeigen, als das, was sie sind: als Gifte" (Schnitzler, "Rezension zu Erlenmeyer," 142).

43. See Herlinghaus, "Towards a Cultural Pharmacology."

44. See Virilio, *A Landscape of Events*. Thanks go to Tom Levin for the hint.

45. See Schnitzler, *Gesammelte Werke in Einzelausgaben*, 1:1017.

46. "von Arzt zu Arzt, von Apotheker zu Apotheker" (*Der Mörder*, 348); "Er . . . suchte . . . nacheinander drei Ärzte auf, gab sich überall als einen von unerträglichen Schmerzen gepeinigten Kranken aus, der, seit Jahren an Morphium, gewöhnt, mit seinem Vorrat zu Ende gekommen sei, nahm die erbetenen Rezepte in Empfang, ließ sie in verschiedenen Apotheken anfertigen und fand sich . . . im Besitze einer Dosis, die er für seine Zwecke mehr als genügend halten durfte" (*Der Mörder*, 348).

47. Wharton, *The House of Mirth*, 281.

48. Davenport-Hines, *The Pursuit of Oblivion*, 259-60. Else's mediation about the amount of Veronal she has at her disposal offers a close equivalent to this analysis: "Gott sei Dank, daß ich die Pulver da habe. Das ist die einzige Rettung. Wo sind sie denn? Um Gottes willen, man wird sie mir doch nicht gestohlen haben. Aber nein, da sind sie ja. Da in der Schachtel. Sind sie noch alle da? Ja, da sind sie. Eins, zwei, drei, vier, fünf, sechs. Ich will sie ja nur ansehen, die lieben Pulver. Es verpflichtet ja zu nichts. Auch daß ich sie ins Glas schütte, verpflichtet ja zu nichts. Eins, zwei, - aber ich bringe mich ja sicher nicht um. Fällt mir gar nicht ein. Drei, vier, fünf—davon stirbt man auch noch lange nicht. Es wäre schrecklich, wenn ich das Veronal nicht mit hätte. Da müßte ich mich zum Fenster hinunterstürzen und dazu hätt' ich doch nicht den Mut. Aber das Veronal, - man schläft langsam ein, wacht nicht mehr auf, keine Qual, kein Schmerz. . . . Vorgestern habe ich auch ein Pulver genommen und neulich sogar zwei. Pst, niemandem sagen. Heut' werden es halt ein bißl mehr sein. Es ist ja nur für alle Fälle" (*FE*, 96-97). Else aestheticizes the Veronal suicide as a potential realization of her volition. She even swaps Veronal's official legal classification—"poison" (*FE*, 101, 130)—for the term "Medizin," a word that is "zweimal unterstrichen" and carries "drei Ausrufungszeichen" (*FE*, 101). Armed with this rhetoric of total control and safety, Else tries to bolster her agency: "Und wenn ich . . . keine Lust habe, mich umzubringen und nur schlafen will, dann trinke ich eben nicht das ganze Glas aus, sondern nur ein Viertel davon oder noch weniger. Ganz einfach. Alles habe ich in meiner Hand" (*FE*, 101).

49. See especially Scheible, "Arthur Schnitzler," 28-29. Scheible's calculation is inherently flawed because he does not reference historical debates and thus overlooks individualizing aspects such as gender, accumulation of the drug in the body, and individual idiosyncrasies in responding to the substance. For more on the dosage controversy in scholarship, see Tebben, "Selbstmörderinnen in der deutschen Literatur," and Aurnhammer, *Arthur Schnitzlers intertextuelles Erzählen*, 167.

50. Contemporary medical sources note that "als tödliche Dosis 10,0 anzusehen ist; eine höhere Dosis ist nur dreimal überstanden worden . . . Dosen von 8-9 g haben sich in einer Reihe von Fällen noch als tödlich erwiesen" (Renner, "Über Schlafmittel und ihre Wirkungen," 327). The dose of ten grams is also significant because it serves as the key reference for the judicial assessment of Veronal's toxicity. This goes back to a prominent case discussed countless times in the medical literature and amply documented in Bayer's corporate archives. In this case (which happened in the town of Holzminden in 1905), the assistant of a pharmacist mistook the name Veronal for Kamala, a fern extract. Instead of ten grams of fern extract, a man thus took ten grams of Veronal and died. In the wake of this incident, Veronal moved to the list of potent substances that were only sold on prescription. Other literary sources likewise refer to ten grams of Veronal as the lethal dose. For example, Bayer also took issue with the novel *Die Kwannon von Okadera* by Ludwig

Wolff, first published in installments in the *Berliner Illustrirte Zeitung* [*sic*], in which a "Glasröhre mit zehn Veronal-Tabletten" serves, in the words of Bayer's case officers Dr. Krüger and Dr. Lomnitz, "als ideales Mittel für Selbstmörder." See also Svevo, *Edizione critica delle opere di Italo Svevo*, 3:368-69, and BAL, 166/8, Pharma, Produkte A-Z, Veronal, 1909-1929, doc. 477, September 16, 1920.

51. In "Zur Kasuistik der Veronalvergiftung," one Bofinger writes in a widely read medical journal two years before *Fräulein Else* was published: "Es steht also fest, daß ein junger Mann sich durch Einnehmen von 4,5 g Veronal eine tödliche Vergiftung zugezogen hat. Der Fall erinnert an den von Rumpel mitgeteilten, bei dem derselbe Erfolg bei einer Dosis von 5 g eintrat. Ob diese großen Unterschiede der tödlichen Dosis die Folge der Verschiedenheit einzelner Präparate oder der individuellen Empfindlichkeit oder der verminderten Widerstandsfähigkeit oder aller zusammen sind, mag ich nicht zu entscheiden. . . . Für den praktischen Arzt läßt sich jedenfalls der Schluß ziehen, daß bei der Verschreibung von Veronal im Interesse des Kranken und des Arztes größte Vorsicht am Platze ist und daß es sich nicht empfiehlt, größere Mengen dieses Mittels nicht ganz zuverlässigen Personen in die Hände zu geben" (1518-19). The pharmaceutical industry—this time the pharmaceutical giant Merck—noted this publication and responded to it. The response in *Deutsche Medizinische Wochenschrift* sought to undermine Bofinger's observation by arguing that industry quality control ascertains that Veronal is always the same so that there can be no variations. See E. Merck, "Zur Kasuistik der Veronalvergiftung," 552.

52. Schnitzler indicates the amount of Veronal in units, not in grams. It thus remains unclear how much grams she ingests in total, especially because Else does not consume the drug in the form of standardized pills, but in the antiquated form of powder (which would make variations plausible). Else herself is uncertain whether the dose at her disposal is sufficient: "[P]erhaps I don t even have enough Veronal. How many packets does one need? Six I think. But ten is safer. I think I still have ten. Yes, that should be enough" (*FE*, 88; *E*, 235). In fact, she seems to have only six units left, but the interruptions of her count could also be interpreted as an incomplete interim conclusion: "Thank God I have the Veronal. That's the only way out. Oh God, they haven't been stolen? No, here they are. There, in the box. Are they all still here? Yes, they are. One, two, three, four, five, six. I just want to look at them, the precious powders. That doesn't commit me to anything. Even pouring them into the glass doesn't commit me to anything. One, two— but I won't kill myself. I'm certain of that. Wouldn't think of it. Three, four, five—that won't really kill anybody by a long shot. It would be terrible if I didn't have the Veronal with me. Then I'd have to throw myself from the window, and I wouldn't have the courage to do that. But with Veronal—you slowly go to sleep and just don't wake up anymore; no agony, no trouble. You lie down in bed, drink the whole thing in one gulp, dream, and then everything's over. The day before yesterday I took one

packet, and the other day I even took two" (*FE*, 97; *E*, 240). Moreover, given the long half period of the soporific, some of that earlier dose might have to be taken into account. All this means that the dose of Veronal ultimately Else ingests is hard to specify.

53. It is evident that the scene marks a caesura, because its construction parallels Else's disrobement in the music room in several regards: there Else is exposed to everyone's eyes, here she is removed from everyone's eyes; there, quotes from the partiture of Schumann's *Karneval* incorporate sound into the interior monologue, here the clunky onomatopoesis "Klirr, klirr" (130) incorporates sound; there, Else contends to be conscious despite having suffered a blackout, here she is somewhat conscious but contends that she is "bewußtlos" (130), even though she has just ingested the Veronal.

54. Schnitzler responds with scorn when Paul Czinner's film version of *Fräulein Else* shows this moment earlier in the plot, despite the expressed wishes of the author. In the film, Else takes in the Veronal before she leaves for the music room. Schnitzler is not amused by this change in the sequence of the scenes. In a letter to Clara Katharina Polaczek, he writes: "Der Einfall gegen den ich mich bei unserem ersten Gespräch (Czinner Mayer) gewendet hatte: dass Else 'Veronal' nimmt, ehe sie unbekleidet unter dem Mantel in die Halle geht—blieb bestehn" (Schnitzler, *Briefe 1913-1931*, 597). On differences between the novella and the film, see Hahn, *Verfilmte Gefühle*, 101-40, Kanzog, "Der innere Monolog in der Novelle und in der Verfilmung," Aurnhammer, *Arthur Schnitzler—Filmarbeiten*, and Ballhausen, *Die Tatsachen der Seele*.

55. My reading builds on their findings: Achim Aurnhammer discovers the intertextual references in the novella's ending; Michaela Perlmann constellates the text with Freud's theories and discusses Schnitzler's techniques for portraying dreams, concluding that the dream of flying relates primarily to a physiological cause. See Aurnhammer, "Selig, wer in Träumen stirbt," and Perlmann, *Der Traum in der literarischen Moderne*, 114-29. Other (often psychoanalytically inspired) readings are less convincing. They have, for example, approached the finale as a dream of asexual fusion with the father, as an oedipal wish fulfillment, or as a trauma-driven booty call. See Lange-Kirchheim, "Adoleszenz, Hysterie und Autorschaft in Arthur Schnitzlers Novelle *Fräulein Else*," Morse, "Decadence and Social Change," 49, and Rabelhofer, *Symptom, Sexualität, Trauma*, 225.

56. For the scene, see Wharton, *The House of Mirth*, 312-15.

57. "The doctor found a bottle of chloral. She had been sleeping badly for a long time, and she must haven taken an over-dose by mistake . . ." (Wharton, *The House of Mirth*, 316).

58. "Ich habe Veronal getrunken. Ich werde sterben. Aber es ist geradeso wie vorher. Vielleicht war es nicht genug . . ." (*FE*, 131).

59. The physician, moreover, senses characteristic changes in Else's pupils and face: "*It looks as though she were trying to open her eyes*" (*FE*, 132; *E,* 261; italics in the original). He also observes facial expressions: "*Look here, Cissy, doesn't it seem to you that she's smiling?*" (*FE*, 133; *E*, 262; italics in the orignal).

60. One might thus speculate whether Scheible's claim that Else was to reawaken emerged from sloppy editing. It is striking that Scheible's edition of the novella omits the paratext "Ende" that appears in the first printing of Schnitzler's *Fräulein Else*. See Schnitzler, "*Fräulein Else*," 620.

61. See Bachem, *Unsere Schlafmittel*, 7, and BAL, 166/8, Pharma, Produkte A–Z, Veronal, 1903-8, "Symptome und Behandlung der Veronalvergiftung," 1. Bayer's leaflet mentions only "tiefer Schlaf." Note that Else calls herself "bewußtlos" (*FE*, 130) right after ingesting the Veronal.

62. BAL, 166/8, Pharma, Produkte A–Z, Veronal, 1903-8, "Symptome und Behandlung der Veronalvergiftung," 1.

63. The references to lullabies were first observed by Aurnhammer, "Selig, wer in Träumen stirbt," 509-10.

64. Here, I allude to the medieval wordplay that reads the image ingrained in Turin's Veil of Veronica as the "vera icon" (true image), playing on the kitchen sink etymology that traces "Veronal" back to the Latin "verus" (true) and posits the drug as the "true" soporific. Of course, one could also read the word "Veronalica" as a plural form. The English translation simply gives "Veronal" (*E*, 263).

65. "'Else! Else!'
   Sie rufen von so weit! Was wollt Ihr denn? Nicht wecken. Ich schlafe ja so gut. Morgen früh. Ich träume und fliege. Ich fliege . . . fliege . . . fliege . . . schlafe und träume . . . und fliege . . . nicht wecken . . . morgen früh . . . ‚El . . . '
   Ich fliege . . . ich träume . . . ich schlafe . . . ich träu . . . träum—ich flie . . ."
   (*FE*, 136).

66. "Schlafe, träume, flieg, ich wecke/bald Dich auf und bin beglückt." This quotation has been identified but not given a sufficiently strong reading by Aurnhammer, *Arthur Schnitzlers intertextuelles Erzählen*, 213, and Aurnhammer, "Selig, wer in Träumen stirbt," 509-10. He argues that Else as a figure appears human and yet that she is entirely composed out of literary quotations. This reading is convincing, but it does not specifically apply to the ending of the text.

67. For Freud, dreams that involve flying (*Flugträume*) are part of an archetypal regression into pleasurable infantile experiences of movement. However, according to Michaela Perlmann, for the English psychologist Havelock Ellis, dreams that feature flying indicate "Atmungs- und Herzstörungen oder Anästhesie der Hautsensationen während des Schlafes" (*Der Traum in der literarischen Moderne*, 127). This somatic interpretation suggests reading the metaphors of movement and especially

the experience of flying as an effect of Veronal poisoning that will lead to a mental blackout and most likely to death. Perlmann does not comment on Veronal, but she stresses Ellis's general impact on Schnitzler's notion of how dreams work (*Der Traum in der literarischen Moderne*, 123).

68. Cohn, *Transparent Minds*, 232-46, here 232. For more recent literature, see Lukas and von Keitz, "'Stimme' und 'Partitur,'" Gess, "Intermedialität Reconsidered," Gomes, *Gedankenlesemaschinen*, and Morris, "Der vollständige innere Monolog."

69. According to Cohn's *Transparent Minds* three criteria especially stand out: first, interior monologues must adhere to a dramatic unity of time, since a simultaneity of experience and enunciation in the first-person present tense is constitutive for this form; second, they must legitimize a verbal showing of the mind in a mode of self-address and dramatize the act of locution, since the voice of the figure eclipses the voice of a narrator and thus eclipses the possibility of 'narration'; finally, they must do so with a minimum of declarative statement and instead indirectly suggest actions and changes of scenes, all filtered through the protagonist's thought quotations: "Since language-for-oneself is by definition the form of language in which speaker and listener coincide, the technique that imitates it in fiction can remain convincing only if it excludes all factual statements, all explicit report on present and past happenings" (226).

70. "In the early section he [Gustl] thinks at the rate of nine pages an hour, in a later section he speeds through three hours in only six pages. These irregularities, if deliberate, would indicate that Gustl's verbalizations are not continuous, hence that the ellipsis marks strewn through the text are literal indicators of time passing between thoughts" (Cohn, *Transparent Minds*, 240). It is thus perhaps not surprising that Cohn returns to the issue of narrative time in the interior monologue in "'I Doze and Wake,'" a much later essay, that again addresses the temporality of locution in Schnitzler's *Fräulein Else* (96-108, 99-100, 104-6). On the canonicity of this account of the interior monologue, see also Schmid, *Elemente der Narratologie*, and Niehaus, "Zur Vorgeschichte des 'inneren Monologs.'" For a critique from a Kittlerian perspective, see Niehaus, *"Ich, die Literatur, ich spreche . . . ,"* 136-52.

71. "Was habe ich denn getan? Was habe ich getan? Was habe ich getan? Ich falle um. Alles ist vorbei. Warum ist denn keine Musik mehr? Ein Arm schlingt sich um meinen Nacken. Das ist Paul. Wo ist denn der Filou? Da lieg ich. ‚Ha, ha, ha!' Der Mantel fliegt auf mich herab. Und ich liege da. Die Leute halten mich für ohnmächtig. Nein, ich bin nicht ohnmächtig. Ich bin bei vollem Bewußtsein. Ich bin hundertmal wach, ich bin tausendmal wach" (*FE*, 118).

72. See Cohn, *Transparent Minds*, 240-41.

73. Richard Beer-Hoffmann, *Der Tod Georgs*, 15.

74. Anders, "Veronal."

Chapter 4. Proust's Sleep Experiments

1. Parenthetical cites to *À la recherche du temps perdu* use the abbreviation *RTP* for the French 1987-89 Pléiade edition, and *ISOLT* for a recent English translation, *In Search of Lost Time*, edited by Christopher Prendergast. Occasionally, I correct translations as indicated. Uncredited translations are my own.

2. Tadié, *Proust*, 100. For guidance through the vast scholarship on Proust and dreams, see Kristeva, "Rêve," Kristeva, *Proust and the Sense of Time*, and Wiseman, "Waking to the Night."

3. Proust and Rivière, *Correspondance, 1914-1922*, 250-51. Published studies illuminate the metapoetic importance of sleep in the novel, examine the relation between sleep and the disorganization of time, offer insights into Proust's nocturnal writing and his insomnia, explore the social realities of sleep, analyze the nexus of sleep and gender, and demonstrate that sleep dissolves traditional notions of the self. See Barthes, "Longtemps, je me suis couché de bonne heure . . . ," Fülöp, *Proust, the One, and the Many*, Greaney, *Sleep and the Novel*, Nemoto, "Le sommeil proustien," Nordholt, "Le dormeur éveillé comme figure du moi proustien," Nordholt, "Proust and Subjectivity," Simon and Serça, "Sommeil," Simon, "The Formalist, the Spider, and the Phenomenologist," Yu, "La pensée du sommeil," Warning, "Supplementäre Individualität," and Déchanet-Platz, *L'écrivain, le sommeil et les rêves*. Greaney holds that Proust was the "very last [author] to be able to write 'innocently' of what we now know about the science of sleep" (*Sleep and the Novel*, 170). Likewise, the sleep sciences and the pharma industry are absent in Ollivier, *Proust et les sciences*, and Wright, *Du discours médical dans "À la recherche du temps perdu."*

4. On Proust's use of soporifics and his inverted sleep rhythm, see Mabin, "Sommeil et automédication de Marcel Proust," Mabin, "Proust ou la parole d'un insomniaque," and Mabin, *Le sommeil de Marcel Proust*. Proust had read texts such as Alfred Maury's *Le sommeil et les rêves* (1878). He was also indirectly familiar with several other important studies, such as those by Édouard Claparède—in this case due to a summary in Henri Bergson's *L'énergie spirituelle* (1919). Still, any account of what Proust might have known or read remains ultimately speculative; a reconstruction of Proust's readings and the furnishing of his mental library poses methodological challenges, as Caroline Szylowicz notes in "Proust's Reading." Proust was an avid reader, but he never collected books, and his library was discarded after his death. Proust's familiarity with period scientific discourse about sleep is apparent in the flaunting in *À la recherche du temps perdu* of arcane knowledge about the therapy of insomnia and the chemical composition of soporifics (see *RTP* 3:351).

5. Mabin, "Sommeil et automédication de Marcel Proust," 73. Up until recently,

however, many scholars have described sleep scenes as late additions, overlooking the fact that *À la recherche du temps perdu* continuously addresses sleep themes.

6. Nemoto, "Le sommeil proustien," 123; Yu, "La pensée du sommeil," 35-36; Nordholt, "Le dormeur éveillé comme figure du moi proustien," 540.

7. On sleep research after the invention of the EEG, see Kroker, *The Sleep of Others*, 255-324. For a history of the EEG, see Borck, *Brainwaves*.

8. Canguilhem, *On the Normal and the Pathological*, 209.

9. "Hé, monsieur, c'est que le mal seul fait remarquer et apprendre et permet de décomposer les mécanismes que sans cela on ne connaîtrait pas. Un homme qui chaque soir tombe comme une masse dans son lit et ne vit plus jusqu'au moment de s'éveiller et de se lever, cet homme-là songera-t-il jamais à faire, sinon de grandes découvertes, au moins de petites remarques sur le sommeil ? A peine sait-il s'il dort. Un peu d'insomnie n'est pas inutile pour apprécier le sommeil, projeter quelque lumière dans cette nuit" (*RTP* 3:51-52).

10. For an overview, see Fraisse, "Longtemps je me suis couché de bonne heure."

11. Traugott, *Die nervöse Schlaflosigkeit und ihre Behandlung*, 20-21, 83, 84 (to show that the neurasthenic half sleep is a widespread medical trope, I have quoted the definition of a random neurologist). For Proust's father's account see Proust and Ballet, *L'hygiène du neurasthénique*, 57. Proust and Ballet write about the perceived insomnia of the neurasthenic: "Parmi les malades qui en sont affectés, il en est qui, dès qu'ils sont couchés, s'endorment facilement, mais après quelques instants de sommeil ils s'éveillent tout à coup dans un état d'excitation qui persiste, quelques efforts qu'ils fassent pour se calmer; ils s'agitent, se retournent au lit, et ce n'est qu'à une heure avancée de la nuit ou aux approches du jour qu'ils parviennent à se rendormir" (57). Marcel Proust most likely provided a model for the "typical neurasthenic" which his father had in mind when writing the textbook. See Finn, "Health and Medicine."

12. Adorno, "Standort des Erzählers im zeitgenössischen Roman," 44.

13. For a persuasive account of Proust and reveries, which is derived from Proust's own comments and focuses on the nexus between reading and reverie, see Deschamps, "Rêverie." See also Freud, "Der Dichter und das Phantasieren."

14. Nordholt, "Le dormeur éveillé comme figure du moi proustien"; Blumenberg, *Höhlenausgänge*, 11-19.

15. Genette, *Narrative Discourse*, 46. Genette counts seven beginnings.

16. Nemoto, "Le sommeil proustien," 123; Yu, "La pensée du sommeil," 35-36; Nordholt, "Le dormeur éveillé comme figure du moi proustien," 540. Despite this research, Proust scholarship often remains oblivious to the formal role of the bedrooms, as in Wickers, *Chambres de Proust*. For a comprehensive discussion of bedrooms in Proust, see Hiramitsu, *Les chambres de la création dans l'œuvre de Marcel Proust*.

17. Bayard, *Le hors-sujet*.

18. The insight that Proust's self-description does not match the immanent poetics of his novel has been fundamental to Proust scholarship of the past decades. See Warning, "Erzählen im Paradigma," 190. For an even more comprehensive exposition, see Warning, *Marcel Proust*.

19. As Genette puts it, "It is always necessary to come back to that position, which is central even though eccentric" (*Narrative Discourse*, 45). The beginning of *La prisonnière* (*RTP* 3:519-20) modifies this pattern, as it begins with an awakening before waking up. Because Proust was unable to publish his novel in one go (as he had hoped), he also integrated reminiscences of the overture and sleep states at volume breaks. See, for example, the dozing Mme Cottard and the satirical discussion about the soporific Trional in the spillover of part 2 of *Sodome et Gomorrhe* in the original publication (*RTP* 3:350-53).

20. For a detailed account of Proust's patient history, see Bogousslavsky, "Marcel Proust's Lifelong Tour of the Parisian Neurological Intelligentsia," 133-35. For pertinent scholarship on the links between Proust as a patient and his writing, see especially Bizub, *Proust et le moi divisé*, 254, Yoshida, "Proust et la maladie nerveuse," and Fraisse, "Longtemps je me suis couché de bonne heure," 219.

21. Genette, *Narrative Discourse*, 43; Nordholt, "Proust and Subjectivity," 84.

22. The constitutive split of the narrative voice has given rise to an extensive body of scholarship in narratology. See Jongeneel, "Silencing the Voice in Narratology?," Weimar, "Wo und was ist der Erzähler?," and Hamburger, *Die Logik der Dichtung*, 111-54. For a concise summary of the debates on the narrative voice, Schmid, "Erzählstimme," esp. 134.

23. "Le Sujet Intermédiaire (qui est parfois l'Insomniaque): le *je* dont le relais est indispensable pour que le Narrateur se souvienne du Héros" (Muller, *Les voix narratives*, 8).

24. Barthes, "Longtemps, je me suis couché de bonne heure . . . ," 280. "Un paradoxe le définit bien: il est un sommeil qui peut être écrit, parce qu'il est une conscience de sommeil; tout l'épisode (et, partant, je le crois, toute l'œuvre qui en sort) se tient ainsi suspend dans une sorte de scandale grammatical: dire 'je dors' est en effet, à la lettre, aussi impossible que de dire 'je suis mort'; l'écriture est précisément cette activité qui travaille la langue—les impossibilités de la langue—au profit du discours" (Barthes, "'Longtemps, je me suis couché de bonne heure . . . ,'" 316).

25. Schlesinger, "Proust als Leser von Flaubert," 310.

26. "l'usage entièrement nouveau et personnel qu'il a fait du passé défini, du passé indéfini, du participe présent" (Proust, "À propos du 'style' de Flaubert," 586).

27. Proust, "À propos du 'style' de Flaubert," 589. Proust quotes the following example from Flaubert: "Ils habitaient le fond de la Bretagne. . . . *C'était* une maison basse . . . , d'où l'on *découvre* la mer" (591, emphasis in the original).

28. Proust, "À propos du 'style' de Flaubert," 587.

29. "Les beaux livres sont écrits dans une sorte de langue étrangère. Sous chaque mot chacun de nous met son sens ou du moins son image qui est souvent un contresens. Mais dans les beaux livres, tous les contresens qu'on fait sont beaux" (Proust, *Contre Sainte-Beuve*, 305).

30. Proust, *Selected Letters*, 4:258; for the original French see Proust, *Correspondance*, 20:496–97: "Il s'agit de tirer hors de l'inconscient, pour la faire entrer dans le domaine de l'intelligence, mais en tâchant de lui garder sa vie, de ne pas la mutiler, de lui faire subir le moins de déperdition possible, une réalité que la seule lumière de l'intelligence suffirait à détruire, semble-t-il. Pour réussir ce travail de sauvetage, toutes les forces de l'esprit, et même du corps, ne sont pas de trop. C'est un peu le même genre d'effort . . . nécessaire à quelqu'un qui, dormant encore, voudrait examiner son sommeil avec son intelligence, sans que cette intervention amenât le réveil." Proust wrote this letter in October 1921 in response to a survey by the journal *Annales politiques et littéraires*.

31. Proust's phrase is "Il y faut des précautions, mais bien qu'enfermant en apparence une contradiction, ce travail n'est pas impossible"; Bergson's is "C'est difficile, ce n'est pas impossible à qui s'y est exercé patiemment" (*L'énergie spirituelle*, 101).

32. For a system-theoretical definition, see, for example, Luhmann, "Observing Re-Entries."

33. Greaney, *Sleep and the Novel*, 155.

34. Proust, *Correspondance*, 20:496–97.

35. "[Mes] parents me disaient de me coucher un peu et de chercher le sommeil. Il n'y a pas besoin pour savoir le trouver de beaucoup de réflexion, mais l'habitude y est très utile et même l'absence de la réflexion. Or, à ces heures-là, les deux me faisaient défaut. Avant de m'endormir je pensais si longtemps que je ne le pourrais, que, même endormi, il me restait un peu de pensée. Ce n'était qu'une lueur dans la presque obscurité, mais elle suffisait pour faire se refléter dans mon sommeil, d'abord l'idée que je ne pourrais dormir, puis, reflet de ce reflet, l'idée que c'était en dormant que j'avais eu l'idée que je ne dormais pas, puis, par une réfraction nouvelle, mon éveil . . . à une nouvelle somme où je voulais raconter à des amis qui étaient entrés dans ma chambre que, tout à l'heure en dormant, j'avais cru que je ne dormais pas" (*RTP* 2:443–44).

36. "On a proposé . . . une méthode pour déterminer la profondeur du sommeil, dans le but de chercher l'intensité minimale capable d'éveiller un sujet; cette méthode consistait à produire des bruits d'intensités différentes" (Vaschide, *Le sommeil et les rêves*, 46). On Proust and Vaschide, see Bogousslavsky, "Marcel Proust's Lifelong Tour of the Parisian Neurological Intelligentsia," 135.

37. For historical context on arousal threshold experiments, see Kinzler, *Das Joch des Schlafs*, 145–48, and Basner, "Arousal Threshold Determination in 1862."

38. "Mais deux ou trois fois . . . le sommeil interposé fut en moi assez résistant pour soutenir le choc de la musique et je n'entendis rien. Les autres jours il céda un instant; mais encore veloutée d'avoir dormi, ma conscience, comme ces organes préalablement anesthésiés, par qui une cautérisation, restée d'abord insensible, n'est perçue que tout à fait à sa fin et comme une légère brûlure, n'était touchée qu'avec douceur par les pointes aiguës des fifres qui la caressaient d'un vague et frais gazouillis matinal; et après cette étroite interruption où le silence s'était fait musique, il reprenait avec mon sommeil avant même que les dragons eussent fini de passer, me dérobant les dernières gerbes épanouies du bouquet jaillissant et sonore. Et la zone de ma conscience que ses tiges jaillissantes avaient effleurée était si étroite, si circonvenue de sommeil, que plus tard, quand Saint-Loup me demandait si j'avais entendu la musique, je n'étais pas certain que le son de la fanfare n'eût pas été aussi imaginaire que celui que j'entendais dans le jour s'élever après le moindre bruit au-dessus des pavés de la ville. Peut-être ne l'avais-je entendu qu'en un rêve par la crainte d'être réveillé, ou au contraire de ne pas l'être et de ne pas voir le défilé. Car souvent quand je restais endormi au moment où j'avais pensé au contraire que le bruit m'aurait réveillé, pendant une heure encore je croyais l'être, tout en sommeillant, et je me jouais à moi-même en minces ombres sur l'écran de mon sommeil les divers spectacles auxquels il m'empêchait mais auxquels j'avais l'illusion d'assister" (*RTP* 2: 384-85).

39. Benjamin, "Das Passagen-Werk," 492. Benjamin states that it is "eine der stillschweigenden Voraussetzungen der Psychoanalyse, daß der konträre Gegensatz von Schlaf und Wachen für die empirische Bewußtseinsform des Menschen keine Geltung hat, vielmehr einer unendlichen Varietät konkreter Bewußtseinszustände weicht, die durch alle denkbaren Gradstufen des Erwachtseins aller möglichen Zentren bedingt sind." I quote the English translation of Heller-Roazen, *The Inner Touch*, 77.

40. Benjamin, "Das Passagen-Werk," 492.

41. Yu, "La pensée du sommeil," 39.

42. On these writers, see, for example, Kohtes, *Der Rausch in Worten*, Millington, "Pameelen in the Snow," Pollock, "Opium and the Occult," and Kemper, *Droge Trakl*.

43. The term "scene of writing" alludes to Rüdiger Campe's classic article, "Writing; the Scene of Writing." He does not discuss Proust.

44. On Proust's bedroom(s) and connections to his writing, see especially Fuss, *The Sense of an Interior*, 102-51. For Proust's writing process, see Tadié, *Marcel Proust*, 533-34.

45. Proust, *Correspondance*, 7:285-86 (qtd. in Mabin, "Sommeil et automédication de Marcel Proust," 66), and 2:135-36 (qtd. in Mabin, "Sommeil et automédication de Marcel Proust," 68); Albaret, *Monsieur Proust*, 337. Proust started his consumption of soporifics during his obligatory stint in the military (1889-90). He

quickly got hooked on Trional, whose dosage he successively increased. Before that, Proust frequented opium dens in Paris. See Ragonneau, "Proust et l'opium." The late Proust also experiments with other drugs, such as adrenalin; sometimes he needs "trois piqûres d'adrénaline pour écrire un mot" (Proust, *Correspondance*, 20:555-57, qtd. in Mabin, "Sommeil et automédication de Marcel Proust," 68).

46. Barthes, *The Preparation of the Novel*, 230.

47. "Psychonautik," seafaring on the psyche, is Ernst Jünger's term for the exploration of altered states of consciousness through drug experiments, for him an adventure that recreates the dangers of physical exploration. See Jünger, *Annäherungen*.

48. This point has been argued for self-experiments in general. See Solhdju, *Selbstexperimente*, 8, and Müller-Funk, "Neugierde und literarisches Selbstexperiment im Essayismus der frühen Neuzeit," 114-15.

49. In the *Recherche*, experiences of altered consciousness that do not involve pharmaceuticals include states like drunkenness (alcohol) and states at the borders of sleep. Some of them have been analyzed by Fülöp, *Proust, the One, and the Many*, 53-101. For a concise overview of the figure of Bergotte, see Hassine, "Bergotte."

50. "Oui, je suis persuadé qu'il a voulu faire l'expérience de la mort, expérimenter la sensation la plus grande de la perte de conscience. Seulement, le connaissant comme je l'ai connu, ma conviction est aussi qu'il avait mûrement calculé la dose—probablement de véronal—pour être sûr de conserver toute la lucidité de l'analyse" (Albaret, *Monsieur Proust*, 337).

51. "Bergotte . . . essaya avec succès, mais avec excès, de différents narcotiques, lisant avec confiance le prospectus accompagnant chacun d'eux. . . . Bergotte les essaya tous. Certains sont d'une autre famille que ceux auxquels nous sommes habitués, dérivés, par exemple, de l'amyle et de l'éthyle. On n'absorbe le produit nouveau, d'une composition toute différente, qu'avec la délicieuse attente de l'inconnu. Le cœur bat comme à un premier rendez-vous. Vers quels genres ignorés de sommeil, de rêves, le nouveau venu va-t-il nous conduire ? Il est maintenant dans nous, il a la direction de notre pensée. De quelle façon allons-nous nous endormir ? Et une fois que nous le serons, par quels chemins étranges, sur quelles cimes, dans quels gouffres inexplorés le maître tout-puissant nous conduira-t-il?" (*RTP* 3:691).

52. See Flatau, *Ueber die nervöse Schlaflosigkeit*: "Leider hat sich bei solchen Empfehlungen ein gewisser Schematismus herausgebildet, fast wie Stereotypdruck muthet es uns an, wenn wir in dem Begleitschreiben und der mitgesandten Litteratur lesen: das Mittel ist geruchlos, geschmacklos und wird auch von Kindern gern genommen . . . ; probiert man die Dinge selbst, so findet man diese Angaben durchaus nicht immer bestätigt" (10-11).

53. Simon and Serça, "Sommeil," 948.

54. For the medical sources, see, for instance, Trömner, *Das Problem des*

Schlafes, 74: "Kurz, der hypnotische Schlaf ist nur ein besonders gestalteter Schlaf, etwa wie auch eine künstlich gezüchtete Blume wohl von der natürlichen Urform abweicht, ihr aber trotzdem artgleich bleibt."

55. Proust, Préface, 11.
56. See Nordholt, "Le dormeur éveillé comme figure du moi proustien," 544-46.
57. Proust, *Correspondance,* 20:496.
58. "En saisant varier l'heure, l'endroit où on s'endort, en provoquant le sommeil d'une manière artificielle, ou au contraire en revenant pour un jour au sommeil naturel . . . on arrive à obtenir des variétés de sommeil mille fois plus nombreuses que, jardinier, on n'obtiendrait de variété d'œillets ou de roses" (*RTP* 3:631).
59. "Je jouissais encore des débris du sommeil, c'est-à-dire de la seule invention, du seul renouvellement qui existe dans la manière de conter, toutes les narrations à l'état de veille, fussent-elles embellies par la littérature, ne comportant pas ces mystérieuses différences d'où dérive la beauté. Il est aisé de parler de celle que crée l'opium. Mais pour un homme habitué à ne dormir qu'avec des drogues, une heure inattendue de sommeil naturel découvrira *l'immensité* matinale d'un paysage aussi mystérieux et plus frais" (*RTP* 3:630-31).
60. See Henry, "Proust du côté de Schopenhauer."
61. "Jeden Morgen, beim Erwachen, ist das Bewußtseyn eine *tabula rasa*, die sich aber schnell wieder füllt. Zunächst nämlich ist es die jetzt wieder eintretende Umgebung des vorigen Abends, welche uns an das erinnert, was wir unter eben dieser Umgebung gedacht haben: daran knüpfen sich die Ereignisse des vorigen Tages, und so ruft ein Gedanke schnell den andern hervor, bis Alles, was uns gestern beschäftigte, wieder daist [sic]. . . . Wie gänzlich aber der Schlaf den Faden der Erinnerung unterbricht, so daß dieser an jedem Morgen wieder angeknüpft werden muß, sehn wir an einzelnen Unvollkommenheiten dieser Operation: z.B. eine Melodie, welche Abends uns zum Ueberdruß im Kopfe herumgieng, können wir bisweilen am andern Morgen nicht wiederfinden" (Schopenhauer, *Die Welt als Wille und Vorstellung*, 3:156-57).
62. In this conversation, the fictional Bergson argues that "hypnotics taken from time to time in moderate doses do not affect the solid memory of our everyday lives, so firmly fixed in us" (*RTP* 3:373; *ISOLT* 4:379). But he adds that there are also "other types of memory, higher and more unstable ones" (*RTP* 3:373; *ISOLT* 4:379) that are affected by taking pills to go to sleep, for example, the recollection of learned quotations. Like Joshua Landy, I read this scene as a critique (if not a gentle parody) of Bergson's philosophy. The narrator explicitly refutes Bergson's reasoning: "We possess all our memories, if not the faculty of recalling them, says, following M. Bergson, the eminent Norwegian philosopher . . . what is a memory that we cannot recall?" (*RTP* 3:374; *ISOLT* 4:380) For comments on readings of Proust vis-à-vis Bergson, see Landy, *Philosophy as Fiction*, 7-8, and esp. 163. Another scholar who stresses the differences between Proust and Bergson is David

Gross; see his "Bergson, Proust, and the Reevaluation of Memory." For an account of Bergson in the context of sleep science, see Kroker, *The Sleep of Others*, 133-45. For Bergson's philosophy of dreams, see also Wortham, *The Poetics of Sleep*, 31-33, 39-41.

63. See Hegel, *Enzyklopädie der philosophischen Wissenschaften im Grundrisse*, esp. §§ 398-99, 87-97.

64. Nancy, *The Birth to Presence*, 17.

65. Schwenger, *At the Borders of Sleep*, viii.

66. Schwenger, *At the Borders of Sleep*, ix.

67. "Only literature . . . has the subtlety to deal with such liminal sensations" (Schwenger, *At the Borders of Sleep*, xi). He goes on to study awakening through the lens of several writers, including Danilo Kiš, Aris Fioretos, Jean-Paul Sartre, Giorgio de Chirico, and Paul Valéry but offers only a short remark on Proust. He elaborates elsewhere in his book on the phenomenon of hypnagogic sensations (esp. 1-49). See also Schwenger, "Writing Hypnagogia."

68. See Dostoyevsky, *Notes from Underground*, 127.

69. "La grande modification qu'amène en nous le réveil est moins de nous introduire dans la vie claire de la conscience que de nous faire perdre le souvenir de la lumière un peu plus tamisée où reposait notre intelligence, comme au fond opalin des eaux. Les pensées à demi voilées sur lesquelles nous voguions il y a un instant encore, entraînaient en nous un mouvement parfaitement suffisant pour que nous ayons pu les désigner sous le nom de veille. Mais les réveils trouvent alors une interférence de mémoire. Peu après, nous les qualifions sommeil parce que nous ne nous les rappelons plus. Et quand luit cette brillante étoile qui, à l'instant du réveil, éclaire derrière le dormeur son sommeil tout entier, elle lui fait croire pendant quelque seconde que c'était non du sommeil, mais de la veille; étoile filante à vrai dire qui . . . permet seulement à celui qui s'éveille de se dire: 'J'ai dormi'" (*RTP* 2:631).

70. Valéry, *Cahiers*, 2:127. Translation quoted in Heller-Roazen, *The Inner Touch*, 76. On Valéry and sleep, see Miura, "Sommeil et réveil chez Valéry." QED means "quod erat demonstrandum," "the proof of the argument is complete."

71. For the choice of my comparison, see William James, *The Principles of Psychology*, 224: "The first and foremost concrete fact which everyone will affirm to belong to his inner experience is the fact that consciousness of some sort goes on. . . . If we could say in English 'it thinks,' as we say, 'it rains' or 'it blows,' we should be stating the fact most simply and with the minimum of assumption. As we cannot, we must simply say that thought goes on."

72. "[Il] semble qu'on soit devenu, soi-même, pendant quelques instants après qu'un tel sommeil a cessé, un simple bonhomme de plomb. On n'est plus personne. Comment, alors, cherchant sa pensée, sa personnalité comme on cherche un objet perdu, unit-on par retrouver son propre moi plutôt que tout autre? Pourquoi, quand

on se remet à penser, n'est-ce pas alors une autre personnalité que l'antérieure qui s'incarne en nous? On ne voit pas ce qui dicte le choix et pourquoi, entre les millions d'êtres humains qu'on pourrait être, c'est sur celui qu'on était la veille qu'on met juste la main. Qu'est-ce qui nous guide, quand il y a eu vraiment interruption (soit que le sommeil ait été complet, ou les rêves entièrement différents de nous)? Il y a eu vraiment mort, comme quand le cœur a cessé de battre et que des tractions rythmées de la langue nous raniment. . . . La résurrection au réveil — après ce bienfaisant accès d'aliénation mentale qu'est le sommeil — doit ressembler au fond à ce qui se passe quand on retrouve un nom, un vers, un refrain oublié" (*RTP* 2: 387).

73. See Woolf, *Orlando: A Biography*, esp. 61-64 and 122-27. On Woolf's knowledge of the *Recherche*, see Shore, "Virginia Woolf, Proust, and Orlando," 232. Shore offers many insights, but she does not pick up on the relationship between sleep and gender changes in both texts. More generally, sleep scenes in Woolf often resemble interludes and are closely associated with representations of passing time. Her texts use such interludes to shift to a narrative mode and to relate events in a compressed fashion without having to dramatize them through the perspective of her characters, as in the case of Orlando's gender change and narrated events such as the death of several members of the Ramsay family in the second part of *To the Lighthouse* (1927), which portrays the dormant state of the Ramsay house. On sleep in Woolf in general, see Carson, "Every Exit Is an Entrance (A Praise of Sleep)," and Trigoni, *The Intelligent Unconscious in Modernist Literature and Science*, 108-44.

74. Valéry, *Cahiers*, 2:1243. English translation in Heller-Roazen, *The Inner Touch*, 75.

75. Valéry, *Cahiers*, 2:181. English translation in Heller-Roazen, *The Inner Touch*, 75.

76. Kafka, *The Metamorphosis*, 3. Kafka, "Die Verwandlung," 115: "Als Gregor Samsa eines Morgens aus unruhigen Träumen erwachte, fand er sich in seinem Bett zu einem ungeheueren Ungeziefer verwandelt. . . . Es war kein Traum."

77. Mann, *The Magic Mountain*, 579.

78. Mann, *The Magic Mountain*, 585-86. For the original German, see Mann, *Der Zauberberg*, 745. For a discussion of dreams in the novel, see Koopmann, "Wie wirklich ist das Unwirkliche?"

79. "Un homme qui dort, tient en cercle autour de lui le fil des heures, l'ordre des années et des mondes. Il les consulte d'instinct en s'éveillant et y lit en une seconde le point de la terre qu'il occupe, le temps qui s'est écoulé jusqu'à son réveil; mais leurs rangs peuvent se mêler, se rompre. . . . Toujours est-il que, quand je me réveillais ainsi, mon esprit s'agitant pour chercher, sans y réussir, à savoir où j'étais, tout tournait autour de moi dans l'obscurité, les choses, les pays, les années. Mon corps, trop engourdi pour remuer, cherchait, d'après la forme de sa fatigue, à repérer la position de ses membres pour en induire la direction du mur, la place des meubles, pour reconstruire et pour nommer la demeure où il se trouvait. Sa

mémoire, la mémoire de ses côtes, de ses genoux, de ses épaules, lui présentait successivement plusieurs des chambres où il avait dormi, tandis qu'autour de lui les murs invisibles, changeant de place selon la forme de la pièce imaginée, tourbillonnaient dans les ténèbres" (*RTP* 1:6).

80. "Et avant même que ma pensée, qui hésitait au seuil des temps et des formes, eût identifié le logis en rapprochant les circonstances, lui, — mon corps, — se rappelait pour chacun le genre du lit, la place des portes, la prise de jour des fenêtres, l'existence d'un couloir, avec la pensée que j'avais en m'y endormant et que je retrouvais au réveil" (*RTP* 1:6).

81. Proust literally compares awakening to the transformation of a caterpillar into a butterfly, but unlike in Kafka's novella, the metamorphosis is successful: "Comme une chrysalide en voie de métamorphose, j'étais une créature double aux diverses parties de laquelle ne convenait pas le même milieu" (*RTP* 2:383) ["like a chrysalis in the process of metamorphosis, I was a dual creature whose various parts were not at home in the same environment"] (*ISOLT* 3:85).

Chapter 5. Undreaming Kafka

1. Kafka to Marderstein, quoted in Neumann, "Der Zauber des Anfangs und das 'Zögern vor der Geburt,'" 439. A November 1, 1912, letter to his fiancée reports in the same vein that his "way of life" centers on creating the best conditions for writing (Kafka, *Briefe 1900-1912*, 203-4). On Kafka's exercise program, see Alt, *Franz Kafka*, 206. Quotations in English from texts cited in other languages are always my translations, unless noted otherwise.

2. "durch viel Schlaf am Nachmittag die Fortsetzung der Arbeit bis tief in die Nacht zu ermöglichen" (January 17, 1915, Kafka, *Tagebücher*, 716). In parenthetical cites to Kafka's diaries, with two sets of volume and page numbers, the first refers to the German original in the *Kritische Ausgabe*, while the second refers to a recent English translation. When a parenthetical citation does not contain a second set, it means the translation is mine.

3. On Kafka's penchant for wax and cotton earplugs by the newly founded Ohropax firm, see Whitney, "Inside the Ear," 302.

4. Alt suggests that Kafka's dream logic is rooted in the practice of journaling his dreams (*Franz Kafka*, 495-96). In contrast, Engel distinguishes between dreamlike states and dreams; he is interested in the "Traumhafte an Kafkas Texten, die keine Träume sind" ("Kulturgeschichte/n?," 173). According to Engel, the conceit of this kind of narration comes down to placing the protagonist in an environment that represents his interiority. In making a claim to dreamlikeness, Engel points to Kafka's noting in a diary entry that he tried to represent his "traumhafte[] innere[] Leben" (August 6, 1914, Kafka, *Tagebücher*, 546).

5. See Alt, "Erzählungen des Unbewussten," 153, and Krings, "Der Tod ein Traum," 204.

6. Kafka, "Beschreibung eines Kampfes," 1:529 ("Es ist keine Freude, sich mit der Psychoanalyse abzugeben, und ich halte mich von ihr möglichst fern"); Kafka, *The Metamorphosis*, 3; Kafka, "Die Verwandlung," 115.

7. Engel, "Dream Theories in Modernist Literature," 383.

8. Examples of characters who work in bed include the lawyer in *Der Proceß* and the officials in *Das Schloss*. Among characters who suffer from chronic sleep disorders is the *chef de cuisine* in *Der Verschollene*, who interprets her insomnia as a chronic adaptation to her previous station in life (176). In *Der Verschollene*, some figures regularly have black coffee at 3 A.M. in order to stay awake (347-48). Kafka himself avoided stimulants such as alcohol, coffee, and tea. See Alt, *Franz Kafka*, 209.

9. Neumann, "Der Zauber des Anfangs und das 'Zögern vor der Geburt,'" 442. It is well known that Kafka published only a fraction of his literary production himself; more than 90 percent of his work remained unpublished during his lifetime. Most of these texts appeared posthumously under the editorship of Max Brod, who aimed to establish Kafka as a great author. To this end, he disguised the fragmentary character of both published and unpublished texts and presented them as completed works. Brod fused different versions of the same piece, obliterated dead ends, added titles to chapters and texts, and so on. Since the 1980s, Kafka's texts have been reedited based on the manuscripts in two competing editions, the *Kritische Ausgabe* and the *Historisch-Kritische Franz Kafka-Ausgabe*. Suffice it to say that this has profoundly affected Kafka studies. The reediting did away with the idea of complete texts and gave rise to studies that focus on the writing process and the materiality of Kafka's texts and also eradicated the distinction between canceled and noncanceled passages in the manuscripts. For a first overview of the history of Kafka editions, see Engel, "Werkausgaben und Editionsgeschichte."

10. See Neumann, "Der verschleppte Prozess," Vogl, *Ort der Gewalt*, Kölbel, *Die Erzählrede*, and Kleinwort, *Der späte Kafka*.

11. Barthes, *The Preparation of the Novel*, 238. The term "scene of writing" references Rüdiger Campe's classic article, "Writing; the Scene of Writing."

12. The essay was first published in 1909; the survey took place in 1927. The survey is accessible in Mann, *["Braucht man zum Dichten Schlaf und Zigaretten?"]*. For the quote, see Mann, *Süßer Schlaf!*: "Der ist gewiß der Größte, welcher der Nacht die Treue und Sehnsucht wahrt und dennoch die gewaltigsten Werke des Tages tut" (208-9).

13. Mann, *Süßer Schlaf!*, 207.

14. On Kafka's scene of writing in general, see Campe, "Schreiben im Prozess," Schütterle, *Franz Kafkas Oktavhefte*, Jahraus, *Kafka*, 76-86, Wolf, "Die Nacht des

Bürokraten," Alt, *Franz Kafka*, 312, and Schwenger, *At the Borders of Sleep*, 63. Schwenger explicitly asks, "How does this nocturnal instruction find its way into Kafka's writing?" (63) Yet he does not answer the question. Kilcher, *Kafkas Werkstatt*, was published too late to be considered in this study.

15. See Deo and Charlier, "For Franz Kafka, Insomnia Was a Literary Method," Perciaccante and Coralli, "Franz Kafka's Insomnia and Parasomnias," Iranzo et al., "The Insomnia of Franz Kafka," Perciaccante and Coralli, "Insomnia," Iranzo et al., "Sleep and Sleep Disorders in Franz Kafka's Narrative Works," and Mishara, "Kafka, Paranoic Doubles and the Brain."

16. Iranzo et al., "The Insomnia of Franz Kafka," 24. On sleep hygiene, see chapter 2 of this book. I concur with Alt, *Franz Kafka*, who notes with regard to the author that "Schlaflosigkeit bildet keineswegs die Folge, sondern die Bedingung seiner literarischen Arbeit" (312). However, although Alt suggests that Kafka changed his schedule, while he did indeed have a plan to do so, he did not end up following it because he concluded it would threaten his power to write: "Nun habe ich mir seit dem gestrigen Vormittag und seit der heutigen ein wenig bessern Nacht das Gelübde gegeben, um 1/2 11 schlafen zu gehen. Das ist fast das Ende des Schreibens" (*Briefe, April 1914-1917*, 79).

17. See Türk, "Health and Illness," 45-46.

18. "Vielleicht gibt es auch ein anderes Schreiben, ich kenne nur dieses, in der Nacht, wenn mich die Angst nicht schlafen läßt, kenne ich nur dieses. Und das Teuflische daran erscheint mir sehr klar" (*Briefe, 1902-1924*, 384-85). On the infernal, see Voigts, *Geburt und Teufelsdienst*.

19. Janouch, *Conversations with Kafka*, 18. Of course, this text cannot be entirely trusted.

20. For this drawing, see Kafka, *"Einmal ein grosser Zeichner,"* 79. For all drawings and sketches, see Kafka, *The Drawings*.

21. See Maury, "Des hallucinations hypnagogiques."

22. See Alt, *Franz Kafka*, 315-16.

23. "It was in 1919, in complete solitude and at the approach of sleep, that my attention was arrested by sentences, more or less complete, which became perceptible to my mind without my being able to discover (even by meticulous analysis) any possible previous volitional effort. One evening in particular, as I was about to fall asleep, I became aware of a sentence articulated clearly to a point excluding all possibility of alteration and stripped of all quality of vocal sound; a curious sort of sentence which came to me bearing—in sober truth—not a trace of any relation whatever to any incidents I may at that time have been involved in; an insistent sentence, it seemed to me; a sentence, I might say, that knocked at the window" (Breton, "What Is Surrealism?," 120). Even though hypnagogia is an important point of reference, Freud (whom Breton discusses immediately before this passage) remains the key theoretical anchor for Breton. For surrealism and sleep, see

especially Conley, *Robert Desnos*, 15-23. On surrealism more broadly, see Foster, *Compulsive Beauty*.

24. The translation is from Kafka, *Letters to Felice*, 270.

25. This sentence calls up associations with Kafka's idol, Gustave Flaubert, who often exchanged his desk for a couch, where new ideas would "marinate." A passage originally written for *Der Proceß* also speaks to this idea: "Gewöhnlich lag er dann auf dem Kanapee seines Bureaus - er konnte sein Bureau nicht mehr verlassen, ohne eine Stunde lang auf dem Kanapee sich zu erholen - und fügte in Gedanken Beobachtung an Beobachtung. Er beschränkte sich nicht peinlich auf die Leute, welche mit dem Gericht zusammenhingen, hier im Halbschlaf mischten sich alle" (348).

26. "Ich brauche zu meinem Schreiben Abgeschiedenheit, nicht 'wie ein Einsiedler,' das wäre nicht genug, sondern wie ein Toter. Schreiben in diesem Sinne ist ein tieferer Schlaf, also Tod, und so wie man einen Toten nicht aus seinem Grabe ziehen wird und kann, so auch mich nicht vom Schreibtisch in der Nacht" (*Briefe, 1913-März 1914*, 221). The English translation comes from Kafka, *Letters to Felice*, 279. I have modified it, however, replacing "seclusion" with "detachment" in order to capture the mental dimension of *Abgeschiedenheit*.

27. For a contextualization of Kafka's reading of Master Eckhart, see Stach, *Kafka*, 254. On detachment in Meister Eckhart, see Bernard McGinn's definitive account in *The Harvest of Mysticism in Medieval Germany*, 164-81.

28. "Mir ist immer unbegreiflich, daß es jedem fast, der schreiben kann, möglich ist, im Schmerz den Schmerz zu objektivieren, so daß ich zum Beispiel im Unglück, vielleicht noch mit dem brennenden Unglückskopf mich setzen und jemandem schriftlich mitteilen kann: Ich bin unglücklich. . . . Und es ist gar nicht Lüge und stillt den Schmerz nicht, ist einfach gnadenweiser Überschuß der Kräfte in einem Augenblick, in dem der Schmerz doch sichtbar alle meine Kräfte bis zum Boden meines Wesens, den er aufkratzt, verbraucht hat. Was für ein Überschuß ist es also?" (*Tagebücher*, 834).

29. Kafka, *Nachgelassene Schriften und Fragmente II*, 1:585.

30. "Es ist Nacht und niemand wird mir morgen vorhalten, was ich jetzt sagen könnte, denn es kann ja im Schlaf gesprochen sein" (Kafka, "Beschreibung eines Kampfes," 110).

31. Kafka, *The Metamorphosis*, 3.

32. Kafka, *The Trial*, 5. The original suggests that he has done nothing "evil" ("Böses").

33. Many scholars have pointed out that the Hebrew word for "land surveyor," "mashoah," resembles the word for "messiah," "mashiah." For readings sympathetic to the idea of the land surveyor as the messiah see Robertson, *Kafka*, and Engel and Robertson, *Kafka und die Religion in der Moderne*. For a critique of theological approaches to Kafka, see North, *The Yield*.

34. "Riß oder Sprung, welcher die Zeit geteilt und die Perspektiven geschieden und in ein und demselben Akt eine erzählte Welt und eine Erzählung aus sich herausgesetzt hat," Mülder-Bach, "Am Anfang war . . . der Fall, " 125. For further explication, see Blumenberg, *Höhlenausgänge*: "Die Welt entstehen zu lassen wird zum Prozeß des Eintritts in sie, gleichbedeutend mit dem Heraustreten aus dem, was sie nicht oder noch nicht ist. . . . Überspitzt darf man sagen, gerade die erfundene Geschichte müsse längst begonnen haben, bevor ihr erster Satz sie 'realisiert'" (13-14).

35. Some scholars argue that Kafka references a book by his friends Max Brod and Felix Weltsch. Other suggest linking the idea of the riskiest moment to a passage in Schopenhauer's *Die Welt als Wille und Vorstellung*. Yet others speculate about reading it as a quotation from Proust, whom Kafka is unlikely to have read. See Alt, *Franz Kafka*, Morris, "Josef K.'s (A + x) Problem," and Stadler, "Halbschlaf-Szenen bei Kafka und Benjamin," 209. On the reason for the elimination of the passage, see Neumann, "Der Zauber des Anfangs und das 'Zögern vor der Geburt,'" 442.

36. Kafka, *Der Proceß*, 168: "Jemand sagte mir . . ., dass es doch sonderbar sei, dass man, wenn man früh aufwacht, wenigstens im allgemeinen [sic] alles unverrückt an der gleichen Stelle findet, wie es am Abend gewesen ist. Man ist doch im Schlaf und im Traum wenigstens scheinbar in einem vom Wachen wesentlich verschiedenen Zustand gewesen, und es gehört . . . eine unendliche Geistesgegenwart oder besser Schlagfertigkeit dazu, um mit dem Augenöffnen alles, was da ist, gewissermaßen an der gleichen Stelle zu fassen, an der man es am Abend losgelassen hat. Darum sei auch der Augenblick des Erwachens der riskanteste Augenblick im Tag, sei er einmal überstanden, ohne dass man irgendwohin von seinem Platze fortgezogen wurde, so könne man den ganzen Tag über getrost sein." My translation modifies the translation by Duttlinger, *The Cambridge Introduction to Franz Kafka*, 60.

37. In his *Poetics*, Aristotle defines the middle of the narration thusly. See Kölbel, *Die Erzählrede in Franz Kafkas "Das Schloss,"* 75.

38. Vogl, "Vierte Person," 745.

39. This is most evident in parodies of Stein's work: "As Alyson Tischler relates, 'At the height of her fame in 1934, Steinian language appeared in newspaper headlines that announced her arrival in America. For example, when she landed in Chicago after lecturing in New York, a *Chicago Herald* headline, 'Understand Einstein? Just Try Stein-Stein,' was accompanied by the subhead: 'She Arrives—She Arrives—She Arrives—She Arrives—Arrives'" (Mieszkowski, *Crises of the Sentence*, 198).

40. Vogl, "Vierte Person," 746.

41. Alt, *Franz Kafka*, 594.

42. On anxiety in "Der Bau," see Wegmann, "The Human as Resident Animal." On the iterative mode, see especially Niehaus, "Iterativität bei Franz Kafka."

43. "Nun aber überkommt mich doch eine gewisse Lässigkeit und auf einem

Platz, der zu meinen Lieblingen gehört, rolle ich mich ein wenig zusammen, noch lange habe ich nicht alles besichtigt, aber ich will ja auch noch weiter besichtigen bis zum Ende, ich will hier nicht schlafen, nur der Lockung gebe ich nach mich hier so einzurichten, wie wenn ich schlafen wollte, nachsehn will ich, ob das hier noch immer so gut gelingt, wie früher. Es gelingt, aber mir gelingt es nicht mich loszureißen, ich bleibe hier in tiefem Schlaf. Ich habe wohl sehr lange geschlafen, erst aus dem letzten von selbst schon sich auflösenden Schlaf werde ich geweckt, der Schlaf muß nun schon sehr leicht sein, denn ein an sich kaum hörbares Zischen weckt mich" (*Nachgelassene Schriften und Fragmente II*, 1:605-6).

44. Kafka, *Der Proceß: Apparatband*, 168.

45. Recent scholarship has commented extensively on the hissing sound. See Whitney, "Inside the Ear," and Gellen, "Noises Off." For an account of earlier scholarship, see Menke, *Prosopopoiia*.

46. Strowick, "Epistemologie des Verdachts," 131.

47. Without ellipses, the passage reads: "Mir ist dann, als stehe ich nicht vor meinem Haus, sondern vor mir selbst, während ich schlafe, und hätte das Glück gleichzeitig tief zu schlafen und dabei mich scharf bewachen zu können. Ich bin gewissermaßen ausgezeichnet, die Gespenster der Nacht nicht nur in der Hilflosigkeit und Vertrauensseligkeit des Schlafes zu sehn, sondern ihnen gleichzeitig in Wirklichkeit bei voller Kraft des Wachseins in ruhiger Urteilsfähigkeit zu begegnen" (Kafka, *Nachgelassene Schriften und Fragmente II*, 1:591) ["I feel then as if I weren't standing and looking at my house, but at myself as I sleep, and as if I had the good fortune to be both deep asleep and at the same time able to observe myself keenly. I am, you might say, marked out to see the ghosts of the night not only in my vulnerable and sweet trustful sleep, but at the same time to encounter them in reality too, awake and energetic, with a strong and steady judgement" (Kafka, "The Burrow," 160-61)].

48. This split of the subject during sleep is deeply enmeshed with the pronominal changes in Kafka's texts, for example, in *The Castle*, which moves from the third person into the first person and back into the third person. On these pronominal changes, see Cohn, "K. Enters *The Castle*." For the consequences for Kafka's narrative perspective, see Vogl, "Vierte Person."

49. See the *Apparatband* volume of *Nachgelassene Schriften und Fragmente II*, 2:447. In the manuscript, Kafka has changed the tense of in "Ich habe wohl sehr lange geschlafen" from the present to the perfect. Michael Niehaus, who first noticed this change, claims that "Ich schlafe wohl sehr lange" is inconsistent and should be altered for this reason ("Das Schreiben interpretieren"). However, descriptions of this kind that have not been changed or suppressed appear in several Kafka texts, for example, in "Beschreibung eines Kampfes" and "Forschungen eines Hundes." On similar cases in more recent texts by other authors than Kafka, see Cohn, "'I Doze and Wake.'"

50. Coetzee, "Time, Tense and Aspect," 564.

51. Coetzee, Time, Tense and Aspect," 576.

52. Coetzee, Time, Tense and Aspect," 571, 575, 576.

53. Hamburger, *Die Logik der Dichtung*, 62. For Hamburger, the I-origio is "gleichbedeutend mit Begriffe Aussagesubjekt" and means "den durch das Ich (das Erlebnis- oder Aussage-Ich) besetzten Nullpunkt, die Origo des raumzeitlichen Koordinationsystems, der zusammenfällt oder identisch ist mit Jetzt und Hier. Die Origio des Jetzt-Hier-Ich-Systems, welche Bezeichnung wir also zu Ich-Origo verkürzen, wird von Brugmann und Bühler zur Beschreibung der Funktionen der deiktischen Pronomina der Rede benutzt" (62). Other scholars have chosen different approaches to unstable subjectivity in the text, focusing on metaphors of writing; see Richter, "Difficile Dwellings," and Menke, *Prosopopoiia*.

54. "Les hommes s'endorment journellement avec une audace qui serait inintelligible si nous ne savions qu'elle est le résultat de l'ignorance du danger" (Baudelaire, *Œuvres complètes*, 1:654).

55. On beds in Kafka's writing, see Goebel, "Der Paria."

56. Kafka, "In der Strafkolonie," 207; Kafka, "In the Penal Colony," 76.

57. Kafka, *Der Verschollene*, 16.

58. Kafka, *Der Proceß*, 348.

59. Duttlinger, "Schlaflosigkeit," 233. See also the Kafka chapter in Duttlinger, *Attention and Distraction*, 85–126.

60. "progressive Ent-Schöpfung," Vogl, "Am Schlossberg," 90.

61. This is at least what Kafka reports to his friend Robert Klopstock in a letter dated January 24, 1922 (*Briefe, 1902–1924*, 369). Kafka further elaborates on this experience in a diary entry from January 16, 1922 (*Tagebücher*, 877).

62. *S* in parenthetical cites refers to *Das Schloss*, while *C* refers to the English translation, *The Castle*.

63. Although it proves wrong, K.'s first thought after being roused for the first time is that he is dreaming. Puzzled, K. repeats the suggestion that he has spent the night in the castle without permission: "Als wollte er sich davon überzeugen, ob er die früheren Mitteilungen nicht vielleicht geträumt hätte" (*S*, 8; *C*, 6).

64. Brod, "'Das Schloss.'" Brod excluded not only the Bürgel episode but also the rest of Kafka's manuscript from his first edition. Even today, some of the most careful scholarly readings concur with Brod's negative assessment of the scene. See Alt, *Franz Kafka*, Kölbel, *Die Erzählrede in Franz Kafkas "Das Schloss,"* 19, and Kleinwort, *Der späte Kafka*, 224. Scholars have also discovered that Kafka continues the scene in one of his notebooks.

65. Hans Castorp, who spends seven years in a Swiss sanatorium even though he is not sick, concludes that he must not let death govern his life and practices kindness and love instead. This implies that he must leave the sanatorium imme-

diately to return to the ordinary world as an active citizen, but, as a matter of fact, he stays on. Alt, *Franz Kafka*, 617, compares the Bürgel episode to the "Snow" chapter.

66. One could sort existing positions into a "tragic" camp and an "ironic" camp. The "tragic" camp argues that the land surveyor could have gained recognition from the castle if he had not fallen asleep at the wrong moment. Because K.'s human condition—his somnolence—undermines his striving, he becomes an allegory for the tragic nature of human existence. In its classic version, this argument goes back to Martini, *Das Wagnis der Sprache*, 317, Emrich, *Franz Kafka*, 386-90, and Philippi, *Reflexion und Wirklichkeit*, 195-96. More recently, this reading has been reintroduced by Duttlinger, "Schlaflosigkeit." Taken together, the tragic reading affirms Bürgel's interpretation of the event, which is organized around the term of the boundary: "No, no, you don't have to apologize for your drowsiness; why should you? Physical strength [*Leibeskräfte*] is enough only up to a certain point; who can help it if that very point is also very significant otherwise? No one can help it. That's the way the world corrects itself in its course and keeps its balance. It's an excellent, incredibly excellent arrangement, although dismal in other respects" (*C*, 236). By contrast, the "ironic" camp holds that the sleep state of the Bürgel episode could never have been anything else than another iteration of the land surveyor's futile quest for access to the castle. See Alt, *Franz Kafka*, 617.

67. On Kafka's interrogations, and nighttime interrogations in particular, see Niehaus, *Das Verhör*, esp. 466-83. The scheduled hearing cannot take place, because an usher determines that Erlanger, who is on nocturnal duty, is asleep by looking into the official's room via a small opening on the top of the door. "The servant got K. to raise him on his shoulders and then looked down into the room through the space above the corridor wall. 'He's lying on his bed,' said the servant, clambering back down to the floor, 'fully clothed, but I think he's asleep. Sometimes weariness overcomes him in the village; it's the different way of life here. We'll have to wait. He'll ring the bell when he wakes up. I've known him to sleep away his entire visit to the village, and then have to go back to the castle as soon as he woke again'" (*S*, 383; *C*, 213). Despite its strangeness, this event is one among many in *The Castle* in which officials on duty seem to be sleeping (see the Klamm episode: *S*, 61-65; *C*, 36-38); the first-person narrator of the story "Investigations of a Dog" likewise "pretend[s] to be asleep" at one point ("Investigations of a Dog," 140).

68. Although one can only speculate whether this is true, it is worth remembering that Bürgel serves as a deputy to the official Friedrich. This is remarkable, because someone named Fritz has appointed K. as a land surveyor during the night of his arrival. Are Friedrich and Fritz the same person? To be sure, similar names are not uncommon among officials in *The Castle*, as in the case of Sordini and Sortini. But while the names of Sordini and Sortini are marked by a binary difference, Fritz

is a conventional diminutive of Friedrich. However, even the existence of both Sordini and Sortini could be just another addition to the villagers' mythology of castle officials.

69. "K. schlief, es war zwar kein eigentlicher Schlaf, er hörte Bürgels Worte vielleicht besser als während des frühern totmüden Wachens, Wort für Wort schlug an sein Ohr, aber das lästige Bewußtsein war geschwunden . . ., er war noch nicht in der Tiefe des Schlafs, aber eingetaucht in ihn war er" (S, 415).

70. Nancy, *The Fall of Sleep*, 7. For more context on the "fall of distinctions," see the discussion in chapter 4 of this book, especially the section "The Angel of Certitude."

71. "K. nickte lächelnd, er glaubte jetzt, alles genau zu verstehen; nicht deshalb, weil es ihn bekümmerte, sondern weil er nun überzeugt war, in den nächsten Augenblicken würde er völlig einschlafen, diesmal ohne Traum und Störung; zwischen den zuständigen Sekretären auf der einen Seite und den unzuständigen auf der anderen und angesichts der Masse der voll beschäftigten Parteien würde er in tiefen Schlaf sinken und auf diese Weise allem entgehen. An die leise, selbstzufriedene, für das eigene Einschlafen offenbar vergeblich arbeitende Stimme Bürgels hatte er sich nun so gewohnt, daß sie seinen Schlaf mehr befördern als stören würde. Klappere, Mühle, klappere, dachte er, du klapperst nur für mich" (S, 419).

72. "Der Müller wacht aus dem Schlafe auf, wenn seine Mühle plötzlich still steht" (Hufeland, *Bemerkungen über die Brownsche Praxis*, 56). This aphorism quickly turned into a mainstay of hygienist discourse and circulated widely as a topos. On hygienist discourse, see the first section of chapter 2 of this book. The reference to Hufeland was first identified by Duttlinger, "Schlaflosigkeit," 231.

Chapter 6. Rilke and Rest

1. I would like to thank Yoann Givry and the Fondation Martin Bodmer, Genève, for permission to reproduce the image. Klossowska first published it in 1950 in a volume with Rilke's letters to her. See Bircher, "Rainer Maria Rilke und Merline." For more information on Rilke's iconography, see Strittmatter, "Strategien der Autorinszenierung."

2. Rilke, *Letters*, 2:320, emphasis in the original. For the original, see Rilke, *Briefe aus Muzot*, 169-70.

3. In parenthetical cites to Rilke's work, *KA* refers to the commonly used German edition of Rilke's works as of 2023, *Kommentierte Ausgabe*, and is followed by the source of the English translation quoted in the text. I use *KA Supp.* to refer to the *Supplementband* that contains Rilke's French poetry. Uncredited translations are my own. "Der Gram ist schweres Erdreich Darin/wurzelt dunkel ein seliger Sinn,/ daß er sich blühend entringe;/wie war in dir, mein stiller Schoß, alles trotzdem namenslos:/draußen erst heißen die Dinge./Heißen nach Zweifel und heißen nach

Zeit,/aber da legen wir Seligkeit/plötzlich zwischen die Namen./Und dann tritt auch die reine Hirschkuh/und der starke Stern dazu/in den befriedeten Rahmen" (*KA*, 2:191). Below the poem is added "(die gleichzeitige, Innen-Ansicht)." The *Kommentierte Ausgabe* dates the poem to October 13, 1921 (2:587). For a reading, see Baer, *The Rilke Alphabet*, 83–85.

4. "On raconte que chaque jour, au moment de s'endormir, Saint-Pol-Roux faisait naguère placer, sur la porte de son manoir de Camaret, un écriteau sur lequel on pouvait lire: Le poète travaille" (Breton, *Manifestes du surréalisme*, 39).

5. Apart from scholarship on Rilke's epitaph "Rose, oh reiner Widerspruch," only a single article, Tina-Karen Pusse's "'Unter schläfernden Lidern'" has attempted to investigate the topic of Rilke and sleep, and it does not cover the fruitful later period in Rilke's work examined here. In addition, some Rilke poems focused on Endymion are discussed in Kocziszky, *Der Schlaf in Kunst und Literatur*, 180–85. Of course, much scholarship exists on Rilke's writings on the night and dreams, but they are not (or are only peripherally) relevant in this context.

6. Among Rilke's German works, these poems include texts such as "Zum Einschlafen zu sagen" (*KA*, 1: 275), "Endymion" (*KA*, 1:441), "Dame vor dem Spiegel" (*KA*, 1:570), "Das Bett" (*KA*, 1:572), "Schlaf-Mohn" (*KA*, 1:574), "Schlaflied" (*KA*, 1:576), "So wie eine Türe" (*KA*, 2:11), "Schläfer, schwarz ist das Naß noch an meinen Füßen" (*KA*, 2:16), "Heute will ich dir zu Liebe Rosen" (*KA*, 2:104), "Kleine Gegengabe ins Gemüt der Schläferin" (*KA*, 2:157), "Aufstehn war Sagen damals" (*KA*, 2:188), several *Sonette an Orpheus* (I.2 [*KA*, 2:241], I.XIV [*KA*, 2:247], II.XIV [*KA*, 2:264], II.XV [*KA*, 2:264-65]), "Jetzt wär es Zeit, daß Götter träten . . ." (*KA*, 2:394), "Idol" (*KA*, 2:395), "Sterne, Schläfer und Geister" (*KA*, 2:369), and "Musik" (*KA*, 2:398-99). In Rilke's French works, sleep-related poems include texts such as "Le dormeur" (*KA Supp.*, 176), "La déesse" (*KA Supp.*, 36), "La dormeuse" (*KA Supp.*, 74), "Voilà la nuit" (*KA Supp.*, 156), "Il faut croire que tout est bien" (*KA Supp.*, 188), "Peur de la table, peur de l'alcôve" (*KA Supp.*, 242), "Chat" (*KA Supp.*, 274), "Divinité du sommeil des chats" (*KA Supp.*, 288), and "Cimetière" (*KA Supp.*, 290).

7. Rilke, *Letters*, 1:26. On social typologies of the insomniac, see Beaumont, "Insomnia and the Late Nineteenth-Century Insomniac." Some scholars believe that Rilke himself had experiences with sleep-inducing drugs. See Kocziszky, *Der Schlaf in Kunst und Literatur*, 180. Another scholar has observed that Rilke moves from an "idealization of insomnia to an idealization of sleep" ("'Unter schläfernden Lidern,'" 153).

8. The scene is preceded by a reference to a sleeping baby who seems unaffected by the urban surroundings. How the protagonist's insomnia in Paris connects with his experiences in the countryside is ripe for scholarly discussion, considering the strong evidence that city life in the novel triggers earlier trauma. For an elaboration of the latter argument, see Huyssen, "Urban Experience and the Modernist Dream of a New Language."

9. At the same time, the novel indicates that the metropolis can only partly be blamed for the insomnia of the protagonist. He had already experienced sleepless nights when he was still living in the countryside: "I could not sleep either. But suddenly, towards morning, I awoke from something that passed for sleep and with a horror that froze my very heart saw something white sitting on my bed. My desperation finally lent me the strength to stick my head under the blanket, where I wept tears of fear and helplessness" (*KA*, 3:447; *Notebooks*, 115). In this state that is sleeplike but does not constitute real sleep, nightmarish apparitions—like this appearance of a ghost—blur the lines between sleeping and waking.

10. "The doctor smiled politely and stood up, walked to the window with his assistants, and uttered a few words accompanied by a horizontal shaking movement of the hand. After three minutes one of the young persons came back to the table, peering short-sightedly and looking agitated; trying to look sternly at me, he said, 'Do you sleep well, sir?' 'No, badly.' Whereupon he quickly returned to the group. There they parleyed for a while and then the doctor turned to me and informed me that they would have me called" (*KA*, 3:494; *Notebooks*, 136-37).

11. "There I sit in the cold night and write and know all of this" (*KA*, 3:611; *Notebooks*, 291).

12. These poems have produced countless convincing interpretations. For an exemplary reading of "Schlaflied" that argues that insomnia is at its core, see Waters, *Poetry's Touch*, 34-38.

13. Lauterbach, "Frankreich," 82-85, here 82. Lauterbach proposes several possible explanations for Rilke's elective affinity with Valéry, a connection that seems surprising at first, since Valéry was an unabashed champion of intellectual complexity, while Rilke is commonly thought to cherish intuition and myth. Lauterbach argues that both respond to symbolist poetics and develop similar aesthetic strategies in its wake while also emphasizing the metapoetic dimensions of poetry.

14. "Rien ne m'a plus frappé que cette propriété essentielle du système de l'homme, de se défaire et dissoudre dans le sommeil, de se reconstruire au réveil—après l'entr'acte" (Valéry, *Cahiers*, 2:187). On Valéry and sleep, see Miura, "Sommeil et réveil chez Valéry."

15. "Le phénomène de l'endormissement et celui du réveil m'ont longtemps occupé l'esprit. . . . Quelle merveille que le pouvoir de n'être pas, propriété de ce qui est" (Valéry, *Cahiers*, 2:183).

16. Valéry, *Lettres à quelques-uns*, 225. For an account of Valéry's rejection of psychoanalysis, see Marx, "Paul Valéry, 'le moins freudien des hommes'?"

17. See Miura, "Sommeil et réveil chez Valéry," esp. 72, 78, 85-86, 92, 98-99. Ironically, Freud had similar intentions of being scientific, as is evident in his early neuroscientific work and by the diagrams he included in *Die Traumdeutung*.

18. See Miura, "Sommeil et réveil chez Valéry."

19. On Valéry's poetics, see Genette, "La littérature comme telle," and Todorov, "Valéry's Poetics."

20. "Le s'éveillant ne sait où il est, qui il est, ce qu' il y a—; il est une pluralité de questions" (Valéry, *Cahiers*, 2:126). For a discussion of *La soirée avec Monsieur Teste*, "Agathe," and *La jeune parque*, see Miura, "Sommeil et réveil chez Valéry," 76-110, Schwenger, *At the Borders of Sleep*, 42-49, and Gifford, "La descente dans le sommeil de la Jeune Parque," 73-81.

21. "Toutes choses doivent s'écrire à partir du sommeil—origine et zéro" (Valéry, *Cahiers*, 2:123).

22. Lauterbach, "Frankreich," 84. It is almost certain that Rilke was aware of a small selection of the thoughts on sleep contained in the *Cahiers*, since a section entitled *Études et fragments sur le rêve* had been compiled for publication in *Nouvelle Revue Française* in 1909 by their mutual friend André Gide. Rilke would also have known *La soirée avec Monsieur Teste* and *La jeune Parque*.

23. König, *"O komm und geh,"* 71: "Paul Valérys Gedichte, Prosastücke und Dialoge, denen er nun mehr Einfluß auf sein Werk einräumte als allem anderen, und die zu übersetzen er sogar seiner eigenen Produktion vorzog."

24. Rilke translated "La dormeuse" in 1922; the translation was published two years later in a Swiss magazine. Rilke's collected translations of Valéry's poems was published by Insel in 1925. On the dates, see Rilke, *Sämtliche Werke*, 7:1274 and 1398. The French original was first published in its complete form in 1922, but Valéry kept revising the poem until 1942. See Crow, *Paul Valéry*, 103.

25. Crow, *Paul Valéry*, 103.

26. *À la recherche du temps perdu* 3:579-83; *The Prisoner and the Fugitive*, 60-64.

27. The observation that "amas doré" can be heard as "âme adorée" owes to Louth, *Rilke*, 517.

28. A similar observation has already been made by König, *"O komm und geh,"* 78, in the context of Rilke's translation of Valéry's poem "Le cimetière marin."

29. See Ryan, *Umschlag und Verwandlung*.

30. The idea of creating a sanctuary in language for the "deity of cat sleep" recalls the opening poem in the *Sonnets to Orpheus*, where an orphic song transforms words into temples for wild animals (see *KA*, 2:241, ll. 10-14).

31. For an account of the poetics of the "double poem," see Louth, *Rilke*, 530-32, Stieg, "Rilkes späteste Gedichte auf deutsch und französisch," 168-78, and Catling, "Rilke's 'Left-Handed Lyre.'"

32. For an elaboration of this position, see the commentary by Manfred Engel and Ulrich Fülleborn in *KA*, 2:772. If we are to believe Engel and Fülleborn, Rilke develops the so-called evocative as an equivalent to Valéry's idea of the calculated poetic spell. "Das Gedicht [Idol] verwirklicht als erstes den neuen Dichtungsent-

wurf, des Auftaktgedichtes *Jetzt wär es Zeit*" (*KA*, 2:771). On the most persuasive interpretation of this intricate textual fabric, the poem exemplifies the recurring poetic principles of Rilke's last period—it interlaces the visible and the invisible, abstracts from concrete empirical phenomena, and embodies a worldview according to which everything can turn into its opposite. At the same time, "Idol" gathers a panoply of poetic forms that contradict and complement each other, balancing composition, rhetorical structures of meaning, images, and sounds, as well as different modes of lyric speech.

33. Fülleborn, *Das Strukturproblem der späten Lyrik Rilkes*, 172.

34. On these poems, see Louth, "Zu Rilkes Gong Gedichten," Stieg, "Rilkes späteste Gedichte auf deutsch und französisch," Riethmüller, "Rainer Maria Rilke, 'Gong,'" and Bauer, "'Un Doux Vent Polyglotte,'" 332-33.

35. For one possible account of Rilke's take on Fechner, see Fick, *Sinnenwelt und Weltseele*, 33-48, esp. 51-54.

36. See Fechner, *Elemente der Psychophysik*, 2:440. On Fechner, see Hagner, "Aufmerksamkeit als Ausnahmezustand," 282-83.

37. See Kohlschütter, *Messungen der Festigkeit des Schlafes*, 11. Kohlschütter dedicated his dissertation to his "beloved teacher" Gustav Fechner (3). For historical context on arousal threshold experiments and their continuation, see also Kinzler, *Das Joch des Schlafs*, 145-48, and Basner, "Arousal Threshold Determination in 1862." A further discussion of these experiments can be found in chapter 1 (Claparède on sleep curves) and again in chapter 4 (Proust and Vaschide) of this book.

38. "Klang, nicht mehr mit Gehör/meßbar." The quote is from a short draft entitled "Gong," written, like "Idol," in October 1925. See Rilke, *Gedichte*, 506. For some reason, the poem has been excluded from the *Kommentierte Ausgabe* (see 2:856). "Gong" radicalizes this thought further: "Nicht mehr für Ohren . . . : Klang/der, wie ein tieferes Ohr,/uns, scheinbar Hörende, hört./Umkehr der Räume" (*KA*, 2:396). On the gong poems, see also Louth, "Zu Rilkes Gong-Gedichten," 139-54.

39. Bauer speaks of "l'idole androgyne" and "dieu-déesse" ("'Un Doux Vent Polyglotte,'" 330).

40. See König, *"O komm und geh,"* esp. 71-72. Rilke completed the fifty-five poems of the *Sonette an Orpheus* in less than three weeks of manic writing in February 1922, at the same time as he wrote the final poems of the *Duineser Elegien*, with which he had struggled for almost a decade. The *Sonette* were conceived as a memorial for the young dancer Wera Ouckama Knoop, who had died of leukemia at the age of nineteen. The *Sonette* are thus often read as a philosophical attempt to interpret death as the condition of life rather than as its end. Formally, they address the mythic poet Orpheus, who is best known for descending into the underworld to regain his deceased wife Eurydice. However, lesser-known parts of the myth

(which Rilke evokes here) portray Orpheus as a figure whose song highlights the animateness of the natural world. For an overview and interpretation of the *Sonette* see especially Louth, *Rilke*, Zanucchi, "Rilkes 'Sonette an Orpheus' (1923)," König and Bremer, *Über "Die Sonette an Orpheus" von Rilke*, Eldridge, *Lyric Orientations*, 118–92, König, *"O komm und geh,"* and Gerok-Reiter, *Wink und Wandlung*.

41. "'L'explication orphique de la Terre, qui est le seul devoir du poëte et le jeu littéraire par excellence.'" (Mallarmé, "Lettre autobiographique à Verlaine" 392–93). For a comment on Mallarmé's "explication orphique de Terre" in relation to Rilke, see Louth, *Rilke*, 456–59, and Gerok-Reiter, *Wink und Wandlung*, 26–27. See also Rilke, "Vorrede zu einer Vorlesung aus eigenen Werken (*KA*, 4:707–9): "Die Arbeiten ... gehen ... aus der Überzeugung hervor, daß es eine/eigene berichtigte Aufgabe sei, die Weite,/Vielfältigkeit/ja Vollzähligkeit der Welt/in reinen Beweisen vorzuführen./Denn: ja! Zu einem derartigen Zeugnis hoffte ich mir das Gedicht zu erziehen, das es mir fähig werden sollte, alle Erscheinung, nicht nur das Gefühlsmäßige allein,/lyrisch zu begreifen" (708).

42. Mario Zanucchi formulates this insight in the following way: the sonnets "inszenieren den Symbolismus noch einmal, relativieren jedoch zugleich seinen Anspruch durch ihren diskursiven Rahmen. Aufgrund ihrer symbolisch-diskursiven Doppelkodierung befinden sich auch die Sonette in einer ständigen contradictio in adjecto" ("Transfer und Modifikation," 538).

43. For a reading of these poems, especially II.28, see König, *"O komm und geh,"* 19–30.

44. I have learned much from the following readings: Nebrig, "I.2," König, *"O komm und geh,"* 125–27, Knoop, "'Und fast ein Mädchen wars,'" and Gerok-Reiter, *Wink und Wandlung*, 150–51.

45. Leisi, *Rilkes Sonette an Orpheus*, 80.

46. Even though in English you can say "the house sleeps fifteen people," the verb "sleep" in that construction does not in fact refer to the act of sleeping but to providing accommodations.

47. "Je n'ai eu de repos que durant les neuf mois où j'ai dormi la vie dans le sein de ma mère" (Chateaubriand, "Préface testamentaire," 1:1047). A version of the *Mémoires d'outre-tombe* is preserved in Rilke's library. See Janssen, "Rilkes Bibliothek," 298.

48. On the "Aktive dieses Schlafens," see Krämer, *Rilkes "Sonette an Orpheus,"* 56. König, *"O komm und geh,"* proposes a similar argument: "The term receives an active meaning," and "'sleeping' is added to the list of terms which express creative processes in Rilke" that König calls "Schaffenswörter," a play on a common synonym for the term "verbs," referred to as "doing words" in primary school. König notes that "these words include, in addition to 'sleeping,' 'sounding' (creating sounds, instead of 'resonating'; on this compare poem I.26 of the *Sonnets of Orpheus*, line 1) and 'happening' (in the newly created sense of 'it is happening,' in the event; on

this compare poem II.1, l. 4).... The genesis of the new expression 'to sleep something' mirrors Rilke's own development as a poet towards this theory" (125-26).

49. "Seit den wunderbaren Schöpfungstagen/Schläft der Gott: wir sind sein Schlaf,/hingenommen, stumpf von ihm ertragen/unter Sternen, die er übertraf" (*KA*, 2:93).

50. See Lessing, "Wie die Alten den Tod gebildet."

51. Nebrig similarly observes an "Entzugsbewegung" in the poem (l. 2, l. 28). Withdrawal has long been identified as a characteristic figure in Rilke. See Mason, "Rilke and the Gesture of Withdrawal."

52. Pusse, "'Unter schläfernden Lidern,'" 162.

53. On the level of form, the performative reversal in sonnet II.XIV leads to an erasure of deictics ("Siehe"; "da"), an appearance of the potentialis ("nähme," "käme," "bliebe," "priese"), a tonal shift from heavy *we* assonances ("wer," "weiß," "wenn," "welken") to light *wie* sounds ("Winde," "Wiesen"), and to a falling silent.

54. Engel and Fülleborn, "Kommentar," 755.

55. One could read the "innige Schlafen" in relation to Rilke's characteristic understanding of "innig" as "a heightened intimacy that is achievable only with distance." For comments on "innig" in Rilke, see Christian, "Air, Ether, Atmosphere," 242.

56. The original reads "Doch aus dem Schlafenden fällt,/wie aus lagernder Wolke,/reichlicher Regen der Schwere" (*KA*, 2:383, ll. 6-8). The previous stanza opens with "Stehender" (standing one) (l. 5). Rilke explicitly rejects the idea that we fall asleep in *Die Aufzeichnungen des Malte Laurids Brigge*: "Der Ausdruck In-den-Schlaf-fallen paßt nicht.... Schlaf war etwas, was mit einem stieg, und von Zeit zu Zeit hatte man die Augen offen und lag auf einer neuen Oberfläche, die noch lang nicht die oberste war" (*KA*, 3:558).

57. "Comment échapper à notre emprise, fleurs? Comment ne pas être *nos* fleurs? Est-ce de tous ses pétales que la rose s'éloigne de nous? Veut-elle être rose-seule, rien-que-rose? Sommeil de personne sous tant de paupières?" (*KA Supp.*, 290, ll. 5-8). For the translation, see Rilke, *The Complete French Poems of Rainer Maria Rilke*, 219.

58. For a short summary of this work, see Stoppel, "Tagesperiodische Erscheinungen bei Pflanzen," 659-61. For a perspective from today's science, see Foster, *Life Time*, 5-6. It is Stoppel who attributes the term "Pflanzenschlaf" to Carl Linneaus.

59. Foster, *Life Time*, 6.

60. "Wie aus der Übersicht hervorgeht, sind unsere Kenntnisse der tagesperiodischen Erscheinungen bei Pflanzen noch sehr lückenhaft. Über die Ursache dieser Peridozität stehen wir vorläufig nur vor Vermutungen.... Wir sind somit in unserer Erkenntnis noch nicht viel weiter als Zinn im Jahre 1759" (Stoppel, "Tagesperiodische Erscheinungen bei Pflanzen," 668). Not much historiographical research

seems to have been undertaken on Stoppel. She is, however, briefly mentioned in Ahlheim, "Die Vermessung des Schlafs und die Optimierung des Menschen": "Als eine der ersten 'Rhythmusforscherinnen' hatte Rose Stoppel die 'tagesperiodischen Erscheinungen bei Pflanzen' untersucht und festgestellt, dass Bohnen, die schon als Keimlinge in dauernder Nacht und bei gleicher Temperatur gehalten wurden, sich in ihrem Stoffwechsel nach dem für sie ja eigentlich kaum wahrnehmbaren Tag- und-Nacht-Rhythmus richteten. Dabei 'schliefen' auch Bohnen, die als Saatgut aus Amerika oder Japan gekommen waren, in Deutschland nach dem europäischen Rhythmus" (16-17).

61. Louth, *Rilke*, 559.
62. Translation by Louth, *Rilke*, 559.
63. Wolff, *Rilkes Grabschrift*, 22.
64. For example, it is obvious that "Lider" (eyelids) implies "Lieder" (songs). Texts such as *Die Rosenschale* connect rose petals, eyelids, and sleep in a logic of overlayering and counting, while other texts that reference the "Schlaf der tausend Rosenaugenlider" identify the lyrical subject with the sleep of the rose: "Rosen- Schlaf, ich bin dein Schläfer" (*KA*, 2:104).
65. For an account of possible readings of this poem, see Wolff, *Rilkes Grabschrift*. Wolff himself stresses the openness of the poem to diverging interpretations. For the emblem, see Selbmann, "Rainers Widersprüche," 171. For the haiku, see Klawitter, "'Komprimierte Kunstpillen,'" Wittbrodt, *Hototogisu ist keine Nachtigall*, 176-98, Motoyoshi, "Das japanische Kurzgedicht in der europäischen Moderne," and Meyer, "Rilkes Begegnung mit dem Haiku."

Conclusion

1. This description of *Sleep Works* goes back to a felicitous suggestion by Tom Levin. Methodologically, it is inspired by Vogl, "Für eine Poetologie des Wissens."
2. The nickname coined by Carus Sterne plays on the then-official company name Chemische Fabrik auf Aktien (which translates as "chemical factory with a stock market listing"). At other times, the company was called Schering. See Kinzler, *Das Joch des Schlafs*, 193.
3. Macho, *Todesmetaphern*, 249-67, here 253. Macho quotes Aristotle, Lessing, Kant, Hegel, and Freud.
4. Hofmannsthal, *Dramen*, 37: "Arzt: Der Schlaftrunk wirkt auf erschreckende Weise.—Es kommt zuerst über den, der getrunken hat, eine grosse Angst und Unruhe. Die elementarischen Lebenskräfte fühlen, dass sie gebunden werden sollen und empören in ihrer ganzen Stärke sich gegen die Überwältigung. Sodann . . . wird dem Herrn ein Anblick zuteil werden, wie dem Priester am Sterbebett eines Gerechten zuteil wird. . . . Dies währt, bis der Leib das Übergewaltige nicht mehr aushält . . . und dumpf hinabstürzt in todesähnlichen Schlaf."

5. On modernism and death in English-language writing, see Sherman, *In a Strange Room*.

6. Mann, *The Magic Mountain*, 656-57. For the original, see Mann, *Der Zauberberg*, 442-44. Woods translates "sinnige Vorstellung" as "sedate notion," which fits Mann's ironic tone, but it could also be rendered as "suggestive notion."

Works Cited

Archives

Archive of Medical History, University of Zürich
Bayer AG Corporate Archives, Leverkusen (abbreviated as BAL)
Deutsche Kinemathek Schering Archiv, Bayer AG, Berlin.
Sigmund Freud Papers, Library of Congress, Washington, DC
Wellcome Collection, London

Primary Literature and Sources

Albaret, Céleste. *Monsieur Proust: Souvenirs recueillis par Georges Belmont*. Paris: Laffont, 1975.
Altenberg, Peter. *Mein Lebensabend*. Berlin: S. Fischer, 1919.
Auerbach, Siegmund. *Die Behandlung der nervösen Schlaflosigkeit*. Munich: Verlag der Aerztlichen Rundschau Otto Gmelin, 1921.
Bachem, Carl. *Unsere Schlafmittel mit besonderer Berücksichtigung der neueren*. 2nd ed. Berlin: August Hirschwald, 1910.
Baudelaire, Charles. *The Flowers of Evil*. Translated by James McGowan. Oxford: Oxford University Press, 2008.
———. *Œuvres complètes*. Edited by Claude Pichois and Jean Ziegler. 2 vols. Paris: Gallimard, 1975-76.
Beer-Hoffmann, Richard. *Der Tod Georgs*. Paderborn: Mentis, 1994.
Benjamin, Walter. "Hashish, Beginning of March, 1930." In *Selected Writings*, vol. 2, edited by Michael W. Jennings, Howard Eiland, and Gary Smith, translated by Edmund Jephcott, 327-30. Cambridge, MA: Belknap Press of Harvard University Press, 1999.
———. "Hashish in Marseilles." In *Selected Writings*, vol. 2, edited by Michael W. Jennings, Howard Eiland, and Gary Smith, translated by Edmund Jephcott, 673-79. Cambridge, MA: Belknap Press of Harvard University Press, 1999.

———. "Main Features of My Second Impression of Hashish." In *Selected Writings*, vol. 2, edited by Michael W. Jennings, Howard Eiland, and Gary Smith, translated by Edmund Jephcott, 85-90. Cambridge, MA: Belknap Press of Harvard University Press, 1999.

———. "Das Passagen-Werk. Aufzeichnungen und Materialien." In *Gesammelte Schriften, Das Passagen-Werk,* vol. 5, pt. 1, edited by Rolf Tiedemann, 79-654. Frankfurt am Main: Suhrkamp, 1991.

———. "Surrealism." In *Selected Writings*, vol. 2, edited by Michael W. Jennings, Howard Eiland, and Gary Smith, translated by Edmund Jephcott, 207-21. Cambridge, MA: Belknap Press of Harvard University Press, 1999.

Benn, Gottfried. *Sämtliche Werke: Stuttgarter Ausgabe*. Vol. 1, poems 1. Edited by Gerhard Schuster. Stuttgart: Klett-Cotta, 1986.

Berger, Hans. "Über das Elektrenkephalogramm des Menschen." *Archiv für Psychiatrie und Nervenkrankheiten* 87, no. 1 (1929): 527-70.

———. "Über das Elektrenkephalogramm des Menschen: Dritte Mitteilung." *Archiv für Psychiatrie und Nervenkrankheiten* 94, no. 1 (1931): 16-60.

———. "Über das Elektrenkephalogramm des Menschen: Vierte Mitteilung." *Archiv für Psychiatrie und Nervenkrankheiten* 97, no. 1 (1932): 6-26.

———. "Über das Elektrenkephalogramm des Menschen: Achte Mitteilung." *Archiv für Psychiatrie und Nervenkrankheiten* 102 (1933): 452-69.

———. "Über das Elektrenkephalogramm des Menschen: Neunte Mitteilung." *Archiv für Psychiatrie und Nervenkrankheiten* 102 (1934): 539-57.

Bergson, Henri. *L'énergie spirituelle*. 3rd. ed. Paris: Presses Universitaires de France, 1990.

Bofinger. "Zur Kasuistik der Veronalvergiftung." *Deutsche Medizinische Wochenschrift* 48, no. 45 (1922): 1518-19.

Breton, André. *Manifestes du surréalisme*. Paris: Gallimard, 1975.

———. "What Is Surrealism?" In André Breton, *What Is Surrealism? Selected Writings*, edited by Franklin Rosement, 112-41. New York: Monad Press, 1978.

Breuer, Josef, and Sigmund Freud. *Studien über Hysterie*. Leipzig: Franz Deuticke, 1895.

Broch, Hermann. *Die Schlafwandler*. Frankfurt am Main: Suhrkamp, 1994.

Charcot, Jean-Martin. *Leçons du mardi à la Salpêtrière: Policlinique, 1888-1889*. Paris: Lecrosnier & Babé, 1889.

Chateaubriand, François-René de. "Préface testamentaire." In *Mémoires d'outre-tombe*, vol. 1, edited by Maurice Levaillant and Georges Moulinier, 1044-48. Paris: Gallimard, 1951.

Claparède, Édouard. "Édouard Claparède." In vol. 1 of *A History of Psychology in Autobiography*, 63-97. Worcester, MA: Clark University Press, 1930.

———. "Esquisse d'une théorie biologique du sommeil." *Archives de Psychologie* 4 (1905): 246-349.

———. "La question du sommeil." *L'année psychologique* 18 (1911): 419-59.
Degner, Ernst. "Das medizinisch-kinematographische Universitäts-Institut, Berlin, Charité, und seine Organisation." *Medizin und Film* 3 (1926): 43-44.
———. "Medizinische Kinematographie." In *Photographisches Praktikum für Mediziner und Naturwissenschaftler*, edited by Alfred Hay, 303-35. Vienna: Springer, 1930.
De Quincey, Thomas. *Confessions of an English Opium-Eater and Other Writings*. New York: Random House, 2013.
Deutsches Adelsblatt: Zeitschrift der Deutschen Adelsgenossenschaft für die Aufgaben des christlichen Adels 51 (1933).
Diderot, Denis. *Entretien entre d'Alembert et Diderot*. Paris: Garnier, 2018.
Dostoyevsky, Fyodor. *Notes from Underground: The Double*. Translated by Jessie Coulson. Harmondsworth, UK: Penguin, 1987.
Dubois, Raphael. "Le centre du sommeil." *Comptes rendus hebdomadaires des séances et mémoires de la société de biologie* 53 (1901): 229-30.
E. Merck. "Zur Kasuistik der Veronalvergiftung." *Deutsche Medizinische Wochenschrift* 49, no. 17 (1923): 55.
Economo, Constantin von. *Cellular Structure of the Human Cerebral Cortex*. Edited by Lazaros Triarhou. Basel: Karger, 2009.
———. "Die centralen Bahnen des Kau- und Schluckactes." *Pflügers Archiv für die gesamte Physiologie des Menschen und der Tiere* 91 (1902): 629-43.
———. "Die Encephalitis lethargica." *Jahrbücher für Psychiatrie und Neurologie* 38 (1917): 253-331.
———. *Die Encephalitis lethargica*. Leipzig: Deuticke, 1918.
———. "Encephalitis lethargica." *Wiener Medizinische Wochenschrift* 73 (1923): 778-82; 836-38; 1114-17; 1243-49; 1334-38.
———. "Die Encephalitis lethargica Epidemia ('Schlafkrankheit') und ihr Verhältnis zu Grippe und Krieg." In *Volksgesundheit im Krieg*, edited by Clemens Pirque von Cesnatico, 67-70. Vienna: Hölder-Pichler-Tempsky, 1926.
———. *Die Encephalitis lethargica: Ihre Nachkrankheiten und ihre Behandlung*. Munich: Urban & Schwarzenberg, 1929.
———. "Neue Beiträge zur Encephalitis lethargica." *Neurologisches Centralblatt* 36 (1917): 866-78.
———. "Nochmals zur Frage der arealen Grenzen in der Hirnrinde (Antwort auf die Vogtschen Darstellungen)." *Zeitschrift für die gesamte Neurologie und Psychiatrie* 124 (1930), 309-16.
———. "Pathologie des Schlafs." In *Handbuch der normalen und pathologischen Physiologie. Mit Berücksichtigung der experimentellen Pharmakologie*, vol. 17, edited by Leo Adler, Julius Bauer, Wilhelm Caspari, and Ulrich Ebbecke, 591-610. Berlin: Springer, 1926.
———. "Professor Emil Redlich (†)." *Zeitschrift für die gesamte Neurologie und Psychiatrie* 133 (1931): 322-28.

———. "Der Schlaf als Lokalisationsproblem." In *Der Schlaf: Mitteilungen und Stellungnahme zum derzeitigen Stand des Schlafproblems*, edited by David Sarason, 38-54. Munich: Lehmann, 1929.

———. "Schlaftheorie." *Ergebnisse der Physiologie* 28 (1929): 312-39.

———. "Sleep as a Problem of Localization." *Journal of Nervous and Mental Disease* 71, no. 3 (1930): 249-59.

———. "Über den Schlaf." *Wiener Medizinische Wochenschrift* 38 (1925): 873-76.

Fechner, Gustav Theodor. *Elemente der Psychophysik*. 2 vols. Leipzig: Breitkopf und Härtel, 1860.

Fischer, Emil, and Josef von Mering. "Ueber eine neue Klasse von Schlafmitteln." *Die Therapie der Gegenwart*, no. 3 (1903): 97-101.

Flatau, Georg. "Ueber die nervöse Schlaflosigkeit und deren Behandlung mit besonderer Berücksichtigung der Psychotherapie." *Berliner Klinik* 157 (1901): 1-16.

Flury, Ferdinand. "Statistik der Vergiftungen." In *Lehrbuch der Toxikologie für Studium und Praxis*, edited by Max Cloetta, Edwin Faust, Ferdinand Flury, Erich Hübener, and Heinrich Zangger, 52-59. Berlin: Springer, 1928.

Freud, Sigmund. "Briefe an Arthur Schnitzler." *Die Neue Rundschau* 66 (1955): 95-106.

———. "Der Dichter und das Phantasieren." In *Werke aus den Jahren 1906-1909*, vol. 7 of *Gesammelte Werke*, edited by Anna Freud et al., 213-23. Frankfurt am Main: S. Fischer, 1966.

———. *The Interpretation of Dreams*. Edited and translated by James Strachey. New York: Basic Books, 2010.

———. *Nachtragsband, Texte aus den Jahren 1885 bis 1938*. Vol. 18 of *Gesammelte Werke*. Edited by Angela Richards. Frankfurt am Main: S. Fischer, 1987.

———. *Die Traumdeutung*. Edited by Alexander Mitscherlich, Angela Richards, and James Strachey. Frankfurt am Main: S. Fischer, 1989.

———. *Schriften über Kokain*. Edited by Albrecht Hirschmüller. Frankfurt am Main: S. Fischer, 1996.

———. *Vorlesungen zur Einführung in die Psychoanalyse*. Vol. 11 of *Gesammelte Werke*. Edited by Edward Bibring, Willi Hoffer, Ernst Kris, and Otto Isakower. Frankfurt am Main: S. Fischer, 1969.

Gaupp, Robert. "Über Wesen und Behandlung der Schlaflosigkeit: Erstes Referat." In *Verhandlungen des Deutschen Kongresses für Innere Medizin. Einunddreißigster Kongress gehalten zu Wiesbaden vom 20.-23. April 1914*, edited by Wilhelm Weintraud, 9-44. Wiesbaden: Bergmann, 1914.

Gélineau, Jean-Baptiste. "De la narcolepsie." *Gazette des hôpitaux* 54 (1880): 626-28; 635-37.

"Gesundheitsrat." *Blatt der Hausfrau* 16, no. 19 (1905): 552.

Hauptmann, A. "Neurasthenische und hysterische Äußerungen und Konstitutionen."

In *Lehrbuch der Nervenkrankheiten*, 2nd ed., edited by Hans Curschmann and Franz Kramer, 612-704. Berlin: Springer, 1925.

Hegel, Georg Friedrich Wilhelm. *Enzyklopädie der philosophischen Wissenschaften im Grundrisse*. Vol. 10 of *Werke*, edited by Eva Moldenhauer and Karl Markus Michel. Frankfurt am Main: Suhrkamp, 1986.

Hess, W. R. *Biological Order and Brain Organization: Selected Works of W. R. Hess*. Edited and translated by Konrad Akert. New York: Springer, 1981.

———. "Der Schlaf." *Klinische Wochenschrift* 12, no. 4 (1933): 129-34.

———. "Über die Wechselbeziehungen zwischen psychischen und vegetativen Funktionen." *Schweizer Archiv für Neurologie und Psychiatrie* 15 (1924): 260-77.

———. "Über die Wechselbeziehungen zwischen psychischen und vegetativen Funktionen." *Schweizer Archiv für Neurologie und Psychiatrie* 16 (1925): 36-55, 285-306.

Hofmannsthal, Hugo von. *Dramen: Der Turm*. Vol. 14, pt. 1, of *Sämtliche Werke:*, edited by Werner Bellmann. Frankfurt am Main: S. Fischer, 1990.

Huelsenbeck, Richard. *En avant Dada: Eine Geschichte des Dadaismus*. Hannover: Paul Steegemann, 1920.

Hufeland, Christoph Wilhelm. *Bemerkungen über die Brownsche Praxis*. Vol. 1. Tübingen: Cotta'sche Buchhandlung, 1799.

"Ein ideales Schlafmittel: Veronal." *Neues Wiener Journal*, May 28, 1903.

"Im 'Bulletin de la Société Royale de Pharmacie de Bruxelles.'" *Apotheker-Zeitung* 23, no. 53 (1908): 476.

Jacobsohn, Leo. *Klinik der Nervenkrankheiten: Ein Lehrbuch für Ärzte und Studierende*. Berlin: August Hirschwald, 1913.

James, William. *The Principles of Psychology*. Vol. 1. New York: Holt, 1890.

Janouch, Gustav. *Conversations with Kafka*. 2nd ed., rev. enl. New York: New Directions, 2012.

Kafka, Franz. "Beschreibung eines Kampfes: Schwarzes Schulheft, 'Fassung A'." In *Nachgelassene Schriften und Fragmente I*, vol. 1, *Textband*, edited by Malcolm Pasley, 54-120. Frankfurt am Main: S. Fischer, 1993.

———. *Briefe, 1900-1912*. Edited by Hans-Gerd Koch. Frankfurt am Main: S. Fischer, 1999.

———. *Briefe, 1913-März 1914*. Edited by Hans-Gerd Koch. Frankfurt am Main: S. Fischer, 1999.

———. *Briefe, April 1914-1917*. Edited by Hans-Gerd Koch. Frankfurt am Main: S. Fischer, 1999.

———. *Briefe, 1902-1924*. Edited by Max Brod. Frankfurt am Main: S. Fischer, 1958.

———. "The Burrow." In *A Hunger Artist and Other Stories*, translated by Joyce Crick, 153-83. Oxford: University Press, 2009.

———. *The Castle*. Translated by Anthea Bell. New York: Oxford University Press, 2009.

———. *The Diaries of Franz Kafka, 1910-23*. New York: Schocken, 1988.

———. *The Drawings*. Edited by Andreas B. Kilcher and translated by Kurt Beals. New Haven, CT: Yale University Press, 2022.

———. *"Einmal ein grosser Zeichner": Franz Kafka als bildender Künstler*. 2nd ed. Edited by Niels Bokhove and Marijke van Dorst. Prague: Vitalis, 2011.

———. *A Hunger Artist and Other Stories*. Translated by Joyce Crick. Oxford: University Press, 2009.

———. "In der Strafkolonie." In *Drucke zu Lebzeiten*, edited by Wolf Kittler, Hans-Gerd Koch, and Gerhard Neumann, 203-48. Frankfurt am Main: S. Fischer 1994.

———. "In the Penal Colony." In *The Metamorphosis and Other Stories*, translated by Joyce Crick, 75-99. Oxford: University Press, 2009.

———. "Investigations of a Dog." In *A Hunger Artist and Other Stories*, translated by Joyce Crick, 121-52. Oxford: University Press, 2009.

———. *Letters to Felice*. New York: Schocken, 1973.

———. *The Metamorphosis*. Translated by Stanley Corngold. New York: Norton, 1996.

———. *Nachgelassene Schriften und Fragmente II*. Vol. 1. *Textband*. Edited by Jost Schillemeit. Frankfurt am Main: S. Fischer, 1992.

———. *Nachgelassene Schriften und Fragmente II*. Vol. 2. *Apparatband*. Edited by Jost Schillemeit. Frankfurt am Main: S. Fischer, 1992.

———. *Der Proceß*. Edited by Malcolm Pasley. Frankfurt am Main: S. Fischer, 1990.

———. *Der Proceß: Apparatband*. Edited by Malcolm Pasley. Frankfurt am Main: S. Fischer, 1990.

———. *Das Schloss*. Frankfurt am Main: S. Fischer, 1982.

———. *Tagebücher*. Edited by Hans-Gerd Koch, Michael Müller, and Malcolm Pasley. Frankfurt am Main: S. Fischer, 1990.

———. *The Trial*. Translated by Michael Mitchell. New York: Oxford University Press, 2009.

———. *Der Verschollene*. Edited by Jost Schillemeit. Frankfurt am Main: S. Fischer, 1983.

———. "Die Verwandlung." In *Drucke zu Lebzeiten*, edited by Wolf Kittler, Hans-Gerd Koch, and Gerhard Neumann, 115-200. Frankfurt am Main: S. Fischer 1994.

Kohlschütter, Ernst. *Messungen der Festigkeit des Schlafes: Inaugural-Dissertation verfasst mit Zustimmung der medizinischen Facultät der Universität Leipzig*. Leipzig: Kreysing, 1862.

Kruse, Uve Jens. *Das Büchlein zum guten Schlaf*. Buchenbach: Felsen, 1920.

Lechner, Karl. *Die klinischen Formen der Schlaflosigkeit*. Leipzig: Deuticke, 1909.

Lessing, Gotthold Ephraim. "Wie die Alten den Tod gebildet." In *Werke und Briefe*, edited by Wilfried Barner, 715-78. Frankfurt am Main: Deutscher Klassiker Verlag, 1985.

Lewy, Friedrich Heinrich. "Akute Encephalitis lethargica." *Medizin und Film* 3, no. 1 (1926): 28-29.
Lhermitte, Jean. *Le sommeil*. Paris: Colin, 1931.
Liébeault, Ambroise-Auguste. "Das Wachen, ein activer Seelenzustand—Der Schlaf, ein passiver Seelenzustand—Physiologisch passive Zustände, beziehentlich pathologische, welche dem Schlaf analog sind—Suggestion." *Zeitschrift für Hypnotismus* 3 (1894-95): 22-28; 33-45.
Mallarmé, Stéphane. "Lettre autobiographique à Verlaine." In *Igitur, Divagations, Un coup de dés*, edited by Bertrand Marchal, 390-96. Paris: Gallimard, 2003.
Manacéïne, Marie de. "Quelques observations expérimentales sur l'influence de l'insomnie absolue." *Archives Italiennes de Biologie* 21 (1894): 322-25.
Mann, Thomas. ["Braucht man zum Dichten Schlaf und Zigaretten?"]. In *Reden und Aufsätze 3*, vol. 11 of *Gesammelte Werke in zwölf Bänden*, 764-66. Frankfurt am Main: S. Fischer 1960.
———. *The Magic Mountain*. Translated by John E. Woods. New York: Everyman's Library, 2005.
———. *Süßer Schlaf!* In *Essays: 1893-1914*, vol. 14, pt. 1, of *Große kommentierte Frankfurter Ausgabe: Werke—Briefe—Tagebücher*, edited by Heinrich Detering, 202-9. Frankfurt am Main: S. Fischer 2002.
———. *Der Zauberberg*. Vol. 5, pt. 1, of *Große kommentierte Frankfurter Ausgabe*, edited by Heinrich Detering, Eckhard Heftrich, Hermann Kurzke, et al. Frankfurt am Main: S. Fischer, 2002.
Marx, Karl, and Friedrich Engels. *Das Kapital*. Vol. 23 of *Werke*. Berlin/East: Dietz, 1968.
Maupassant, Guy de. *Notre cœur: Illustrations de René Lelong*. Paris: Société d'éditions littéraires et artistiques, 1902.
Maury, Alfred. "Des hallucinations hypnagogiques, ou des erreurs des sens dans l'état intermédiaire entre la vielle et le sommeil." *Annales médico-psychologiques* 11 (1848): 26-40.
———. *Le sommeil et les rêves: Études psychologiques sur ces phénomènes et les divers états qui s'y rattachent*. Paris: Didier et cie, 1861.
Mauthner, Ludwig. "Zur Pathologie und Physiologie des Schlafes nebst Bemerkungen über die 'Nona.'" *Wiener Medizinische Wochenschrift* 40, nos. 23-28 (1890): 962-64; 1002-4; 1050-52; 1144-46; 1185-88.
Mingazzini, Giovanni. "Klinischer und anatomisch-pathologischer Beitrag zum Studium der Encephalitis epidemica (lethargica)." *Zeitschrift für die gesamte Neurologie und Psychiatrie* 63 (1921): 199-244.
Mosso, Angelo. *La fatica*. 3rd ed. Milano: Frat. Treves, 1891.
———. *Fatigue*. Translated by Margaret Drummond and W. B. Drummond. London: Sonnenschein, 1904.
———. *La paura*. Milano: Frat. Treves, 1884.

Nietzsche, Friedrich. *Nachgelassene Fragmente, 1887-1889*. Vol. 13 of *Sämtliche Werke*. Edited by Giorgio Colli and Mazzino Montinari. Munich: Deutscher Taschenbuch Verlag, 1999.

Oppenheim, Hermann. "Die Neurasthenie oder Nervenschwäche." In *Lehrbuch der Nervenkrankheiten für Ärzte und Studierende*, 1008-1148. Berlin: Karger, 1923.

Pawlow, Ivan. "Innere Hemmung" der bedingten Reflexe und der Schlaf—ein und derselbe Prozeß." *Skandinavisches Archiv für Physiologie* 44, no. 1 (1923): 42-58.

Piéron, Henri. *Le problème physiologique du sommeil*. Paris: Masson, 1913.

Plötzl, Otto. "Der Schlaf als psychisches Problem." In *Der Schlaf: Mitteilungen und Stellungnahme zum derzeitigen Stand des Schlafproblems*, edited by David Sarason, 24-38. Munich: Lehmann, 1929.

———. "Zur Physiologie des Schlafes." In *Der Schlaf: Mitteilungen und Stellungnahme zum derzeitigen Stand des Schlafproblems*, edited by David Sarason, 54-64. Munich: Lehmann, 1929.

Proust, Adrien, and Gilbert Ballet. *L'hygiène du neurasthénique*. Paris: Masson & Cie, 1897.

Proust, Marcel. *Contre Sainte-Beuve*. Edited by Pierre Clarac. Paris: Gallimard, 1971.

———. *Correspondance*. 21 vols. Edited by Philip Kolb. Paris: Plon, 1970.

———. *À la recherche du temps perdu*. 4 vols. Paris: Gallimard, 1987-89.

———. *In Search of Lost Time*. Vol 6: *Finding Time Again*. 6th ed. Edited by Christopher Prendergast. Translated by Ian Patterson. London: Penguin Classics, 2003.

———. *In Search of Lost Time*. Vol. 2: *In the Shadow of Young Girls in Flower*. 2nd ed. Edited by Christopher Prendergast. Translated by James Grieve. London: Penguin Classics, 2003.

———. *In Search of Lost Time*. Vol. 4: *Sodom and Gomorrah*. 4th ed. Edited by Christopher Prendergast. Translated by John Sturrock. London: Penguin Classics, 2003.

———. *In Search of Lost Time*. Vol. 3: *The Guermantes Way*. 3rd ed. Edited by Christopher Prendergast. Translated by Mark Treharne. London: Penguin Classics, 2003.

———. *In Search of Lost Time*. Vol. 5: *The Prisoner and the Fugitive*. 5th ed. Edited by Christopher Prendergast. Translated by Carol Clark. London: Penguin Classics, 2003.

———. *In Search of Lost Time*. Vol. 1: *The Way by Swann's*. Edited by Christopher Prendergast. Translated by Lydia Davis. London: Penguin Classics, 2003.

———. Préface. In *Préface, traduction et notes à "La Bible d'Amiens" de John Ruskin*, edited by Yves-Michel Ergal, 11-84. Paris: Bartillat, 2007.

———. *Selected Letters*. Vol. 4: *1918-1922*. Edited by Philip Kolb. Translated by Joanna Kilmartin. London: Collins, 2000.

Proust, Marcel, and Jacques Rivière. *Correspondance, 1914-1922*. Edited by Philip Kolb. Rev. ed. Paris: Gallimard, 1976.

Redlich, Emil. "Über Narkolepsie." *Zeitschrift für die gesamte Neurologie und Psychiatrie* 95 (1925): 256-70.
———. "Zur Narkolepsiefrage." *Monatsschrift für Psychiatrie und Neurologie* 37 (1915): 85-94.
Renner, Albrecht. *Schlafmittel-Therapie*. Berlin: Springer, 1925.
———. "Über Schlafmittel und ihre Wirkungen (einschließlich Nebenwirkungen und Vergiftungen)." *Ergebnisse der Inneren Medizin und Kinderheilkunde* 23 (1923): 234-336.
Rilke, Rainer Maria. *Briefe aus Muzot: 1921 bis 1926*. Leipzig: Insel, 1935.
———. *The Complete French Poems of Rainer Maria Rilke*. Translated by Alfred Poulin Jr. Saint Paul, MN: Graywolf Press, 1986.
———. *Gedichte*, pt. 2. Vol. 2 of *Sämtliche Werke in sieben Bänden*, edited by Ernst Zinn and Ruth Sieber-Rilke. Wiesbaden: Insel, 1956.
———. *Kommentierte Ausgabe*. 4 vols. Edited by Manfred Engel, Ulrich Fülleborn, Horst Nalewski, and August Stahl. Frankfurt am Main: Insel, 1996-2003.
———. *Letters of Rainer Maria Rilke*, vol. 1: *1892-1910*. Translated by Jane Greene and M. D. Herter Norton. New York: Norton, 1969.
———. *Letters of Rainer Maria Rilke*, vol. 2: *1910-1926*. Translated by Jane Greene and M. D. Herter Norton. New York: Norton, 1969.
———. *New Poems*. Translated by Len Krisak. Woodbridge: Boydell and Brewer, 2015.
———. *The Notebooks of Malte Laurids Brigge*. Translated by Robert Vilain. Oxford: Oxford University Press, 2016.
———. *Sonnets to Orpheus*. Translated by Edward Snow. Bilingual ed. New York: North Point Press, 2014.
———. *Sonnets to Orpheus with Letters to a Young Poet*. Translated by Stephen Cohn. Manchester, UK: Carcanet, 2000.
———. *Supplementband* to *Kommentierte Ausgabe*. Edited by Manfred Engel, Ulrich Fülleborn, Horst Nalewski, and August Stahl. Frankfurt am Main: Insel, 2003.
———. *Übertragungen*. Vol. 7 of *Sämtliche Werke*, edited by Walter Simon, Karin Wais, and Ernst Zinn. Wiesbaden: Insel, 1997.
Sarason, David. "Zur Einführung." In *Der Schlaf: Mitteilungen und Stellungnahme zum derzeitigen Stand des Schlafproblems*, edited by David Sarason, 5-9. Munich: Lehmann, 1929.
Schenk, Paul. *Versuch einer psychologischen Theorie des Schlafes*. Leipzig: Druck der Werkgemeinschaft, 1928.
Schopenhauer, Arthur. *Die Welt als Wille und Vorstellung*. Vol. 3 of *Zürcher Ausgabe: Werke in zehn Bänden*, edited by Angelika Hübscher. Zürich: Diogenes, 1977.
Schnitzler, Arthur. *Briefe*, vol. 2: *1913-1931*. Edited by Peter Michael Braunwarth et al. Frankfurt am Main: S. Fischer, 1984.
———. *Fräulein Else*. Vienna: Paul Zsolnay, 1925.

———. *Fräulein Else*. In *Desire and Delusion: Three Novellas*, translated by Margret Schaefer, 192-264. Chicago: Dee, 2003.

———. "Genese von *Fräulein Else*." In Arthur Schnitzler, *Arthur Schnitzler Digital: Historisch-Kritische Werkausgabe*, https://www.schnitzler-edition.net/chronologie/9257#.

———. *Gesammelte Werke in Einzelausgaben: Das Dramatische Werk*. Vol. 1: *Liebelei und andere Dramen*. Frankfurt am Main: S. Fischer Taschenbuch, 1986.

———. *Medizinische Schriften*. Edited by Horst Thomé. Vienna: Zsolnay, 1988.

———. "Der Mörder." In *Erzählungen*, edited by Hartmut Scheible, 332-52. Düsseldorf: Artemis & Winkler, 2002.

———. "Rezension zu Erlenmeyer, 'Die Morphiumsucht und ihre Behandlung.'" In *Medizinische Schriften*, edited by Horst Thomé, 141-45. Vienna: Zsolnay, 1988.

———. *Traumnovelle*. In *Gesammelte Werke: Die Erzählenden Schriften*, edited by Heinrich Schnitzler, 2:434-505. Frankfurt am Main: S. Fischer, 1961.

"Selbstmordversuch oder Unfall des Filmschauspielers Max Linder." *Neue Freie Presse*, February 23, 1924.

Seyfarth, Carl. *Strümpell-Seyfarth Lehrbuch der speziellen Pathologie und Therapie der inneren Krankheiten: Für Studierende und Ärzte*. 27th ed. Leipzig: F. C. W. Vogel, 1928.

Siemerling, Ernst. *Schlaf und Schlaflosigkeit*. Berlin: Schwabacher'sche Verlagsbuchhandlung, 1923.

Sommer, Ernst. *Kraft durch Ruhe: Wie man nach Belieben einschläft und die Schlaflosigkeit bemeistert*. 11th ed. Oranienburg-Berlin: Orania, 1913.

Starck, Fritz. *Die Kunst gut zu schlafen und früh aufzustehen: Eine Anleitung, sich einen gesunden Schlaf zu erhalten, die Schlaflosigkeit zu heilen, plötzliches Aufschrecken, Schnarchen, Alpdrücken zu beseitigen, schön zu träumen und früh aufzustehen*. Munich: Melchior Kupferschmid, 1908.

Stoppel, Rose. "Tagesperiodische Erscheinungen bei Pflanzen." In *Handbuch der normalen und pathologischen Physiologie: Mit Berücksichtigung der experimentellen Pharmakologie*, vol. 17, edited by Leo Adler, Julius Bauer, Wilhelm Caspari, and Ulrich Ebbecke, 659-68. Berlin: Springer, 1926.

Svevo, Italo. *La coscienza di Zeno*. Vol 3. of *Edizione critica delle opere di Italo Svevo*, edited by Bruno Maier. Rome: Studio Tesi, 1985.

Tomanek, Eduard. "Ueber den Einfluss des Čechischen auf die Deutsche Umgangssprache in Österreich-Schlesien, besonders in Troppau und Umgebung: Ein Beitrag zur Sprachmischung." In *Jahresbericht des k.k. Staats-Gynmasiums in Troppau für das Schuljahr 1890-91*, 3-39. Troppau: Adolf Drechsler, 1891.

Traugott, Richard. *Die nervöse Schlaflosigkeit und ihre Behandlung*. 3rd ed. Würzburg: Curt Kabitzsch, 1913.

Trömner, Ernst. *Das Problem des Schlafes: Biologisch und psychophysiologisch betrachtet*. Wiesbaden: Bergmann, 1912.

———. "Schlaf und Encephalitis." *Zeitschrift für die gesamte Neurologie und Psychiatrie* 101 (1926): 786-97.
"Unter der sehr bezeichnenden Überschrift 'Die Tablettenseuche.'"*Apotheker-Zeitung* 23, no. 44 (1908): 388-89.
Valéry, Paul. *Album de vers anciens, Jeune Parque, Charmes*. Vol. 3 of *Œuvres de Paul Valéry*. Paris: Nouvelle Revue Française, 1931.
———. *Cahiers*. 2 vols. Edited by Judith Robinson. Paris: Gallimard, 1973.
———. *Lettres à quelques-uns*. 7th ed. Paris: Gallimard, 1952.
———. *Poems*. Vol. 1 of *Collected Works of Paul Valéry*, translated by David Paul. Princeton, NJ: Princeton University Press, 1971.
Vaschide, Nicolas. *Le sommeil et les rêves*. Paris: Flammarion, 1911.
Vogt, Oskar. "Zur Kenntniss [sic] des Wesens und der psychologischen Bedeutung des Hypnotismus." *Zeitschrift für Hypnotismus, Suggestionstherapie, Suggestionslehre und verwandte psychologische Forschungen* 3 (1894-95): 277-340.
———. "Zur Kenntniss [sic] des Wesens und der psychologischen Bedeutung des Hypnotismus." *Zeitschrift für Hypnotismus* 4-5 (1895-96): 32-45; 122-67; 229-44.
Wharton, Edith. *The House of Mirth*. Edited by Martha Banta. New York: Oxford University Press, 1994.
Winternitz, H. "Über Veronalnatrium." *Medizinische Klinik* 4, no. 31 (1908): 1189-90.
Woolf, Virginia. *Orlando: A Biography*. Edited by Suzanne Raitt and Ian Blyth. Cambridge: Cambridge University Press, 2018.
Wundt, Wilhelm. *Grundzüge der physiologischen Psychologie*. 6th rev. ed. Vol. 3. Leipzig: Engelmann, 1911.

Secondary Literature

Adorno, Theodor W. "Standort des Erzählers im zeitgenössischen Roman." In *Noten zur Literatur I*, 41-48. Darmstadt: Wissenschaftliche Buchgesellschaft, 2015.
Aebischer, Gaspard. "De la veille à l'insomnie: Une histoire des nuits sans sommeil au 19e siècle." PhD diss., University of Geneva, 2018. https://archive-ouverte.unige.ch/unige:108475.
Aebischer, Gaspard, and Philip Alexander Rieder. "Awaking Insomnia: Sleeplessness in the 19th Century through Medical Literature." *Medical Humanities* (November 2019): 1-8.
Ahlheim, Hannah, ed. *Kontrollgewinn—Kontrollverlust: Die Geschichte des Schlafs in der Moderne*. Frankfurt am Main: Campus, 2014.
———. *Der Traum vom Schlaf im 20. Jahrhundert: Wissen, Optimierungsphantasien und Widerständigkeit*. Göttingen: Wallstein, 2018.
———. "Die Vermessung des Schlafs und die Optimierung des Menschen: Eine

deutsch-amerikanische Geschichte (1930-1960)." *Zeithistorische Forschungen* 10, no. 1 (2013): 13-37.

Akert, Konrad. "Walter Rudolf Hess (1881-1973) and His Contribution to Neuroscience." *Journal of the History of the Neurosciences* 8, no. 3 (1999): 248-63.

Alt, Peter-André. "Erzählungen des Unbewussten: Zur Poetik des Traums in Franz Kafkas Romanen." In *Der europäische Roman zwischen Aufklärung und Postmoderne: Festschrift zum 65. Geburtstag von Jürgen C. Jacobs*, edited by Jürgen Jacobs, Friedhelm Marx, and Andreas Meier, 153-74. Weimar: VDG, 2001.

———. *Franz Kafka: Der ewige Sohn*. Munich: Beck, 2005.

———. *Der Schlaf der Vernunft: Literatur und Traum in der Kulturgeschichte der Neuzeit*. Munich: Beck, 2002.

Anders, Ruth H. "Veronal: Geschichte eines Schlafmittels." *Pharmazeutische Zeitung* 47 (2003). https://www.pharmazeutische-zeitung.de/inhalt-47-2003/magazin-47-2003/.

Anderson, Wilda C. *Diderot's Dream*. Baltimore, MD: Johns Hopkins University Press, 1990.

Andretta-Purtschert, Daniela Doris Anna. *Zur Entwicklungsgeschichte der Hypnotika und Sedativa in der ersten Hälfte des 20. Jahrhunderts im deutschsprachigen Raum*. Dietikon: Juris Druck + Verlag, 1998.

Andriopoulos, Stefan. *Possessed: Hypnotic Crimes, Corporate Fiction, and the Invention of Cinema*. Chicago: University of Chicago Press, 2008.

Anonymous. "Joseph von Mering (1849-1908)." *Nature* 164, no. 4182 (1949): 1076.

Aurnhammer, Achim. *Arthur Schnitzler—Filmarbeiten: Drehbücher, Entwürfe, Skizzen*. Würzburg: Ergon 2015.

———. *Arthur Schnitzlers intertextuelles Erzählen*. Berlin: De Gruyter, 2013.

———. "Selig, wer in Träumen stirbt. Das literarisierte Leben und Sterben von Fräulein Else." *Euphorion* 77 (1983): 500-510.

Bachelard, Gaston. *The New Scientific Spirit*. Translated by Arthur Goldhammer. Boston: Beacon Press, 1984.

Bachmann-Medick, Doris. *Cultural Turns: New Orientations in the Study of Culture*. Berlin: De Gruyter, 2016.

Baer, Ulrich. *The Rilke Alphabet*. Translated by Andrew Hamilton. New York: Fordham University Press, 2014.

Ballhausen, Thomas. *Die Tatsachen der Seele: Arthur Schnitzler und der Film*. Vienna: Verlag Filmarchiv Austria, 2006.

Barkhoff, Jürgen. *Magnetische Fiktionen: Literarisierung des Mesmerismus in der Romantik*. Stuttgart: Metzler, 1995.

Barthes, Roland. " Longtemps, je me suis couché de bonne heure." In *Le bruissement de la langue*, 313-25. Paris: Seuil, 1984.

———. "Longtemps, je me suis couché de bonne heure . . ." In *The Rustle of Lan-*

guage, translated by Richard Howard, 277-90. Berkeley: University of California Press, 1989.

———. *The Preparation of the Novel: Lecture Courses and Seminars at the Collège de France, 1978-1979 and 1979-1980*. Edited by Kate Briggs. New York: Columbia University Press, 2011.

Basner, Mathias. "Arousal Threshold Determination in 1862: Kohlschütter's Measurements on the Firmness of Sleep." *Sleep Medicine* 11, no. 4 (2010): 417-22.

Bauer, Roger. "'Un doux vent polyglotte': Les poèmes en double version, allemande, et française, de Rainer Maria Rilke." *Revue d'Allemagne* 13 (1981): 313-37.

Bayard, Pierre. *Le hors-sujet: Proust et la digression*. Paris: Minuit, 1996.

Beaumont, Matthew. "Insomnia and the Late Nineteenth-Century Insomniac: The Case of Albert Kimball." *Interface Focus* 10, no. 3 (2020): 1-8.

Beer, Gillian. *Darwin's Plots: Evolutionary Narrative in Darwin, George Eliot and Nineteenth-Century Fiction*. 3rd ed. Cambridge: Cambridge University Press, 2009.

Beer, John Joseph. *The Emergence of the German Dye Industry*. New York: Arno Press, 1981.

Bellettini, Lorenzo. "Das 'Handbuch des perfekten Rezensenten': Arthur Schnitzlers Zeitungsausschnittsammlung als zeithistorisches Archiv." In *Akten-kundig? Literatur, Zeitgeschichte, Archiv*, edited by Marcel Atze, Michael Hansel, Thomas Degener, and Volker Kaukoreit, 188-200. Vienna: Praesens, 2009.

Bentivoglio, Marina, and Gigliola Grassi-Zucconi. "The Pioneering Experimental Studies on Sleep Deprivation." *Sleep* 20, no. 7 (1997): 570-76.

Beradt, Charlotte. *The Third Reich of Dreams*. Chicago: Quadrangle Books, 1968.

Berger, Joseph R., and Joel A. Vilensky. "Encephalitis Lethargica (von Economo's Encephalitis)." In *Handbook of Clinical Neurology*, vol. 123, edited by Alex C. Tselis and John Booss, 745-61. Amsterdam: Elsevier, 2014.

Berlant, Lauren Gail. *Cruel Optimism*. Durham, NC: Duke University Press, 2011.

Biagioli, Mario. *Galileo's Instruments of Credit: Telescopes, Images, Secrecy*. Chicago: University of Chicago Press, 2006.

———. "Postdisciplinary Liaisons: Science Studies and the Humanities." *Critical Inquiry* 35, no. 4 (2009): 816-35.

Bircher, Martin. "Rainer Maria Rilke und Merline: Zum Erwerb von Baladine Klossowskas Nachlass durch die Bibliotheca Bodmeriana, Cologny." *Librarium: Zeitschrift der Schweizerischen Bibliophilen Gesellschaft* 47 (2004): 107-15.

Bizub, Edward. *Proust et le moi divisé: La "Recherche"; Creuset de la psychologie expérimentale (1874-1914)*. Geneva: Droz, 2006.

Blanchot, Maurice. "Dreaming, Writing." In *Friendship*, translated by Elizabeth Rottenberg, 140-48. Stanford, CA: Stanford University Press, 1997.

Bloom, Peter J. "Diagnosing Invisible Agents: Between the Microbiological and the

Geographic." In *French Colonial Documentary: Mythologies of Humanitarianism*, 95-123. Minneapolis: University of Minnesota Press, 2008.

Blumenberg, Hans. *Höhlenausgänge*. Frankfurt am Main: Suhrkamp, 1989.

Bogousslavsky, Julien. "Marcel Proust's Lifelong Tour of the Parisian Neurological Intelligentsia: From Brissaud and Dejerine to Sollier and Babinski." *European Neurology* 57, no. 3 (2007): 129-36.

Böhme, Hartmut. "Das Gefühl der Schwere: Historische und phänomenologische Ansichten der Müdigkeit, Erschöpfung und verwandter Emotionen." *Figurationen* 16, no. 1 (2015).

Bono, James J. "Science Studies as Cultural Studies." In *The Cambridge Companion to Literature and Science*, edited by Steven Meyer, 156-75. Cambridge: Cambridge University Press, 2018.

Bono, James J. "Making Knowledge: History, Literature, and the Poetics of Science." *Isis* 101, no. 3 (2010): 555-59.

Borbély, Alexander. *Das Geheimnis des Schlafes: Neue Wege und Erkenntnisse der Forschung*. Stuttgart: DVA, 1984.

Borck, Cornelius. *Brainwaves: A Cultural History of Electroencephalography*. Translated by Ann Hentschel. New York: Routledge, 2018.

———. *Hirnströme: Eine Kulturgeschichte der Elektroenzephalographie*. Göttingen: Wallstein, 2005.

———. "Writing Brains: Tracing the Psyche with the Graphical Method." *History of Psychology* 8, no. 1 (2005): 79-94.

Borgards, Roland, Harald Neumeyer, Nicolas Pethes, and Yvonne Wübben, eds. *Literatur und Wissen: Ein interdisziplinäres Handbuch*. Stuttgart: Metzler, 2013.

Brandstetter, Gabriele. "Ökonomie und Vergeudung: Performance und Nacktheit bei Arthur Schnitzler und Marina Abramovic." In *Transgressionen: Literatur als Ethnographie*, edited by Gerhard Neumann, 287-313. Freiburg im Breisgau: Rombach, 2003.

Brandt, Christina. "Kulturwissenschaften und Wissenschaftsgeschichte." In *Handbuch Wissenschaftsgeschichte*, edited by Marianne Sommer, Staffan Müller-Wille, and Carsten Reinhardt, 92-106. Stuttgart: Metzler, 2017.

Brod, Max. "'Das Schloss': Nachwort zur ersten Auflage." In *Franz Kafka*, edited by Heinz Politzer, 39-47. Darmstadt: Wissenschaftliche Buchgesellschaft, 1973.

Bronfen, Elisabeth. "1924, October: Arthur Schnitzler's Novella *Fräulein Else* Published in *Die Neue Rundschau*." In *A New History of German Literature*, edited by David E. Wellbery, Judith Ryan, Hans Ulrich Gumbrecht, Anton Kaes, Joseph Leo Koerner, and Dorothea von Mücke, 738-43. Cambridge, MA: Belknap Press of Harvard University Press, 2004.

———. "Weibliches Sterben an der Kultur." In *Die Wiener Jahrhundertwende: Einflüsse, Umwelt, Wirkungen*, edited by Jürgen Nautz and Richard Vahrenkamp, 464-80. Vienna: Böhlau, 1996.

Brooker, Peter, Andrzej Gasiorek, Deborah Longworth, and Andrew Thacker, eds. *The Oxford Handbook of Modernisms*. Oxford: Oxford University Press, 2010.

———. Introduction to *The Oxford Handbook of Modernisms*, edited by Peter Brooker et al., 1-16 Oxford: Oxford University Press, 2010.

Campe, Rüdiger. "Schreiben im Prozess: Kafkas ausgesetzte Schreibszene." In *"Schreibkugel ist ein Ding gleich mir: von Eisen": Schreibszenen im Zeitalter der Typoskripte*, edited by Davide Giuriato, Martin Stingelin, and Sandro Zanetti, 115-32. Munich: Fink, 2005.

———. "Writing; the Scene of Writing." Translated by Bryan Klausmeyer and Johannes Wankhammer. *MLN* 136, no. 5 (2021): 971-83.

Canguilhem, Georges. "Le concept de réflexe au XIXe siècle." In *Études d'histoire et de philosophie des sciences concernant les vivants et la vie*, 295-304. Paris: Vrin, 1968.

———. *La formation du concept de réflexe aux XVIIe et XVIIIe siècles*. Paris: Presses Universitaires de France, 1955.

———. *On the Normal and the Pathological*. Translated by Carolyn Fawcett. Boston: Reidel, 1978.

Carson, Anne. "Every Exit Is an Entrance (A Praise of Sleep)." In *Creative Criticism: An Anthology and Guide*, edited by Stephen Benson and Clare Connors, 82-102. Edinburgh: Edinburgh University Press, 2014.

Caspari, Martina. "Durchkreuzungen des zeitgenössischen Hysterie-Diskurses." *Germanic Notes and Reviews* 36, no. 1 (2006): 5-28.

Catling, Jo. "Rilke's 'Left-Handed Lyre': Multilingualism and the Poetics of Possibility." *Modern Language Review* 102, no. 4 (2007): 1084-1104.

Chan, Roy Bing. *The Edge of Knowing: Dreams, History, and Realism in Modern Chinese Literature*. Seattle: University of Washington Press, 2017.

Christian, Margareta Ingrid. "Air, Ether, Atmosphere: Space in Rilke's *Duineser Elegien*." *Oxford German Studies* 49, no. 3 (2020), 228-48.

Clarke, Bruce, and Manuela Rossini, eds. *The Routledge Companion to Literature and Science*. New York: Routledge, 2010.

Class, Monika. "Medical Case Histories as Genre: New Approaches." *Literature and Medicine* 32, no. 1 (2014): vii-xvi.

Coen, Deborah R. *Vienna in the Age of Uncertainty: Science, Liberalism, and Private Life*. Chicago: University of Chicago Press, 2007.

Coetzee, J. M. "Time, Tense and Aspect in Kafka's 'The Burrow.'" *MLN* 96, no. 3 (1981): 556-79.

Cohn, Dorrit. "'I Doze and Wake': The Deviance of Simultaneous Narration." In *The Distinction of Fiction*, 96-108. Baltimore, MD: Johns Hopkins University Press, 1999.

———. "K. Enters *The Castle*: On the Change of the Person in Kafka's Manuscript." *Euphorion* 62, no. 1 (1968): 28-45.

———. *Transparent Minds: Narrative Modes for Presenting Consciousness in Fiction*. Princeton, NJ: Princeton University Press, 1978.
Cohn, Elisha. *Still Life: Suspended Development in the Victorian Novel*. New York: Oxford University Press, 2016.
Compagnon, Antoine. *Proust between Two Centuries*. Translated By Richard Goodkin. New York: Columbia University Press, 1992.
Conley, Katharine. *Robert Desnos, Surrealism, and the Marvelous in Everyday Life*. Lincoln: University of Nebraska Press, 2003.
Crary, Jonathan. *Suspensions of Perception: Attention, Spectacle, and Modern Culture*. Cambridge, MA: MIT Press, 2001.
———. *24/7: Late Capitalism and the Ends of Sleep*. London: Verso, 2013.
Crow, Christine Mary. *Paul Valéry and the Poetry of Voice*. Cambridge: Cambridge University Press, 1982.
Daston, Lorraine J. "British Responses to Psycho-Physiology, 1860-1900." *Isis* 69, no. 2 (1978): 192-208.
Daston, Lorraine J., and Peter Galison. "The Image of Objectivity." *Representations* 40 (1992): 81-128.
———. *Objectivity*. New York: Zone, 2010.
Davenport-Hines, R. P. T. *The Pursuit of Oblivion: A Global History of Narcotics, 1500-2000*. London: Weidenfeld and Nicolson, 2001.
De Warren, Nicolas. "The Inner Night: Towards a Phenomenology of (Dreamless) Sleep." In *On Time: New Contributions to the Husserlian Phenomenology of Time*, edited by Dieter Lohmar and Ichiro Yamaguchi, 273-94. Dordrecht: Springer, 2010.
Déchanet-Platz, Fanny. *L'écrivain, le sommeil et les rêves: 1800-1945*. Paris: Gallimard, 2008.
Dement, William C. "The History of Narcolepsy and Other Sleep Disorders." *Journal of the History of the Neurosciences* 2, no. 2 (1993): 121-34.
———. "The Study of Human Sleep: A Historical Perspective." *Thorax* 53, supp. 3, (1998): 2-7.
Deo, Saudamini, and Philippe Charlier. "For Franz Kafka, Insomnia Was a Literary Method." *Lancet Neurology* 15, no. 12 (2016): 1207.
Derrida, Jacques. *L'écriture et la différence*. Paris: Seuil, 1967.
Deschamps, Nicole. "Rêverie." In *Dictionnaire Marcel Proust*, edited by Annick Bouillaguet, 869-72. Paris: Champion, 2004.
Dibie, Pascal. *Ethnologie de la chambre à coucher*. Paris: Grasset, 1987.
Didi-Huberman, Georges. *Invention of Hysteria: Charcot and the Photographic Iconography of the Salpêtrière*. Cambridge, MA: MIT Press, 2004.
Diener, Leander. "Krieg und Frieden im vegetativen Nervensystem: Körpermodelle der experimentellen Physiologie im 20. Jahrhundert." *Body Politics—Zeitschrift für Körpergeschichte* 7 (2019): 97-121.

Dieterle, Bernard, and Manfred Engel, eds. *Historizing the Dream*. Würzburg: Königshausen & Neumann, 2019.
Dieterle, Bernhard. "Das übersetzerische Werk." In *Rilke-Handbuch: Leben, Werk, Wirkung*, edited by Manfred Engel, 454-79. Stuttgart: Metzler, 2010.
Dolar, Mladen. "The Burrow of Sound." *Differences* 22, nos. 2-3 (2011): 112-39.
Drucker-Colín, Réne, and Hugo Merchant-Nancy. "Evolution of Concepts of Mechanisms of Sleep." In *The Pharmacology of Sleep*, edited by Anthony Kales, 1-28. Berlin: Springer, 2012.
Duflo, Colas. *Diderot philosophe*. Paris: Champion, 2013.
Dufoe, Nicole. "Bram Stoker's Sleep Work." *Representations* 156, no. 1 (2021): 1-26.
Duttlinger, Caroline. *Attention and Distraction in Modern German Literature, Thought, and Culture*. Oxford: Oxford University Press, 2022.
———. *The Cambridge Introduction to Franz Kafka*. Cambridge: Cambridge University Press, 2013.
———. "Psychology and Psychoanalysis." In *Franz Kafka in Context*, edited by Carolin Duttlinger, 216-24. Cambridge: Cambridge University Press, 2017.
———. "Schlaflosigkeit: Kafkas Schloss zwischen Müdigkeit und Wachen." In *"Schloss"-Topographien: Lektüren zu Kafkas Romanfragment*, edited by Malte Kleinwort and Joseph Vogl, 219-43. Bielefeld: Transcript, 2013.
Economo, Karoline von, and Julius von Wagner-Jauregg. *Baron Constantin von Economo: His Life and Work*. Translated by Ramsay Spillman. Burlington, VT: Free Press Interstate, 1937.
Ekirch, A. Roger. *At Day's Close: Night in Times Past*. New York: Norton, 2005.
———. "The Modernization of Western Sleep: Or, Does Insomnia Have a History?" *Past and Present* 226, no. 1 (2015): 149-92.
Eldridge, Hannah Vandegrift. *Lyric Orientations: Hölderlin, Rilke, and the Poetics of Community*. Ithaca, NY: Cornell University Press, 2015.
Emrich, Wilhelm. *Franz Kafka*. 3rd ed. Frankfurt am Main: Athenäum, 1961.
Engel, Manfred. "Dream Theories in Modernist Literature: Proust's *Recherche*, Joyce's *Ulysses*, and Kafka's *The Castle*." In *Theorizing the Dream*, edited by Bernard Dieterle and Manfred Engel, 341-91. Würzburg: Königshausen & Neumann, 2018.
———. "Kafka und die moderne Welt." In *Kafka-Handbuch: Leben, Werk, Wirkung*, edited by Manfred Engel and Bernd Auerochs, 498-515. Stuttgart: Metzler, 2010.
———. "Kulturgeschichte/n? Ein Modellentwurf am Beispiel der Kultur- und Literaturgeschichte des Traumes." *KulturPoetik* 10, no. 2 (2010): 153-76.
———. "Die 'Sonette an Orpheus' als Beginn des spätesten Werks." In *Nach Duino*, edited by Karen Leeder and Robert Vilain, 15-27. Göttingen: Wallstein, 2010.
———. "Werkausgaben und Editionsgeschichte." In *Kafka-Handbuch: Leben, Werk, Wirkung*, edited by Manfred Engel and Bernd Auerochs, 517-23. Stuttgart: Metzler, 2010.

Engel, Manfred, and Ulrich Fülleborn, "Kommentar." In Rainer Maria Rilke, *Kommentierte Ausgabe*, 4 vols., edited by Manfred Engel and Ulrich Fülleborn, 2:413-873. Frankfurt am Main: Insel, 1996-2003.

Engel, Manfred, and Ritchie Robertson, eds. *Kafka und die Religion in der Moderne/ Kafka, Religion, and Modernity*. Würzburg: Königshausen & Neumann, 2014.

Epicurus. "Letter to Menacceus." In *The Epicurus Reader*, translated and edited by Brad Inwood and Lloyd P. Gerson, 28-31. Indianapolis, IN: Hackett, 1997.

Fick, Monika. *Sinnenwelt und Weltseele: Der psychophysische Monismus in der Literatur der Jahrhundertwende*. Tübingen: Niemeyer, 1993.

Fiedler, Theodore. "Psychoanalyse." In *Rilke-Handbuch: Leben, Werk, Wirkung*, edited by Manfred Engel, 165-74. Stuttgart: Metzler, 2010.

Finn, Michael R. "Health and Medicine." In *Marcel Proust in Context*, edited by Adam A. Watt, 123-29. Cambridge: Cambridge University Press, 2013.

Fliedl, Konstanze. *Arthur Schnitzler*. Stuttgart: Reclam, 2005.

Foley, Paul Bernard. *Encephalitis Lethargica: The Mind and Brain Virus*. New York: Springer, 2018.

———. "The Encephalitis Lethargica Patient as a Window on the Soul." In *The Neurological Patient in History*, edited by Jacyna L. Stephen and Casper Stephen T., 184-211. Woodbridge, UK: Boydell and Brewer, 2012.

Forrester, John. *Thinking in Cases*. Malden, MA: Polity Press, 2017.

Foster, Hal. *Compulsive Beauty*. Cambridge, MA: MIT Press, 1995.

Foster, Russell G. *Life Time: The New Science of the Body Clock, and How It Can Revolutionize Your Sleep and Health*. London: Penguin, 2022.

———. "Sleep, Circadian Rhythms and Health." *Interface Focus* 10, no. 3 (2020): 1-18.

Foucault, Michel. *The Order of Things: An Archaeology of the Human Sciences*. Translated by Alan Sheridan. New York: Pantheon, 1970.

Fraisse, Luc. "Longtemps je me suis couché de bonne heure." *Romanistische Zeitschrift für Literaturgeschichte/Cahiers d'Histoire des Littératures Romanes* 40, nos. 1-4 (2016): 217-35.

Friedman, Susan Stanford. "Definitional Excursions: The Meanings of Modern/ Modernity/Modernism." *Modernism/Modernity* 8, no. 3 (2001): 493-513.

Fülleborn, Ulrich. *Das Strukturproblem der späten Lyrik Rilkes*. Heidelberg: Winter, 1960.

Fuller, Matthew. *How to Sleep: The Art, Biology and Culture of Unconsciousness*. London: Bloomsbury, 2018.

Fülöp, Erika. *Proust, the One, and the Many: Identity and Difference in "À la recherche du temps perdu."* London: Legenda, 2012.

Fuss, Diana. *The Sense of an Interior: Four Writers and the Rooms That Shaped Them*. London: Routledge, 2004.

Garnier, Guillaume. *L'oubli des peines: Une histoire du sommeil (1700-1850)*. Rennes: Presses Universitaires de Rennes, 2013.

Gellen, Kata. "Noises Off: Cinematic Sound in Kafka's 'The Burrow.'" In *Mediamorphosis: Kafka and the Moving Image*, edited by Shai Biderman and Ido Lewit. 111-29. London: Wallflower, 2016.
Genette, Gérard. "La littérature comme telle." In *Figures*, vol. 1, 253-65. Paris: Seuil, 1966.
———. *Narrative Discourse: An Essay in Method*. Ithaca, NY: Cornell University Press, 1990.
Gerok-Reiter, Annette. *Wink und Wandlung: Komposition und Poetik in Rilkes "Sonette an Orpheus."* Tübingen: Niemeyer, 1996.
Gess, Nicola. "Intermedialität Reconsidered: Vom Paragone bei Hoffmann bis zum Inneren Monolog bei Schnitzler." *Poetica* 42, nos. 1-2 (2010): 139-68.
Gifford, Paul. "La descente dans le sommeil de la Jeune Parque." In *Paul Valéry à tous les points de vue: Hommage à Judith Robinson-Valéry*, edited by Robert Pickering and Jürgen Schmidt-Radefeldt, 73-81. Paris: L'Harmattan, 2003.
Gijswijt-Hofstra, Marijke, and Roy Porter, eds. *Cultures of Neurasthenia from Beard to the First World War*. Amsterdam: Rodopi, 2001.
Gomes, Mario. *Gedankenlesemaschinen: Modelle für eine Poetologie des Inneren Monologs*. Freiburg im Breisgau: Rombach, 2008.
Gottesmann, Claude. *Henri Piéron and Nathaniel Kleitman: Two Major Figures of 20th Century Sleep Research*. New York: Nova Biomedical, 2013.
Gradmann, Christoph. "Africa as a Laboratory." In *Epidemics and Pandemics in Historical Perspective*, edited by Jörg Vögele, Stefanie A. Knöll, and Thorsten Noack, 337-54. Wiesbaden: Springer, 2016.
Greaney, Michael. "'Observed, Measured, Contained': Contemporary Fiction and the Science of Sleep." *Contemporary Literature* 56, no. 1 (2015): 56-80.
———. *Sleep and the Novel: Fictions of Somnolence from Jane Austen to the Present*. New York: Palgrave Macmillan, 2018.
———. "Terribly Strange Beds: Conrad, Sleep, and Modernism," *Conradian* 37, no. 1 (2012): 1-19.
Griffiths, Devin. *The Age of Analogy: Science and Literature between the Darwins*. Baltimore, MD: Johns Hopkins University Press, 2016.
Goebel, Eckart. "Der Paria: Kafkas Betten." In *Glücksritter: Risiko und Erzählstruktur*, edited by Wolfram Ette and Bernhard Teuber, 213-37. Paderborn: Brill | Fink, 2021.
Gross, David. "Bergson, Proust, and the Reevaluation of Memory." *International Philosophical Quarterly* 25 (1985): 369-80.
Gross-Elixmann, Klara. *Poetologie und Epistemologie: Schreibstrategien und Autorschaftskonzepte in Arthur Schnitzlers medizinischen Texten*. Würzburg: Königshausen & Neumann, 2016.
Guenther, Katja. *Localization and Its Discontents: A Genealogy of Psychoanalysis and the Neuro Disciplines*. Chicago: University of Chicago Press, 2015.

Hagner, Michael. "Aufmerksamkeit als Ausnahmezustand." In *Aufmerksamkeit*, vol. 3 of *Lichtensteiner Exkurse*, edited by Norbert Haas, Rainer Nägele, and Hans-Jörg Rheinberger, 273-94. Eggingen: Klaus Isele, 1998.

———. *Der Geist bei der Arbeit: Historische Untersuchungen zur Hirnforschung*. Göttingen: Wallstein, 2006.

———. "Gehirnführung: Zur Anatomie der geistigen Funktionen, 1870-1930." In *Ecce Cortex: Beiträge zur Geschichte des modernen Gehirns*, edited by Michael Hagner, 177-205. Göttingen: Wallstein, 1999.

———. "Lokalisationstheorien." In *Enzyklopädie Medizingeschichte*, edited by Werner Gerabek, 862-63. New York: De Gruyter, 2005.

Hahn, Henrike. *Verfilmte Gefühle: Von "Fräulein Else" bis "Eyes Wide Shut."* Bielefeld: Transcript, 2014.

Hamburger, Käte. *Die Logik der Dichtung*. 2nd ed. Stuttgart: Klett, 1968.

Handley, Sasha. *Sleep in Early Modern England*. New Haven, CT: Yale University Press, 2016.

Hansen, Maike. *Somniloquies: Communication entre veille et sommeil dans des textes dramatiques de William Shakespeare, Denis Diderot, Heinrich von Kleist, Eugène Scribe et Richard Wagner*. Paderbon: Brill | Fink, 2022.

Harvey, David. *Paris, Capital of Modernity*. New York: Routledge, 2003.

Hassine, Juliette. "Bergotte." In *Dictionnaire Marcel Proust*, edited by Annick Bouillaguet, 130-32. Paris: Champion, 2004.

Healy, David. *The Creation of Psychopharmacology*. Cambridge, MA: Harvard University Press, 2002.

Heesen, Anke te. *Der Zeitungsausschnitt: Ein Papierobjekt der Moderne*. Frankfurt am Main: S. Fischer, 2006.

Heller-Roazen, Daniel. *The Inner Touch: Archaeology of a Sensation*. Cambridge, MA: Zone, 2007.

Henry, Anne. "Proust du côté de Schopenhauer." In *Schopenhauer et la création littéraire en Europe*, edited by Anne Henry, 149-64. Paris: Klincksieck, 1989.

Hellmann, Kai-Uwe. *Fetische des Konsums: Studien zur Soziologie der Marke*. Wiesbaden: Springer, 2011.

Herlinghaus, Hermann. "Towards a Cultural Pharmacology." In *The Pharmakon: Concept Figure, Image of Transgression, Poetic Practice*, edited by Hermann Herlinghaus, 1-20. Heidelberg: Winter, 2018.

Herold, Thomas. "The Paradox of Time in Hermann Broch's *Die Schlafwandler*." *Oxford German Studies* 43, no. 2 (2014): 156-71.

Herzberg, David L. *Happy Pills in America: From Miltown to Prozac*. Baltimore, MD: Johns Hopkins University Press, 2009.

———. *White Market Drugs: Big Pharma and the Hidden History of Addiction in America*. Chicago: University of Chicago Press, 2020.

Herzog, Hillary. "'Medizin ist eine Weltanschauung': On Schnitzler's Medical

Writings." In *A Companion to the Works of Arthur Schnitzler*, edited by Dagmar Lorenz, 227-42. Woodbridge, UK: Camden House, 2003.
Hess, Christian W. "Walter R. Hess (17.3.1881-12.8.1973)." *Schweizer Archiv für Neurologie und Psychiatrie* 159, no. 4 (2008): 255-61.
Hesse, Heidrun. "'Ästhetik der Existenz.' Foucaults Entdeckung des ethischen Selbstverhältnisses." In *Michel Foucault: Zwischenbilanz einer Rezeption*, edited by Axel Honneth and Martin Saar, 300-08. Frankfurt am Main: Suhrkamp 2003.
Hiramitsu, Ayano. *Les chambres de la création dans l'oeuvre de Marcel Proust*. Paris: Champion, 2019.
Hoffert, Margarethe. "Warum 'Veronal'?" *Zeitschrift für romanische Philologie* 74 (1958): 147-49.
Homburg, Ernst, Anthony S. Travis, and Harm G. Schröter, eds., *The Chemical Industry in Europe, 1850-1914: Industrial Growth, Pollution, and Professionalization*. Dordrecht: Kluwer, 1998.
Huyssen, Andreas. "Urban Experience and the Modernist Dream of a New Language." In *A New History of German Literature*, edited by David E. Wellbery, Judith Ryan, Hans Ulrich Gumbrecht, Anton Kaes, Joseph Leo Koerner, and Dorothea von Mücke, 668-72. Cambridge, MA: Belknap Press of Harvard University Press, 2004.
Iranzo, Alex, Ambra Stefani, Birgit Högl, and Joan Santamaria. "The Insomnia of Franz Kafka." *Sleep Medicine* 50 (2018): 24-28.
———. "Sleep and Sleep Disorders in Franz Kafka's Narrative Works." *Sleep Medicine* 55 (2019): 69-73.
Jahraus, Oliver. *Kafka: Leben, Schreiben, Machtapparate*. Stuttgart: Reclam, 2006.
Janssen, Hans. "Rilkes Bibliothek." *Philobiblon* 33, no. 4 (1989): 293-319.
James, Tony. *Dream, Creativity, and Madness in Nineteenth-Century France*. Oxford: Oxford University Press, 1995.
Jongeneel, Els. "Silencing the Voice in Narratology? A Synopsis." In *Stimme(n) im Text: Narratologische Positionsbestimmungen*, edited by Andreas Blödorn, Daniela Langer, and Michael Scheffel, 9-30. Berlin: De Gruyter, 2006.
Jorek, Adriane. *Das Pulver als Arzneiform: Ein Überblick über seine Entwicklung vom 18. bis 20. Jahrhundert*. Stuttgart: Wissenschaftliche Verlagsgesellschaft, 1998.
Jünger, Ernst. *Annäherungen: Drogen und Rausch*. Stuttgart: Klett, 1970.
Jung, Richard. "W. R. Hess und das Ordnungsprinzip in der Physiologie." *Schweizer Archiv für Neurologie und Psychiatrie* 132 (1983): 277-308.
Kaes, Anton. *Shell Shock Cinema: Weimar Culture and the Wounds of War*. Princeton, NJ: Princeton University Press, 2009.
Kanzog, Klaus. "Der innere Monolog in der Novelle und in der Verfilmung." In *Arthur Schnitzler: Zeitgenossenschaften = Contemporaneities*, edited by Ian Foster and Florian Krobb, 359-72. Bern: Peter Lang, 2002.
Karsten, Arne. "Ein Urbild *Fräulein Elses*? Das Leben und Sterben der Stephanie

Bachrach (1887-1917)." In *Erzählte Moderne*, edited by Andreas Blödorn, Christof Hamann, and Christoph Jürgensen, 204-13. Göttingen: Wallstein, 2018.

Keating, Peter, and Alberto Cambrosio. "Does Biomedicine Entail the Successful Reduction of Pathology to Biology?" *Perspectives in Biology and Medicine* 47, no. 3 (2004): 357-71.

Kemper, Hans-Georg. *Droge Trakl: Rauschträume und Poesie*. Salzburg: Otto Müller, 2014.

Kilcher, Andreas. *Kafkas Werkstatt: Der Schriftsteller bei der Arbeit*. München: C.H. Beck, 2024.

Kinzler, Sonja. *Das Joch des Schlafs: Der Schlafdiskurs im bürgerlichen Zeitalter*. Köln: Böhlau, 2011.

Klawitter, Arne. "'Komprimierte Kunstpillen': Das moderne hai-kai bei Yvan Goll." *Études Germaniques* 68, no. 3 (2013): 475-88.

Klinger, Sebastian Paul. "Veronal Sleep: White Market Drugs and Public Health in Arthur Schnitzler's *Fräulein Else*." *Deutsche Vierteljahrsschrift für Literaturwissenschaft und Geistesgeschichte* 98, no. 1 (2024): 83-104.

Kleinwort, Malte. *Der späte Kafka: Spätstil als Stilsuspension*. Munich: Fink, 2013.

Knoop, Christine A. "'Und fast ein Mädchen wars': Zur Darstellbarkeit von Inspiration bei Rainer Maria Rilke." *German Quarterly* 85, no. 3 (2012): 253-74.

Kocziszky, Eva. *Der Schlaf in Kunst und Literatur: Konzepte im Wandel von der Antike zur Moderne*. Berlin: Reimer, 2019.

Kohtes, Michael. *Der Rausch in Worten: Zur Welt- und Drogenerfahrung der Surrealisten und Beatniks*. Marburg an der Lahn: Jonas, 1987.

Kölbel, Martin. *Die Erzählrede in Franz Kafkas "Das Schloss."* Frankfurt am Main: Stroemfeld, 2006.

König, Anna Maria. "Erwachen. Ein leibzeitliches Übergangsphänomen." In *Der Leib und seine Zeit: Temporale Prozesse des Körpers und deren Dysregulationen im Burnout und bei anderen Leiberfahrungen*, edited by Reinhold Esterbauer, Andrea Paletta, and Julia Meer, 167-87. Freiburg im Breisgau: Karl Alber, 2020.

König, Christoph. *"O komm und geh": Skeptische Lektüren der "Sonette an Orpheus" von Rilke*. Göttingen: Wallstein, 2014.

König, Christoph, and Kai Bremer. *Über "Die Sonette an Orpheus" von Rilke: Lektüren*. Göttingen: Wallstein, 2016.

Koopmann, Helmut. "Wie wirklich ist das Unwirkliche? Hans Castorp träumt." In *Lebenstraum und Todesnähe: Thomas Manns Roman "Der Zauberberg,"* edited by Helmut Koopmann and Thomas Sprecher, 59-78. Frankfurt am Main: Klostermann, 2015.

Kovalzon, Vladimir M. "Some Notes on the Biography of Maria Manasseina." *Journal of the History of the Neurosciences* 18, no. 3 (2009): 312-19.

Krämer, Thomas. *Rilkes "Sonette an Orpheus," erster Teil: Ein Interpretationsgang*. Würzburg: Königshausen & Neumann, 1999.
Krings, Marcel. "Der Tod ein Traum: Methode und Grenzen der Literatur in Kafkas Erzählung 'Ein Traum.'" *Zeitschrift Für Deutsche Philologie* 130, no. 2 (2011): 197-216.
Kristeva, Julia. *Proust and the Sense of Time*. New York: Columbia University Press, 1993.
——. "Rêve." In *Dictionnaire Marcel Proust*, edited by Annick Bouillaguet, 862-64. Paris: Champion, 2004.
Kroker, Kenton. "Configuring Epidemic Encephalitis as a National and International Neurological Concern." In *The History of the Brain and Mind Sciences: Technique, Technology, Therapy*, edited by Stephen T. Casper and Delia Gavrus, 77-106. Woodbridge, UK: Boydell and Brewer, 2017.
——. "Creatures of Reason? Picturing Viruses at the Pasteur Institute during the 1920s." In *Crafting Immunity: Working Histories of Clinical Immunology*, edited by Kenton Kroker, Jennifer Keelan, and Pauline M. H. Mazumdar, 145-63. Burlington, VT: Ashgate, 2008.
——. "The First Modern Plague: Epidemic Encephalitis in America, 1919-39." *Transactions and Studies of the College of Physicians of Philadelphia* 23 (2001): 63-67.
——. *The Sleep of Others and the Transformations of Sleep Research*. Toronto: University of Toronto Press, 2007.
Krovoza, Alfred, and Christine Walde, eds. *Traum und Schlaf: Ein interdisziplinäres Handbuch*. Stuttgart: Metzler, 2018.
Landy, Joshua. *Philosophy as Fiction: Self, Deception, and Knowledge in Proust*. Oxford: Oxford University Press, 2004.
Lane, Jeremy. "Falling Asleep in the Wake: Reading as Hypnagogic Experience." In *Re: Joyce: Text, Culture, Politics*, edited by John Brannigan, Geoff Ward, and Julian Wolfreys, 163-81. New York: Palgrave Macmillan, 1998.
Lange-Kirchheim, Astrid. "Adoleszenz, Hysterie und Autorschaft in Arthur Schnitzlers Novelle *Fräulein Else*." *Jahrbuch Der Deutschen Schillergesellschaft* 42 (1998): 265-300.
Latham, Sean, and Gayle Rogers. *Modernism: Evolution of an Idea*. London: Bloomsbury, 2015.
Lauterbach, Dorothea. "Frankreich." In *Rilke-Handbuch: Leben, Werk, Wirkung*, edited by Manfred Engel, 60-88. Stuttgart: Metzler, 2010.
Lavie, Peretz. "The Sleep Theory of Constantin von Economo." *Journal of Sleep Research* 2, no. 3 (1993): 175-78.
Leahy, Richard. *Literary Illumination: The Evolution of Artificial Light in Nineteenth-Century Literature*. Cardiff: University of Wales Press, 2018.

Leisi, Ernst. *Rilkes Sonette an Orpheus: Interpretation, Kommentar, Glossar*. Tübingen: Narr, 1987.

Le Rider, Jacques. "Tiefenpsychologie und Psychiatrie." In *Schnitzler-Handbuch: Leben, Werk, Wirkung*, edited by Christoph Jürgensen, Wolfgang Lukas, and Michael Scheffel, 35-39. Stuttgart: Metzler, 2014.

Lesch, John. *The German Chemical Industry in the Twentieth Century*. Dordrecht: Springer, 2000.

Lesky, Erna. *Die Wiener medizinische Schule im 19. Jahrhundert*. Graz: Böhlau, 1965.

Lewis, Pericles, ed. *The Cambridge Companion to European Modernism*. Cambridge: Cambridge University Press, 2011.

———, ed. *The Cambridge Introduction to Modernism*. Cambridge: Cambridge University Press, 2007.

Lodge, David. *Consciousness and the Novel: Connected Essays*. Cambridge, MA: Harvard University Press, 2002.

López-Muñoz, Francisco, Ronaldo Ucha-Udabe, and Cecilio Alamo. "The History of Barbiturates a Century after Their Clinical Introduction." *Neuropsychiatric Disease and Treatment* 1, no. 4 (2005): 329-43.

Louth, Charlie. *Rilke: The Life of the Work*. New York: Oxford University Press, 2020.

———. "Zu Rilkes Gong Gedichten." In *Rilkes Musikalität*, edited by Thomas Martinec, 139-54. Göttingen: V&R Unipress, 2019.

Ludtke, Laura E. "Sleep, Disruption and the 'Nightmare of Total Illumination' in Late Nineteenth- and Early Twentieth-Century Dystopian Fiction." *Interface Focus* 10, no. 3 (2020): 1-13.

Luhmann, Niklas. "Observing Re-Entries." In *Protosoziologie im Kontext: "Lebenswelt" und "System" in Philosophie und Soziologie*, edited by Gerhard Preyer, Georg Peter, and Alexander Ulfig, 290-301. Würzburg: Königshausen & Neumann, 1996.

Lukas, Wolfgang. *Das Selbst und das Fremde: Epochale Lebenskrisen und ihre Lösung im Werk Arthur Schnitzlers*. Munich: Fink, 1996.

Lukas, Wolfgang, and Ursula von Keitz. "'Stimme' und 'Partitur': Zu Arthur Schnitzlers Fräulein Else." In *Textschicksale: Das Werk Arthur Schnitzlers im Kontext der Moderne*, edited by Michael Scheffel and Wolfgang Lukas, 185-210. Berlin: De Gruyter, 2017.

Lyons, Maryinez. *The Colonial Disease: A Social History of Sleeping Sickness in Northern Zaire, 1900-1940*. New York: Cambridge University Press, 1992.

Ma, Jean. *At the Edges of Sleep: Moving Images and Somnolent Spectators*. Oakland, CA: University of California Press, 2022.

Mabin, Dominique. "Proust ou la parole d'un insomniaque." *La Presse Médicale* 22 (1993): 1663-65.

———. *Le sommeil de Marcel Proust*. Paris: Presses Universitaires de France, 1992.

―――. "Sommeil et automédication de Marcel Proust: Une analyse à partir de sa correspondance." *Neurophysiologie clinique* 24, no. 1 (1994): 61-74.

Macho, Thomas. *Todesmetaphern: Zur Logik der Grenzerfahrung*. Frankfurt am Main: Suhrkamp 1987.

Mao, Douglas. *The New Modernist Studies*. Cambridge: Cambridge University Press, 2021.

Mao, Douglas, and Rebecca l. Walkowitz. "The New Modernist Studies." *PMLA* 123, no. 3 (2008): 737-48.

Marshall, Jonathan. "Dynamic Medicine and Theatrical Form at the Fin de Siècle: A Formal Analysis of Dr Jean-Martin Charcot's Pedagogy, 1862-1893." *Modernism/Modernity* 15, no. 1 (2008): 131-53.

Martini, Fritz. *Das Wagnis der Sprache: Interpretation deutscher Prosa von Nietzsche bis Benn*. Stuttgart: Klett, 1954.

Marx, William. "Paul Valéry, 'le moins freudien des hommes'?" In *Freud au Collège de France, 1885-2016*, edited by Antoine Compagnon and Céline Surprenant. Paris: Collège de France, 2018. https://books.openedition.org/cdf/5709.

Mason, Eudo C. "Rilke and the Gesture of Withdrawal." In *Rilke, Europe, and the English-Speaking World*, 176-78. Cambridge: Cambridge University Press, 1961.

Matthias, Bettina. "Arthur Schnitzler's *Fräulein Else* and the End of the Bourgeois Tragedy." *Women in German Yearbook* 18, no. 1 (2002): 248-66.

Mauss, Marcel. "Techniques du corps." *Journal de psychologie normale et pathologique* 32 (1935): 241-90.

―――. "Techniques of the Body." In *Incorporations*, edited by Jonathan Crary and Sanford Kwinter, 455-77. New York: Zone, 1992.

Mavromatis, Andreas. *Hypnagogia: The Unique State of Consciousness between Wakefulness and Sleep*. New York: Routledge, 1987.

Mayer, Andreas. *Freud zur Einführung*. Hamburg: Junius, 2016.

―――. *Sites of the Unconscious: Hypnosis and the Emergence of the Psychoanalytic Setting*. Chicago: University of Chicago Press, 2013.

McGinn, Bernard. *The Harvest of Mysticism in Medieval Germany (1300-1500)*. Vol. 4 of *The Presence of God: A History of Western Christian Mysticism*. New York: Crossroad, 2005.

Menke, Bettine. *Prosopopoiia: Stimme und Text bei Brentano, Hoffmann, Kleist und Kafka*. Munich: Fink, 2000.

Metzl, Jonathan. *Prozac on the Couch: Prescribing Gender in the Era of Wonder Drugs*. Durham, NC: Duke University Press, 2003.

Meyer, Hermann. "Rilkes Begegnung mit dem Haiku." In *Spiegelungen: Studien zu Literatur und Kunst*, 147-86. Tübingen: Niemeyer, 1987.

Meyer, Steven, ed. *The Cambridge Companion to Literature and Science*. Cambridge: Cambridge University Press, 2018.

Michelson, Eduard. *Untersuchungen über die Tiefe des Schlafes: Inaugural-Dissertation zur Erlangung des Grades eines Doctors der Medizin*. Dorpat: Schnakenburg's Buchdruckerei, 1891.

Mieszkowski, Jan. *Crises of the Sentence*. Chicago: University of Chicago Press, 2019.

Millington, Richard. "Pameelen in the Snow: Towards a Reading of Gottfried Benn's 'Episode with Cocaine.'" *Seminar: A Journal of Germanic Studies* 40, no. 4 (2004): 349-67.

Mishara, Aaron L. "Kafka, Paranoic Doubles and the Brain: Hypnagogic vs. Hyper-Reflexive Models of Disrupted Self in Neuropsychiatric Disorders and Anomalous Conscious States." *Philosophy, Ethics, and Humanities in Medicine* 5, no. 13 (2010): 1-37.

Miura, Nobutaka. "Sommeil et réveil chez Valéry: D'Agathe à La jeune parque." *Etudes de langue et littérature françaises* 38 (1981): 72-110.

Montiglio, Silvia. *The Spell of Hypnos: Sleep and Sleeplessness in Ancient Greek Literature*. London: Tauris, 2016.

Morris, Craig. "Der vollständige innere Monolog: eine erzählerlose Erzählung? Eine Untersuchung am Beispiel von 'Leutnant Gustl' und 'Fräulein Else.'" *Modern Austrian Literature* 31, no. 2 (1998): 30-51.

Morris, Joel. "Josef K.'s (A + x) Problem: Kafka on the Moment of Awakening." *German Quarterly* 82, no. 4 (2009): 469-82.

Morse, Margaret. "Decadence and Social Change: Arthur Schnitzler's Works as an Ongoing Process of Destruction." *Modern Austrian Literature* 10, no. 2 (1977): 37-52.

Moser, Jeannie. *Psychotropen: Eine LSD-Biographie*. Konstanz: Konstanz University Press, 2013.

Motoyoshi, Mizue. "Das japanische Kurzgedicht in der europäischen Moderne." In *Humanität in einer pluralistischen Welt? Themengeschichtliche und formanalytische Studien zur deutschsprachigen Literatur*, edited by Christian Kluwe, 203-18. Würzburg: Königshausen & Neumann, 2000.

Mülder-Bach, Inka. "Am Anfang war . . . der Fall: Ursprungsszenen der Moderne." In *Am Anfang war . . . Ursprungsfiguren und Anfangskonstruktionen der Moderne*, edited by Inka Mülder-Bach and Eckhard Schumacher, 107-30. Munich: Fink, 2008.

Mülder-Bach, Inka, and Michael Ott. *Was der Fall ist*. Paderborn: Fink, 2014.

Muller, Marcel. *Les voix narratives dans la "Recherche du temps perdu."* Geneva: Droz, 1965.

Müller-Funk, Wolfgang. "Neugierde und literarisches Selbstexperiment im Essayismus der frühen Neuzeit. Montaigne und die Folgen." In *"Es ist nun einmal zum Versuch gekommen": 1580-1790*, edited by Michael Gamper, 111-30. Göttingen: Wallstein, 2009.

Müller-Jahncke, Wolf-Dieter, Christoph Friedrich, and Ulrich Meyer. *Arzneimittelgeschichte*. 2nd ed. Stuttgart: Wissenschaftliche Verlagsgesellschaft, 2005.

Müller-Seidel, Walter. *Arztbilder im Wandel: Zum literarischen Werk Arthur Schnitzlers*. Munich: Beck, 1997.

Nancy, Jean-Luc. *The Birth to Presence*. Translated by Brian Holmes and others. Stanford, CA: Stanford University Press, 2007.

———. *The Fall of Sleep*. New York: Fordham University Press, 2009.

Nebrig, Alexander. "I.2." In *Über "Die Sonette an Orpheus" von Rilke: Lektüren*, edited by Christoph König and Kai Bremer, 28-31. Göttingen: Wallstein, 2016.

Nemoto, Misako. "Le sommeil proustien ou une nouvelle phénoménologie du présent." *Marcel Proust Aujourd'hui* 2 (2004): 121-38.

Neumann, Gerhard. "Träume als Abfederungsritual der Kultur." In *Kafka-Lektüren*, 531-61. Berlin: De Gruyter, 2013.

———. "Der verschleppte Prozess: Literarisches Schaffen zwischen Schreibstrom und Werkidol." *Poetica* 14 (1982): 92-112.

———. "Der Zauber des Anfangs und das 'Zögern vor der Geburt': Kafkas Poetologie des 'riskantesten Augenblicks.'" In *Nach erneuter Lektüre: Franz Kafkas "Der Proceß,"* edited by Hans Dieter Zimmermann, 121-42. Würzburg: Königshausen & Neumann, 1992.

Neymeyr, Barbara. "'Fräulein Else': Identitätssuche im Spannungsfeld von Konvention und Rebellion." In *Arthur Schnitzler: Dramen und Erzählungen*, edited by Hee-Ju Kim and Günter Sasse, 190-208. Stuttgart: Reclam, 2007.

Niehaus, Michael. *"Ich, die Literatur, ich spreche . . .": der Monolog der Literatur im 20. Jahrhundert*. Würzburg: Königshausen & Neumann, 1995.

———. "Iterativität bei Franz Kafka: Vorläufige Bemerkungen." In *Kafkas narrative Verfahren*, edited by Harald Neumeyer and Wilko Steffans, 111-28. Würzburg: Königshausen & Neumann, 2015.

———. "Das Schreiben interpretieren: Zum Beispiel Kafka." In *Schreiben*, edited by Martin Stingelin and Ludger Hoffmann, 273-92. Paderborn: Fink, 2017.

———. *Das Verhör*. Literatur und Recht. Munich: Fink, 2003.

———. "Zur Vorgeschichte des 'inneren Monologs.'" *Arcadia* 29, no. 3 (1994): 225-39.

Nordholt, Annelies Schulte. "Le dormeur éveillé comme figure du moi proustien." *Neophilologus* 80, no. 4 (1996): 539-54.

———. "Proust and Subjectivity." In *Subjectivity*, edited by Willem van Reijen and Willem G. Weststeijn, 81-106. Amsterdam: Rodopi, 2000.

North, Paul. *The Yield: Kafka's Atheological Reformation*. Palo Alto, CA: Stanford University Press, 2015.

Ollivier, Jean-Pierre. *Proust et les sciences*. Paris: Champion, 2018.

Otis, Laura. *Membranes: Metaphors of Invasion in Nineteenth-Century Literature, Science, and Politics*. Baltimore, MD: Johns Hopkins University Press, 1999.

Otter, Chris. *The Victorian Eye: A Political History of Light and Vision in Britain, 1800-1910*. Chicago: University of Chicago Press, 2008.

Osten, Philipp. *Das Tor zur Seele: Schlaf, Somnambulismus und Hellsehen im frühen 19. Jahrhundert*. Paderborn: Schöningh, 2015.

———. "Über Wachen und Schlafen: Medizinische Schlafdiskurse im 19. Jahrhundert." In *Kontrollgewinn—Kontrollverlust: Die Geschichte des Schlafs in der Moderne*, edited by Hannah Ahlheim, 73-98. Frankfurt am Main: Campus, 2014.

Parris, Benjamin. "'The Body Is with the King, but the King Is Not with the Body': Sovereign Sleep in *Hamlet* and *Macbeth*." *Shakespeare Studies* 40 (2012): 101.

———. "Seizures of Sleep in Early Modern Literature." *SEL Studies in English Literature, 1500-1900* 58, no. 1 (2018): 51-76.

———. *Vital Strife: Sleep, Insomnia, and the Early Modern Ethics of Care*. Ithaca, NY: Cornell University Press, 2022.

Paulin, Roger, and Helmut Pfotenhauer. "Einleitung." In *Die Halbschlafbilder in der Literatur, den Künsten und den Wissenschaften*, edited by Roger Paulin and Helmut Pfotenhauer 205-23. Würzburg: Königshausen & Neumann, 2011.

Penzin, Alexei. *Rex Exsomnis*. Ostfildern: Hatje Cantz, 2012.

Perciaccante, Antonio, and Alessia Coralli. "Franz Kafka's Insomnia and Parasomnias." *Lancet Neurology* 15, no. 10 (2016): 1014.

———. "Insomnia: The Enemy Feeding the Literary Genius of Franz Kafka." *Sleep Medicine* 52 (2018): 232.

Pergnier, Maurice. *Le sommeil et les signes: Arts, science, littérature et mystère d'hypnos*. Lausanne: L'Age d'Homme, 2004.

Perlmann, Michaela L. *Der Traum in der literarischen Moderne: Untersuchungen zum Werk Arthur Schnitzlers*. Munich: Fink, 1987.

Peter, Helga. "Schlafhygiene." In *Enzyklopädie der Schlafmedizin*, edited by Thomas Penzel, Jörg Hermann Peter, and Helga Peter, 1090-92. Berlin: Springer, 2007.

Pethes, Nicolas. "Telling Cases: Writing against Genre in Medicine and Literature." *Literature and Medicine* 32, no. 1 (2014): 25-45.

Pethes, Nicolas, and Susanne Düwell. *Fall—Fallgeschichte—Fallstudie: Theorie und Geschichte einer Wissensform*. Frankfurt am Main: Campus, 2014.

Pethes, Nicolas, and Sandra Richter, eds. *Medizinische Schreibweisen: Ausdifferenzierung und Transfer zwischen Medizin und Literatur (1600-1900)*. Tübingen: Niemeyer, 2008.

Pfotenhauer, Helmut, and Sabine Schneider. *Nicht völlig Wachen und nicht ganz ein Traum*. Würzburg: Königshausen & Neumann, 2006.

Philippi, Klaus-Peter. *Reflexion und Wirklichkeit: Untersuchungen zu Kafkas Roman "Das Schloss."* Tübingen: Niemeyer, 1966.

Pinel, John P. J. *Biopsychology*. 6th ed. Boston: Pearson Allyn and Bacon, 2006.

Plumpe, Gottfried. *Die I.G. Farbenindustrie AG: Wirtschaft, Technik und Politik, 1904-1945*. Berlin: Duncker & Humblot, 1990.

Politzer, Heinz. *Franz Kafka: Der Künstler*. Frankfurt am Main: S. Fischer, 1965.

Pollock, Jonathan. "Opium and the Occult: Antonin Artaud and Samuel Taylor Coleridge," *Revue de Littérature Comparée* 300, no. 4 (2001): 567-77.
Pomata, Gianna. "The Medical Case Narrative: Distant Reading of an Epistemic Genre." *Literature and Medicine* 32, no. 1 (2014): 1-23.
Pontalis, Jean-Bertrand, and Jean Laplanche. *The Vocabulary of Psychoanalysis*. Paris: Karnac, 1988.
Pottbeckers, Jörg. "Hatte Leutnant Gustl Hunger? Einige späte Bemerkungen zur Entstehung des inneren Monologs bei Arthur Schnitzler und Knut Hamsun." *Studia austriaca* 20 (2012): 85-105.
Pross, Caroline, Klaus Müller-Wille, and Maximilian Bergengruen, eds. *Neurasthenie: Die Krankheit der Moderne und die moderne Literatur*. Freiburg im Breisgau: Rombach, 2010.
Pusse, Tina-Karen. "'Unter schläfernden Lidern': Dämmerzustände in Rainer Maria Rilkes später Lyrik." In *Der Traum im Gedicht*, 153-67. Würzburg: Königshausen & Neumann, 2017.
Rabaté, Jean-Michel, ed. *A Handbook of Modernism Studies*. Hoboken, NJ: Wiley, 2013.
Rabelhofer, Bettina. *Symptom, Sexualität, Trauma: Kohärenzlinien des Ästhetischen um 1900*. Würzburg: Königshausen & Neumann, 2006.
Rabinbach, Anson. "Ermüdung, Energie und der menschliche Motor." In *Physiologie und industrielle Gesellschaft: Studien zur Verwissenschaftlichung des Körpers im 19. und 20. Jahrhundert*, edited by Philipp Sarasin and Jakob Tanner, 286-312. Frankfurt am Main: Suhrkamp, 1998.
———. *The Human Motor: Energy, Fatigue, and the Origins of Modernity*. Berkeley: University of California Press, 1992.
Radkau, Joachim. "Die wilhelminische Ära als nervöses Zeitalter, oder: Die Nerven als Netz zwischen Tempo- und Körpergeschichte." *Geschichte und Gesellschaft* 20, no. 2 (1994): 211-41.
———. *Das Zeitalter der Nervosität: Deutschland zwischen Bismarck und Hitler*. Hanser, 1998.
Ragonneau, Nicolas. "Proust et l'opium: un passage oublié du *Journal des Goncourt*." *Proustonomics* (blog), April 1, 2021. https://proustonomics.com/proust-opium-sur-un-passage-oublie-du-journal-des-goncourt/.
Rancière, Jacques. *Proletarian Nights: The Workers' Dream in Nineteenth-Century France*. Translated By John Drury. London: Verso, 2012.
Reckwitz, Andreas. *Subjekt*. 2nd ed. Bielefeld: Transcript, 2010.
Reents, Friederike. "Suicidal Tendencies in Modern German Literature." In *Suicidality in the Media: Interdisciplinary Contributions*, edited by Arno Herberth, Thomas Niederkortenthaler, and Benedikt Till, 135-42. Vienna: Lit, 2008.
Reiss, Benjamin. *Wild Nights: How Taming Sleep Created Our Restless World*. New York: Basic Books, 2017.

Rheinberger, Hans-Jörg. *On Historicizing Epistemology: An Essay*. Translated by David Fernbach. Stanford, CA: Stanford University Press, 2010.
———. "Representation in Scientific Practice." *Studies in History and Philosophy of Science, Part A* 25, no. 4 (1994): 647-54.
———. *Toward a History of Epistemic Things: Synthesizing Proteins in the Test Tube*. Stanford, CA: Stanford University Press, 1997.
Richter, Gerhard. "Difficile Dwellings: Kafka's 'The Burrow.'" In *The Poetics of Reading*, edited by Eitel Timm and Kenneth Mendoza, 1-18. Columbia, SC: Camden House, 1992.
Riethmüller, Albrecht. "Rainer Maria Rilke, 'Gong': An den Grenzen von Musik und Sprache." In *Gedichte über Musik: Quellen ästhetischer Einsicht*, 183-209. Laaber: Laaber-Verlag, 1996.
Robertson, Ritchie. *Kafka: Judaism, Politics, and Literature*. Oxford, UK: Clarendon Press, 1985.
Rodriges e Silva, Antonio Manuel. "Das Leben von Prof. Dr. Fritz Jakob Heinrich Lewy (1885-1950)." PhD diss., Philipps-Universität Marburg, 2013. https://archiv.ub.uni-marburg.de/diss/z2015/0518.
Rose, Nikolas. "Neurochemical Selves." *Society* 41, no. 1 (2003): 46-59.
Ryan, Judith. *Rilke, Modernism and Poetic Tradition*. Cambridge: Cambridge University Press, 1999.
———. *Umschlag und Verwandlung: Poetische Struktur und Dichtungstheorie in R. M. Rilkes Lyrik der mittleren Periode (1907-1914)*. Munich: Winkler, 1972.
Sacks, Oliver. *Awakenings*. London: Duckworth, 1973.
Saint-Amour, Paul K. "Stillness and Altitude: René Clair's *Paris Qui Dort*." In *Moving Modernisms: Motion, Technology, and Modernity*, edited by David Bradshaw, Laura Marcus, and Rebecca Roach, 217-35. Oxford: Oxford University Press, 2016.
Sarasin, Philipp. *Reizbare Maschinen: Eine Geschichte des Körpers, 1765-1914*. Frankfurt am Main: Suhrkamp, 2001.
Schäfer, Armin. "Poetologie des Wissens." In *Literatur und Wissen: Ein interdisziplinäres Handbuch*, edited by Roland Borgards et al., 36-41. Stuttgart: Metzler, 2013.
Scheible, Hartmut. "Arthur Schnitzler." In *Deutsche Dichter des 20. Jahrhunderts*, edited by Hartmut Steinecke, 11-31. Berlin: Schmidt, 1994.
Scheidhauer, Marcel. *Freud et ses visiteurs: Français et suisses francophones, 1920-1930*. Toulouse: Erès, 2010.
Schivelbusch, Wolfgang. *Lichtblicke: Zur Geschichte der künstlichen Helligkeit im 19. Jahrhundert*. Munich: Hanser, 1983.
Schlesinger, Renate. "Proust als Leser von Flaubert." *Poetica* 43, nos. 3-4 (2011): 301-17.
Schmid, Wolf. *Elemente der Narratologie*. 3rd ed. Berlin: De Gruyter, 2014.

———. "Erzählstimme." In *Handbuch Erzählliteratur*, edited by Matías Martínez, 131–38. Stuttgart: Metzler, 2011.
Schmidt-Hannisa, Hans Walter. "Das eiserne Szepter des Schlafes: Über die Unzurechnungsfähigkeit von Schlaftrunkenen, Nachtwandlern und Träumern im 18. Jahrhundert." In *Unzurechnungsfähigkeiten: Diskursivierungen unfreier Bewußtseinszustände seit dem 18. Jahrhundert*, edited by Michael Niehaus and Hans-Walter Schmidt-Hannisa, 57–84. Frankfurt am Main: Peter Lang, 1998.
———. "Halbschlafbilder: Zur Ästhetik des Kontrollverlusts." In *Kontrollgewinn—Kontrollverlust: Die Geschichte des Schlafs in der Moderne*, edited by Hannah Ahlheim, 51–72. Frankfurt am Main: Campus, 2014.
Schmitz, Rudolf. *Geschichte der Pharmazie: Von der Frühen Neuzeit bis zur Gegenwart*. Eschborn: Govi, 2005.
Schneuwly, Bernard. "La psychologie appliquée à l'enseignement du français: L'exemple de Claparède." *Histoire Épistémologie Langage* 17, no. 1 (1995): 143–61.
Schößler, Franziska. "Börse und Begehren: Schnitzlers Monolog 'Fräulein Else' und seine Kontexte." In *Arthur Schnitzler: Affairen und Affekte*, edited by Evelyne Polt-Heinzl and Konstanze Fliedl, 119–29. Vienna: Brandstätter, 2006.
Schorske, Carl E. *Fin-de-Siècle Vienna Politics and Culture*. New York: Knopf, 1980.
Schulz, Hartmut, and Piero Salzarulo. "The Evolution of Sleep Medicine in the Nineteenth and the Early Twentieth Century." In *Sleep Medicine: A Comprehensive Guide to Its Development, Clinical Milestones, and Advances in Treatment*, edited by Sudhansu Chokroverty and Michel Billiard, 75–90. New York: Springer, 2015.
Schütterle, Annette. *Franz Kafkas Oktavhefte: Ein Schreibprozess als "System des Teilbaues."* Freiburg im Breisgau: Rombach, 2002.
Schwenger, Peter. *At the Borders of Sleep: On Liminal Literature*. Minneapolis: University of Minnesota Press, 2012.
———. "Writing Hypnagogia." *Critical Inquiry* 34, no. 3 (2008): 423–39.
Scrivner, Lee. *Becoming Insomniac: How Sleeplessness Alarmed Modernity*. New York: Palgrave Macmillan, 2014.
———. "That Sweet Secession: Sleep and Sleeplessness in Western Literature." In *Sleep: Multiprofessional Perspectives*, edited by Andrew Green and Alexander Westcombe, 268–90. London: Kingsley, 2012.
Seitter, Walter. *Geschichte der Nacht*. Berlin: Philo, 1999.
Selbmann, Rolf. "Rainers Widersprüche: zu Rilkes Grabspruch 'Rose, oh reiner Widerspruch.'" In *Die Welt ist in die Hände der Menschen gefallen*, 165–75. Frankfurt am Main: Insel, 2002.
Serres, Michel. *The Parasite*. Translated by Lawrence R. Schehr. Baltimore, MD: Johns Hopkins University Press, 1982.

Sharpe, William. *New York Nocturne: The City after Dark in Literature, Painting, and Photography, 1850-1950*. Princeton, NJ: Princeton University Press, 2008.

Sherman, David. *In a Strange Room: Modernism's Corpses and Mortal Obligation*. New York: Oxford University Press, 2014.

Sherry, Vincent, ed. *The Cambridge History of Modernism*. Cambridge: Cambridge University Press, 2017.

Shore, Elizabeth. "Virginia Woolf, Proust, and Orlando." *Comparative Literature* 31, no. 3 (1979): 232-45.

Shorter, Edward. *Before Prozac: The Troubled History of Mood Disorders in Psychiatry*. Oxford: Oxford University Press, 2008.

Shuttleworth, Sally. "Fagged Out: Overwork and Sleeplessness in Victorian Professional Life." *Interface Focus* 10, no. 3 (2020): 1-10.

———. *The Mind of the Child: Child Development in Literature, Science, and Medicine 1840-1900*. Oxford: Oxford University Press, 2010.

Shuttleworth, Sally, and Russell G. Foster. "Sleep and Stress." *Interface Focus* 10, no. 3 (2020): 1-4.

Simon, Anne. "The Formalist, the Spider, and the Phenomenologist: Proust in the Magic Mirror of the Twentieth Century." In *The Strange M. Proust*, edited by André Benhaïm, 23-35. London: Legenda, 2009.

Simon, Anne, and Isabelle Serça. "Sommeil." In *Dictionnaire Marcel Proust*, edited by Annick Bouillaguet, 947-50. Paris: Champion, 2004.

Solhdju, Katrin. *Selbstexperimente: Die Suche nach der Innenperspektive und ihre epistemologischen Folgen*. Munich: Fink, 2011.

Solms, Mark. "Sleep." In *The Freud Encyclopedia: Theory, Therapy, and Culture*, edited by Edward Erwin, 528-30. New York: Routledge, 2002.

Spector, Scott. *Prague Territories: National Conflict and Cultural Innovation in Franz Kafka's Fin de Siècle*. Berkeley: University of California Press, 2000.

Stach, Reiner. *Kafka: The Early Years*. Translated by Shelley Laura Frisch. Princeton, NJ: Princeton University Press, 2016.

Stadler, Ulrich. "Halbschlaf-Szenen bei Kafka und Benjamin." In *Die Halbschlafbilder in der Literatur, den Künsten und den Wissenschaften*, edited by Roger Paulin and Helmut Pfotenhauer, 205-23. Würzburg: Königshausen & Neumann, 2011.

Steger, Brigitte. *Inemuri: Wie die Japaner schlafen und was wir von ihnen lernen können*. Reinbek: Rowohlt, 2007.

Steger, Brigitte, and Lodewijk Brunt, eds. *Night-Time and Sleep in Asia and the West: Exploring the Dark Side of Life*. London: Routledge, 2003.

Steinfeld, Thomas. *Ich will, ich kann: Moderne und Selbstoptimierung*. Konstanz: Konstanz University Press, 2016.

Steinlechner, Gisela. "*Fräulein Else*: Eine Zeitreise zwischen Fin de Siècle und Roaring Twenties." In *Arthur Schnitzler: Affairen und Affekte*, edited by Evelyne Polt-Heinzel and Gisela Steinlechner, 131-41. Vienna: Brandstätter, 2006.

Stern, Felix. *Die epidemische Encephalitis*. Berlin: Springer, 1922.
Stieg, Gerald. "Rilkes späteste Gedichte auf deutsch und französisch: Ein Vergleich am Beispiel von 'Gong.'" In *Nach Duino*, edited by Karen Leeder and Robert Vilain, 168-78. Göttingen: Wallstein, 2010.
Strittmatter, Ellen. "Strategien der Autorinszenierung. Über Rilkes Verhältnis zum fotografischen Porträt." In *Die Präsentation kanonischer Werke um 1900: Semantiken, Praktiken, Materialität*, edited by Philip Ajouri, 217-42. Berlin: De Gruyter, 2017.
Strowick, Elisabeth. "Epistemologie des Verdachts: zu Kafkas 'Bau.'" In *The Parallax View: Zur Mediologie der Verschwörung*, edited by Marcus Krause, Arno Meteling, and Markus Stauff, 123-35. Munich: Fink, 2011.
Summers-Bremner, Eluned. *Insomnia: A Cultural History*. London: Reaktion, 2010.
Surprenant, Céline. "Freud and Psychoanalysis." In *Marcel Proust in Context*, edited by Adam A. Watt, 107-14. Cambridge: Cambridge University Press, 2013.
Szylowicz, Caroline. "Proust's Reading." In *Marcel Proust in Context*, edited by Adam A. Watt, 43-50. Cambridge: Cambridge University Press, 2013.
Tacke, Alexandra. *Schnitzlers "Fräulein Else" und die nackte Wahrheit: Novelle, Verfilmungen und Bearbeitungen*. Köln: Böhlau, 2017.
Tadié, Jean-Yves. *Marcel Proust*. Translated by Euan Cameron. New York: Viking, 2000.
———. *Proust*. Paris: Belfond, 1983.
Tebben, Karin. "Selbstmörderinnen in der deutschen Literatur des 19. und 20. Jahrhunderts—zur poetologischen Signifikanz ihrer Todesarten." *Colloquia Germanica* 35, no. 1 (2002): 1-25.
Thomé, Horst. *Autonomes Ich und "Inneres Ausland": Studien über Realismus, Tiefenpsychologie und Psychiatrie in deutschen Erzähltexten (1848-1914)*. Tübingen: Niemeyer, 1993.
———. "Die Beobachtbarkeit des Psychischen bei Arthur Schnitzler und Sigmund Freud." In *Arthur Schnitzler im zwanzigsten Jahrhundert*, edited by Konstanze Fliedl, 51-66. Vienna: Picus, 2003.
Thrift, Nigel. "The Material Practices of Glamour." *Journal of Cultural Economy* 1, no. 1 (2008): 9-23.
Travis, Anthony S. et al., eds., *Determinants in the Evolution of the European Chemical Industry, 1900-1936: New Technologies, Political Frameworks, Markets, and Companies*. Dordrecht: Springer, 1998.
Triangle Collective, ed. *The Palgrave Handbook of Twentieth and Twenty-First Century Literature and Science*. Cham: Palgrave Macmillan, 2020.
Triarhou, Lazaros C. "The Percipient Observations of Constantin von Economo on Encephalitis Lethargica and Sleep Disruption and Their Lasting Impact on Contemporary Sleep Research." *Brain Research Bulletin* 69, no. 3 (2006): 244-58.

———. "The Signalling Contributions of Constantin von Economo to Basic, Clinical and Evolutionary Neuroscience." *Brain Research Bulletin* 69, no. 3 (2006): 223-43.

Trigoni, Thalia. *The Intelligent Unconscious in Modernist Literature and Science*. New York: Routledge, 2021.

Turek, Fred W. "Melatonin : Pathway from Obscure Molecule to International Fame." *Perspectives in Biology and Medicine* 41, no. 1 (1997): 8-20.

Türk, Johannes. "Health and Illness." In *Franz Kafka in Context*, edited by Carolin Duttlinger, 44-53. Cambridge: Cambridge University Press, 2017.

Turner, Henry S. "Lessons from Literature for the Historian of Science (and Vice Versa): Reflections on 'Form.'" *Isis* 101, no. 3 (2010): 578-89.

Todorov, Tzvetan. "Valéry's Poetics," *Yale French Studies* 44 (1970): 65-71.

Uhlig, Ingo. *Traum und Poiesis: Produktive Schlafzustände, 1641-1810*. Göttingen: Wallstein, 2015.

Ulrich, Gerd. *"Wirkungen, die an Wunder grenzen": Arzneimittelwerbung in Deutschland (1830 bis 1930)*. Norderstedt: Books on Demand, 2007.

Uttal, William R. *The New Phrenology: The Limits of Localizing Cognitive Processes in the Brain*. Cambridge, MA: MIT Press, 2001.

Vidal, Fernando. *The Sciences of the Soul*. Chicago: University of Chicago Press, 2011.

Vilensky, Joel A., ed. *Encephalitis Lethargica: During and after the Epidemic*. New York: Oxford University Press, 2011.

Virilio, Paul. *A Landscape of Events*. Cambridge, MA: MIT Press, 2000.

Vogl, Joseph. "Am Schlossberg." In *Über Berge*, edited by Susanne Goumegou, Brigitte Heymann, Dagmar Stöferle, and Cornelia Wild, 83-90. Berlin: Kadmos, 2012.

———. "Für eine Poetologie des Wissens." In *Die Literatur und die Wissenschaften, 1770-1930: Walter-Müller Seidel zum 75. Geburtstag*, edited by Karl Richter, 107-27. Stuttgart: M & P, 1997.

———. *Ort der Gewalt. Kafkas literarische Ethik*. Zürich: Diaphanes, 2010.

———. "Vierte Person: Kafkas Erzählstimme." *Deutsche Vierteljahrsschrift für Literaturwissenschaft und Geistesgeschichte* 68, no. 4 (1994): 745-56.

Voigts, Manfred. *Geburt und Teufelsdienst: Franz Kafka als Schriftsteller und als Jude*. Würzburg: Königshausen & Neumann, 2008.

Wallace, Nathaniel Owen. *Scanning the Hypnoglyph: Sleep in Modernist and Postmodern Representation*. Boston: Brill, 2016.

Warning, Rainer. "Erzählen im Paradigma: Kontingenzbewältigung und Kontingenzexposition." *Romanistisches Jahrbuch* 52, no. 1 (2001): 176-209.

———. *Marcel Proust*. Paderborn: Fink, 2016.

———. "Supplementäre Individualität: Prousts 'Albertine endormie.'" In *Proust-Studien*, 77-108. Munich: Fink, 2000.

Waters, William. *Poetry's Touch: On Lyric Address*. Ithaca, NY: Cornell University Press, 2003.

Webb, Wilse B. "Sleep as a Biological Rhythm: A Historical Review." *Sleep* 17, no. 2 (1994): 188-94.

Weber, Matthias. *Die Entwicklung der Psychopharmakologie im Zeitalter der naturwissenschaftlichen Medizin: Ideengeschichte eines psychiatrischen Therapiesystems*. Munich: Urban & Vogel, 1999.

Weber, Nicholas Fox. *Balthus: A Biography*. New York: Knopf, 1999.

Wegmann, Thomas. *Dichtung und Warenzeichen: Reklame im literarischen Feld, 1850-2000*. Göttingen: Wallstein, 2011.

———. "The Human as Resident Animal: Kafka's 'Der Bau' in the Context of His Later Notebooks and Letters." *Monatshefte* 103, no. 3 (2011): 360-71.

Weimar, Klaus. "Wo und was ist der Erzähler?" *MLN* 109, no. 3 (1994): 495-506.

Weyand, Björn. *Poetik der Marke: Konsumkultur und literarische Verfahren, 1900-2000*. Berlin: De Gruyter, 2013.

Whitney, Tyler. "Inside the Ear: Silence, Self-Observation, and Embodied Spaces in Kafka's 'Der Bau.'" *Germanic Review: Literature, Culture, Theory* 92, no. 3 (2017): 301-19.

Wickers, Olivier. *Chambres de Proust*. Paris: Flammarion, 2013.

Williams, Simon J. *Sleep and Society: Sociological Ventures into the (Un)Known*. New York: Routledge, 2005.

Wimmer, Wolfgang. *"Wir haben fast immer was Neues": Gesundheitswesen und Innovationen der Pharma-Industrie in Deutschland, 1880-1935*. Berlin: Duncker & Humblot, 1994.

Wiseman, Martha. "Waking to the Night: Proust's Dream Theater." *Marcel Proust Aujourd'hui* 2 (2004): 83-102.

Wittbrodt, Andreas. *Hototogisu ist keine Nachtigall: Traditionelle japanische Gedichtformen in der deutschsprachigen Lyrik (1849-1999)*. Göttingen: V&R unipress, 2005.

Wittgenstein, Ludwig. *Philosophical Investigations*. Translated by G. E. M. Anscombe. Oxford: Blackwell, 1953.

———. *Zettel*. Edited by G. E. M. Anscombe and G. H. von Wright and translated by G. E. M. Anscombe. Berkeley: University of California Press, 1967.

Wöhrle, Georg. *Hypnos, der Allbezwinger: Eine Studie zum literarischen Bild des Schlafes in der griechischen Antike*. Stuttgart: Steiner, 1995.

Wolf, Burkhardt. "Die Nacht des Bürokraten: Franz Kafkas statistische Schreibweise." *Deutsche Vierteljahrsschrift für Literaturwissenschaft und Geistesgeschichte* 80, no. 1 (2006): 97-127.

Wolff, Joachim. *Rilkes Grabschrift: Manuskript- und Druckgeschichte, Forschungsbericht, Analysen und Interpretation*. Heidelberg: Stiehm, 1983.

Wolf-Meyer, Matthew. "Biomedicine, the Whiteness of Sleep, and the Wages of Spatiotemporal Normativity in the United States." *American Ethnologist* 42, no. 3 (2015): 446-58.

———. "Natural Hegemonies : Sleep and the Rhythms of American Capitalism." *Current Anthropology* 52, no. 6 (2011): 876-95.

———. *The Slumbering Masses: Sleep, Medicine, and Modern American Life*. Minneapolis: University of Minnesota Press, 2012.

———. "What's So Natural about Sleep?" *Anthropology Now* 5, no. 3 (2013): 9-17.

———. "Where Have All Our Naps Gone? Or Nathaniel Kleitman, the Consolidation of Sleep, and the Historiography of Emergence." *Anthropology of Consciousness* 24, no. 2 (2013): 96-116.

Wollaeger Mark A., and Matt Eatough, eds. *The Oxford Handbook of Global Modernisms*. New York: Oxford University Press, 2012.

Worbs, Michael. *Nervenkunst: Literatur und Psychoanalyse im Wien der Jahrhundertwende*. Frankfurt am Main: Europäische Verlagsanstalt, 1983.

Wortham, Simon Morgan. *The Poetics of Sleep: From Aristotle to Nancy*. London: Bloomsbury, 2014.

Wright, Donald. *Du discours médical dans "À la recherche du temps perdu": Science et souffrance*. Paris: Champion, 2007.

Yoshida, Jo. "Proust et la maladie nerveuse." *Marcel Proust* 96, no. 2 (1992): 101-19.

Yu, Cécile. "La pensée du sommeil dans *À la recherche du temps perdu*." *Littérature* 129 (2003): 33-46.

Zanucchi, Mario. "Rilkes *Sonette an Orpheus* (1923)." In *Transfer und Modifikation: Die französischen Symbolisten in der deutschsprachigen Lyrik der Moderne (1890-1923)*, 517-80. Berlin: De Gruyter, 2016.

Index

Page numbers in *italics* indicate an illustration.

24/7 society, 3, 6, 14, 35, 114. *See also* capitalism; modernity
active sleep, 12-13, 20, 21-23, 24, 28-30, 33-34. *See also À la recherche du temps perdu*; passive sleep
active subject, 21-22
African trypanosomiasis, 25
Ahlheim, Hannah, 17
À la recherche du temps perdu (Proust): awakening, memory, and self, 90-91, 93-94, 95-96, 135-36, 137; centrality of sleep, 73-74, 81, 88; connection between sleep and writing, 74, 80-81, 87-88, 90; consciousness, 84-85, 86-87, 93-94; elusiveness of sleep, 75; insomnia portrayed, 75, 76, 90; narrator and protagonist, 77-80, 81; natural vs artificial sleep, 88-90; neurasthenic half sleep, 75-76; reentry into sleep, 82-83; sleep as active process, 22, 88-90; sleep as metamorphosis of self, 97, 220n81; soporifics' role, 85-90; sound events tracing borders of sleep, 84-85; structural function of sleep, 74, 76-77; tenses (grammatical) in, 76, 78-81, 88, 95, 96
Albaret, Céleste, 86-87
Alt, Peter-André, 106
Altenberg, Peter, 35-36
arousal thresholds, 83-84, 124-25
Artaud, Antonin, 85

automatic writing, 15, 134
autonomous subject, 31, 32-33. *See also* waking
awakening: dreams legible through, 71; motif in literature, 76-79; reentries of somnolence and wakefulness, 81-83; threatening sleep, 23; Valéry on, 118-19. *See also À la recherche du temps perdu*; Kafka, Franz; waking

barbiturates, 43, 44, 45-46, 87. *See also* Veronal
Barthes, Roland, 80, 86, 99
Baudelaire, Charles, 109-10
Baum, Vicki, 63
Bayer: about, 36; Adamon, 43; advertising, 41, 42, 43, 44, 53-54; Luminal, 43; response to fictional depictions of Veronal, 13-14, 58, 60, 63-64, 201n15; sleeping pills, 50; Voluntal, 43. *See also* sleep-inducing drugs; Veronal
Beard, George, 37
Beer, Gillian, 11
Beer-Hoffmann, Richard, 72
Benjamin, Walter, 50, 60, 85
Benn, Gottfried, 38, 85
Berger, Hans, 7, 33-34
Bergson, Herni, 22, 81, 91
Bernard, Claude, 28, 75
Birlo, Eduard, 56, 57
Bismarck, Otto von, 51
Blumenberg, Hans, 76

brain: brain sleep vs body sleep, 29; functional localization, 26-27, 31; mesencephalon, 29; sleep centers in, 23, 26-28, 30, 32-33; sleep hardwired function of, 24, 26; sleep hormones, 47; sleep regulation centers in, 23-24, 28-30, 31; sleep regulation mechanism in, 26
Brentano, Clemens, 70
Breton, André, 101
Breuer, Josef, 3
Broch, Hermann, 54-55
Brod, Max, 111, 221n9
Bronfen, Elisabeth, 204n34

caffeine, 86
Canguilhem, Georges, 26, 74, 188n48
capitalism: assaulting restful sleep, 6, 35; branding, modern practices of, 50; consumption reclaiming agency, 41; insomnia proliferating under, 35, 37-38; sleeping pills and aesthetics of consumption, 52-53; sleep tied to, 6. *See also* insomnia; modernity
Chateaubriand, François-René, 128
circadian rhythms, 47, 131-32. *See also* periodicity
Claparède, Édouard, 12, 18, 20-24, 34, 47, 185n33
Cocteau, Jean, 85
Coetzee, J. M., 109
Cohn, Dorrit, 71
Cohn, Elisha, 177n15
consciousness, 82, 84, 92-93, 118. *See also* À la recherche du temps perdu (Proust); waking
Crary, Jonathan, 3, 35

death, 2, 128-29, 133, 136-37. *See also* Fräulein Else; sleep-inducing drugs; Veronal
deep sleep, 82
Diderot, Denis, 10, 40-41, 180n49
dietetics, 40-41, 193n31
dogs, sleep deprivation experiments, 20, 47, 195n60
Dostoyevsky, Fyodor, 92
dreams: flying in, 70, 209n67; guardian of sleep, 23, 182n4; hypnagogic experiences, 15, 101, 104-5; legible through awakening, 71; link with sleep severed, 16-17, 176n12, 182n4; means of sustaining sleep, 23; as sleep action, 23; somniloquy, 10, 105, 180n49
Dujardin, Édouard, 72
Duttlinger, Carolin, 110

Economo, Constantin von, 12-13, 24-26, 27-32, 34, 47
EEG (electroencephalograph). *See* electroencephalograph
Ekirch, Roger, 3, 6
EL (encephalitis lethargica). *See* encephalitis lethargica
electroencephalograph (EEG), 7, *33*, 33-34
Ellis, Havelock, 70
encephalitis lethargica (EL), 25; active sleep and, 12-13, 24, 28; sleep-brain link, 26, 28; sleep reconsidered due to, 24-26, 31-32; symptoms and sequel conditions, 186n38; willpower and, 31-32
Enlightenment, 40
exhaustion: Claparède's revision of, 20; danger of, 20-21; as inability to work, 17-18; normal sleep and, 20-21; sleep as defense against, 21; sleep as special case of, 18; waking due to, 23. *See also* fatigue; sleep deprivation; sleep-inducing drugs
Exner, Sigmund, 31

fatigue, 18, 20, 21, 47-48. *See also* exhaustion; sleep deprivation; sleep-inducing drugs
fatigue substances, 47-48
Fechner, Gustav, 124
Federal Law for the Protection of Commodity Brands, 50
Fischer, Emil, 46-47
Flaubert, Gustave, 62, 80, 223n25
Flury, Ferdinand, 63
Foucault, Michel, 9, 193n31
Fräulein Else (Schnitzler): Czinner's film version, 208n54; desire for glamour, 62-63; Else as body made from text, 68-70; interior monologues, 14, 58, 62, 69-72, 203n25; newspaper report catalyst, 61-62; pharmaceutical industry's reaction to, 13-14, 58, 60, 63-64; suicide by Veronal, 59, 60, 61-62, 63-64,

66-72, 207n52; Veronal as possessing agency, 59, 66, 68-69; Veronal's foundational role, 59, 60, 61, 63; Veronal's quotidianness, 60
Freud, Sigmund: on Claparède, 21; dream as guardian of sleep, 23, 182n4; flying in dreams, 209n67; sleep as disinterest in one's surroundings, 22; sleep-dreams link severed, 3-4, 16-17, 182n4
Fülleborn, Ulrich, 123

Galen, 40-41, 42
Garshin, Vsevolod, 72
Gélineau, Jean-Baptiste-Édouard, 27
gender: cures for insomnia and, 38, 39, 117; deity of cat sleep, 125; in *Fräulein Else* (Schnitzler), 58; male gaze, 121-22; medical dosages for women vs men, 55, 57; norms and politics, 121; sleeping pills targeting women, 13, 50, 53, 55, 57; sleeping women, 119-22, 126-29; sleep interrupting self and, 92, 94, 125, 132; women in science 20-21, 132, 188n61, 189n64. *See also* Veronal
Genette, Gérard, 76
Grand Hotel (film), 63

Hamburger, Käte, 80, 109
Hegel, Georg Wilhelm Friedrich, 10, 91-92, 181n50
Hofmannsthal, Hugo von, 137
hormones, 47-48
Huelsenbeck, Richard, 50
Hufeland, Christoph Wilhelm, 113
hypnagogic experiences, 15, 101, 104-5

insomnia: capitalism proliferating, 35, 37-38; characterizations of, 36; cures for, 36, 38, 39, 40; defined, 35; social causes and conditions, 35, 37-38. *See also* À *la recherche du temps perdu*; Kafka, Franz; neurasthenia; Rilke, Rainer Maria; sleep-inducing drugs
interior monologues: criteria for, 210n69; expression of collective *Mittelbewusstsein*, 204n33; in *Fräulein Else* (Schnitzler), 14, 58, 62, 69-72, 203n25; in *Recherche* (Proust), 76. *See also* language of sleep
intermediary subjects, 77-78

Joyce, James, 9

Kafka, Franz: awakening in works by, 15, 94, 105-9; connection between writing and sleeping, 103-4; diaries, 99-105; dream logic tradition of interpreting, 98-99; falling asleep in works by, 109-13; hypnagogic experiences, 15, 104-5; insomnia of, 100-101, 103, 105, 110, 136; nighttime writing, 14-15, 98, 99-101, 104-5, 136; sleep deprivation as creative technique, 14-15, 100-101, 103, 105; somnambulism, 101, *102*; somnolent and waking states in works by, 110-14, 136; tense (grammatical) in works by, 108-9; work-related sleep issues in works by, 99, 112, 114; *The Castle* (*Das Schloss*), 105, 110-14; "Blumfeld," 107; "The Burrow" ("Der Bau"), 107-9; "In the Penal Colony" ("In der Strafkolonie"), 110; "Investigations of a Dog" ("Forschungen eines Hundes"), 227n67; *The Man Who Disappeared* (*Der Verschollene*), 110; "The Metamorphosis" ("Die Verwandlung"), 94, 105; *The Trial* (*Die Verwandlung*), 94, 105-6
Klossowska, Baladine, 115
Kohlschütter, Ernst, 124-25
König, Christoph, 126
Kraepelin, Emil, 18, 23
Kroker, Kenton, 17, 24

Landy, Joshua, 217n62
language of sleep, 2, 4-5, 20, 21-22, 32-33, 78-80. *See also* Claparède, Édouard; Economo, Constantin von; *Fräulein Else* (Schnitzler); Kafka, Franz; Proust, Marcel; Rilke, Rainer Maria; Valéry, Paul
Lechner, Karl, 35
Lessing, Gotthold Ephraim, 129
Linnaeus, Carl, 131
Lomnitz, Ernst, 48
Luhmann, Niklas, 81

Mairan, Jean-Jacques d'Ortous de, 131
Mallarmé, Stéphane, 126
Manacéïne, Marie de, 12, 20, 47
Mann, Thomas, 94-95, 100, 111, 137
Marx, Karl, 6

Maupassant, Guy de, 63
Maury, Alfred, 101
Mauss, Marcel, 3
medicine: barbiturates, 43, 44, 45-46, 87; branded medications, 50; dosage problems, 55, 57, 64-65, 66; health-care system transformed, 51; morphine, 64-65; as techno-fix, 59, 64. *See also* gender; pharmaceutical industry; sleep-inducing drugs; Veronal
Meister Eckhart, 103
memory, 90-96, 135-36, 137
men. *See* gender
Merck, 46, 50. *See also* Veronal
Mering, Josef Freiherr von, 45-47, 64
Mesmer, Franz Anton, 5
Meyer, Steven, 11
Meynert, Theodor, 31
Miura, Nobutaka, 118
modernism, 7-9, 179n36. *See also* Kafka, Franz; Proust, Marcel; Rilke, Rainer Maria; Schnitzler, Arthur
modernity: attacking sleep, 116-17; insomnia side-effect of, 6-7, 35-36, 38; shifts in sleep behavior, 5-6; sleep aids as shelter from, 36, 45; soporifics solving a problem of, 37, 53-54, 135. *See also* capitalism
morphine, 64-65
Mosso, Angelo, 17-18, 23
Muller, Marcel, 77-78

Nancy, Jean-Luc, 91, 113, 184n19
narcolepsy, 25, 27
national socialists, 43
Neal, Josephine, 188n61
nervousness. *See* neurasthenia
neurasthenia: insomnia prime symptom of, 36, 37; rising concerns over, 37
neurasthenic half sleep, 75-76, 77
Nordholt, Annelies Schulte, 76

Otis, Laura, 11

Parris, Benjamin, 5
passive sleep, 12, 20, 28. *See also* active sleep
pathology, 25, 26, 75. *See also* encephalitis lethargica (EL); sleep disorders
Paul, David, 120-21

Pavlov, Ivan, 31
Pearl, Raymond, 188n61
periodicity: circadian rhythms, 47, 131-32; early characterizations of, 27; endocrine sleep-wake rhythm, 30; monophasic sleep, 6; polyphasic sleep, 6, 177n22; self-regulating cycles, 30; sleep regulation centers, 29, 30. *See also* regulating sleep
pharmaceutical industry: advertising, 41, 48; chemical sleep medication, 38; fatigue substances, 48; insomnia, struggles to address, 38; mass marketing of pharmaceuticals, 51-52; narrative of medical authority, 72; pills, development of, 51-52; rise of, 36-37; sociotope of, 10; trademarks and branding, 50. *See also* Bayer; *Fräulein Else*; Merck; sleep-inducing drugs; Veronal
phenomenology of sleep, 184n19
physiology, 17, 31-32, 45. *See also* sleep deprivation; thermodynamic theory
Pierce, C. S., 121
Piéron, Henri, 12, 20, 37, 47, 195n60
plant sleep, 129, 131-33
Plötzl, Otto, 32
poetry. *See* Rilke, Rainer Maria; Valéry, Paul
Proust, Marcel: connection between writing and sleeping, 74, 81, 87-88; insomniac and sleeping pill addict, 14, 73-74, 77, 85-87, 89-90, 135-36; knowledge of sleep science, 14, 73-74, 135, 211n4; sanatorium stay, 77; *À propos du «style» de Flaubert*, 80. *See also À la recherche du temps perdu*
psychoanalysis, 7-8, 16-17, 99, 135, 204n33
psychonautics, 86-90

Quincey, Thomas de, 59

Rabinbach, Anson, 17
reflex theory, 31, 33
regulating sleep, 23-24, 26, 28-30, 31. *See also* periodicity
Ribot, Théodule Armand, 75
Rilke, Rainer Maria: agency of sleep, 125-26; anthropocentric sleep, 129, 131, 132-33, 136; arousal thresholds in works by, 124, 125; cat sleep, 122-26; connection

Index

between writing and sleeping, 115, 117; insomnia of, 116; language and grammar of sleep, 122, 123-26, 128-29, 130-31, 133; lullaby genre, 125; nighttime writing, 117-18; overview, 15; *Rilke on His Sofa in Muzot* (Klossowska), 115, *116*; sleep and death, 128-29, 133; sleep as state of potentiality, 125; sleep disturbances in works by, 116-17; sleep-wake transitions, 122; synesthesia in works by, 124; textual order of somnific states, 129, 130-31; translation of Valery's "La dormeuse," 119, 120, 122; Valéry's influence on, 118, 119, 123, 126; *Die Aufzeichnungen des Malte Laurids Brigge*, 116-17; *Cimetière*, 131; "Divinité du sommeil des chats," 122-23, 126; "Idol," 123-24, 125-26, 132; *Der Neuen Gedichte anderer Teil*, 117; *Sonette an Orpheus*, 126-30

Rilke on His Sofa in Muzot (Klossowska) (watercolor), 115, *116*

Romantic literature, 5, 70, 128

Ryan, Judith, 122

Scheible, Hartmut, 206n49

Schlesinger, Renate, 80

Schnitzler, Arthur: engagement with public health issues, 13-14, 58-59, 61-62, 72, 135; medicine as techno-fix, 59, 64; theory of public health crises, 63-66; *Leutnant Gustl*, 72; *Der Mörder*, 65; *Der Ruf des Lebens*, 65; *Sterben*, 61; *Traumnovelle*, 61; *Der Weg ins Freie*, 62. See also *Fräulein Else*

Schopenhauer, Arthur, 91

Schwenger, Peter, 92

Serres, Michel, 4

Seyfarth, Carl, 192n6

Shore, Elizabeth, 219n73

Shorter, Edward, 44

Shuttleworth, Sally, 11, 183n7

sleep: death and, 2, 128-29, 133, 136-37; as form of work, 23; fragility of, 22; lifestyle choice governing, 40-41; natural vs artificial, 45, 48, 88-90; reentries of somnolence and wakefulness, 81-83, *82*; who sleeps during sleep?, 9-10, 23, 31-33, 79-80, 90, 91-92. *See also* active sleep; active subject; brain; deep sleep; dreams; exhaustion; fatigue; language of sleep; passive sleep; periodicity; physiology; reflex theory; regulating sleep; tiredness; waking

sleep as passive, 16, 18, 21, 135. *See also* passive sleep

sleep deprivation, 20, 21, 47, 195n60

sleep disorders, 36, 39. *See also* African trypanosomiasis; *À la recherche du temps perdu*; encephalitis lethargica (EL); insomnia; Kafka, Franz; narcolepsy; neurasthenic half sleep; sleep-inducing drugs; somnambulism; somniloquy

sleep hygiene, 40-41

sleep-inducing drugs: Adalin, 41, 42; Adamon, 43; asylum patients, 38; barbiturates, 43, 44; chemical sleep medications, 38; chloral hydrate, 37; death by, in literature, 65-66, 67; as deathlike sleep, 137; Diaethylmalonylharnstoff, 46-47, 49; distrust of, 38, 40, 41, 52-53; dosages for women vs men, 55; effects on memory, 91; Hedonal, 51; hygiene and, 41; ideal soporific, search for, 46-48; introduction of, 37; as lifestyle agents, 51, 53; linked with hygiene, 41; Luminal, 43; mechanism for effect unclear, 46-47; Medinal, 55; modern technology of the self, 13; naming of, 196n68; overview, 13; reproducing fatigue substances, 47; sleeping pills, 44, 50-54, 91; solving problem of modernity, 37, 53-54; Sulfonal, 51; taste and sugarcoating, 53; tree diagram of drugs, 43, 44; Voluntal, 43. *See also À la recherche du temps perdu*; *Fräulein Else*; pharmaceutical industry; Proust, Marcel; Veronal

sleepiness, 21. *See also* fatigue; tiredness

sleeping sickness. *See* African trypanosomiasis; encephalitis lethargica; narcolepsy

sleeplessness. *See* insomnia; sleep disorders

sleep science: Claparède's work on active sleep, 18, 20-24; epistemic shift in, 9-10; pathology, history within, 24-26; physiology, history within, 17-18; sleeping sicknesses and, 24-31. *See also* brain; electroencephalograph (EEG)

sleep studies: arousal thresholds, 83–84, 124–25; Bertino (cracked skullcap), 18, *19*; experiments vs experience, 21; graphical method, 18, *19*; sound responsiveness, 18. See also electroencephalograph (EEG); sleep deprivation
somnambulism (sleep-walking), 5, 101, *102*, 181n50. See also Broch, Hermann
somniloquy (sleep-talking), 10, 105, 108n49
soporifics. See sleep-inducing drugs
sound, 18, 83–84, 124–25
Stein, Gertrude, 106
Stern, Felix, 188n61
Stoppel, Rose, 132
suicide. See also death; *Fräulein Else*; sleep-inducing drugs; Veronal
surrealists, 12
Svevo, Italo, 60, 136
synesthesia, 124

thermodynamic theory, 18
tiredness, 18, 21. See also exhaustion; fatigue; sleep deprivation; sleepiness
Trakl, Georg, 85
trance, 60, 104, 107, 110
Trömner, Ernst, 9
Turner, Henry S., 11

Valéry, Paul, 3, 93, 94, 118–22, *123*, 126
Vaschide, Nicolas, 20, 83–84
Veronal: advertising, 44, 45, 48, 50, *52*; antidote to modernity, 45, 57; Bayer's prospectus for, *49*; commercialization and licensing, 46; as dangerously glamorous, 63; death by, in literature, 60, 65–66; dosage problems, 55, 57, 66, 206n50; endocrine fatigue substances, 48; gender norms and politics, 50, 53, 55, *56*, 57, 58, 72; as ideal soporific, 48, 50, 54, 57, 72; large-scale use of barbiturates, 43, 45; as lifestyle agent, 53–54; natural vs artificial sleep, 45, 48; from over-the-counter to prescription, 54–55; overview, 13; pills (tablets), 51–52, *52*; Proust's use of, 14, 86–87, 136; success of, 54; sugarcoating of, 53; suicide and accidents linked to, 54–55, 57, 61, 63, 66, 68, 72; transformed drug scene, 43, 45. See also *Fräulein Else*; gender
"Veronal" (Birlo) (photograph), *56*, 57
Virilio, Paul, 65
Vogt, Oskar, 30

waking: arousal thresholds, 83–84, 124–25; complementary relationship with sleep, 29–30; exhaustion causing, 23; memory, consciousness, and self, 82, 90–95; reentries of somnolence and wakefulness, 81–83, *82*; restoring distinctions sleep has undone, 91–92; riskiness of, 106; spatio-temporal orientation, 108–9; wakefulness within sleep, 82. See also *À la recherche du temps perdu*; awakening; Kafka, Franz; neurasthenic half sleep; periodicity
weariness. See fatigue
Weber, Matthias, 55
Wernicke, Carl, 27
Wharton, Edith, 65–66, *67*
Wittgenstein, Ludwig, 4, 9–10
Wolff, Ludwig, 60, 201n15
women. See gender
Woolf, Virginia, 94, 125
Wundt, Wilhelm, 27

Explore other studies in Modernism from **HOPKINS PRESS**

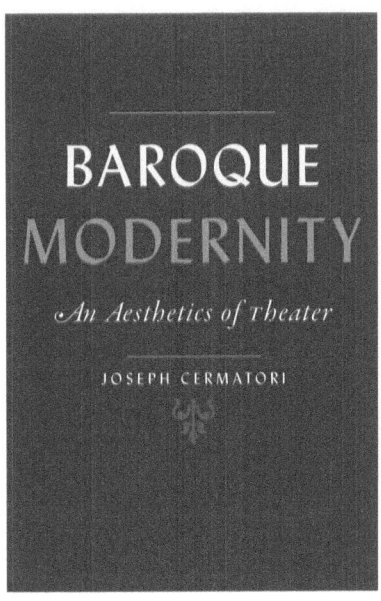

www.ingramcontent.com/pod-product-compliance
Lightning Source LLC
Chambersburg PA
CBHW032036300426
44117CB00009B/1081